SPECIFYING AND SECURING A SOCIAL MINIMUM IN THE BATTLE AGAINST POVERTY

This book addresses a topic that is currently high on the agenda in many fora: how to specify and secure a social minimum. The term 'social minimum' has different meanings, depending on the context. These contexts are examined in this book from different perspectives, including law, sociology, philosophy, politics and economics.

In the first part, the social minimum is discussed from a conceptual and theoretical point of view.

The second part shows the various ways in which the social minimum can be specified and measured. There is a need for new indicators that take into account, for instance, aspects of adequate social participation. As this part shows, the choice of indicators is closely intertwined with political choices.

The third part approaches the social minimum from the perspective of legal obligations, addressing the nature of different obligations imposed on individuals and states.

The fourth part deals with the question of social minimum in the context of courts, adjudication and justiciability. The role of international treaties and national constitutions – the interpretation of the rights they enshrine and the way these are dealt with by expert committees and courts – is discussed with a view to understanding how the guarantee of a social minimum can be promoted within individual countries.

Besides being of interest for academics in fields ranging from legal theory and human rights to the social sciences, the book also serves as an important source for students as well as practitioners interested in the social minimum, and anyone who wants to gain an insight into the current debates on this extremely important issue.

Volume 24: Human Rights Law in Perspective

Human Rights Law in Perspective

The language of human rights figures prominently in legal and political debates at the national, regional and international levels. In the UK the Human Rights Act 1998 has generated considerable interest in the law of human rights. It will continue to provoke much debate in the legal community and the search for original insights and new materials will intensify.

The aim of this series is to provide a forum for scholarly reflection on all aspects of the law of human rights. The series will encourage work which engages with the theoretical, comparative and international dimensions of human rights law. The primary aim is to publish over time books which offer an insight into human rights law in its contextual setting. The objective is to promote an understanding of the nature and impact of human rights law. The series is inclusive, in the sense that all perspectives in legal scholarship are welcome. It will incorporate the work of new and established scholars.

Human Rights Law in Perspective is not confined to consideration of the UK. It will strive to reflect comparative, regional and international perspectives. Work which focuses on human rights law in other states will therefore be included in this series. The intention is to offer an inclusive intellectual home for significant scholarly contributions to human rights law.

Recent titles in this series

Property and Human Rights in a Global Context
Edited by Ting Xu and Jean Allain

Governing (Through) Rights
Bal Sokhi-Bulley

Gender Equality in Law: Uncovering the Legacies of Czech State Socialism
Barbara Havelkova

Investment and Human Rights in Armed Conflict:
Charting an Elusive Intersection
Daria Davitti

For the complete list of titles in this series,
see 'Human Rights Law in Perspective' link at
www.bloomsburyprofessional.com/uk/series/
human-rights-law-in-perspective/

Specifying and Securing a Social Minimum in the Battle Against Poverty

Edited by
Toomas Kotkas
Ingrid Leijten
and
Frans Pennings

•HART•
OXFORD • LONDON • NEW YORK • NEW DELHI • SYDNEY

HART PUBLISHING

Bloomsbury Publishing Plc

Kemp House, Chawley Park, Cumnor Hill, Oxford, OX2 9PH, UK

HART PUBLISHING, the Hart/Stag logo, BLOOMSBURY and the Diana logo are trademarks of Bloomsbury Publishing Plc

First published in Great Britain 2019

A catalogue record for this book is available from the British Library.

Library of Congress Cataloging-in-Publication data

Names: Kotkas, Toomas, 1970- editor. | Leijten, Ingrid, 1984- editor. | Pennings, F. (Frans), editor.

Title: Specifying and securing a social minimum in the battle against poverty / Toomas Kotkas, Ingrid Leijten, Frans Pennings.

Description: Oxford ; New York : Hart , 2019. | Series: Human rights law in perspective; volume 24 | "the sociology of law in June 2017, during which the first drafts of papers on minimum income were discussed. In September 2018 we had a follow-up workshop at Gothenburg University ..." —ECIP Introduction, page 11. | Includes bibliographical references and index.

Identifiers: LCCN 2019034064 (print) | LCCN 2019034065 (ebook) | ISBN 9781509926022 (hardback) | ISBN 9781509926039 (Epub)

Subjects: LCSH: Public welfare—Law and legislation—Congresses. | Basic needs—Law and legislation—Congresses.

Classification: LCC K1960.A6 .S64 2019 (print) | LCC K1960.A6 (ebook) | DDC 344.03/25—dc23

LC record available at https://lccn.loc.gov/2019034064

LC ebook record available at https://lccn.loc.gov/2019034065

ISBN: HB: 978-1-50992-602-2
ePDF: 978-1-50992-604-6
ePub: 978-1-50992-603-9

Typeset by Compuscript Ltd, Shannon

To find out more about our authors and books visit www.hartpublishing.co.uk. Here you will find extracts, author information, details of forthcoming events and the option to sign up for our newsletters.

Contents

PART 3
SECURING A SOCIAL MINIMUM:
OBLIGATIONS FOR STATES AND INDIVIDUALS

PART 4
SECURING A SOCIAL MINIMUM:
THE ROLE OF COURTS AND SUPERVISORY BODIES

List of Authors

Michael Adler is Emeritus Professor of Socio-Legal Studies at the University of Edinburgh. His academic interests lie at the interface between social policy and public law. In the course of his career, he has carried out empirical research in several fields of policy, including education, criminal justice and social security but, in recent years, his interests have focused on administrative justice and redress mechanisms in relation to social rights. Together with Frans Pennings, he has edited the *European Journal of Social Security* since 1999.

David Bilchitz is Professor at the University of Johannesburg and Director of the South African Institute for Advanced Constitutional, Public, Human Rights and International Law; he is also Secretary-General of the International Association of Constitutional Law.

Katie Boyle is Associate Professor in International Human Rights Law at the School of Law, University of Stirling. She has published widely on human rights and in particular models of incorporation and justiciability for economic, social and cultural rights and human rights reform during periods of constitutional transition. She was a member of the First Minister's Advisory Group on Human Rights Leadership (Scotland) and previously qualified as a lawyer with the Government Legal Service for Scotland.

Eberhard Eichenhofer is Professor Emeritus for civil law, social security and social welfare law at the universities of Osnabrück (1989–1997) and Jena (1997–2016). Now he is retired and living in Berlin.

Tim Goedemé is Senior Research Officer at the Institute for New Economic Thinking at the Oxford Martin School and Department of Social Policy and Intervention, University of Oxford. He is also a Research Coordinator at the Herman Deleeck Centre for Social Policy, University of Antwerp and Associate Member of Nuffield College. He studies poverty, inequality and social policy.

Dimitrios Kagiaros is a Lecturer in Law at the University of Exeter. He previously taught on constitutional law, administrative law and human rights law courses at the Universities of Edinburgh and Hull. His research interests include whistleblower protection, the impact of the European sovereign debt crisis on human rights and the case law of the European Court of Human Rights in relation to Freedom of Expression.

Toomas Kotkas is Professor of Jurisprudence and Social Law at the University of Eastern Finland. He is doing research on social law from both doctrinal and socio-legal/historical perspectives. His recent publications include T Kotkas and K Veitch (eds), *Social Rights in the Welfare State: Origins and Transformations* (Abingdon, Routledge, 2017).

Ingrid Leijten is Assistant Professor of Constitutional and Administrative Law at Leiden University, the Netherlands. In 2019, she is a Guest Professor at the Friedrich Alexander University Erlangen-Nuremberg in Germany. Her research deals with the protection of fundamental rights at the international, European and national levels, with a focus on socio-economic rights and the role of courts. Leijten is the author of *Core Socio-Economic Rights and the European Court of Human Rights* (Cambridge, Cambridge University Press, 2018).

Colm O'Cinneide is Professor of Constitutional and Human Rights Law, UCL and formerly Vice-President of the European Committee of Social Rights 2008–14. All opinions expressed are personal to the author.

Tess Penne is a PhD student at the Herman Deleeck Centre for Social Policy at the University of Antwerp. Since 2015, she receives a fellowship of the Research Foundation Flanders. In her PhD project, she makes use of reference budgets to study income adequacy and poverty in Europe.

Frans Pennings is Professor of Labour Law and Social Security Law at Utrecht University. He has published several books and articles on international standards in social security, coordination of social security and on national and comparative topics.

David Piachaud is Emeritus Professor of Social Policy at the London School of Economics and Associate of the Centre for Analysis of Social Exclusion. His research and publications are on poverty, social security and the future of social policy.

Elena Pribytkova obtained a Doctor of the Science of Law (JSD) degree at Columbia Law School and a PhD at the Russian Academy of Sciences. She is Post-Doctoral Global Fellow at the Center for Human Rights and Global Justice at New York University.

Sara Stendahl is Professor of Public Law at Gothenburg University. Research interests include the regulation of social security and welfare with particular focus on questions of legality and legitimacy, justice, social human rights, law and society, inclusion/exclusion, social sustainability, legal pluralism and developments in the interface of private/public law.

Bérénice Storms is research coordinator at the Center for Budget Advice & Research (CEBUD, Thomas More Kempen). She also works as a senior researcher at the Herman Deleeck Center for Social Policy (CSB, University of Antwerp). Her main research topics are reference budgets, income adequacy, local and regional anti-poverty policies and budget and debt counseling practices.

Otto Swedrup is a doctoral candidate in Public Law at Gothenburg University. His areas of interest include welfare law, social rights and the civil society and his research focuses particularly on the legal obligations and responsibilities of the public sector and questions of how public authorities act in order to secure social rights.

Malcolm Torry is Director of the Citizen's Basic Income Trust and a Visiting Senior Fellow in the Social Policy Department at the London School of Economics. He researches the reform of social security benefits systems, and particularly the desirability and feasibility of a Citizen's Basic Income (also called a Basic Income, a Universal Basic Income, or a Citizen's Income): an unconditional income for every individual. A further research interest is the characteristics and management of religious and faith-based organisations. He is a priest in the Church of England, and for 34 years served in full-time posts in south London parishes.

Karel Van den Bosch works since 2009 at the Belgian Federal Planning Bureau. He is also affiliated to the Herman Deleeck Centre for Social Policy of the University of Antwerp. His research is about poverty, income distribution, pensions and long-term care.

Ben TC Warwick is a Lecturer in the Birmingham Law School at the University of Birmingham. His research explores how economic factors affect human rights (and especially socio-economic rights). He is interested in the ways that laws and the institutions that enforce them change under such pressures. This has led him to write on the related questions of crisis, neoliberalism, and the reversal of rights protections. He is a specialist in international human rights and the United Nations human rights bodies.

List of Abbreviations

ACHPR	African Commission on Human and Peoples' Rights
App	Application
Art	Article
BE	Belgium
BL	German Basic Law
CCPR	Committee on Civil and Political Rights (The Human Rights Committee)
CEDAW	Convention on the Elimination of all Forms of Discrimination Against Women
CESCR	Committee on Economic, Social and Cultural Rights
cf	compare
Ch	Chapter
CRC	Convention on the Rights of the Child
CPR	Civil and political rights
CRPD	Convention on the Rights of Persons with Disabilities
CSOs	Civil Society Organisations
DE	Germany
DK	Denmark
ECHR	European Convention on Human Rights
ECSR	European Committee on Social Rights
ECtHR	European Court of Human Rights
EL	Greece
(R)ESC	(Revised) European Social Charter
ESR	economic and social rights
eg	for example
et al	and others

et seq	and what follows
etc	etcetera
EU	European Union
EU-SILC	European Union Statistics on Income and Living Conditions
ff	following
FCC	German Federal Constitutional Court
FI	Finland
GDP	Gross domestic product
GNI	Gross national income
HDI	Human development indicator
IACtHR	Inter-American Court of Human Rights
ibid	ibidem (in the same source)
ICCPR	International Covenant on Civil and Political Rights
ICESCR	International Covenant on Economic, Social and Cultural Rights
IGOs	intergovernmental organisations
ILA	International Law Association
ILO	International Labour Organization
IMF	International Monetary Fund
IT	Italy
JRF	Joseph Rowntree Foundation
JSA	Jobseeker's Allowance
LIS	Luxembourg Income Study
MCO	minimum core obligations
MPI	Multidimensional Poverty Index
MT	Malta
NGO	Non-governmental Organisation
n	footnote
NHS	National Health Service (UK)
NHSL	Swedish New Health and Medical Services Act

ODA	Official Development Assistance
OECD	Organisation for Economic Cooperation and Development
OHCHR	Office of the United Nations High Commissioner for Human Rights
OPHI	Oxford Poverty and Human Development Initiative
para	paragraph
Prop	Proposition
PT	Portugal
SDGs	Sustainable development goals
SER	socio-economic rights
SERAC	Social and Economic Rights Action Center
SM	social minimum
SOL	Swedish Social Services Act
UDHR	Universal Declaration of Human Rights
UK	United Kingdom
UN	United Nations
UNDP	United Nations Development Programme
USA	United States of America
USD	United States Dollar
v	versus
WHO	World Health Organization
WTO	World Trade Organization
WWII	World War II

1

Introduction

INGRID LEIJTEN, TOOMAS KOTKAS AND FRANS PENNINGS

I. POVERTY, INEQUALITY AND THE SOCIAL MINIMUM

According to the 2018 global Multidimensional Poverty Index (MPI), some 1.3 billion people live in multidimensional poverty, and half of them are younger than 18.[1] The MPI is published by the United Nations Development Programme (UNDP) and the Oxford Poverty and Human Development Initiative (OPHI). The 'multidimensional poverty' the MPI refers to includes health, education and living standards, measured with the help of 10 indicators such as child mortality, nutrition, school attendance, drinking water, sanitation and housing. Deprived people live in all regions, though their number is most significant in sub-Saharan Africa and South Asia, and mostly they live in rural areas. Moreover, millions of people face the prospect of falling into multidimensional poverty, given, for example, risks of crisis, natural disasters or the effects of climate change.[2]

Against this background, the UN 2030 Agenda for Sustainable Development aims to end poverty in all its forms.[3] And regardless of the large number of poor people, it cannot be said that no progress at all has been made – to the contrary. According to the UNDP report Work for Human Development from 2015, income poverty in developing country regions fell by more than two-thirds between 1990 and 2015. The number of extreme poor people worldwide, ie people living on less than US $1.25 a day, fell from 1.9 billion to 836 million.[4]

[1] See the report, Oxford Poverty and Human Development Initiative, *Global Multidimensional Poverty Index 2018: The Most Detailed Picture To Date of the World's Poorest People* (Oxford, University of Oxford, 2018), as well as S Alkire and S Jahan, 'The New Global MPI 2018: Aligning with the Sustainable Development Goals', HDRO Occasional Paper (New York, UNDP, 2018).

[2] See UNDP, 'Beyond Income: A Broader Picture of Poverty' (New York, UNDP, 2018) see https://feature.undp.org/multidimensional-poverty.

[3] United Nations General Assembly, 'Transforming our World: the 2030 Agenda for Sustainable Development', 25 September 2015, A/RES/70/1.

[4] UNDP, 'Human Development Report 2015: Work for Human Development' (New York, UNDP, 2015) 4. In 2018, the international poverty line is valued at US $1.90 in terms of 2011 purchasing power parity.

In line with the MPI, however, Special Rapporteur on extreme poverty and human rights, Philip Alston, warns that measuring poverty solely on the basis of income, fails to capture the depth and complexity of this issue.[5] Extreme poverty has a significant impact on the full enjoyment of human rights: it often means a lack of access to education, health services and safe drinking water, but also affects possibilities to participate meaningfully in the political process and causes human rights violations relating to, eg, working in an unsafe environment. The elimination of poverty, in this line of thinking, should not be a matter of charity, but rather a matter of right.[6]

Effectively combatting poverty requires a plethora of actions and measures. One of the key normative concepts in regard to this battle against poverty, is the concept of the social minimum, which can be understood as the floor of socio-economic protection states are required to provide. Rather than dealing with poverty as such, this book brings together insights concerning this social minimum as a matter of justice and rights. That every person should be able to rely on a minimum social protection hardly needs stating. In this regard, we 'may continue to disagree about what is good, but nevertheless agree about what is insufferably, unarguably wrong'.[7] No one should find him- or herself without access to basic social means necessary for living a life in dignity.

Yet with every definition of a social minimum, the problems inherent in this concept surface: what exactly should a social minimum include and how can it be secured? How minimal can a social minimum be? Is it universal or rather dependent on context and therefore country- or even region-specific, and who should be entitled to it where? It can be asked what constitutes the 'social' in the social minimum: which aspects of individuals' lives should be perceived as social and therefore included in such a minimum? Is that, in line with the MPI, income, health and education? What about the possibility to partake in social and cultural life?

The tendency to focus on a floor, rather than a more ambitious level of protection, intrinsically is linked to the fact that resources are limited and political views on the provision of social goods are diverse. The question of what states need to provide and to whom divides those with different political convictions and philosophical ideas on the good life and the role of the state therein. Modern societies care about the well-being of their members, which can however be understood as a matter of political will or of right. Indeed, where it is agreed that a (legal) entitlement to a social minimum exists, this does not yet answer the question of how we can best secure that all members of a particular society or community are provided with this minimum. Just like the

[5] See the homepage of the Special Rapporteur of Extreme Poverty and Human Rights, www.ohchr.org/EN/Issues/Poverty/Pages/SRExtremePovertyIndex.aspx.

[6] ibid.

[7] *cf* M Ignatieff, 'Human Rights as Ideology' in M Ignatieff and A Gutmann (eds), *Human Rights as Politics and Idolatry* (Princeton, NY, Princeton University Press, 2001) 56.

eradication of poverty, the provision of a social minimum can be perceived as a right rather than a privilege. More precisely, a social minimum can be codified as a constitutional (or human) right, and as such claimed before the courts. Due to its potential indeterminacy, however, it can just as well be concluded that we need to rely on the other branches for securing a social minimum, and thus on political deliberation on who deserves what. A social minimum could be guaranteed by means of a Basic Income, but it could also take the form of particular benefit for those in need or (a mixture of) payments in cash or in kind. And once it is provided, is the social minimum in fact unconditional for those in need or can it instead be required that conditions must be met and that individuals be subject to sanctions?[8]

In the light of this, the question that is central to this volume is how we can specify and secure a social minimum. We do not intend to present definite answers as these may differ from one context to the other, or depending on who you ask. Our aim is rather to provide an array of academic and other insights concerning the issue of the social minimum. Bringing together various disciplines relevant to this topic, namely social policy, law and legal theory, and economics, this book offers a broad and unique outlook of topical aspects related to the social minimum. This will offer a deeper understanding of a topic that is well worth our attention in times of great inequality and continuing (and new) social threats. Whereas for lawyers it is interesting to engage with the ways in which a social minimum is calculated and features in policy-making, for non-lawyers concerned with this topic it will be illuminating to see what law does, and what it cannot do, in order to make the social minimum real.

Before turning to the structure of this book, a few more things must be noted on minimalism and its relation to equality. Even though the number of people living in extreme poverty has significantly decreased during the past few decades, burning problems such as income inequality still remain. In this regard, the 2015 UNDP report mentioned earlier states that the technological revolution has been accompanied by rising income inequality. Even people with better education and training who can work more productively may not receive commensurate rewards in income, stability or social recognition. Workers overall are getting a smaller share of total corporate income – both in developed countries and in developing countries.[9] Income inequality is illustrative of the broader gap between the rich and the poor. A UNDP update report in his regard continues that 'inequality is not only normatively wrong; it is also dangerous' as it can fuel extremism and have adverse consequences for social cohesion.[10]

[8] On the main philosophical views concerning the various aspects of the social minimum see S White, 'Social Minimum' in EN Zalta (ed), *The Stanford Encyclopedia of Philosophy*, Winter 2015 edn, available at plato.stanford.edu/archives/win2015/entries/social-minimum.

[9] UNDP, 'Human Development Report 2015' (2015) 100.

[10] UNDP, 'Human Development Indices and Indicators: 2018 Statistical Update' (New York, UNDP, 2018) 4. See also the Gini Index on global income distribution, eg, https://data.worldbank.org/indicator/si.pov.gini.

It is true that the provision of a social minimum does not do away with inequalities. It does not place a ceiling on wealth. At the same time, redistribution will have some effect in terms of controlling the gap between rich and poor. Is it problematic that we focus on a minimum level of social protection, rather than on economic equality? The difference between the two is not merely one of degree; whereas the first entails an individual, independent entitlement, the latter is relative as it concerns deprivation measured in comparison to what others have. How just is a world where everyone has a sufficient level of social protection, though more or less nothing compared to the wealthy few?

This dilemma is vividly presented in Samuel Moyn's recent book, *Not Enough. Human Rights in an Unequal World.*[11] Telling the story of Croesus, who was wonderfully rich yet insisted on a floor of protection for everyone subject to his totalitarian power, Moyn asks whether this 'utopia' – enough basic means for everyone – could ever be enough given the inequality it represents. In his book, Moyn sets out that human rights have failed to provide material equality and that the sufficiency human rights have come to stand for, shows their failure in today's world of great inequalities. Human rights have proven to be the companion of neoliberalism rather than its antidote.

The pejorative way in which 'sufficiency' can be used, however, does not do justice to the importance and promise of minimalism and, indeed, a social minimum. Admittedly, the danger when focusing on a social minimum is that this distracts from more encompassing protection while legitimating minimalist efforts.[12] The floor of protection that is offered, in other words, runs the risk of becoming the ceiling instead. This goes for government action as well as for courts' determination of minimum levels of social protection. But the choice for a book on the social minimum is evidence of our belief in the value of this notion, rather than of skepticism as to what it has to offer. This book engages with what poverty means, and addresses the gap between the rich and the poor as a necessary aspect of the discussion of the social minimum. What is more, even an isolated discussion of different facets of the social minimum does not signal a lack of ambition but instead underlines the reality that for many individuals even enjoying a basic, minimum level of protection is something very remote. It can moreover be argued that minimum protection can be seen as a prerequisite of achieving a more (materially) just society, as a starting point for addressing the enormous gap between the rights and the poor. Not least because a social minimum – including (access to) health care and education – will also benefit the enjoyment of civil and political rights, lead to better possibilities for political participation and increased (economic) chances. In the light of this,

[11] S Moyn, *Not Enough. Human Rights in an Unequal World* (Cambridge, MA, Belknap Press, 2018).

[12] *cf* K Young, 'The Minimum Core of Economic and Social Rights: A Concept in Search of Content' 33 (2008) *Yale Journal of International Law* 113.

engaging with the question of how best to specify and secure a social minimum is a worthwhile aim.

The remainder of this introduction serves to further introduce the overall topic of the book and the different parts thereof in particular. This book consists of four parts, namely: (1) Conceptual Questions; (2) Specifying a Social Minimum; (3) Securing a Social Minimum: Obligations for States and Individuals, and (4) Securing a Social Minimum: the Role of Courts and Supervisory Bodies. In this way, the book moves from the more abstract issues to concrete (case law) examples; from, first, considering why we need a social minimum and what it entails, to, thereafter, seeing how it is or should be given 'bite'. Below, under the headers of the different parts, the chapters that constitute these will be introduced. This overview will assist the reader who wants to connect the dots and navigate the book in order to find what he or she is looking for.

II. CONCEPTUAL QUESTIONS

As we mentioned above, the social minimum continues to be highly debated. The questions it brings up can be of a more practical nature, but also entail conceptual and theoretical issues that are fundamental to our understanding – and acceptance – of the social minimum as a matter of social justice. In the first part of the book, several of these fundamental points are taken up in a way that helps clearing the path for the parts to follow.

To start with, in chapter two, David Bilchitz takes up the fundamental yet difficult question of the justification for thinking in terms of minimum thresholds when it comes to the distribution of goods. Minimalism can first be justified by a set of *normative* arguments that demonstrate that the notion of justice itself can be connected analytically to the notion of its encompassing a minimum set of demands of morality. An *instrumental* justification instead involves reasons for why developing minimum thresholds is valuable for attaining other, greater aims. The third set of arguments Bilchitz presents are *democratic* in nature and involve considering the role of disagreement in democratic societies and its relations to notions of distributive justice. By means of these justifications, he defends conceptual and practical approaches involving the setting of minimum thresholds. There can be different thresholds, namely a basic threshold that can be termed the 'minimum core' as well as a more demanding 'sufficiency' threshold.

Minimum social protection serves the aim of eradicating poverty. Since the United Nations Declaration of Human Rights was adopted in 1948, a life free from poverty has been widely accepted as a fundamental human right – albeit one far from being achieved. What does such a right mean? In chapter three, Malcolm Torry contributes to the discussion on the social minimum by outlining a three-dimensional matrix as a way of a conceptualising the social minimum. The three dimensions are resources, characteristics, and mode of delivery.

Each of the resources – healthcare, education, income, and so on – can be delivered by a variety of modes; and, in relation to each mode, such characteristics as quality, ease of access, efficiency, and equity, can be scored. Torry argues that constructing such a three-dimensional matrix and giving scores to the characteristics enables us to choose the modes of delivery for the different resources that would deliver the best available social minimum.

Deciding to whom, in the face of destitution, a social minimum is to be allocated, is a question of scope. The chapter by Sara Stendahl and Otto Swedrup (chapter four) deals with this issue and while it discusses this topic in a national context, at its core the question 'who counts?' is philosophical and has divided writings on ethics and justice for centuries. The chapter puts forward two contrasting approaches on how to understand 'who counts' in a Swedish setting, one more particularist (based on a historic narrative) and another more universalist (based on a legal narrative). The more universalist version provides an explanation for a Swedish solidarity that evidently encompasses not only citizens and residents but also strangers and outcasts, people with distinctly weak civil and social rights. This is solidarity at a minimal level, sometimes handed out harshly and with no reference to rights – but it does exist, and the authors propose that it plays an important role in the intricate web of values that forms the Swedish welfare state. In an effort to identify the core characteristics of this tradition it is described as based on a normative pattern of 'pragmatic decency'.

III. SPECIFYING A SOCIAL MINIMUM

To justify a focus on minimum thresholds and a social minimum is one thing. Discussing the possibilities related to scope and modes of delivery makes the social minimum more tangible. It is still something else, however, to engage with what a social minimum exactly entails. In other words, how can this minimum be specified? In Part 2 of the book, the authors provide interdisciplinary insights on this topic.

In chapter five, Michael Adler discusses the thesis that the worldwide concern with human rights and the prevalence of neoliberalism are the main reasons for the disappearance of material inequality from the political agenda. It is argued that champions of human rights were simply 'out of position' to challenge abuses of social and economic rights and the explosion of inequality. As a result, the main focus of concern turned to the social minimum, which became the hand-maiden of neoliberalism. Adler now considers alternative ways of *defining* the social minimum, by focusing on material inequality and makes the case for redistribution from rich to poor and, in particular, from the super-rich to the extremely poor. In doing so, he raises the question of whether there ought to be a social maximum as well as a social minimum.

In chapter six, Tim Goedemé, Tess Penne and Otto Swedrup argue that without comparable benchmarks cross-national monitoring of the adequacy of minimum income schemes is impossible. Yet it is not that straightforward to define what comparability means in this context, and how it should be operationalised. At minimum, comparability would require that people have a broadly similar understanding of what adequate social participation means. Even though resources that households require vary across time and space, such a shared understanding is needed and investigated in this chapter. For this purpose, the essential social positions that one should be able to take are taken into account. In addition, the authors examine the need that should be satisfied in order to be able to fulfil in an adequate way the social roles associated with these positions. A large-scale project that involved country teams in all EU Member States enabled the authors to develop a core list of social positions, and to validate these as well as a list of intermediate needs across EU Member States. On the basis of this, benchmarks are developed to assess the adequacy of social protection schemes that are comparable in a meaningful way.

To conclude this part, in chapter seven Eberhard Eichenhofer examines what characterises and constitutes poverty (and thus informs the social minimum). The social policy concept of poverty refers to the interrelationship between the living conditions of an individual and the average individual or a particular segment of the entire population of a given society. When determining these interrelations, empirical denominators that are built on economic indicators and open to be measured in monetary terms are identified as personal income or wealth. Social welfare law entails a different concept of poverty: its notion of need is broad and can be characterised as a physical, mental, social or economic deficit. In any respect a normative and an empirical dimension of poverty can be identified and thus poverty becomes both an absolute and relative concept. First, poverty indicates the living conditions which require a poverty alleviation measure as such. Second, it is necessary to specify the individual needs a person cannot satisfy him- or herself. Both dimensions have to be approached in an appropriate manner. The interplay between them is complex, as there are empirical facts that do not count and norms that do not convince.

IV. SECURING A SOCIAL MINIMUM: OBLIGATIONS FOR STATES AND INDIVIDUALS

Obligations stemming from the social minimum were discussed conceptually in chapter three. But what is it that can be required from states more precisely, within and beyond their borders? The issue of obligations for individuals in relation to the(ir) social minimum is a tricky one. After all, if a minimum that is provided is of a basic nature and involves what is minimally necessary for living a life in dignity, can we expect individuals to contribute and even impose sanctions on them if they fail to do so? Indeed, conditionality and minimum protection may seem at odds with one another, yet are a reality in many states. This is the topic of Part 3, Securing a Social Minimum: Obligations for States and Individuals.

Elena Pribytkova discusses, in chapter eight, what territorial and extraterritorial duties correspond to basic human rights indispensable for a decent social minimum. This question requires an examination of the nature, status, content and scope of these obligations and also which entities are responsible for securing access to a decent social minimum nationally and universally. The chapter provides a preliminary outline of a conception of territorial and extraterritorial obligations relating to a decent social minimum; it addresses their interpretations in moral, legal and political philosophy, in international and regional human rights instruments, as well as in the practice of international, regional and national monitoring and accountability bodies. Can theories of social and global justice contribute to justifying, conceptualising, and allocating territorial and extraterritorial human rights obligations to guarantee a decent social minimum?

Besides for states, the provision of a social minimum is sometimes also mirrored in obligations for individuals. What kind of citizenship ideally counterparts the minimum social protection by the state? In chapter nine, David Pichaud discusses the obligations of citizenship and compares two paths to ending poverty. One places all responsibility on the state, which is what proponents of a Universal Basic Income propose. The other shares responsibility between the state and individuals with the state being responsible for ensuring employment opportunities, training and child care and for social security. In this understanding, individuals who can work would have a responsibility to do so. Responsibilities for global poverty are discussed and ways in which advanced nations contribute to the poverty of poorer nations are considered.

In chapter ten, Frans Pennings discusses the conditions that can be imposed on recipients of a minimum income, specifically in this chapter, public assistance. He starts with a description of the early Poor Laws where the concept of 'deserving poor' was still used. However, also when a general and enforceable right is created it appears that in some systems specific conditions are attached to the receipt of social assistance, such as the obligation to do community work or other voluntary work. Where this happens, it appears, in his case study of the Netherlands, courts can mitigate too heavy obligations set by the administration, and international (human rights) standards can be very helpful for this purpose. Overall this leads to a hybrid legal position, where social assistance is still regarded with suspicion, but the legal context can place some helpful limits.

V. SECURING A SOCIAL MINIMUM: THE ROLE OF COURTS AND SUPERVISORY BODIES

The issue of conditionality and the response of courts brings us to the broader issue of what role there is or should be for (semi-)judicial bodies in securing a social minimum. Usually this issue comes up in relation to the judicial protection of fundamental social rights enshrined in constitutions or human rights documents. Are courts capable of adjudicating these rights and the right to a social minimum in particular? And if so, what approach will best serve the aim of protecting a robust social minimum and moving towards a more socially just society? These questions provide plenty of food for debate, which is reflected in the chapters that constitute this book's final part.

In chapter eleven, Colm O'Cinneide takes up the issue of the role of courts in protecting access to a social minimum. Rights discourse in this regard provides significant normative weight and could push back against the dominant influence of neoliberal orthodoxy. This however requires that we find legal tests to identify breaches of social and economic rights that are sufficiently clear, determinate and demanding to play a useful role in protecting access to the social minimum. Courts as well as scholars tend to evade the minimum and focus on process rather than substance. According to O'Cinneide, however, without a doctrine specifying the scope and content of socio-economic rights, reasonableness and similar kinds of review can lead to inconsistent or incoherent case law that fails to show respect for the social minimum. Instead, a substantive approach has the advantage of focusing attention on the positive entitlements of individuals and provides courts with a clearer normative steer. Templates for how this can be done exist at both national and international level: examples are presented from the German Federal Constitutional Court and the European Committee on Social Rights, showing that it is possible to provide social and economic rights with minimum content whilst sticking to the boundaries of one's (semi-)judicial task.

Indeed, it is generally agreed that the task of courts is a limited one that must be in line with the balance of powers struck in a given context. Acknowledging this point, Toomas Kotkas discusses the various ways in which the legal system deals with the question of the social minimum (chapter twelve). By using Niklas Luhmann's systems theory as an interpretative framework, Kotkas argues that rather than defining a precise pecuniary minimum limit for social security benefits, the legal system – courts in particular – adheres to particular juridical strategies that include, among others, legal syllogism, the proportionality principle and the principle of equality. Kotkas's argument is based on an analysis of three statements given by the Constitutional Law Committee of the Finnish Parliament on governmental bills relating to the social minimum. From the point of view of Luhmannian social theory, legal programming is indispensable for the maintaining of the functional differentiation of social subsystems. Without legal programming the systemic demarcation between law and politics would be in danger of blurring which, in turn, would be detrimental to the primary function of the legal system, ie, the stabilisation of normative expectations in modern complex societies. However, the role of the legal system can vary, and this depends on the developmental stage of a given society.

Ben Warwick's chapter (chapter thirteen) addresses the use of social minima (minimum core obligations, minimum essential levels) by the UN bodies.

After discussing the history of these terms in the UN context, he goes on to map the current practice of the treaty bodies as to their use of social minima. On the basis of a comprehensive analysis, it is shown that other bodies than the CESCR only refer to minimum concepts in a limited way. And what explains the limited consistence of the use of minimum concepts? Warwick illustrates the utility of different minima, including the Social Protection Floor developed by the ILO. Because of their different benefits, the retirement of several minimum concepts in order to focus on one particular approach, would come with certain costs. Reconciliation, on the other hand, also has its problems, although the moment surrounding the Social Protection Floor is worth capturing by the treaty bodies to develop a future proof approach.

At the international level, even though semi-judicial review on the basis of economic and social rights norms is increasingly possible, these possibilities still lag behind compared to the binding judgements resulting from civil and political rights review. The following two chapters deal with the indivisible protection of socio-economic rights, that is, how they can be protected through civil and political rights review, and in particular the practice of the European Court of Human Rights in this regard. In chapter fourteen, Ingrid Leijten illustrates this protection at the same time showing that it involves an inherent bias against social protection due to the lack of identifying prima facie social content and an emphasis on balancing and the margin of appreciation. A way out of this problem seems to be the reliance on procedural review, which arguably helps secure what could be understood as a (substantive) social minimum. This is the case when courts like the ECtHR require states to take into account the (minimum) interests of persons involved in their proportionality tests. Yet procedural review in not entirely unproblematic, and Leijten identifies several risks that must be addressed in order to ensure its potential.

Dimitrios Kagiaros, in chapter fifteen, emphasises a different subset of the ECtHR's case law, namely that in which positive obligations are found in cases concerning vulnerable applicants. Vulnerability has begun to feature prominently in the ECtHR's work, and according to Kagiaros, it can serve as a useful normative justification for the Court to be less deferential to the respondent state and to interpret the Convention in a manner that generates obligations in the direction of a social minimum. This is explained by discussing the meaning of positive obligations as obligations of means that can be seen as subjective as they vary among states. However, objective requirements are formulated when the applicant is member of a vulnerable group and is wholly reliant on state support for her subsistence. In addition to this, the chapter discusses the limitations of vulnerability analysis in this context and makes suggestions on how this tool could be developed to further build a path towards a social minimum under the ECHR.

Our volume concludes with a chapter by Katie Boyle providing an overall argument for constitutional and judicial protection of a social minimum, without losing sight of bigger ambitions. More precisely, Boyle argues for the protection of a social minimum to be included in the constitution as a part of multi-institutional approach to economic and social rights that enhances democracy by enabling participation. She addresses questions around relative and absolute thresholds in the legal enforcement of a social minimum/minimum core, as well as the substantive and procedural components of their enforcement by courts. Both absolute and relative standards can apply; an ideal combination of the two requires courts to use a hybrid approach to procedural and substantive review and remedies. It is nevertheless crucial not to forget that the minimum is not sufficient to meet the full international obligations of states to achieve progressively the different economic and social rights.

This book is the result of a workshop at the Oñati International Institute for the sociology of law in June 2017, during which the first drafts of papers on minimum income were discussed. In September 2018 we had a follow-up workshop at Gothenburg University, where we debated the contributions for this book. In this way authors were able to benefit from the suggestions from their peers in finalising their work. We are grateful to both the Oñati organisation and Gothenburg University for their hospitality.

Part 1

Conceptual Questions

2

What is the Relationship between Minimum Thresholds and Distributive Justice?

DAVID BILCHITZ

I. THE QUESTION OF MINIMUMS IN DISTRIBUTIVE JUSTICE

HUMAN BEINGS HAVE a penchant for thinking about minimum thresholds when it comes to the distribution of goods. Indeed, this way of thinking has influenced many practices of both international and domestic institutions. For instance, the World Bank initially developed a measurement of US $1 a day to capture the threshold below which individuals can be said to live in extreme poverty: this amount is supposed to translate into the minimum basic level of resources an individual can command to avoid severe deprivation.[1] Similarly, many countries in the world have developed a 'poverty line' which sets out the domestic understanding of the minimum income or control of resources that is necessary to escape the worst depredations of poverty.[2] The Millennium Development Goals and, more recently, the Sustainable Development Goals, set targets, many of which seek to establish a minimum level of well-being below which individuals should not fall – such as, for instance, eradicating hunger.[3]

[1] The US $1 a day measure was set out in the World Development Report of 1990 available at https://openknowledge.worldbank.org/handle/10986/5973 (last accessed 10 May 2017) and was increased with the cost of living to US $1.90/day in 2015.

[2] In South Africa, for example, the statistics agency, Statistic South Africa, has set out no less than three poverty thresholds, the lowest of which (the food poverty line) expresses the level below which people lack sufficient income to purchase food that meets minimum energy requirements: see https://beta2.statssa.gov.za/publications/Report-03-10-06/Report-03-10-06March2014.pdf (last accessed 10 May 2017) 64.

[3] See www.un.org/sustainabledevelopment/sustainable-development-goals.

The question that arises and is the subject of this chapter concerns what the justification is for thinking in terms of minimum thresholds at all. This might seem like a rather basic question but, examining the reasons that lie behind it allows us not only to understand the practice but also to shape its usage. I use the term 'minimalism' in this chapter as a shorthand: by that, I do not mean an approach to adjudication in courts whereby judges avoid expansive reasoning (an approach familiar to lawyers); rather, the term references an approach to distributive justice that is focused on setting and achieving minimum thresholds.

I consider three justifications for doing so. The first set of arguments is *normative* in nature: I first seek rather foundationally to demonstrate that the notion of justice itself can be connected analytically to the notion of its encompassing a minimum set of demands of morality.[4] It also seeks to provide an argument for why minimum thresholds may be of normative relevance within any adequate conception of distributive justice. A second set of arguments are *instrumental* in nature: they provide what may be more familiar reasons for why developing minimum thresholds is valuable for attaining other ends, and, in particular, the eventual full requirements of distributive justice. Finally, I consider a third set of argument which are *democratic* in nature: these arguments involve considering the role of disagreement in democratic societies and its relationship to the notions of distributive justice that we develop. The goal of this chapter will be to defend the conceptual and practical approaches to distributive justice which involve the setting of minimum thresholds as well as to distinguish between some of the different thresholds that can be developed and their deeper justification(s). Through doing so, I hope to provide a defence of how they can play a crucial role in the trajectory towards creating a more just distribution of resources within and between societies.

II. MINIMALISM AND ITS DISCONTENTS

Before engaging in a detailed discussion of minimalism, it will be helpful to understand a little bit more about what it involves. In doing so, it is helpful to consider the following quotation by Martha Nussbaum in outlining her capability view of justice:

> A list of central capabilities is not a complete theory of justice. Such a list gives us the basis for determining a decent social minimum in a variety of areas. I argue that the structure of social and political institutions should be chosen, at least in part, with a view to promoting at least a threshold level of human capabilities.

[4] A more ambitious claim could be that the notion of justice *necessarily* is connected to the notion of minimums: this may well be true (and is worth engaging with further); however, the limitations of a book chapter do not allow for an attempt to defend this more ambitious claim.

> But, the provision of a threshold level of capability, exigent though that goal is, may not suffice for justice.[5]

In this passage, Nussbaum gives expression to a number of key features of minimalism. First, the setting of minimum thresholds does not claim to offer a complete theory of justice but involves a partial understanding of what justice involves. Secondly, it involves setting a threshold of provision of goods below which individuals should not be allowed to fall. Finally, it is meant to guide the structure and policies of institutions in the society. Before elaborating on the case for minimalism as expressed, it is worth exploring an initial intuitive challenge to it which may help us with its justification.

Distributive justice concerns the manner in which benefits and burdens and, in particular, resources should be distributed in a society. Let us take the figurative cake that has to be distributed between eight members of Bongani's family. Without knowing more about the individuals concerned, our intuitions suggest that a fair distribution would involve cutting the cake into eight equal slices. It would seem strange to say that we should give Thulani at least a minimum of 1/16th of the cake. It seems unclear why such a minimum would have any justifiability, without knowing more about the people concerned. To give Thulani less than his full share would be to treat him unequally and, thus, would fail to achieve the requirements of distributive justice.

This example is clearly rather simplistic as the 'without knowing more' requirement makes a major difference.[6] Nevertheless, it illustrates the tenor of a particular objection to minimalism which has a strong appeal in the real world too: if there are requirements of distributive justice, then no question of minima arises. We are required to realise these requirements and, to the extent we fall short, we are under an obligation continually to achieve them. We may of course set indicators and benchmarks on the road to improvement, but these have no appeal or normative basis in and of themselves. The full ideal of distributive justice sets the goal from which we must measure any departures. A second but related objection suggests that minimalism can in fact inhibit the achievement of the ideal. It allows people to have a sense that they have achieved something by reaching the minimum and can also lead to a situation where the minimum becomes a substitute for the ideal itself: ie the minimum becomes the maximum. These objections raise the fundamental question: what is the point of recognising minimum thresholds in relation to distributive justice? Responses to these objections can take at least three forms, and I consider each in turn.

[5] M Nussbaum, *Women and Human Development: the Capabilities Approach* (Cambridge, Cambridge University Press, 2000) 75. I have made similar claims in D Bilchitz, *Poverty and Fundamental Rights* (Oxford, Oxford University Press, 2007) 64–69.

[6] Does Thulani perhaps have many opportunities to have cake whereas the other seven lack it? Could having too much sugar in the cake harm Thulani but not the others? Is there some reason why some of the others should be given a greater slice?

III. THE CASE FOR MINIMALISM: NORMATIVE FOUNDATIONS

The first set of responses consider the normative foundations for setting minimum thresholds in relation to distributive justice. I consider here two distinct arguments: the first essentially involves the claim that the notion of justice itself – as it has been understood and explicated by some of the most influential philosophers – in some sense is tied to the notion that it captures a minimum threshold of morality to be reached in interactions between individuals in society. The second argument provides a normative justification for minimum thresholds *within* the structure of distributive justice.

A. The Notion of Justice and the Minimum

Justice is, we are told by John Rawls, the 'first virtue of social institutions, as truth is of systems of thought'.[7] Moreover, for Rawls, 'the primary subject of justice is the basic structure of society, or more exactly, the way in which the major social institutions distribute fundamental rights and duties and determine the division of advantages from social cooperation'.[8] Rawls here, in a sense, suggests that justice is itself a normative notion which governs the most basic institutions in our society: it is something that relates to the foundational structure of the way in which societies are designed.[9] Indeed, he is at pains to point out that justice does not exhaust the domain of the normative in our lives but rather is a particular part thereof.[10] We might be tempted to conclude from this understanding that justice is in some sense intimately connected to the dimensions of minimalism articulated above. Indeed, Rawls' view impresses upon us the notion that justice engages the most pressing, and foundational normative concerns: why would this be so?

In answering this question and considering the place of justice within the normative domain more generally, it is useful to go back to the classic discussion of the relationship between justice and utility in the work of John Stuart Mill. Mill was faced with a difficult problem: utilitarianism seems to offer a comprehensive account of what constitutes a good state of affairs that focuses on achieving the greatest happiness overall: in other words, the normative domain seems to be specified in terms of a maximum rather than a minimum. Yet, what role then does a notion of justice play within the normative domain? Is it co-extensive with all the requirements of the principle of

[7] J Rawls, *A Theory of Justice*, revd edn (Cambridge, Belknap Harvard, 1999) 3.

[8] ibid, 6.

[9] Some philosophers have challenged this restriction of justice to the basic structure for reasons slightly different to the focus of this chapter: see, for instance, GA Cohen, 'Where the Action is: on the Site of Distributive Justice' (1997) 26 *Philosophy and Public Affairs* 3.

[10] Rawls, *Theory of Justice* (1999) 9 and 15. Rawls, for instance, suggests his theory leaves out how we are to conduct ourselves towards animals and the rest of nature.

utility or is it some sub-set of that domain? Mill sets out to explain why the notion of justice has the peculiar normative force it does and his answer is illuminating and, indeed, remains of great relevance for those of us concerned with this idea.

Mill argues that justice relates to an 'extraordinarily important and impressive kind of utility'.[11] The interest involved when we discuss justice, for Mill, is

> that of security, to everyone's feeling the most vital of all interests … security no human being could possibly do without; on it we depend for all our immunity from evil, and for the whole value of all and every good, beyond the passing moment.[12]

He goes on to say that:

> Our notion, therefore of the claim we have on our fellow creatures to join in making safe for us the very groundwork of our existence, gathers feelings around it so much more intense than those concerned in any of the more common cases of utility.[13]

Justice, Mill explains, has a peculiar strength, force and fundamental quality (as it has for Rawls). These characteristics thereof, however, are explained by its being deeply rooted in the most basic interests of individuals. Mill focuses on security though the way in which he explicates the idea is expansive and could include a wide range of interests we have in, for instance, our basic social and economic well-being. The simple point is that justice involves protection for the most basic interests of individuals: these interests are the foundation for attaining any other goods we might value and relate to the very basis of our existence and the meaning of our lives. We could reframe this and say that, according to Mill, justice is about a minimum set of protections for the most basic interests we have that can enable us to achieve a range of other goods in our lives.[14] Without such protections, any possibility of realising maximum utility for individuals fades from view: an attention to these minimum conditions is thus essential to attain a more expansive state of affairs in future.

Understood in this way, the notion of a social minimum flows very naturally from the very analytical features of the concept of justice itself. People will demand and be entitled to claim from any society in which they live the necessary conditions for being able to live decent lives and to achieve other goods they may value. Justice provides, in this view, the necessary foundation – which can be seen to provide a conception of the social minimum – for individual existence and flourishing.

The argument thus far seeks to show that justice already in and of itself articulates a limited domain of the normative realm and one which seeks to

[11] JS Mill, *Utilitarianism* (1863), ch 5 available at www.utilitarianism.com/mill1.htm.

[12] ibid, ch 5.

[13] ibid, ch 5.

[14] There are strong similarities here between Mill's account and what Rawls refers to as primary goods: see Rawls (n 7) 348: 'rational individuals, whatever else they want, desire certain things as prerequisites for carrying out their plans of life'.

specify minimum conditions for individuals in the social domain. It is, in some sense, thus intimately connected to the idea of a minimum threshold. However, this view is compatible with a wide variety of views as to what falls within the domain of justice. Are there good normative reasons then for including minimum thresholds *within* a conception of distributive justice itself?

B. Justice and the Minimum Core

In providing such a justification, it is necessary to justify the idea that there are distinct thresholds that are themselves normatively relevant to distributive justice. What might be said for this particular view?

To argue in favour of a 'tiered' version of distributive justice[15] returns to a deep point about the structure of individual interests. Let us take an interest in having access to adequate food, which is intimately tied to Mill's notion of being secure in the 'groundwork of one's existence'.[16] There are varying degrees to which this interest can be realised:

(i) individuals may lack food or any ability to gain access to it and be slowly wasting away;
(ii) they may have some income but not enough to eat healthily and display signs of malnutrition;
(iii) they may have enough income not to be malnourished but be in a continual state of worry as to whether that income source will last or whether it would be adequate;
(iv) they may have food guaranteed but only be able to gain access to repetitive and unattractive meals; and
(v) they may have sufficient income to be able to acquire healthy, diverse and attractive food and not have to worry about where their next meal will come from.

Clearly, it would be desirable for everyone to be in the latter category as that is necessary for individuals to flourish and be able to achieve so many other goods and goals. Yet, even if that is not possible, it is important to recognise that there is a significant improvement to move someone from the first state to the fourth (for instance).

The idea here is that certain forms of deprivation are more serious than others in how they affect the interests of individuals. Consequently, those states of deprivation place more urgent demands on us than others. Such urgency is normatively relevant and moving someone from one state to a better one in

[15] I have explored the notion of tiers in the structure of distributive justice in D Bilchitz, 'Equality, Liberty and Modern Constitutionalism' in G Hull (ed), *The Equal Society* (Maryland, Lexington Books, 2015) 236.

[16] Mill, *Utilitarianism* (1863) ch 5.

fact achieves something that is normatively significant. The key point here is to understand that individual well-being is not an all-or-nothing matter: improvements can come in degrees and those degrees matter. It is thus possible to talk about a state of affairs as being more or less just than another. Justice is not only a once-and-for-all achievement where any non-realisation of the full ideal is as serious as any other. Instead, there are degrees to which a society can fall short of achieving the full ideal. The crossing of various threshold matters and significantly improves individual lives: moving someone from stage (i) to (iv) above cannot be seen as normatively insignificant even if it is not fully adequate. There remains the recognition that there is a need to strive to achieve the full requirements of justice. Consequently, understanding the normative relevance of various thresholds does not detract from a continuous pressure for improvement until the complete requirements of justice are realised.

A crucial point flowing from this understanding of individual interests is that there is not only one standard against which individual lives are improved, but multiple standards. These standards each have normative relevance. This notion is important when dealing with justice in the real world: perhaps, if by magic it were possible to bring everyone to the high social minimum demanded by distributive justice, it would not be necessary to think in these terms. Since the real world does not involve such attractive but fantastical possibilities, it is necessary to recognise that there will be no automatic achievement of a high social minimum. If the only process that is feasible is a gradual attainment of various distributive justice ideals, then it seems necessary to recognise not just the pragmatic importance (a matter which will be elaborated on further below) but also the normative relevance of improvements in people's lives that meet various thresholds. In determining those thresholds, normatively relevant criteria can be used.

Perhaps the clearest example of a normatively relevant threshold concerns enabling individuals to have the necessary conditions to be free from threats to survival: without survival, there is no possibility of further flourishing. Consequently, this is a threshold which provides the basics for any further improvement in individual well-being.[17] That threshold also has a deep connection to the original impetus for a conception of justice at all, namely identifying necessary conditions for flourishing. The threshold, though, identifies those things that are so central, so fundamental, so urgent that no flourishing is possible without them.

These ideas are centrally connected to the notion of the 'minimum core' that has been developed in the field of socio-economic rights. The idea of the minimum core as initially articulated in General Comment 3 of the United Nations Committee on Economic, Social and Cultural Rights was designed to create a

[17] I have attempted to articulate the minimum core threshold in this way in D Bilchitz, *Poverty* (2007) 187. I have also suggested a second higher threshold which identifies the general necessary conditions for the fulfilment of a wide range of purposes at 188.

strong obligation on State parties to the International Covenant on Economic, Social and Cultural Rights to achieve 'minimum essential levels' of each of the rights contained therein.[18] The notion connects strongly with the idea that priority attention must be given to realising the most urgent needs of the most vulnerable.[19] That idea is intimately tied to the very basic impetus around the concept of justice (as articulated by Mill): to protect the most vital interests of individuals. It, however, conceives of the minimum deliberately in a reduced way that is not meant to exhaust the domain of what is protected by justice but to provide a normatively relevant conception of a minimum below which severe injustice results. Crossing this threshold is normatively significant: it achieves a certain amount of good in the world even if it does not exhaust all the good that must be achieved.[20]

It is important to recognise the various notions of the minimum that have been at play in this section. On the one hand, there is the notion that justice itself requires identifying minimum demands of morality and thus specifying a social minimum that a just society should establish. On the other hand, there is the idea of minimum thresholds or tiers within the notion of justice itself which attempt to capture the fact that the realisation of individual interests is a matter of degree and, consequently, that the realisation of justice itself can involve questions of degree. One such threshold is what has been termed the 'minimum core' which relates to a particularly fundamental threshold of having sufficient resources to survive. It is important to distinguish these different ideas of the minimum which are justified and capable of application in different ways.[21]

IV. THE CASE FOR MINIMALISM: INSTRUMENTAL ARGUMENTS

Having outlined the fact that thinking in terms of minima can have normative relevance, I turn to consider a second set of arguments for minimalism which

[18] CESCR, General Comment 3, para 10, available at www.refworld.org/docid/4538838e10.html (last accessed 11 May 2017).

[19] I sought to explore the underpinnings of this idea and elaborate upon it in Bilchitz (n 5).

[20] This can be seen to accord, perhaps with the vision of justice articulated by Amartya Sen that is not focused per se on the articulation of ideals of perfect justice for their own sake, but on the identification and elimination of concrete injustices in the world around us: see A Sen, *The Idea of Justice* (Cambridge, Harvard University Press, 2009) 7 and 21.

[21] K Young, 'The Minimum Core of Economic, and Social Rights: a Concept in Search of Content' (2008) 33 *Yale Journal of International Law* 113 identifies various ways in which the notion of the minimum core has been used. I argue in this chapter that, actually, there are different understandings of minimum thresholds in a theory of justice (or in giving expression to socio-economic rights) and the 'minimum core' language should be utilised as only one understanding of a social minimum. It identifies a normative concept of the general necessary conditions to be free from threats to survival. Young criticises the latter view: I do not find her critiques convincing, yet to address them properly would require a different chapter. Her alternative of focusing on indicators and benchmarks itself is insufficient as it too requires a normative foundation (indicators do not simply identify themselves). I attempt to justify the use of this minimum core standard in this piece (and elsewhere), but the scope of this chapter does not allow for a more detailed response to Young.

focuses upon their 'instrumental value'. In doing so, I set aside the argument above concerning the normative foundations of minima and, instead, focus on the instrumental benefits of 'thresholds' and 'tiers' in the context of distributive justice.

Instrumental arguments are essentially pragmatic in nature and are of the following form: achieving X is a valuable ideal; achieving Y, given reasonable assumptions is likely to contribute to the achievement of X; therefore, it is valuable to seek to achieve Y. We can replace these terms in this context with the following: achieving a just distribution of resources is a valuable ideal; achieving a minimum set of thresholds of social provision, given reasonable assumptions, is likely to contribute to the achievement of a just distribution of resources; therefore, it is valuable to seek to achieve that minimum set of thresholds. The question that we need to address before we can accept this argument is why thinking in terms of minimum thresholds is likely to achieve a just distribution of resources?

The one set of reasons we can give fall under the broad heading of 'possibility'. These arguments suggest that, in many societies across the world, the full achievement of distributive justice is either not attainable or does not appear to be attainable. Let us consider the first of these possibilities: in a number of poorly developed countries, the attempt to ensure everyone has a fully adequate level of resources they can command is simply not possible in the near future, in the context of existing global institutional arrangements (ie in the absence of large transfers of wealth from the rich to the poor). Malawi, for instance, has a population of 17 million people and a GDP per capita of US $381. Over 50 per cent of the population live below the national poverty line.[22] In such a context, the claim is that we need to focus on what is attainable in achieving a minimum threshold which will significantly help improve the lives of those who are worst off. Developing minimum thresholds allows for a focus on improvements which are clearly feasible and challenges a fatalism that suggests nothing can be done to improve people's lives. It is important, however, to connect this instrumental argument with the normative discussion above: setting minimum thresholds must not be utilised to avoid achieving the more expansive ideals with which it is connected. That means that these minimum thresholds should not be seen as final ends in themselves but stages in the process of continuous development towards the achievement of the final goal: the ideal just distribution of resources.

This connects with an idea of fundamental rights which I've termed the 'bridging conception'.[23] This involves conceiving of such right as moral ideals which create a pressure for legal institutionalisation. It is not always possible to introduce concrete measures to achieve the full realisation of rights immediately.

[22] Statistics are from World Bank Data available at http://data.worldbank.org/country/malawi.

[23] D Bilchitz, 'Fundamental Rights as Bridging Concepts: Straddling the Boundary between Ideal Justice and an Imperfect Reality' (2018) 40 *Human Rights Quarterly* 119, 124–32.

Amartya Sen, for instance, writes about 'the need to work towards changing the prevailing circumstances to make the unrealized rights realizable and ultimately realized'.[24] Sen writes further that '[to] see the ethical force of some claims is also a demand to consider what one should do to make them realizable, for example through working for the development of new institutions'.[25] The fact that a right cannot be fully realised now does not mean that nothing can be done to help achieve it. Thinking in terms of minima can help in two ways: first, connected with the first argument, it can focus on a particularly urgent set of individual needs and render their realisation a priority, something that is also often more feasible. Secondly, it can help focus our attention on what can be done to alleviate the plight of individuals in these circumstances and set targeted and achievable goals to improve their conditions.[26] In this way, setting minimum thresholds can help address the gap between ideals and the concrete and difficult real-life circumstances faced by individuals.

Whilst minimum thresholds have these very concrete advantages, a challenge could be that they take away the focus from the achievement of the ultimate goal of a decent social minimum that meets the full requirements of distributive justice. It could also be argued that such thresholds could render people satisfied with the status quo and lead them to fail to see that justice creates a much wider and deeper challenge to existing distributions. These objections suggest the importance of ensuring that minimum thresholds are not themselves seen as a substitute for a more expansive conception of what justice requires (and the consequent more expansive social minimum). In the Malawian example above, for instance, I stated that it is not possible to bring everyone out of poverty quickly, given – as one part of an explanation – the structure of global institutional arrangements. The recognition that minimum thresholds can help us on the path to distributive justice should not preclude a wider critique of those global institutional arrangements (and wider global economic structures) which could reasonably require greater transfers of wealth from rich to poor countries. The two are not mutually exclusive. The point, even in such circumstances, is that minimum thresholds may allow for the recognition that there are targets short of full realisation of distributive justice which can be achieved and represent progress; in contrast, the alternative approach would recognise no progress until the full requirements of distributive justice are achieved.

Indeed, these concerns are connected to the second dimension I mentioned above about the perceptions of what is possible in correcting the current wrongs of resource distribution in the world. Addressing the poverty in Malawi overall may well seem like a gargantuan task that simply goes beyond

[24] A Sen, 'Elements of a Theory of Human Rights' (2004) 32 *Philosophy and Public Affairs* 315, 348.

[25] ibid, fn 55.

[26] There is a connection between the normative and instrumental arguments here: the normatively relevant set of urgent interests can help guide what must be done in the interim.

what well-off countries are able to sell to their populace (even if it is right). Political feasibility is a real constraint in the achievement of greater distributive justice. We know how difficult it is to ensure, for instance, that desperate refugees are provided with homes in Europe, even if that is what justice requires. Minimum thresholds may well help with this problem: particularly, if connected to the minimum core, they provide an understanding of a threshold of great urgency below which people are in terrible desperation. Marshalling the resources to address such circumstances may well be more politically feasible than attempting fully to achieve a wider global distributive justice ideal (and higher social minimum). This reasoning requires us to accept that the 'best must not be the enemy of the good': achieving some advances should not be hindered as a result of our inability to do even better. Of course, that should not stop us from pushing for greater improvements beyond the minimum thresholds, but provides a reason why it may be effective to think politically in such terms.

Connected with these reasons is also the idea that a focus on achieving minimum thresholds is important from a perspective focused on efficient realisation of distributive justice ideals. Performance management today often focuses on the achievement of particular targets, goals and benchmarks: if these are not set, then individual performance tends to be worse. Minimum thresholds can be seen as defining such targets and providing the basis for efficient management of performance in the context of a problem which is truly difficult and cannot be solved immediately. Once again, such arguments do not provide the basis for such minima to be fixed for all time: there is a need for a baseline (the minimum core, as suggested above) and then a continuous setting of further goals for improvement. The usefulness of this reasoning is borne out by the international community recognising the need to set targets such as the Millennium Development Goals and Sustainable Development Goals (SDGs).

Indeed, an important instrumental benefit of thinking in terms of minimum thresholds also relates to the very *process* involved in setting thresholds and goals in a manner that is in some sense separate from the content of those standards. When thinking about, for example, the SDGs, cross-disciplinary approaches were taken seriously in achieving the minimum ideals contained therein. Since many groups wanted their projects to fit under an SDG rubric, real negotiation had to go into defining these aims. Similarly, the development of these thresholds requires thinking carefully about the normative factors that should influence how they are conceived. That, in turn, can aid in the better articulation of those thresholds. The development of such goals and thresholds thus can help encourage discussion, research and consensus around what the basic conditions of distributive justice are and so provide some real progress in advancing those ideals.[27]

[27] I am grateful to Robert Freeman for pressing this point on me.

Some of these ideas are also based upon a recognition that the achievement of a just state of affairs is not something that happens immediately. It is something that takes time and requires gradual improvement. Indeed, this argument again could be connected with the first set of normative arguments provided above to create a strong, pressing urgent demand for the achievement of the minimum core. This is important so that no individual is left in conditions of extreme deprivation. At the same time, there is the need for the recognition that moving beyond the minimum core will require gradual but definite processes for the realisation of a higher and more adequate social minimum which represents a just distribution of resources.

V. THE CASE FOR MINIMALISM: DEMOCRATIC ARGUMENTS

The third set of arguments in defence of minimalism are democratic ones. They concern, on the one hand, an epistemological set of reasons why it may be difficult to know what the complete requirements of distributive justice are. On the other hand, a related concern involves the difficulty of reaching consensus around the requirements of distributive justice: indeed, we see a large amount of disagreement, even amongst philosophers who professionally are required to think about these matters. We can, for instance, think about the implications of a theory such as that of John Rawls, which requires us to think about providing the greatest benefit to the least advantaged;[28] there is then the theory of Ronald Dworkin, which involves a conception of equality of resources;[29] and Robert Nozick's provides a contrasting entitlement theory of justice.[30] The lack of consensus around how resources should be distributed in society may well be connected to the epistemological problems of knowing what constitutes a complete understanding of a just distribution. The reason for such difficulties may lie in an account such as that offered by Rawls concerning the 'burdens of judgment': this seeks to explain why reasonable people differ concerning major questions in a democracy such as distributive justice.[31] The evidence, for instance, is often complex to assess, different weightings are given to different pieces of evidence, and there are a range of different normative considerations which often pull in different directions.[32]

Of course, such disagreement does not mean that there is not a correct approach to distributive justice or that, sometimes, disagreement may not be manufactured for purposes of maintaining an unjust status quo. It would, however, also not be true to suggest that the full requirements of distributive

[28] See, for instance, Rawls (n 7) 53.
[29] R Dworkin, *Sovereign Virtue* (Cambridge, Harvard University Press, 2000).
[30] R Nozick, *Anarchy, State and Utopia* (Oxford, Blackwell, 1974).
[31] J Rawls, *Political Liberalism* (New York, Columbia University Press, 1993) 55–57.
[32] ibid, 56–57.

justice are clear and simple. In a democratic space, thus, it would seem necessary in the face of persistent disagreement, to subject decisions about the full understanding of which distribution is just to popular discussion and voting. A society may, in this way, decide on what the requirements of justice are: arriving at such a decision could be one conception of what constitutes the social minimum in that society. This approach would connect with the manner in which justice and the idea of a social minimum overlap as was argued in section III of this chapter: the social minimum would simply be what individuals in that society determine constitutes the threshold which gives expression to a just distribution in that society.

The notion of the social minimum though is slightly ambiguous and it could have other meanings too. This alternative view flows from a further thought: if we do not fully agree on or know what the full requirements of distributive justice are, could we nevertheless not reach a partial agreement in this regard on what clearly falls within its domain? Are there perhaps minimum requirements of justice that we do clearly know exist and which are much less the subject of reasonable disagreement? A strong argument for approaches which set minimum thresholds of distributive justice is that they articulate and give expression to much less controversial requirements that everyone acknowledges (or should acknowledge) form part of any reasonable conception thereof. Why would this be the case?

The reasons again go back to some of the claims made in relation to the first normative argument in section III of this chapter. The minimum thresholds of distributive justice relate to individual needs and interests which are particularly urgent in the lives of any individual. Not having food, or any shelter is something every human being can relate to; and it is not something that anyone can reasonably want to be without, assuming they want to achieve anything else in their lives. Of course, there are those who deliberately fast out of, for example, religious conviction – but they have the choice to eat: if we lack food at all, and we value our own existence, then we must wish to change our situation. Every individual who values their existence has an interest in having sufficient food at least to survive – and this situation flows from uncontroversial facts about human biology. It is hard to see then how we cannot at least know with a high level of confidence that a distribution which denies individuals the resources necessary to survive is unjust. Such a level of resources is also necessary for an individual to be able to participate in any democratic decision-making: an argument for participation based upon disagreement thus assumes there is a certain minimum level of resources that individuals have access to. Consequently, it seems quite clear that individuals should assent to recognising that any conception of distributive justice must at least ensure that individuals have the general resources necessary to survive. Not to do so would also involve individuals in holding a contradictory, or at least hypocritical position: of needing to claim such a level of resource provision themselves, but denying it to others. Such a guarantee of a minimum core level of resource distribution also need not be put to the popular vote in a democracy: it is a precondition for democratic participation itself and so can be placed beyond the realm of popular approval (and guaranteed in constitutional rights upon which the judiciary may legitimately pronounce).

Whereas there is a reasonable degree of certainty around the minimum core level, it might also be possible to reach significant consensus about a sufficiency threshold above this very minimal threshold. Such a threshold could well be defended in philosophical terms: as articulating a minimum level of general resources people require in order to be in a position to achieve their purposes or goals. This idea would be connected to Rawls' notion of primary goods discussed above: they are necessary conditions for achieving any of the conceptions of the good people may want.[33] This threshold would involve a more complex series of considerations than the purely survival-based one: it could include, for instance, psychological interests such as the notion that individuals require self-respect in order to be able to achieve their goals and so need the resources in a society necessary to experience such self-respect. That might not just entail having, for instance, warm clothing, but also a particular type of clothing which is necessary to appear in public without shame. Adam Smith mentions, in his time, a linen shirt;[34] in many societies today, possessing a mobile phone would perhaps fall into this category. Thus, it may well be that we can philosophically defend guaranteeing such a level of resources to individuals with a relatively high degree of certainty concerning its justifiability. At the same time, such a level may also be defensible from a democratic point of view: there could be very limited disagreement amongst individuals in a society around the need for certain resources to live a decent life in that community if that is already widely accepted (the linen shirt or mobile phone). As such, given the high level of consensus that should be forthcoming on such a socially accepted minimum, it would be possible to provide strong guarantees for such a higher social sufficiency threshold too. That higher threshold could also, in a significant manner, be termed a social minimum: in this context, it would not fully realise the conception of distributive justice in that society. Instead, it would represent the minimum level of resources which it is widely accepted every individual must have in order to function well within that community.

It is clear that the more extensive the resources that are claimed, and the more expansive any threshold becomes, the higher the level of disagreement around it that is likely to occur. There are significant objective measures today as to what resources humans need to survive and thus what is required for a minimum core; deciding on what a sufficient or adequate amount of resources is, once again, open to a higher level of uncertainty and, consequently, higher levels of disagreement. As we saw, determining a complete understanding of distributive

[33] See n 14 (Rawls (n 7) 348).
[34] See A Sen, *Development as Freedom* (Oxford, Oxford University Press, 1999) 73–74.

justice would be the least certain and most controversial. Minimalism thus takes on an important democratic hue in providing a basis on which to maximise the agreement and knowledge that we have while also allowing adequate space for discussion and disagreement about the dictates of distributive justice. It would thus support stronger entitlements to be guaranteed for the first threshold and, also, in all likelihood the second social sufficiency threshold too. In relation to these thresholds, courts would have a role in setting the normative standards involved and determining whether government action complies with them. In relation to the wider question of what a completely just distribution should be, in a democracy, such a matter would not be capable of a definitive substantive solution but need to be addressed procedurally: it would be for public participation and the political process to decide on these more ultimate matters.

VI. CONCLUSION

This chapter has focused on considering the deeper reasons for a practice we commonly utilise: namely, providing an account of minimum thresholds of resource distribution that must be guaranteed in a society. In so doing, it has rendered more complex our conception of what constitutes such a minimum. I first provided an argument which sought to show that the very domain of justice in some sense is conceptually connected with the notion of there being a minimum set of moral demands. The justice social minimum would thus be the distribution of resources that would fully meet the requirements of distributive justice. The chapter then turned to consider what the justification was for determining minimum thresholds within the domain of justice itself. I identified at least two meaningful thresholds that could be justified on the basis of the grounds provided in this chapter. First, there is a minimalist understanding which is very basic and which can be termed the 'minimum core'. This identifies the general necessary preconditions to be free from threats to survival. It is a conception of the minimum without which individuals cannot continue and which, if they value their existence, they cannot deny wanting to achieve. Finally, there is an intermediate idea of a sufficiency social minimum which identifies the general conditions necessary for individuals to achieve their purposes and goals. It is an idea which may vary in different societies but could lead to large-scale agreement on a threshold below which individuals should not fall in order to succeed in their goals and be treated with respect in that society.

The distinction between these different ideas of the social minimum is important as our approach to them, and uses thereof may vary depending on which idea we are concerned with. The last two visions of the minimum, for instance, may allow also for a distinction between what societies guarantee to their own citizens and what they must guarantee minimally to all within their borders. The minimum core, it could be recognised, arises as a duty that flows to all individuals who have value. A society may decide that it does not wish to provide individuals with a sufficiency threshold who lack strong ties to their political community. Similarly, a minimum core might be guaranteed to individuals without any concern for their responsibility in bringing about their desperate plight; however, a society may be less inclined to guarantee individuals the sufficiency threshold if individuals have deliberately squandered away their prior holdings of resources. These are just some of the uses to which these distinctions could be put in a theory of distributive justice as well as within political processes and constitutional jurisprudence. The goal of this chapter was to provide arguments as to why engaging with the idea of minimum thresholds is strongly defensible in any theory of distributive justice and to articulate the different understandings thereof.

3

An Essential Dimension of the Social Minimum[1]

MALCOLM TORRY

I. INTRODUCTION

THIS CHAPTER CONTRIBUTES to the discussion of the social minimum by conceptualising it in three dimensions: the different resources that need to be provided; the characteristics of the provision of those resources; and the ways in which delivery methods are structured.

The *Stanford Encyclopedia of Philosophy* defines a social minimum as 'that bundle of resources which suffices in the circumstances of a given society to enable someone to lead a minimally decent life', and a social minimum policy regime as 'a set of policies and institutions that serve to secure reasonable access to this social minimum for all members of the society'.[2] For the purposes of this chapter, 'resources' means such different types of welfare provision as education, healthcare, income, and so on; 'characteristics' means such measurable characteristics of the resources as their quality, the level of equality of their provision, the ease with which the resources can be accessed, and the efficiency with which the resources are provided; and 'mode of delivery' means the way in which delivery is structured: for instance, whether healthcare is funded by individual insurance policies or by general taxation.

This chapter will construct a partial and provisional categorisation of the 'bundle of resources', and also a list of the characteristics of those resources that would be required if those resources are to promote a minimally decent life. Relationships between the various resources and the various characteristics will then be discussed, and then the characteristics' relationships with different modes of delivery.

[1] I am most grateful to Jeff King for the commentary on the paper offered at the seminar, and for subsequent written comments; to Ben Warwick for commentary on a first draft of this chapter at the authors' meeting; and to all of the participants at both the seminar and the authors' meeting.

[2] S White, 'Social Minimum' in EN Zalta, *The Stanford Encyclopedia of Philosophy*, Winter 2015 edn, available at plato.stanford.edu/archives/win2015/entries/social-minimum.

II. DIMENSIONS

In the academic literature the welfare state is often discussed in terms of a number of dimensions of welfare, but the word 'dimension' can have a variety of meanings. Bo Rothstein defines the dimensions of the welfare state as: (i) coverage; and (ii) allocation method.[3] Gilbert and Specht define four dimensions of social policy as (i) the bases of social allocation; (ii) the types of social provision; (iii) the strategies for delivery; and (iv) the ways to finance the provision made.[4] Gilbert and Terrell reiterate these dimensions, and add some more: equality, equity, and adequacy; and then still more: work incentives, childbearing, family stability, stigma/social integration; and such dimensions of allocation as attributed need, compensation, diagnostic differentiation, and means-tested need;[5] and then more again. Rothstein's and Steinmo's institutional understanding of the welfare state suggests a spectrum along which we might locate 'client institution', 'user institution' and 'customer institution': a spectrum along which empowerment is at a minimum at the 'client institution' end, and at its maximum at the 'customer institution' end.[6] Such a spectrum suggests a definition of 'dimension' with similarities to the word's core usage in relation to three-dimensional space. By the end of this chapter we shall find ourselves with reasons for using the concept of a dimension in a similar way.

III. RESOURCES REQUIRED FOR A 'MINIMALLY DECENT LIFE'

For the purposes of this chapter I shall assume that 'a minimally decent life' and 'the avoidance of poverty' mean much the same. This does not mean that 'dimensions of poverty' and 'dimensions of the social minimum' are synonymous. Dimensions of poverty might be 'intensity', 'duration', or 'type' (poverty as the norm, poverty for the few, poverty as a constant risk, and so on).[7] These would not apply to a social minimum. And we shall find ourselves formulating

[3] B Rothstein, *Just Institutions Matter: The Moral and Political Logic of the Universal Welfare State* (Cambridge, Cambridge University Press, 1998) 20.

[4] N Gilbert and H Specht, *Dimensions of Social Welfare Policy* (Englewood Heights, NJ, Prentice Hall, 1974) 29.

[5] N Gilbert and P Terrell, *Dimensions of Social Welfare Policy* (Upper Saddle River, NJ, Pearson Education, 2013) 76–78, 102–06, 108–11.

[6] B Rothstein and S Steinmo 'Restructuring Politics: Institutional Analysis and the Challenges of Modern Welfare States' in Rothstein and Steinmo (eds) *Restructuring the Welfare State: Political Institutions and Policy Change* (New York, Palgrave Macmillan, 2002) 15; S Kumlin, 'Institutions – Experiences – Preferences: How Welfare State Design Affects Political Trust and Ideology' in Rothstein and Steinmo (ibid) 26.

[7] S Paugam, 'What Forms does Poverty take in European Societies at the Beginning of the Twenty-first Century?' in K De Boyser, C Dewilde, D Dierickx and J Friedrichs (eds) *Between the Social and the Spatial: Exploring the Multiple Dimensions of Poverty and Social Exclusion* (Farnham, Ashgate, 2009) 8–9, 17.

dimensions for the social minimum that do not apply to poverty. They would, of course, apply to the alleviation or abolition of poverty that the provision of a social minimum would imply.

I shall also leave to one side two somewhat extreme definitions of the social minimum: (i) an equal distribution of a society's wealth;[8] and (ii) the 'minimum level of material well-being required before people are plunged into despair'.[9] Instead, I shall ask what we might mean by 'a minimally decent life', and work out from that what resources might be required.

How should we decide what constitutes a minimally decent life? One approach to the avoidance of poverty, often called the 'Breadline Britain' tradition after the 1983 book of that title, is to ask a representative sample of a population what resources they think are required to enable someone to live a minimally decent life. (This is the process employed to set the Minimum Income Standards published annually by the Joseph Rowntree Foundation.)[10] A second approach is the kind of social minimum that Barrientos suggests Rawls has in mind: a 'justice-based social minimum' constructed via a society's democratic institutions.[11] Rawls proposes a social minimum that 'together with the whole family of social policies, maximises the life prospects of the least advantaged over time'.[12] A third approach is to set out from the concept of 'human need', with 'need' defined in what might look like a normative fashion. This was the approach taken by Seebohm Rowntree in York 100 years ago;[13] and a similar approach stems from Abraham Maslow's hierarchy of human needs: first 'safety needs', then 'love needs', and finally 'esteem needs',[14] with 'safety needs' understood as biological (food, drink, and shelter) and as safety and security. A similar and fourth approach emerges from Amartya Sen's 'capabilities' approach to poverty. Here the question is this: What are the resources required to enable someone to exercise capabilities? Or, to state the obverse: What resources are required to avoid capabilities poverty?[15] This approach suggests that human need is in some way normative, whereas in fact

[8] J Waldron, 'John Rawls and the Social Minimum' (1986) 3 *The Journal of Applied Philosophy* 21, 30; K Widerquist, 'How the Sufficiency Minimum becomes a Social Maximum' (2010) 22 *Utilitas* 474.

[9] Waldron, 'John Rawls' 21.

[10] S Lansley and J Mack, *Breadline Britain* (London, London Weekend Television, 1983); S Lansley and J Mack, *Breadline Britain* (London, Oneworld, 2015); A Davis, K Hill, D Hirsch and M Padley, *A Minimum Income Standard for the UK in 2016* (York, Joseph Rowntree Foundation, 2016). In this volume see ch 6 for a discussion of minimum income standards.

[11] A Barrientos, 'Justice-based Social Assistance' (2016) 16 *Global Social Policy* 151, 154–56.

[12] J Rawls, *Justice as Fairness: A Restatement* (London, The Belknap Press of Harvard University Press, 2001) 129–30.

[13] P Townsend, *Poverty in the United Kingdom* (London, Allen Lane, 1979) 32–34.

[14] A Maslow 'A Theory of Human Motivation' (1943) 50 *Psychological Review* 370, 376–82.

[15] S Alkire, 'Choosing Dimensions: The Capability Approach and Multidimensional Poverty' in N Kakwani and J Silber (eds), *The Many Dimensions of Poverty* (Basingstoke, Palgrave Macmillan, 2007) 91; S Reader, 'Does a Basic Needs Approach need capabilities?' (2006) 14 *The Journal of Political Philosophy* 337.

it is to a large extent socially constructed,[16] but it remains true that someone for whom such lower level needs as food, drink and shelter have not been fulfilled will find their very existence threatened, their needs for affiliation, esteem, knowledge, the aesthetic, transcendence and self-realisation[17] difficult to fulfil, and any potential capabilities difficult to exercise.

The 'Breadline Britain' approach to the social minimum automatically generates a list of resources required for a minimally decent life. The justice-based approach requires a similar method to be applied to the least advantaged individual. The third and fourth approaches can be understood either as similar one-stage processes (we need food, so food has to be provided), or as a two-stage process (we need health, so we need a healthcare system).[18]

In a modern society, an income can substitute for some of these resources. This is clearly true of food and drink; it might or might not be true of shelter, although for most households it will be; and it might not be true of healthcare and other public services. The problems related to income are that the different approaches to the social minimum can deliver very different suggestions as to how much income is required for a social minimum, and that the income intended to provide for a social minimum might be chosen in relation to political and affordability constraints rather than in relation to any of the methods discussed above.[19] The problem with healthcare is rather different. The problem here is that two different individuals might need radically different amounts of healthcare if they are both to live minimally decent lives: so in order to ensure that everyone in a society can lead a minimally decent life, healthcare itself has to be provided rather than an income with which to purchase it. It might be objected that an income can be used to purchase healthcare insurance. It can be for some, but not for everyone, as some individuals would be regarded as uninsurable; and, for society as a whole, an insurance-based healthcare system suffers from multiple market failures, and so is less efficient than government-provided universal and unconditional healthcare.[20] This means that income and healthcare are not substitutes, and it is no surprise that Stuart White defines a 'civic minimum' as constituted by both income and healthcare,[21] and that Erik Thorbecke suggests that an income measure is not sufficient because 'it does not incorporate key dimensions of poverty such as life-expectancy (longevity),

[16] H Dean, *Understanding Human Need: Social Issues, Policy and Practice* (Bristol, Policy Press, 2010) 46–47.

[17] Maslow, 'Human Motivation' (1943) 376–82.

[18] S Reader, 'Does a Basic Needs Approach need Capabilities?' (2006) 14 *The Journal of Political Philosophy* 337.

[19] AB Atkinson, *A National Minimum? A History of Ambiguity in the Determination of Benefit Scales in Britain* (London, London School of Economics, 1990).

[20] M Torry, 'Primary Care, the Basic Necessity: Part I: Explorations in Economics' in A Papanikitas and J Spicer (eds) *Handbook of Primary Care Ethics* (Boca Raton, FL, CRC/Francis and Taylor, 2017).

[21] S White, *The Civic Minimum: On the Rights and Obligations of Economic Citizenship* (Oxford, Oxford University Press, 2003) 99, 131–32.

literacy, the provision of public goods, freedom and security': the attributes of social provision required to enable every individual to experience the 'capabilities and functioning' that Amartya Sen believed necessary for the avoidance of poverty.[22] A further reason for separating healthcare and income is offered by Atkinson:

> Whereas a relative income standard has come to be used within country groupings, such as the EU [because the income required for participation in society will differ between different societies], there are good grounds for applying an absolute health deprivation standard [age at death, infant mortality rate, etc.], certainly when comparing across countries and, if adjustments are made over time, they are likely to be infrequent rather than annual.[23]

Sufficient income to pay for food, drink, and shelter (including clothing), and publicly provided healthcare will be essential members of any list of necessary resources. Others might be education, public transport, policing, a courts system, legal representation, and perhaps social cohesion.[24] For the purposes of this chapter, I shall concentrate on income and healthcare.

IV. CHARACTERISTICS OF THE RESOURCES

Each of these resources possesses a variety of characteristics – such as efficiency and equity – and, in different countries, different ways of delivering the resources will mean that the resource will be characterised by more or less equity, more or less efficiency, and so on.

Take healthcare as an example. The Commonwealth Fund, based in New York, has evaluated 11 OECD countries' healthcare systems in relation to a variety of characteristics and sub-characteristics:

- quality (effectiveness, safety, co-ordination, and person-centredness);
- ease of access (affordability and timeliness);
- efficiency (expenditure, administrative costs, administrative efficiency, appropriate use of resources, non-duplication);
- equity (understood as equality);
- 'healthy lives', in terms of 'mortality amenable to medical care, infant mortality, and healthy life expectancy at age 60'[25] (a more general term is 'outcome').

[22] E Thorbecke, 'Multidimensional Poverty: Conceptual and Measurement Issues' in Kakwani and Silber (eds) *Dimensions of Poverty* (2007) 17.

[23] AB Atkinson, 'Income, Health and Multi-dimensionality' in De Boyser et al *Between the Social and the Spatial* (2009) 24.

[24] De Boyser et al (n 7) 220.

[25] K Davis, K Stremikis, D Squires and C Schoen, *Mirror, Mirror, on the Wall: How the Performance of the US Healthcare System Compares Internationally* (New York, Commonwealth Fund, 2014) 28–29.

The researchers find that the United Kingdom is ranked first overall and first in relation to most of the characteristics, and that the United States is ranked last overall, and either last or a long way down the rankings in relation to most of the characteristics.

Each of the first four main indicators that the Commonwealth Fund measured relates to a characteristic of a healthcare system: its quality, its ease of access, its efficiency, and its equity. The fifth is somewhat different: healthy lives. A healthcare system is only partially responsible for the healthiness or otherwise of people's lives, and other factors can be more important. I therefore translate this characteristic as 'outcome'.

The fact that the UK's healthcare system is doing so well in relation to most of the indicators, and that the US system is doing so badly, is an issue to which we shall return.

The first thing to say about the list above is that the division between characteristics and sub-characteristics (which the Commonwealth Fund calls 'indicators' and 'general characteristics') is somewhat arbitrary: both because any such categorisations are largely matters of subjective choice, and because each of the sub-characteristics could be regarded as characteristics. It is because the boundary between 'indicator' and 'general characteristic' is far from clear that I prefer the terminology 'characteristic' and 'sub-characteristic'.

The second and equally important question raised by this list is whether these characteristics are applicable to the other resources required for a minimally decent life in society. Take education as an example: all four characteristics are meaningful, as are their sub-characteristics. In relation to quality, all of effectiveness, safety, co-ordination, and person-centredness would apply; in relation to ease of access, affordability and timeliness are important; in relation to efficiency, expenditure, administrative costs, administrative efficiency, appropriate use of resources and non-duplication, are relevant; equity matters; and the 'outcome' would be a well-educated population. The list feels as complete in relation to education as it does in relation to healthcare. The same might be true of emergency services and public transport, and might potentially be true of other resources that we might wish to add to the list.

However, the list of characteristics that might seem obvious in relation to healthcare and education might not be quite so appropriate in relation to income provision. So here we might require a different set of characteristics: or, if we employ the same list of characteristics, we shall find that the characteristics will mean different things in relation to the different resources, and that the lists of sub-characteristics will be different. None of this is a problem, as we can see if we study the method employed by the Commonwealth Fund. The Commonwealth Fund's researchers employed surveys and other empirical data to generate measurements of their chosen healthcare sub-characteristics in different countries, then combined those scores into scores for each characteristic, and then ranked countries in relation to those scores: and finally they employed a variety of methods to generate overall scores for each country's healthcare system.[26] We shall always be able to construct lists of characteristics and sub-characteristics, we shall always be able to conduct surveys to evaluate to what extent the characteristics are met in different contexts, and although it will never be possible to compare scores across different resources, we shall always be able to rank different contexts in relation to the characteristics of each individual resource, and we shall always be able to ascribe an overall ranking to each context for each resource. This is what matters: so it is not a problem that the lists of characteristics and sub-characteristics might be different for different resources.

Suppose that we wished to conduct a survey and collect other data to discover how people regard the income maintenance system in the UK. First of all, we would need to distinguish between earnings, other forms of income, the tax system, and the benefits system, and we would need to treat each of them separately. We would also need to treat different types of social security benefit differently: for instance, Child Benefit behaves very differently from such means-tested benefits as Jobseeker's Allowance, Child Tax Credits, Working Tax Credits, and Universal Credit. If we decided to set out from the list of characteristics employed by the Commonwealth Fund, we would quickly find ourselves dividing them. 'Effective' could mean 'prevents poverty' and 'incentivises employment'. 'Safety' could mean 'avoids bureaucratic intrusion' and 'ensures continuity of provision'. 'Co-ordinated' could mean 'fits with desired family and employment structure' and 'co-ordinates with other income streams'. 'Person-centred' could mean any or all of 'adapts to individual needs', 'avoids stigmatisation', and 'encourages personal choice'. 'Affordable' needs to apply to the claimant, so it could mean 'the claiming process is not costly in terms of money' and 'the claiming process is not costly in terms of time', and it might also mean 'does not result in overpayments that have to be paid back'. 'Timely' could mean 'payments are always made on time' and 'correct payments are made from the date of the claim'. 'Expenditure' refers to the total cost of each benefit, and 'administrative costs' and 'administrative efficiency' are what they say they are, but 'appropriate use of resources' could mean 'those who need more should receive more' and 'the benefits system should provide everyone with the income that they need in order to live a minimally decent life in society'. 'Non-duplication' might or might not be a desirable feature of benefits systems. Non-duplication suggests administrative efficiency, but it might also be desirable for one income source, such as social security benefits, to incentivise the pursuit of other income sources, such as earnings.

Whether or not we choose to use the Commonwealth Fund's list of characteristics, once we have listed all of the possible sub-characteristics, we can employ the same method as the Commonwealth Fund.[27] We can use survey and

[26] Davis et al, *Mirror, Mirror, on the Wall* (2014) 28–29.
[27] ibid.

other methods to construct scores for the different sub-characteristics, and then use a method similar to that used by the Commonwealth Fund researchers to construct overall scores for the characteristics, and from those we can construct rankings and overall rankings.

What the method does not require is that sub-characteristics should appear to be consistent. This is fortunate. 'Those who need more should receive more' and 'the benefits system should provide everyone with the income that they need to provide themselves with a minimally decent life in society' appear to be inconsistent because 'the benefits system should provide everyone with the income that they need to live a minimally decent life in society' might suggest universal and unconditional benefits, and 'those who need more should receive more' might suggest means-tested benefits. However, the inconsistency might be more linguistic than actual. The same amount of money given to everyone will always increase the net incomes of low earners by a higher proportion than it increases the net incomes of higher earners;[28] and research on proposals to pay an unconditional income to every member of a population shows that such schemes can be designed to redistribute from rich to poor, to reduce poverty, to reduce inequality, to achieve zero net cost, to ensure almost zero losses for low income households on the point of implementation, and to require minimal increases in rates of income tax.[29] But whether or not different characteristics are or are not consistent, and whether or not they appear to be consistent, the method is not compromised. Each sub-characteristic can always be separately scored for each resource in each context; the scores can be combined to create scores for characteristics (whether or not the same characteristics are listed for each resource), rankings can be calculated, and then overall rankings can be ascribed.

It therefore appears that the 'characteristics and subcharacteristics' method can be used in relation to income provision in much the same way as it can be used in other social policy fields. The kinds of surveys and other data-gathering exercises that have generated the international comparisons delivered by the Commonwealth Fund in relation to healthcare systems could easily be used to compare the benefits systems in different countries, and to compare different kinds of benefits within the same country. Equally interesting would be to spread the net further in order to take in other types of income provision, because the

[28] B Rothstein, 'The Universal Welfare State as a Social Dilemma' in Rothstein and Steinmo (eds) *Restructuring the Welfare State* (2002) 210–11.

[29] M Torry, 'A Variety of Indicators Evaluated for Two Implementation Methods for a Citizen's Basic Income', Institute for Social and Economic Research Working Paper EM12/17 (Colchester, Institute for Social and Economic Research, University of Essex, 2017); M Torry, 'An Update, a Correction, and an Extension of an Evaluation of an Illustrative Citizen's Basic Income Scheme – Addendum to EUROMOD Working Paper EM12/17', Institute for Social and Economic Research Working Paper EM12/17a (Colchester, Institute for Social and Economic Research, University of Essex, 2018), available at www.iser.essex.ac.uk/research/publications/working-papers/euromod/em12-17a.

same method could just as easily be employed in relation to earned income and pensions income.

When we set out to construct a list of sub-characteristics to enable us to evaluate income maintenance, we set out from the list of characteristics appropriate for the evaluation of healthcare. The risk of doing this is that we might miss important characteristics and sub-characteristics that might relate to income provision, but not to healthcare. One important characteristic that might be important in relation to income is revealed when we think of the social minimum in terms of its obverse: poverty. A poverty trap occurs where institutional arrangements trap people in poverty. The more positive social minimum characteristic would be ease of progression. Means-tested benefits can constitute traps, because, as earnings rise, benefits can be reduced at the same time as tax is paid, imposing a high marginal deduction rate, of up to 96 per cent in some cases in the UK.[30] Such universal and unconditional benefits as Child Benefit and the Winter Fuel Allowance do not cause such traps, and so offer ease of progression. Do such traps exist in the context of other social minimum resources? Arguably, yes. The question to be asked is whether the institutions involved prevent progress towards achieving a minimally decent life.[31] So, for instance: in healthcare, do the budgetary and institutional boundaries between hospital care and local authority social care prevent progress towards independence following an accident or illness? What we are discussing here is the 'process freedom' that Amartya Sen discusses alongside the 'capabilities' freedom experienced in the situation to which process freedom will take us, and it suggests that there is a characteristic missing from all of our lists – effective pathways – and that this needs to be applied to all of the resources.[32]

We have shown that the characteristics employed by the Commonwealth Fund to rank healthcare systems can also be employed for education provision, and might be useful in relation to income provision if different lists of sub-characteristics are employed. What we have not so far shown to be legitimate is to compare the scores generated by a characteristic of income provision across different countries with the scores generated by the same characteristic of healthcare. The indicators used would be different, which suggests that comparison would be impossible. What we *would* be able to compare would be the two rankings of the different countries in relation to that characteristic.

A similar question arises in relation to each country: in the Commonwealth Fund project each of the different scores given to characteristics is constructed from a wide variety of indicators for sub-characteristics: for instance, the 'quality'

[30] R Murphy and H Reed, *Financing the Social State: Towards a Full Employment Economy* (London, Centre for Labour and Social Studies, 2013) 25–27.

[31] A Sindzingre 'The Multidimensionality of Poverty: An Institutionalist Perspective' in Nanak Kakwani and Jacques Silber (eds) *The Many Dimensions of Poverty* (Basingstoke, Palgrave Macmillan, 2007) 63.

[32] A Sen, *The Idea of Justice* (London, Allen Lane, 2009) 225–52, 370–71.

score is constructed from 44 different indicators.[33] A similar project for education provision would employ some indicators that might look similar, but there could also be substantial differences. The question to ask, therefore, is whether the fact that the quality scores across the different resources are constructed using different groups of indicators means that it is not possible to ask how a country's healthcare system compares with its education system. The answer is surely that it might not be possible to compare them in relation to their scores, but that it might be possible to compare them in relation to their rankings. So, in the same way that the Commonwealth Fund researchers were able to arrive at rankings for the healthcare systems of OECD countries, it might also be possible to arrive at rankings for the quality, access, efficiency, equity and outcomes of each country's other resources, and also to arrive at overall rankings for those resources. This is the kind of exercise that Thorbecke envisages when he asks for a welfare function that incorporates attributes of welfare provision, weights, thresholds of attributes, marginal benefits of attributes and joint interactions,[34] and that Atkinson is looking for when he explores the possibility of a welfare function with both income and health components. Atkinson of course recognises the difficulty of constructing overall scores, because methods for constructing scores will need to be agreed, and weights will need to be applied.[35] As we have suggested, it might be easier to create and compare rankings, and to create overall rankings out of rankings, than to create and compare scores, and create overall scores out of scores; but the question of how the different scores for characteristics are to be weighted in order to create the overall rankings at national level and between countries does not go away. The Commonwealth Fund applied a variety of methods for creating rankings and overall rankings out of multiple indicators:

> We found that these alternative methods tended to consistently yield the same top-performing countries (the U.K. and Switzerland) and worst-performing countries (the U.S. and Canada). However, there was a fair amount of fluidity among the countries in the middle of the performance range, whose rankings were sensitive to relatively small changes in data or methodology. For this reason, overall rankings may overshadow important absolute differences in performance, warranting closer examination of the data when describing a particular country's performance.[36]

I suspect that we would find the same combination of consistency and fluidity with the other social minimum resources.

[33] A Davis, K Hill, D Hirsch and M Padley, 'A Minimum Income Standard for the UK in 2016' (York, Joseph Rowntree Foundation, 2016) 28.

[34] E Thorbecke, 'Multidimensional Poverty: Conceptual and Measurement Issues' in Kakwani and Silber (n 15) 17.

[35] Atkinson, 'Income, Health and Multi-dimensionality' (2009) 31–33; C de Neuberg, K Roelen, and F Gassmann, 'Making Policy Analysis Richer: Multi-dimensional Poverty Research and Social Policy Design' in De Boyser et al (n 7) 52.

[36] Davis et al (n 25) 28–29.

A final question is this: Are the characteristics independent of each other? For instance, might there be a trade-off between equity and efficiency? Le Grand suggests that in relation to means-tested benefits there is such a trade-off between equity, understood as a reduction in poverty, and efficiency, understood as employment and savings incentives.[37] However, such a trade-off does not necessarily exist in relation to unconditional benefits, which, because they provide a higher proportion of net income for the poor than they do for the rich, can result in reductions in poverty and inequality; and because they are not withdrawn as earned and investment incomes rise, they do not compromise efficiency.[38] Trade-offs might or might not exist, but whether they do or not does not compromise the usefulness of generating rankings of characteristics.

V. THE CONSTRUCTION OF A SOCIAL MINIMUM POLICY REGIME

The Commonwealth Fund evaluates each country's healthcare system in relation to its characteristics, suggesting that there are two dimensions to healthcare provision: country, and characteristics. We have now extended the method to a variety of different resources, so we have added a third dimension: resources. However, in relation to the Commonwealth Fund's evaluation, the independent variable is better understood as a particular country's healthcare system's *mode of delivery*. It is the way that a healthcare system is structured that is being evaluated in relation to a variety of characteristics. It is the UK NHS's mode of delivery – that it is publicly funded, and free at the point of use – that makes it the highest ranked, and not the fact that it happens to be in the UK. It is not difficult to conclude that any country attempting to construct an ideal social minimum policy regime will choose to construct a healthcare system that shares characteristics with the UK's NHS: that is, a system publicly funded, and free at the point of use, with General Practitioners providing the essential rationing system.[39] We can draw this conclusion in relation to healthcare in the UK because there is one dominant system, the NHS, and a subsidiary system, private healthcare, largely funded by insurance companies. It is therefore legitimate to say that the UK's healthcare system *is* the NHS.

With other resources it is less straightforward. For instance, in relation to income, different modes of delivery for the income required to provide food, drink, shelter, clothing and the other necessities of a minimally decent life in society, could all be compared with each other. Where a country exhibits a variety of modes of delivery for one of the resources – for instance, in relation to

[37] J Le Grand, 'Equity versus Efficiency: The Elusive Trade-off' (1990) 100 *Ethics* 554, 554.

[38] Torry, 'Two Implementation Methods for a Citizen's Basic Income' (2017); Torry, 'An Update, a Correction, and an Extension' (2018).

[39] M Torry, 'Primary Care, the Basic Necessity: Part I' (2017); M Torry, 'Primary Care, the Basic Necessity: Part II' (2017).

income provision – each of the different modes of delivery (social insurance benefits, means-tested benefits, unconditional benefits, etc) could be ranked separately. So if we were to construct a three-dimensional matrix, and the third dimension of our matrix were to be 'countries', then each country would need to be subdivided into its different systems. This offers the possibility of a further refinement. If systems can be grouped – with, for instance, social insurance systems in different countries being grouped into 'social insurance' rather than into their separate countries, then, as in Figure 3.1, the third dimension of the matrix becomes 'modes of delivery' rather than 'countries'. This is probably right: because, as we have recognised, it is systems that are being tested, and not countries. This third dimension could be understood as a generalisation of the empowerment spectrum developed by Kumlin:[40] a spectrum that enables him to conclude that means-testing and other forms of selectivity hamper citizen empowerment, whereas universal and unconditional provision would not. Along the same spectrum Atkinson concludes that in today's employment market social insurance needs to be complemented by an unconditional income rather than by a means-tested one because we no longer expect governments to ensure the full employment that would enable social insurance on its own to sustain a constant and stable income.[41]

Figure 3.1 A three-dimensional matrix: dimensions of a social minimum

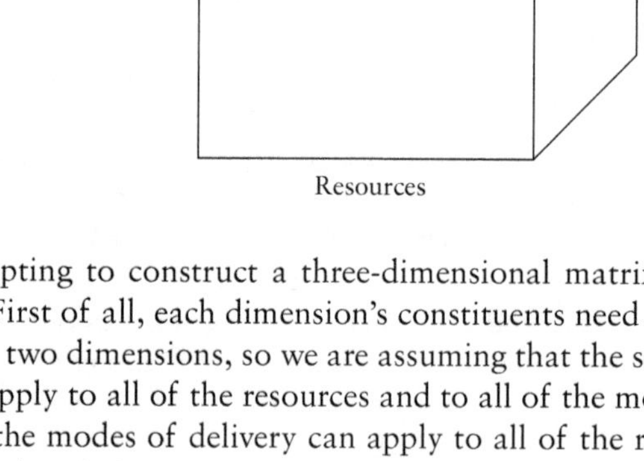

However, attempting to construct a three-dimensional matrix raises at least two questions. First of all, each dimension's constituents need to be consistent across the other two dimensions, so we are assuming that the same set of characteristics can apply to all of the resources and to all of the modes of delivery, and that all of the modes of delivery can apply to all of the resources. Is this legitimate? As a heuristic exercise, yes. However, we have already recognised

[40] Kumlin, 'Institutions – Experiences – Preferences' (2002) 26.

[41] AB Atkinson, *Beveridge, the National Minimum, and its Future in the European Context* (London, London School of Economics, 1993) 9, 19.

that each different resource requires its own set of characteristics, and that categorisations of characteristics and sub-characteristics are always somewhat arbitrary. Similarly, we need to recognise that each mode of delivery will function differently in relation to the different resources. Unconditionality in relation to healthcare means unconditional access when healthcare is needed, whereas unconditionality in relation to income means a constant unconditional provision.

Secondly, attempting to construct a three-dimensional matrix raises the question: To what extent are the different dimensions independent of each other? For instance, in relation to the UK's healthcare system, a 'low administrative costs' sub-characteristic will be intimately related to a mode of delivery characterised by unconditionality. This raises a further question: Where characteristics and modes of delivery appear to be related to each other, what are the causal connections? As Rothstein and Steinmo suggest,[42] the ways in which welfare state institutions evolve through time determines the way that they function, and it is these institutions and their histories that to a large extent determine both the modes of delivery and the characteristics of welfare provision – so it is institutions that constitute the connection between the 'characteristics' and 'modes of delivery' dimensions of our matrix, and it is institutions that generate the mutual dependence of modes of delivery and characteristics. It is, after all, a *social* minimum that we are discussing, so we should not be surprised to find that the different dimensions might be connected to each other by institutions in society.

These connections between dimensions are not a problem. In fact, because the construction of the matrix enables us to evaluate resources' characteristics in relation to a variety of modes of delivery, a completed matrix would provide us with a better understanding of the connections between characteristics and modes of delivery than we might otherwise possess.

Once we have constructed the three dimensions of the matrix, the next task must be to carry out for a wide variety of resources the kind of research carried out by the Commonwealth Fund in relation to healthcare, and to carry it out across a broad range of countries, including developing countries, which will generate the need for a broader range of resources and characteristics.[43] Also required will be research that distinguishes between different modes of delivery within each country, and so the kind of research that Kakwani and Son carried out that showed that 'universal transfers will provide more absolute benefits to children from poor families than to those from non-poor families'.[44] We shall

[42] Rothstein and Steinmo 'Restructuring Politics' (2002) 15–17.

[43] R Chambers, R Longhurst, D Bradley and R Feacham, *Seasonal Dimensions to Rural Poverty* (Brighton, University of Sussex, 1979) 1–2; de Neuberg, Roelen and Gassmann, 'Making Policy Analysis Richer' (2009) 37.

[44] N Kakwani and HH Hyun, 'On Assessing Pro-poorness of Government Programmes: International Comparisons' in Nanak Kakwani and Jacques Silber (eds) *The Many Dimensions of Poverty* (Basingstoke, Palgrave Macmillan, 2007) 269.

then be in a position to construct a three-dimensional matrix, with 'resources', 'characteristics', and 'modes of delivery' on the three axes; and from the completed matrix we shall be able to construct a social minimum policy regime. This is a considerable research agenda, but to pursue it could enable countries' populations to reach social minima, and the global population to reach a global social minimum.

Thorbecke suggests that 'there are too many unresolved questions left over to consider seriously using multidimensional measures in any truly operational sense'.[45] Yes, there are unresolved questions, particularly in relation to the consistency of the same-named characteristics across the different resources, and in relation to the ways in which the different resources affect each other. However, as we have recognised, we are *ranking* modes of delivery rather than applying scores, so to list broad characteristics along an axis is not a problem.

In relation to the connections between different resources: if certain characteristics were not met in relation to income, such as timeliness, then health might be damaged; if the inequality of incomes were to increase, then again health might be damaged; with insufficient income, education might be compromised; and without sufficient education, there might be less income. Some of these relationships might be circular. Without sufficient income, health might be compromised; and ill health can compromise income. There might be unresolved questions here, but that does not compromise our ability to create a legitimate and comprehensible matrix, or our ability to employ the overall rankings for the modes of delivery of the different resources to construct the best available social minimum policy regime.

VI. CONCLUSION

I have now defined the 'dimensions' of the social minimum to mean not the different resources that we need, or the different characteristics that resources might possess, but rather the 'resources', 'characteristics' and 'modes of delivery' dimensions of a matrix: a usage of 'dimension' closer to the word's core meaning in relation to three-dimensional space. An outstanding question is this: Which is the dimension to which we should pay most attention when constructing our social minimum policy regime? The first two dimensions of our matrix – resources and characteristics – are clearly essential to the provision of a social minimum. It now transpires that the third dimension – the 'mode of delivery' dimension – might be even more important in relation to the construction of the policy regime required, because it is this dimension that generates the different outcomes represented by the different rankings.

[45] Thorbecke, 'Multidimensional Poverty' (n 22) 18.

What is now required is further research to tackle the following questions:

- Is it possible to separate out the different modes of delivery of a resource, such as healthcare, within a country? That is, can the Commonwealth Fund's approach be employed in practice in relation to modes of delivery rather than to countries?
- Can the characteristics and sub-characteristics employed by the Commonwealth Fund in relation to healthcare be employed in practice to such other resources as education and income?
- Can the same ranking exercise that the Commonwealth Fund employed in relation to healthcare be transferred to income systems, education, public transport, and so on?
- When applied to different resources, how different would characteristics with the same name need to be for us to have to conclude that the three-dimensional matrix would need to be replaced by a series of 'mode of delivery/characteristics' grids, one for each resource?

What we have not attempted to state in this chapter is a set of levels that the characteristics of the different resources have to reach in order to constitute a social minimum. As we recognised when we studied a number of attempts to achieve that, there will always be a certain subjectivity related to the method chosen and to the way in which the method is constructed. What we have offered, as the chapter title suggests, is a conceptualisation of the social minimum: it will consist of a number of different resources; there will be a variety of modes of delivery for each of those resources; and it will be possible to choose and evaluate characteristics for each resource, and to rank different modes of delivery in relation to the extent to which those characteristics are achieved. Whether or not any of the modes of delivery would deliver a somehow acceptable level of a social minimum is not here at issue. What the method would be able to offer would be a collection of modes of delivery for the different resources that together would achieve the maximum social minimum possible.

4

A Social Minimum for Whom? Making a Case for a Normative Pattern of Pragmatic Decency

SARA STENDAHL AND OTTO SWEDRUP

I. POINTS OF DEPARTURE AND WHERE THEY TAKE US

ARE THERE POSITIONS of social destitution that in themselves trigger a public responsibility to act? And if so, why? Or why not? The reason we ask, and the reason we find it urgent to develop an answer, is that the normative response to the opening question seems to be increasingly contested also in established universal welfare states, such as Sweden. This is a chapter on scope and while it discusses this topic in a local context, we acknowledge that the question 'who counts?' is philosophical and has divided scholars in ethics and justice for centuries. Onora O'Neill describes it as an area challenging for both universalists and particularists, as well as an issue that is far from settled, in spite of increased agreement that all human beings should at least be seen as subjects of justice.[1] Scope is admittedly a difficult topic, but also, from a perspective of justice and ethics, one of paramount importance.

In this chapter we take our point of departure in a set of arguments based on a notion of a social contract. According to this line of reasoning, Swedes, in order to be to be true to the Swedish way, should discard the values embedded in an external human rights ideology and return to a 'we' determined by contract and citizenship.

While we are initially somewhat sceptical, we do take the proposition seriously. We know that stories about nation and nationality are formative and

[1] Onora O'Neill, *A Constructive Account of Practical Reasoning. Towards Justice and Virtue* (Cambridge, Cambridge University Press, 1996) 91. In this text we borrow some of O'Neill's terminology (such as the terms 'universialists' and 'particularists') and we are also indebted to her specific writings on 'scope' (ibid, 91–121). We will reconnect to O'Neill in the concluding section of this chapter.

guide not only perceptions about the past but also point to the future. The present chapter is written in some urgency as we recognise the attractiveness in simplicity and the seductiveness of a grand narrative that like a Columbus' egg, absolves from moral and ethical responsibilities. As the chapter moves forward, we persist in presenting a foundation for alternative approaches, more complex, less straightforward, but also more promising in terms of options for western welfare states, such as Sweden.

In present times, the contextual background is familiar to many western countries. It is a discourse embedded in socio-political developments that include increased economic gaps, tensions between rural and urban regions, demographical changes and impacts of migration, all set in a competitive global economy, spurring technological developments and escalating environmental concerns. In Sweden we see a deepening divide between proponents of different ideological positions. The left and the right on the traditional political scale stand far apart and proponents of a potential middle ground are often described as lacking visions or answers responding to global challenges mirrored in unemployment, violence, hate crime, insecurity, discrimination and social exclusion.

When the abstract social contract argument appears in everyday life in Sweden, the position of 'the foreigner' becomes increasingly exposed and vulnerable. At the core of debates on whether, for instance, hospitals should treat the undocumented or whether the social services should be obliged to provide financial assistance and emergency housing for transit refugees, is the question whether or not there is some understanding of a *social minimum* covering every person present within the borders of the sovereign state. The question about how society deals with those in vulnerable positions is sharply invoked in the face of migration; still, no doubt, the chosen response to the question 'who counts?' cuts deeply also into demarcations among those with more secure positions in society.

In this chapter, we look closer at a line of arguing that takes its point of departure in a defence of the nation-state, proceeds in portraying welfare and democracy as threatened and ends by pointing accusingly at the idea of universalistic human rights. We are specifically interested in arguments delimiting with *whom* we are morally and legally bound to share resources. Today we can see, within the Swedish political and academic debate, a renewed interest in categories such as citizenship and nation-state.[2] Established scholars argue that

[2] One reason to look closer at this discourse comes from the interest in 'Swedish values' and a 'Swedish social contract' among politicians and others who are active in the public debate. See, for example, Radio Sweden (2016) 'Just what are "Swedish Values"?', http://sverigesradio.se/sida/artikel.aspx?programid=2054&artikel=6469485 (accessed 14 May 2017). In the spring of 2017, the Conservative Party (the leading opposition party) proposed welfare reform, suggesting a shift from more universal welfare systems towards a system with social benefits made dependent on work or 'legal and permanent residence'. Moderaterna, 'Hela Sverige ska

the post-WWII embrace of human rights perhaps was a bit hasty. One influential voice that could be linked to this line of argument can be found in Lars Trägårdh, a Swedish professor of history who has become a leading academic arguing the relevance of a Swedish social contract perspective. As we continue, we do this in a close dialogue with the work of Trägårdh. For an alternative reading we turn to Anna Christensen's work on *basic normative patterns* as a theoretical venue to discover other narratives on the constitutive marks of what she labels the 'social dimension' of the Swedish welfare state.[3] A given condition for the claims made by Christensen is that positive legal material, enacted laws and regulations, can be studied for the purpose of disclosing basic normative patterns in society. Christensen's work takes an interest in change, thus she studied legal developments in different, often overlapping but also contradictory normative fields primarily in the areas of work, housing, family and social security.[4] Christensen's analytical contribution is a theory about underlying patterns that discloses tensions and compromises made between core values and principles that guide different welfare reforms.[5] This study explores demarcations made in law that are decisive for delimiting public solidarity and thus determining who counts and who doesn't, a perspective that highlights the question of personal scope.[6]

There are three working hypotheses that have steered the work on this chapter; initially we found Trägårdh's description of the Swedish social contract to be incomplete and that an analysis of legal material would suggest that there is more of contradiction and complexity to be found in a normative account of the Swedish welfare state. In addition, we recognised in Trägårdh's narrative values related to one of the normative patterns found in Christensen's analytical scheme: the *protection of established position.* Yet, no acknowledgment of other strong, but coexisting normative patterns such as *just redistribution* or the *market functional pattern.* Finally, as our work proceeded, we saw potential to further Christensen's conceptual terminology by exploring the presence of a fourth normative pattern that might have evaded attention during

Jobba – Moderaternas Ekonomiska Vårmotion' (2017) www.moderat.se/sites/default/files/attachments/hela_sverige_ska_jobba-varmotion_2017_0.pdf (accessed 11 May 2017) 48. This proposal was motivated by a questioning by the party of whether individuals with temporary residence permits should have the right to access Swedish welfare systems with reference to the notion of a social contract. www.dn.se/debatt/begransa-valfarden-for-de-med-tillfalliga-uppehallstillstand/ (in Swedish).

[3] A Christensen, 'Protection of the Established Position. A Basic Normative Pattern' (2000) 40 *Scandinavian Studies in Law* 285. Anna Christensen (1936–2001) was a professor of law at Lund University.

[4] Christensen, 'Protection of the Established Position' (2000) 287ff.

[5] Christensen's theory and work has been the basis of the Norma Research Programme at the Faculty of Law, Lund University. For more on the legal research conducted within the Norma Research Programme, see www.law.lu.se/#!TheNormaResearchProgramme.

[6] See, eg S Stendahl and O Swedrup 'Social Human Rights as a Legal Strategy to Enhance EU Citizenship' in F Pennings and M Seeleib-Kaiser (eds) *EU Citizenship and Social Rights* (Cheltenham, Edward Elgar 2017) 107.

past decades: a pattern of *pragmatic decency*.[7] Of relevance to this chapter is the proposed identification of a legally framed public practice, that targets profound social need, with universal scope. We suggest that a fruitful way to explain the normative rationale of this practice is to note its strong aspect of pragmatism (a willingness to handle problems) in combination with some sense of a collective moral baseline, a safeguard against shame and disgrace for the community as such.

Against this background we set out to perform a critical reading of some recent and reoccurring statements made about the so-called Swedish social contract, its rationale, content and implications, and in so doing also explore alternative narratives about the Swedish welfare state based on the theory of basic normative patterns. We ask: What distinctions determining eligibility (limits of solidarity) can be found in the two potentially conflicting narratives; an historic notion of a Swedish social contract and a legal notion on basic normative patterns? What implications do these differences have for the delimiting of a social minimum?

The chapter is outlined as follows: In the introduction we have sought to present the problem along with our main arguments. We proceed in section II with a description of how to understand the demarcations of redistribution and solidarity according to the Swedish social contract argument as put forward by Trägårdh. We continue in section III by analysing regulations on social provisions made to the most vulnerable to see what distinctions that can be found in regulations determining eligibility in Sweden. In section IV we discuss the implications of our findings for the delimiting of a social minimum and argue for the existence of a normative pattern characterized by what we choose to call 'pragmatic decency'.

II. THE NOTION OF A 'SWEDISH SOCIAL CONTRACT'

The proposed notion of a Swedish social contract borrows its rhetoric and imagery from a long line of contractarian theory prevalent in political thought. The use of the 'social contract' as a device dates back to ancient Greece and takes its path into present-day political philosophy via classic contractarians such as Hobbes, Locke, Rousseau and Kant.[8] Our ambition is not to delve deeper into contractarian theory but instead to look closer at a proposed Swedish social contract as a basis for arguing demarcations of redistribution and solidarity.

In this section of the chapter we seek to work our way through an argument that begins and ends with the nation-state and results in a claim that it

[7] The rationale for establishing a pattern of pragmatic decency is elaborated on in section IV.

[8] For more on the contractarian theory and discussions, see, eg D Boucher and P Kelly (eds) *The Social Contract from Hobbes to Rawls* (London and New York, Routledge, 1994).

is necessary and legitimate to question the validity of the human rights stand as a normative delimitation of state sovereignty, thus implying, in effect, that it is external to the content of what is conceptualised as 'the Swedish social contract'. While it is rare that Trägårdh or other participants in this discourse directly approach questions on poverty alleviation, we find the potential impact of the social contract argument on this topic fundamental.

A. In Defence of 'Good Nationalism' and the Sovereign State

The Trägårdh 'good nationalism'[9] argument is presented below in a sequence where one argument leads to another as stepping stones towards the normative conclusion, ie the primacy of nation-state, the externality of human rights and the need to choose between the two.[10] The presentation is a simplification – it reduces the details of the argument – but it should provide a fair synthesis of the position taken. This overview of a broader argument becomes more distinct in section B, where we probe further into the description made of the Swedish social contract.

The good nationalism argument (according to Trägårdh):

The sovereign state. All challenges against the state as an organising entity are a threat to democracy and solidarity as developed in the post-WWII welfare state. The state has functioned as a liberator of the individual and as a basis for developing solidarity beyond friendship, family or clan. These achievements justify the existence of borders (states defined by borders).

Nationalisms. All states able to provide democracy, welfare and solidarity are built on some sense of national community or fellowship that is protected by the state (they are nation-states). A sense of national community or identity is based on shared ideological conceptions. One ideological basis for nationality can be found in ideas about the people, ethnicity or race. Historically, Sweden as a nation-state, was far too tolerant to such notions which post-WWII made it ideologically absolutely necessary to draw sharp lines of disassociation with an ethnically based nationalism. Nationalism can also be based on a collective identification with democratically formulated ideas (which has been the Swedish model post-WWII). Such a basis for nationalism can according to Trägårdh be described in terms of a social contract.

[9] In a 2016 text the word 'nationalism' is changed to 'civic statism' and explained: 'what we can call "civic statism", that is a preference for the nation-state rooted in an enduring commitment to the traditional social contract that allies citizens and state through the elaborate system of taxes paid and rights earned.' See L Trägårdh, 'Between Two Models of Solidarity: Sweden, The Welfare State and Globalization' in D Cagan (ed) *Nordic Ways* (Washington DC, Brookings Institution press, 2016) 267–68.

[10] The presentation of arguments in section II A is based on a reading of Trägårdh's academic as well as popular texts, see below n 16 as well as L Trägårdh 'Ett val Mellan två Modeller för Sverige', *Göteborgs-Posten*, 2 December 2015, 2 and L Trägårdh 'Förneka Inte Nationen', *Axess,* 1 February 2016, 37–40.

The Swedish social contract. The Swedish social contract reflects a specific solidarity ideal. It is based on formal citizenship (legal residency) and it is compared to a gigantic insurance company where, in exchange for labour market participation and tax payments, citizens earn their social rights.[11] It is a contract based on an individualised family policy but has low demands on adherence to a coherent community ideology. Other values mentioned are: secularism; an emancipating majority culture; tolerance towards multiculturalism [within the collective of citizens]; and *state individualism*.[12]

The conflict of ideals. In the wake of large migration flows the social contract (as described above) is challenged and a conflict of ideals becomes visible as a politics of double standards is revealed.[13] Against the primacy of the nation-state stands a post-national project, normatively based (or argued) on human rights. This leads to a situation where the 'construction' citizen is put in opposition to the 'construction' human being.

The primacy of citizenship. While there exist in Sweden two contradicting ideals of solidarity, both traceable decades back, only one of these ideals is founded on ideas of nationalism and citizenship (the social contract), the other ideal is based on internationalism. Against this background Trägårdh describes the ideals of human rights as a quasi-religious trump advocated by spokespersons who think themselves better informed, of higher moral and in possession of grander perspectives. There is also a claim that the proponents of human rights describe the 'nation' as artificial and false, as a social and political strait-jacket that proposes a (false) conception of shared community.[14]

In conclusion, we find that the argument starts and ends with the nation-state. In defence of the nation-state it becomes legitimate (necessary) to repudiate the normative foundation that is built on a notion of indivisible, fundamental and universal human rights in favour of citizenship rights. While the account of arguments presented above is intended to provide a short overview of statements that together lead up to the incompatibility stance, we will in the next section stay closer to specific descriptions of the Swedish social contract.

B. The Social Contract and the Basis for Solidarity

We asked in the beginning what distinctions determining eligibility (limits of solidarity) could be found in the historic notion of a Swedish social contract, and in this section we try to find an answer. We set out to understand the content of the proposed 'Swedish social contract' as it is portrayed from an historical

[11] Trägårdh (n 9) 264.
[12] For more on state individualism, see section II B on personal scope.
[13] Trägårdh (n 9) 263.
[14] Trägårdh. 'Ett val mellan två modeller för Sverige' (2015) 2.

perspective and thus also the argument made that not only is it possible to make a distinction between human rights and citizens' rights, but that they are also at least in Sweden, by principle, incompatible.

The Swedish welfare state has been a recurrent theme in the writings of Trägårdh, and in order to grasp his argument in more depth we have included a wide range of key texts.[15] We are interested in: i) descriptions of the personal scope; ii) descriptions of content; iii) descriptions on rights and duties; iv) descriptions on entry and exit; and v) the historical rationale.

Personal scope. In a 2007 article, Trägårdh turns to Rousseau's the *Social Contract* and finds a passage he claims 'could serve as a motto for at least the Swedish welfare state'.[16] The chosen passage from Rousseau ends: 'it is the power of the state alone which makes the freedom of its members'.[17] After citing Rousseau, Trägårdh writes: 'This statism that links social equality, national solidarity, and individual autonomy to the beneficial power of the state makes Sweden, Swedish democracy, and the Swedish social contract profoundly different from those of most other countries [...].'[18] In a text from 2010, Trägårdh elaborates on a type of individualism presented as distinctly Swedish:

> The Swedish pre-occupation – some might even say obsession – with individual autonomy cannot be understood simply as a cultural idiosyncracy. It is, in fact, rooted in a historically grounded praxis that has to a high degree been institutionalized in the institutions of the Swedish welfare state. What is unique about Swedish social policy is neither the extent to which the state has intervened in society nor the generous insurance schemes, but the underlying moral logic. Though the path in no way has been straight, one can discern over the course of the twentieth century an overarching ambition to liberate the individual citizen from all forms of subordination and dependency in civil society: the poor from charity, the workers from their employers, wives from their husbands, children from parents (and vice versa when the parents have become elderly). In practice, the primacy of individual autonomy has been institutionalised through a plethora

[15] We base this part of the chapter on a reading of four texts by Lars Trägårdh: H Berggren and L Trägårdh, *Är Svensken Människa* (Stockholm, Norstedts, 2006 [2015]); L Trägårdh, L (ed) *State and Civil Society in Northern Europe: The Swedish Model Reconsidered* (Oxford, Berghahn Books, 2007); 'Rethinking the Nordic Welfare State through a neo-Hegelian theory of state and civil society' (2010) 15 *Journal of Political Ideologies* 227; L Trägårdh, 'Between Two Models of Solidarity: Sweden, The Welfare State and Globalization' in D Cagan (ed) *Nordic Ways* (Washington DC, Brookings Institution Press, 2016). As the first text, a book, is only published in Swedish we have looked for texts where Trägårdh refers to these ideas in English and found an article from 2010: H Berggren and L Trägårdh, 'Pippi Longstocking: The Autonomous Child and the Moral Logic of the Swedish Welfare State' in H Mattsson and SO Wallenstein (eds) *Swedish Modernism: Architecture, Consumption and the Welfare State* (London, Black Dog Publishing, 2010) 10–23. Of the selected texts it is the last one, published in 2016, that distinctly includes the full line of argument accounted for above in section II A.

[16] Trägårdh (ed) *State and civil society in Northern Europe* (2007) 30.

[17] Rousseau cited by Trägårdh (ibid, 30).

[18] ibid, 28.

> of laws and policies affecting individual Swedes in matters minute and mundane as well as large and dramatic.[19]

We can conclude that the idea of a Swedish social contract is centred on a contract between the state and the individual. The state creates, makes possible, the independence, the level of autonomy, that Trägårdh describes as a foundation of 'the Swedish theory of Love': a theory where true love is only possible between autonomous individuals, freed from hierarchies and dependencies.[20] The liberator according to this narrative is the welfare state. The social rights of the welfare state are described as limited in scope to citizens and those with legal residence.[21] The distancing from human rights is a demarcation necessary to uphold such a distinction.

Rights, obligations and content. The rights emanating from the social contract are according to Trägårdh founded on two logics: a primary rights logic based on conditional reciprocity and a secondary rights logic based on solidarity within the nation-state. These two sets of rights are both described as budget-dependent or relative:

> The social rights that constitute central parts of the Swedish welfare state are ultimately products of national, democratic, political processes /…/. Even though one often talks of 'rights' these are not rights in a strict legal sense, i. e. rights that are claimable in a court of law. Rather they take the form of legislation through which the state takes a broad but unspecified responsibility for providing collective goods, such as healthcare, on equal terms for all citizens and legal residents. These rights are at heart political and collective rights, rather than juridical and individual rights.[22]

There is in the description of the nature of the contract an emphasis on reciprocity: the individual citizen is obliged to work and pay taxes and in return earns a right to welfare. In the text from 2016, legal residents are also mentioned as a category included in the contract (thus, citizens and legal residents). Trägårdh summarizes the content of the social contract by describing it as an 'alliance between state and citizen, whereby citizens work, pay taxes and earn their fundamental social rights'.[23] When elaborating further on the content of the contract he returns to the two different so-called rights logics:

> The primary rights logic is conditional reciprocity tied to earned income (pensions, unemployment insurance, parental insurance, and sick-insurance); the secondary logic rights logic is solidarity within the nation-state covering the young, the elderly, the infirm, and the disabled (healthcare, schools, elderly care and disability rights).[24]

[19] Berggren and Trägårdh, 'Pippi Longstocking' (2013) 13.
[20] ibid, 12.
[21] Trägårdh (n 9) 264.
[22] ibid, 264.
[23] ibid, 263.
[24] ibid, 264.

It is made clear that the 'solidarity within the nation-state' mentioned above and visible for instance in the provision of healthcare, should be interpreted as a solidarity incorporating citizens and legal residents.[25]

Entry and exit. We find little in Trägårdh's texts that elaborate on entrance and exit. In later texts not only citizens but also legal residents are mentioned. Thus 'citizenship' in a formal sense is not the central dividing line, you can be part of the contract without citizenship, in some cases. What, more specifically, does it take for individuals to enter the contract? Could an individual at any point lose his or her position? What happens in case of breach of contract? There are legal responses to these questions but to the extent there is a historical narrative we have not been able to identify it.

The historical rationale. Maybe the text that is most explicit in its account of the historical rationale for the description of the Swedish social contract, is the fairly short Pippi Longstocking text from 2010. In this text we find the following account taking the roots of the argument on human rights versus citizens' rights back to medieval times:

> This self-conscious, politically influential and culturally homogenous [medieval] peasantry was both narrow-mindedly Lutheran and, quite understandably, strongly defensive of their property rights. But it was also deeply suspicious of all forms of aristocratic privilege. Without espousing any liberal ideas in terms of universal human rights or the importance of pluralism, Swedish peasants were socially and politically inclined to egalitarianism. The important thing was not that every human being was of equal worth, but that no individual person was above anybody else – except the king. For this reason, the peasantry proved quite willing throughout history to form alliances with the monarchy and the state to suppress all forms of aristocratic pretension.[26]

There is also a more recent history; Trägårdh refers repeatedly to a Swedish national identity interlinked with a perception of the welfare state, understood as a realisation of *Folkhemmet*, 'the people's home', a slogan that for decades was associated with the politics of the Social Democratic Party.[27] The Swedish Model (the welfare state) is described by Trägårdh as a vision of a social contract where

> the state and the people were conceived of as intrinsically linked; the people's home was a *folkstaat* the state was the homely domain of the national community, the context in which the ideal of solidarity could be joined to that of equality.[28]

There is in this line of argument hard to find a distinction between the Swedish social contract and the Swedish welfare state; to defend the Swedish social contract seems to be the same as to defend the welfare state.[29]

[25] Trägårdh (n 9).
[26] Berggren and Trägårdh, 'Pippi Longstocking' (2010) 10, 14.
[27] Trägårdh (n 16) 27.
[28] ibid, 28.
[29] ibid, 14.

C. Summary

The Trägårdh historic narrative on the Swedish social contract begins in medieval times; it is guided by strong norms on autonomy, individuality, the state and ownership. These norms influence the understanding of the welfare state and will, according to the above narrative, also influence the description of the social contract. It is underlined that human rights are perceived as distinctly external in relation to the Swedish welfare state project, lacking a democratic foundation. Redistribution within the social contract is guided by two logics: reciprocity (earned rights) and solidarity (with fellow citizens and other lawfully residing individuals). It is not transparent what the social contract says about the potential responsibility for the well-being of non-fellow citizens or non-residents living in Sweden.

III. SOCIAL PROVISIONS MADE TO THE MOST VULNERABLE IN SWEDEN

In this section, our intention is to present an alternative narrative to the one that emphasises the social contract when describing and understanding the Swedish welfare state. This alternative narrative takes its starting point in Anna Christensen's legal theory on basic normative patterns. We begin by identifying regulations on social provisions made to the most vulnerable and continue with an analysis of current legislation and examples of legal practices, in order to distinguish patterns that tend to resurface with a degree of consistency.[30] Writing about the basic normative patterns, Christensen says that they 'resurface now and again in different connections' which can be identified in studies of legal material, but that these patterns still tend to retain a 'certain degree of constancy'.[31]

The theme of a social minimum gives us a starting point to identify what Christensen might refer to as a 'subject area'. Christensen has studied, for example, 'the right to property' as a subject area where she studies different elements of that particular right, as a way of highlighting if and how different normative patterns are manifested in the legal rules constituting the right to property in Sweden.[32] Examples are presented below, from two different areas of the welfare state, selected for the quality of being of essential importance for individuals in vulnerable positions: *social assistance* and *health care*.[33] Our examples are

[30] For a study on the history of social rights discourse in the Nordic welfare states see, eg T Kotkas, 'The Short and Insignificant History of Social Rights Discourse in the Nordic Welfare States' in T Kotkas and K Veitch (eds) *Social Rights in the Welfare State* (Abingdon, Routledge, 2017). According to Kotkas, three 'themes' emerge when studying the post-war social security legislation in Sweden and Finland: (1) collective social justice, (2) responsibility of the state/society; and (3) rights in a technical meaning.

[31] Christensen, 'Protection of the Established Position' (2000) 289.

[32] ibid, 293.

[33] In a purer legal sense, both social assistance and health care can be understood and described as social rights. Here, we adopt a broader perspective as we look at a set of different rules determining eligibility within these two areas of the welfare state.

limited to Swedish national legislation. In both of them, the primary and sometimes default, legal rationale in delimiting access to different social schemes revolves around the concept of *residency*.

A. Distinctions Determining Eligibility: Residence-based Schemes and Beyond

In Sweden, historically as well as today, a number of regulations have used some form of residence status as a criterion to determine eligibility for social benefits and services delivered by municipalities.[34] In the past, it was rare that anyone's status as resident as such was questioned, although municipalities could argue about on what side of an administrative border such residence was upheld.[35] In contrast, today, the usage of residency as a means to demarcate the personal scope as such has increased. Thus, a situation is created where individuals may find themselves excluded from accessing legal rights.[36] Taking an interest in the demarcation of personal scope, through studying legal regulations, we find examples of this but also provisions that go beyond, to secure basic needs for an individual who does not fulfil the legal criteria of being a resident. In section IV, we will return to Anna Christensen's theory of basic normative patterns to further explore a possible rationale behind the examples presented below.

i. *Social Assistance*

The responsibility for providing to the basic social needs of destitute individuals in Sweden has historically been placed on and taken by local communities, from parishes to the municipalities, and still is today. From the days of poor relief through to the days of the social democratic welfare regime, the local communities have been responsible to care for those of its members who have been destitute and unable to support themselves.[37] The logic of geographically demarcating and dividing responsibility between municipalities, that can be found in Poor Relief Ordinances from the 1800s, is still very much present with residence as the guiding legal concept deciding on which municipality is responsible to provide assistance in each given case.[38] The Social Services Act makes the distinction between municipality of temporary residence and municipality of habitual residence. If someone is not considered a resident of a municipality, the support offered by the local Social Services will be limited

[34] See, eg S Stendahl, 'To Reside: To Live, Be Present, Belong' (2016) 2 *European Journal of Social Security* 232, 235 ff.

[35] SOU 1950:11, 171.

[36] Stendahl, 'To Reside' (2016).

[37] See, eg H Johansson, *I det Sociala Mmedborgarskapets Skugga: Rätten till Socialbidrag under 1980- och 1990-Talen* (Lund, Arkiv Förlag, 2001) 49.

[38] See, eg Thomas Erhag, 'Under Pressure? – Swedish Residence-based Social Security and EU Citizenship' (2016) 2 *European Journal of Social Security* 207, 224 ff.

to emergency help.[39] If the Social Services finds that the individual cannot be granted social assistance through the individual rights provision in the Social Services Act (Ch 4 §1 SOL) there is still an opportunity for the municipality to provide support in accordance with local rules (Ch 4 §2 SOL). This logic, of an 'extra opportunity' for the municipalities to offer support where the legal basis is not framed as an individual right but rather an opportunity for the municipality, originates from the Poor Relief Ordinance of 1871.[40]

Regarding eligibility, there is no requirement or mention of nationality or citizenship in the Social Services Act. This means that anyone can apply for social assistance in a Swedish municipality, regardless of legal status. Nevertheless, two current debates, relating to the question of personal scope and the right to social assistance in Sweden has to do with the right to social assistance for individuals who lack formal residency and, in some cases, legal status (undocumented).[41] A first example is the situation for destitute EU migrants, individuals who often lack formal residency and therefore only receive emergency support from the Social Services. This support is constituted by minimal level subsistence benefits intended to finance a bus journey back to the origin EU Member State of the individual, or food and short-term shelter. The issues of personal scope in these cases are often closely connected with the question of residence, in that the individuals are not registered in the Population register (civil registration) and thereby do not fall under the responsibility of a municipality of habitual residency, as set out in the Social Services Act.[42]

A second example of issues concerning social assistance and personal scope has to do with the situation for undocumented migrants, and especially the situation for unaccompanied minors who reside in Sweden on a temporary residence permit. A number of reports show how young persons who arrived in Sweden applying for asylum as unaccompanied minors are living homeless in Swedish municipalities.[43] One reason for this, that has been presented from a municipal standpoint, is that the minors are in an 'unclear' legal position. If they can be included in the group of persons covered by the provisions in

[39] Chapter 2a 2 § Socialtjänstlag (2001:453) [Social Services Act].

[40] SOU 1950:11, 63 f.

[41] See, eg P Kjellbom and A Lundberg, 'Olika Rrättsliga Rum för en Skälig Levnadsnivå? En Rättskartografisk Analys av SoL och LMA i Domstolspraktiken' (2018) *Nordisk Socialrättslig Tidskrift* 17–18.

[42] See, eg Erhag, 'Under Pressure?' (2016) about the municipal responsibility to provide support in emergency situations, and S Stendahl, 'Welfare State Borders: On Local Initiatives to Cater to the Needs of Destitute EU Migrants in Swedish Cities' in *Invisible Social Security Revisited. Essays in Honour of Jos Berghman* (Leuven, Lannoo Campus Publishers, 2014) on the situation for the group of destitute EU migrants and the local responses to provide for the basic social needs of this group.

[43] Even though unaccompanied minors and migrant EU citizens are not included in official homelessness statistics from Swedish public authorities, there are still plenty of news reports and NGO reporting on the situation for both groups. See, eg www.svt.se/nyheter/lokalt/uppsala/ensamkommande-blir-hemlosa-i-vantan-pa-besked.

the Swedish Reception of Asylum Seekers' Act, this would mean that they are excluded from the possibility to receive social assistance from the municipal Social Services according to the individual rights provision in Ch 4 § 1 SoL.[44] The issue here of personal scope is perhaps not so much an issue of residency but more who should be responsible to provide and finance services and support, the Swedish Migration Agency (a government agency) or the municipalities through the Social Services. The personal scope, which in practice decides who receives social assistance, is in these cases based on the migration status of the person (if he/she has a decision on asylum, residence permit, expulsion, or not).[45]

The long-standing practice of local authorities to take care of the social needs of people has to a large extent been characterised by the norm of local autonomy. The legal framework giving municipalities acting space in meeting local challenges and individual needs is, however, not a guarantee for equal treatment across the country. Håkan Johansson and Alexandru Panican highlight the city of Malmö as an example of a Swedish municipality where 'socio-economic challenges are reflected in the local social-policy discourses and local social intervention programmes'. The municipality, in addition to maintaining a fairly consistent level of social assistance in terms of monetary benefits, is also an active actor in developing local job-activation programmes in order to combat poverty at a local level. Johansson and Panican study the efforts made by the local social services in response to relatively high levels of unemployment and poverty, and conclude that the city still only pursues 'regular policies under non-regular circumstances'.[46]

One thing the two examples mentioned above have in common, together with the example of the city of Malmö, is how the exclusion from even a minimal level social assistance benefits, has triggered responses from the civil society to take care of basic social needs of the groups mentioned above. These responses are, in many cases, carried out through partnerships where local civil society organisations (CSOs) take the role of service providers and the municipality finances the services through taxpayer money. In the city of Gothenburg among others, this type of partnership ('voluntary sector organisation public partnership') has been used as a legal format in order for the municipality to finance local CSOs providing emergency shelter and other minimal level services to the group of destitute EU-migrants living in the city.[47]

[44] § 1 The Swedish Reception of Asylum Seekers' Act (lag (1994:137) om mottagande av asylsökande m.fl.).

[45] See, eg Kjellbom and Lundberg, 'Olika Rättsliga Rum' (2018).

[46] H Johansson and A Panican, 'Strategies Against Poverty in a Social Democratic Local Welfare System: Still the Responsibility of Public Actors?' in H Johansson and A Panican (eds) *Combating Poverty in Local Welfare Systems: Active Inclusion Strategies in European Cities* (London, Palgrave Macmillan, 2016) 155, 157ff.

[47] See, eg Stendahl, 'Welfare State Borders' (2014). This is also part of an ongoing PhD project 'The outermost responsibility' ('Det yttersta ansvaret'), Swedrup, O (forthcoming).

ii. Healthcare

In keeping with our interest in social provisions made for the most vulnerable, we now turn to the area of healthcare in search for examples that show distinctions determining eligibility. Looking closer at the regulations in the area of healthcare, emphasis is, to a large extent, put on regulating responsibilities for public authorities rather than to formulate individual rights provisions, and especially the responsibilities of the county councils to provide 'good health and care' to all 'inhabitants' (Ch 8 § 1 NHSL).[48] The responsibilities of the county councils are aimed primarily at 'inhabitants', who according to preparatory works should be understood as individuals who are formal residents according to the civil registration procedures. However, the demarcation of personal scope is reminiscent of the provisions in the Social Services Act (SOL) in the sense that there are no references made in the NHSL to nationality nor citizenship.[49] The Act even takes it further and includes the 'whole population' when prescribing the aims and goals of the healthcare system in Sweden (Ch 3 § 1 NHSL).

Even though the NHSL can be read as an example of regulation central to providing the most vulnerable with emergency healthcare, the law does not include any individual rights provisions. Instead, access, as mentioned, relies on meeting the requirements of residency set out in the Act. However, there are a couple of examples of provisions that go beyond the requirement of residency, that could be read as to broaden the scope of individuals so that all persons in need of, at least, emergency health care in Sweden should not be denied. One such example would be the provision in Ch 8 § 4 NHSL where it is stated that: 'If someone staying in the county, who is not a resident, should be in need for emergency health care, the county council should offer that person such care.' This statement is in line with the fundamental human rights law principle of human dignity that is central to the NHSL.[50]

Another example, of provisions securing at least the need for emergency health care to all, is the Law Concerning Health Care for Asylum Seekers and Others, passed by the Riksdag in 2008. Although this Act sets out to secure access to emergency health care for undocumented individuals it does not go beyond securing that minimum level of subsidised healthcare in emergency situations. The passing of the 2008 Act has been described as a way to 'codify existing practice'.[51] This 'existing practice' refers to the way many county councils had worked out local guidelines advocating that undocumented individuals in need

[48] 'NHSL' is short for the 'New Health and Medical Services Act', and refers to Hälso- och sjukvårdslag (2017:30) [Health and Medical Services Act].

[49] See, eg Erhag (n 38) 221 ff.

[50] Ch 3 § 1 NHSL.

[51] See, eg Shannon Alexander, 'Humanitarian Bottom League? Sweden and the Right to Health for Undocumented Migrants' (2010) 12 *European Journal of Migration and Law* 215, 216ff.

should be given access to emergency care and that the cost for the provided care should be dealt with at a later stage.[52]

iii. Summary

As we have shown in this section, a number of regulations in Sweden have used and still use some form of residence status as a criterion to determine eligibility to benefits and services. Regarding eligibility, there is no requirement or mention of nationality or citizenship in the Social Services Act nor in the New Health and Medical Services Act.

However, there are some examples of legal provisions that go beyond the requirement of residency, that seem to broaden the scope of individuals so that all persons in need of, at least, minimal level subsistence benefits as well as emergency health care in Sweden should not be denied. In the field social assistance, we see examples of local civil society organisations in cooperation with municipalities arranging partnerships to be able to provide basic social needs of individuals. In the area of healthcare, practices can be found where county councils have gone beyond the obligations set out in national legislation to provide emergency healthcare to undocumented individuals. These practices are, however, not based on a logic of individual rights, but rather examples of ways that the public sector is given legal space for securing a social minimum for everybody living in Sweden.

IV. SCOPE AND A BASIC NORMATIVE PATTERN OF PRAGMATIC DECENCY

In this final section we draw together the different strands of thought that constitute the rationale of this chapter. We asked in our chapter heading: 'A social minimum for whom?' The word 'minimum' literally means 'the least or smallest amount or quantity possible, attainable or required'. While the concrete content of a social minimum is the topic of other contributions in this volume, our interest is in scope. Deciding to whom, in the face of destitute poverty a social minimum is to be allocated. An including response could, with a reference to O'Neill, be described as more universalist in character, while an excluding response could be described as particularist.[53]

[52] Prop 2012/13:109, 36.

[53] O'Neill, *Practical Reasoning* (1996). O'Neill's own response to scope is that both universalists and particularists have difficulties as both branches of thought, in different ways, in defining scope tend to be 'fixed by providing definitive analyses of the concepts of agents or subject' (p 91). In contrast, O'Neill proposes a constructive approach that enable 'agents to construct an account of the scope of ethical consideration to which they are committed at a given juncture' (ibid, 120ff), and combines this open notion of scope with obligations of justice (rejection of injury) and obligations of virtue (rejection of indifference and neglect) (ibid, 205).

In a legal context we find regulated state responsibilities with universal personal scope in the international human rights framework. Within this framework, social and economic rights have a given place. A signifier for legal arguments based on human rights is the rejection, in principle, of practices that make distinctions as concern personal scope. This is also where the abstract human rights framework seems to clash with a proposition of a social contract where social rights are described as distributed based on particular, locally embedded norms framed by for instance citizenships, legal residence and performance (work and taxes). It is in this clash our chapter starts, as we describe Trägårdh's (particularist) historic narrative of a Swedish social contract and its rejection of a (universalist) human rights agenda as 'non-Swedish'. Anna Christensen's way to portray basic normative patterns became a venue to investigate the potential of an alternative approach.

We formulated two questions: What distinctions determining eligibility (limits of solidarity) can be found in the two potentially conflicting narratives; a historic notion of a Swedish social contract and a legal notion on basic normative patterns? and What implications do these differences have in terms of delimiting the personal scope of a social minimum?

When looking for answers to the first question in Trägårdh's historic narrative we find that eligibility and solidarity overall are framed by a requirement of formal citizenship (including legal residence). He compares the Swedish welfare state to a gigantic insurance company where social rights are earned by good citizenship behaviour, defined as a commitment to work and payment of taxes. He calls this a logic of conditional reciprocity, equalled in large to active labour market participation. There is also in his historic narrative a broader framework of Swedish solidarity described as built on a logic of solidarity within the nation-state (in contrast and addition to the social rights earned by good behaviour). This second logic of solidarity reaches out to the young, the elderly, the infirm and the disabled, given that they are citizens or legal residents. The historic narrative thus points at different distinctions of eligibility where the primary distinction is made between formal citizens (including legal residents) and others. Within this framing two logics of solidarity are presented as a distinction is made between those who work (and earn rights) and those who don't.

While it is obvious that Sweden as a state has ratified international human rights conventions and also implemented such norms into Swedish constitutional and statutory law, it is reasonable to assume that the argument that human rights are non-Swedish rather points at the normative foundation of such norms. Thus, the proposition that to be human in itself is a legitimate basis from which to claim a right to a life in dignity. The particularist disassociation with human rights seems to denounce the moral basis for a 'we' that is universal in scope.

When we looked for eligibility criteria to social rights as they are formulated in law, we found that access to social assistance and healthcare was established in a consistent mode by the use of a residence criteria. In order to access rights-based social assistance and healthcare, to be a resident is also to meet the core qualification criteria. This said, in order to meet the required criteria there is a need to be registered in the Population register (civil registration). If you are not a legal resident, this can be complicated. We find nothing in the regulation on social assistance and healthcare that confirms Trägårdh's framing of his two logics of solidarity in ideas about citizenship. There are no conceptual links between citizenship (or nationality) and the legal residence criteria; you can be a citizen and lose your status as resident and you can be a non-citizen with a resident status.

In the legal narrative, contrary to the historic, we find no emphasis on citizenship, but similar to the historic narrative we note that there are different levels of access to social rights, some more generous than others. For those who fail the residence requirement, we found that there is within the legal framework a discretionary space that public authorities can use to meet what could be described as aspects of the social (minimum) needs of humans living within their territory. The only eligibility criteria to receive such help is need. The historic narrative is silent on how to meet the social needs of those who fall between the cracks, and it could be that this is the kind of redistribution that in the historic narrative is portrayed as non-Swedish and human-rights based.

The overall impression, based on the legal material, of whether the fundamental claim of universality embedded in human rights determine the scope and outreach of social solidarity in Sweden is not clear-cut. Thus, while the legal framework that provide municipalities with enough mandate and discretion to handle urgent social needs is not characterised by a human rights language, there are indications that the explicit presence of social human rights norms in statutory law has increased. A development visible for instance in the new regulation of access to healthcare (see section III above). Still, human rights are not used as legal norms motivating the discretionary practice that seem to establish local social minimums: a social content with a universal scope based on collective solidarity in the face of destitution. It could be argued that these local practices, establishing de facto social minimums, form an adequate, or limited, response to a state commitment to safeguard the most basic level of fundamental human dignity as set out in international law, yet, we would argue, it is not evident that 'human dignity' or 'human rights' are adequate descriptions of the normative pattern that characterize this legal practice. More on this below.

The second question asked if the two alternative narratives had implications for the determination of scope for a social minimum. The historic narrative, as we interpret it, would allow for a social minimum delimited in scope to those with a formal status as citizens or legal residents. With this follows a normative affirmation that even basic social rights can be denied those who lack the required formal status; there are those who count and those who don't, to paraphrase O'Neill. The legal narrative, on the other hand, seems to indicate that there is a normative basis that can be used to explore and further elaborate a social minimum that is more inclusive.

We would expect our findings on scope to reflect one or more of Anna Christensen's three identified core patterns: the protection of established position, the market functional pattern and just distribution. These patterns have also proven to form a fairly consistent nexus of values that keep influencing relevant aspects of the normative field in focus. Thus, we can conclude that our expectations are met, at least to some degree. The historic narrative has a strong linkage to what Christensen described as a conservative pole of values protecting status quo and ownership to established social positions, in particular the position earned by participation on the labour market. In Trägårdh's description of the Swedish social contract we recognise some of the well-known characteristics of how social security is distributed in Sweden: there is indeed a strong emphasis on individual labour market participation where those who are in full-time work until retirement are rewarded fairly generous, income-related, cash benefits and in recent years also tax deductions. In this aspect we find the two narratives, law and history, converging.

However, in Christensen's work the status of citizenship did not appear as a protected position (which is understandable given that citizenship is absent as a legal requirement to determine eligibility to social benefits and services). Still, the value provided to citizenship in the historic narrative reflect a similar conservative, status quo, logic that Christensen attributes to ownership of a specific social status. In a similar way the position of being resident could also be understood as a position protected by the normative pattern of established position, a fact that at times might have been taken for granted, but has become more visible as the awareness of the privileges linked to residency has increased. The notion of 'citizen' is similar in some respects to the notion of 'resident' as both identify a position that at least potentially rewards a behaviour of immobility (staying put, anchoring, remaining). This is an understanding of the position of being resident that the legal narrative brings to the forefront.

A. A Normative Pattern of Pragmatic Decency

As noted, Christensen identified three basic normative patterns when studying different aspects of what she labelled the social dimension. Christensen's analytical terminology has contributed to clarify and make more transparent not least how the conservative normative value protecting ownership of an 'established position' transcended the legislative framework establishing social security protection in the reign of a welfare regime labelled 'social-democratic' by Esping-Andersen and others.[54] However, Christensen's work did not include

[54] See, eg G Esping-Andersen, *Three Worlds of Welfare Capitalism* (Cambridge, Polity Press, 1989).

studies on social assistance nor social protection for people living at the very margins of society.

It is quite clear that in order to meet the social needs of the most vulnerable, the outreach of legislation constructed as rights is limited.[55] The residence criteria functions, as described above, increasingly as protection of an established position, admittedly, in some aspects, securing a position with harsher conditions than the protection given to those engaged in paid work.

While there have been periods when the criteria 'resident' had a meaning that did better correspond to its everyday use and all those living their lives within a given municipality also was understood as included within the responsibilities of the municipalities in terms of being residents, this has been challenged.[56] In this development increased attention, also in field of social protection, has been directed to the responsibility of the municipalities to secure what might be called a 'social minimum' also for those who are not, for whatever reason, acknowledged any rights. In section III above we outlined some of the ongoing practices that the municipalities engage in, often in cooperation with organised civil society, and often by contributing means to enable their work.

We suggest that there is a need for an addition to the conceptual terminology elaborated by Christensen to normatively explain the discretion awarded municipalities as a platform for public accountability. It is reasonable to assume that there is a strong normative pattern at work that explains this construction of law and its functions. It is also reasonable to argue that this pattern is different from the previously identified normative patterns: *established position* (there are no established positions to be protected), *market functional ideas* (while there are distinct traces of such values in the social dimension at large, they are not dominating in this sector) or *just distribution* (the handling of the social problems at hand is not primarily driven by values associated with justice nor redistribution).

What we can observe is a legally framed practice that is pragmatic and driven by a capacity to handle problems (not solve them). There seems to be some level of minimal decency that must be upheld in society also for those who do not meet the qualifications. Some kind of moral agreement, that in no municipality should anyone have to freeze to death, or starve, or be denied treatment if seriously ill. The content of this 'minimum' is not laid down in law or practice, and thus it is not transparent. However, we would argue that the scope at this level is broad and inclusive. We would suggest that this is a normative pattern viable at present and that it has a trajectory that could be traced far back. In its universalistic and including scope, it corresponds to a fundamental aspect of human rights norms, but there is still little in law and municipal practices that reflect an awareness of this body of norms or its ambitions in terms of equality and dignity.

[55] See, eg Stendahl and Swedrup, 'Social Human Rights' (2017) 107ff.
[56] See, eg Stendahl (n 34).

We propose to call this set of values a normative pattern of 'pragmatic decency'. A pattern of norms linked to pragmatism (methods of problem solving at a local level that are based less on principle and more on results) and decency used by us to indicate an important but basic, maybe even minimalistic, quality of interaction between public entities and individuals, to make possible co-living in societies that aspire to be more than civilised.[57]

B. Conclusion

The particularist response to the question about scope, drives towards anchoring ethical values in the traditions and practices of distinct communities, and is not without merits.[58] Yet, history provides nauseating examples of what such ideals might lead to in terms of delimiting ethical scope and ethical consideration. A universalist response is more inclusive and defines the domain of ethical consideration as including, for instance, all human beings or all living beings, or maybe all beings with certain characteristics (as soul, reason, personhood, consciousness).[59] Yet, philosophers, such as O'Neill, will argue that the logical coherence of each such given, pinpointed, parameter can be questioned. Maybe, the scope determined by pragmatic decency can be described, in principle, as less fixed and rather delimited by a constructive, ongoing process aimed at determining who is within the domain of our ethical consideration at each time and place.[60] In practice, this delimitation of scope is more universalist than particularist in character.

We have put forward two contrasting narratives on how to understand 'who counts' in a Swedish setting, one more particularist (the historic) and another more universalist (the legal). Of these two it is only the more universalist version that provides an explanation for a Swedish solidarity that evidently encompasses not only citizens and residents but also strangers and outcasts, people with distinctly weak civil and social rights. This is solidarity at a minimal level, sometimes handed out harshly and always with no reference to rights – but it does exist and we propose that it plays an important role in the intricate and non-coherent web of values that form the social dimension of the Swedish welfare state. In an effort to identify the core characteristics of this tradition we have described it as a normative pattern of 'pragmatic decency'.

[57] A notion of decency framed by O'Neill's obligations of justice (rejection of injury) and obligations of virtue (rejection of indifference and neglect) see O'Neill (n 1) and Avishai Margalit, who makes a distinction between a decent society (in which institutions do not humiliate people) and a civilised society in which people do not humiliate each other. See A Margalit, *The Decent Society* (Cambridge, MA, Harvard University Press, 1996).

[58] O'Neill (n 1) 13.

[59] ibid, 92.

[60] ibid, 91–121.

Such a description should hopefully invite a discussion on how to improve the quality of pragmatism as well as the level of decency in a continuing analysis of the function of a more transparent commitment to a social minimum. Returning again and finally to the work of O'Neill, it does provide some hope for the future that the construction of scope within the practice of pragmatic decency is not fixed, but for the values embedded in decency, and thus it should allow for an ongoing, practical and constructive procedure, to be used to determine at each given time and place who (or what) is within our domain of ethical consideration.

Part 2

Specifying a Social Minimum

5

The Social Minimum in the Context of Inequality

MICHAEL ADLER

I. INTRODUCTION

A RECENT BOOK by the American legal historian Samuel Moyn[1] argues that the worldwide concern with human rights and the prevalence of neoliberalism are the main reasons for the disappearance of material inequality from the political agenda. According to Moyn, 'human rights stigmatised only the shame of material insufficiency while turning a blind eye to galloping material inequality'.[2] He argued that champions of human rights, who focused their attention on the abuse of civil and political rights, were simply 'out of position' to challenge abuses of social and economic rights and the explosion of inequality. As a result, the main focus of concern turned to the social minimum, which became the hand-maiden of neoliberalism. He concluded that 'The critical reason that human rights have been a powerless companion to market fundamentalism is that they simply have nothing to say about material inequality'.[3]

This chapter has a great deal to say about material inequality. It considers alternative ways of *defining* the social minimum and discusses the problems of measuring the number of people with incomes below the social minimum, whatever that may be. It does not deal with the normative foundations of the right to a social minimum or its legal status but deals instead with empirical methods and statistical problems. It is also about *enforcing* the social minimum, although it has a rather different take on this issue than the other chapters in the book. It is not about adjudication or the role of the courts, international conventions, international organisations or other regulatory bodies. It is, however, normative

[1] S Moyn, *Not Enough: Human Rights in an Unequal World* (Cambridge, MA, Belknap Press of Harvard University Press, 2018), esp ch 7.

[2] ibid, 176.

[3] ibid, 216.

in the sense in that, like Samuel Moyn,[4] it makes the case for redistribution from rich to poor and, in particular, from the super-rich to the extremely poor. In doing so, it raises the question of whether there ought to be a social maximum as well as a social minimum. The chapter is, above all, contextual. It seeks to put the discussion of a social minimum and a social maximum into context by describing, in broad terms, the extent of extreme poverty and excessive affluence in different countries, indicating how these have changed since the financial crisis 10 years ago.

The chapter is in three parts; the first focuses on the poor and the destitute, the second on the rich and the 'super-rich', and the third attempts to provide a holistic picture of global trends in inequality. These three parts are presented as 'the bottom-up view', 'the top-down view' and 'the integrated view'. They are followed by a short normative discussion of what can and should be done about the levels of inequality that exist in the world today.

II. THE BOTTOM-UP VIEW

A. Some Old Debates Revisited

In the first paragraph of his monumental study 'Poverty in the United Kingdom',[5] Peter Townsend asserted that:

> Poverty can be defined objectively and applied consistently in terms of the concept of relative deprivation. ... Individuals, families and groups can be said to be in poverty when they lack the resources to obtain the types of diets, participate in activities and have the living conditions and amenities which are customary or, at least, encouraged and approved in the societies to which they belong. Their resources are so seriously below those commanded by the average individual or family that they are, in effect, excluded from ordinary living patterns, customs and activities.[6]

It follows that poverty, understood in terms of a lack of resources, leads to social exclusion, and Townsend's study attempted to identify the point at which, as resources decline, relative deprivation increase disproportionately. The basis of Townsend's study was a survey of 2,000 households carried out in 1969/70. A reasonably exhaustive list of 60 indicators of the 'style of living' of the population was constructed,[7] covering diet, clothing, fuel and light, home amenities, housing and living facilities, the immediate environment of the home, the characteristics,

[4] ibid, 218, where he argues that 'economic justice requires either redesigning markets or, at least, redistributing from the rich to the poor'.

[5] P Townsend, *Poverty in the United Kingdom* (Harmondsworth, Penguin Books, 1979).

[6] ibid, 1.

[7] ibid, 249 explains that the list of indicators appears to be 'built up'. It seems to have included all the indicators of 'style of living' that Townsend could think of and was not based on what members of the public thought its constituent parts were.

security, general conditions and welfare benefits of work, family support, recreation, education, health and social relations, etc. By applying these indicators to individuals and families, a score was built up – the higher the score, the lower their participation in activities that people ought to have been able to enjoy. From this list, Townsend then selected a representative sub-set of 12 indicators[8] that were used to construct an index of deprivation.

The incomes of everyone in the survey, which were used as a measure of their resources, were adjusted for the size of the household and the modal value of the deprivation index was calculated for each adjusted income level. This was then plotted against the income level (expressed in logarithmic form). Townsend concluded that 'as income diminishes from the highest level, so deprivation steadily increases but, below 150 per cent of the supplementary benefit standard,[9] it begins to increase swiftly'.[10] He argued that the poverty level was represented by this threshold and that, at the time, 25 per cent of the UK population were living in poverty. This compared with an estimated seven per cent who were living at or below supplementary benefit levels.

Two years after the publication of Townsend's study, it was subjected to a devastating critique by David Piachaud.[11] While recognising Townsend's achievement, Piachaud criticised his study on three grounds. First, he argued that it wasn't clear how the deprivation index had been constructed, ie how the 60 indicators of 'style of living' had been identified or how the 12 that were used to construct the index of deprivation had been chosen, and that many of them had nothing to do with poverty. Secondly, he argued that the modal score of the deprivation index concealed considerable variation between people at the same income level. Thirdly, he questioned whether there was, in fact, a threshold below which the deprivation index increased particularly sharply. He concluded that there was 'no satisfactory evidence to suggest that there is any such threshold of deprivation'.[12]

While Townsend had argued that poverty and deprivation were the result of low income and that, for different types of household, there was a level of income below which members of the household experienced deprivation and could be said to be 'poor', Piachaud questioned this logic and suggested that deprivation, defined as the lack of socially recognised necessities, could exist at all income levels. His critique encouraged the search for an alternative approach to the conceptualisation and measurement of poverty and informed Joanna Mack and Stewart Lansley's study, which was carried out for the documentary series *Breadline Britain*,[13] which was the next major study of poverty in the UK.

[8] Once again the choice was made by Townsend. The correlations between all of them and net disposable income were highly significant. See ibid, 251.

[9] The level at which social assistance would have been paid.

[10] Townsend, *Poverty* (1979) 260–61.

[11] D Piachaud, 'Peter Townsend and the Holy Grail' (1981) *New Society*, 10 September.

[12] ibid, 420.

[13] J Mack and S Lansley, *Poor Britain* (London, George Allen and Unwin, 1985).

Taking their lead from Piachaud, Mack and Lansley defined poverty as 'an enforced lack of socially perceived necessities'. The lack of 'socially perceived necessities' was not enough in itself – it had to be due to a lack of income and to the fact that these necessities could not be afforded. The basis of their study was a survey in which 1,174 members of the public were asked whether they thought that individual items on a list were necessities in the sense that people should be able to afford them and should not have to do without them. The list covered a wide range of goods and activities including heating, household goods, food, clothing, personal possessions, leisure and social activities. People were then asked which of these items they did not have, which they did not have because they could not afford them and which they did not have because they did not want them. 26 of the 33 items on the list were described as necessities by a majority of those who were asked, and these constituted an empirically validated list of socially perceived necessities. The number of people who lacked three or more of these items because they could not afford them was selected as the appropriate criterion[14] and constituted the number experiencing material deprivation.

The main difference between the two approaches to the measurement of poverty outlined above is that Townsend's approach focuses on income and seeks to identify the level of income below which people experience deprivation while Mack and Lansley's approach focuses on deprivation and uses income to distinguish between those who experience deprivation because they cannot afford to purchase the items in question from those who could afford to do so but, for whatever reason, choose not to. Townsend's approach, which focuses on low income, can be described as an 'indirect' approach while Mack and Lansley's approach, which focuses on material deprivation, can be described as a 'direct' approach'.[15] The problem is that neither of these approaches is a particularly good one. As Brian Nolan and Christopher Whelan have pointed out, income measures are unsatisfactory because a substantial proportion of those below a given poverty line do not experience deprivation while deprivation measures are likewise unsatisfactory because a substantial proportion of those reporting what they consider to be enforced deprivation do not have low current incomes.[16] The first group are those who, because they have stocks of capital, are supported by family and friends, are unusually good at budgeting or for some other reason, manage to ensure that they and their families do not go short; the second group are those who go short for reasons other than a lack of resources, eg because

[14] Very few of the better off, ie of those in the top half of the income distribution, lacked three or more of these necessities and nearly all who did so reported that they had cut back on non-necessities. See Mack and Lansley (ibid, 176).

[15] This distinction was highlighted by Stein Ringen. See S Ringen, *The Possibility of Politics: A Study in the Political Economy of the Welfare State* (Oxford, Oxford University Press, 1987) and 'Direct and Indirect Measures of Poverty' (1988) 17 *Journal of Social Policy* 351.

[16] B Nolan and CT Whelan, *Resources, Deprivation and Poverty* (Oxford, Oxford University Press, 1996) 116.

a member of the household, or someone for whom they feel responsible, has additional needs, is mentally or physically unwell, has a drink, drug or gambling problem, or is just not good at budgeting.

B. Some Recent Developments

Brian Nolan and Christopher Whelan, and Rod Hick in his review of their work,[17] argue against having to choose one or other of these approaches and have advocated what they call a 'consistent' measure of poverty that identifies the 'poor' as being those who experience *both* a lack of resources, as measured by an income poverty line, *and* a low standard of living, as measured by deprivation indicators. This is an important advance, not least because the people identified as being in poverty using indirect and direct measures tend to be different people. In their more recent book,[18] Nolan and Whelan constructed a set of poverty profiles for respondents in 26 European countries[19] and explored the relationship between them and economic stress, defined as reporting 'difficulty' or 'great difficulty' in making ends meet. In each of the 26 countries, respondents who were 'consistently poor', ie those who were poor on both measures, were most likely to report economic stress and respondents who were deprived but not income poor were more likely to do so than those who were income poor but not deprived.[20] According to Hick, this suggests that indicators of material deprivation are particularly useful in identifying respondents who claim to be at risk of economic stress.[21] On the basis of these findings, and his own analysis of 4,858 respondents aged between 16 and 59 in the 2006/07 wave of the British Household Panel Survey, Hick concludes that material deprivation measures should be given greater weight than low income measures.[22] This is because, on six of seven dimensions of multiple deprivation (ill-health, mental ill-health, housing deprivation, lack of autonomy, low life satisfaction and financial stress, but not unemployment),[23] the material deprivation measure rather than the low income measure makes the decisive difference in identifying individuals at risk. However, Hick does not say what the balance between the two measures ought to be.

[17] R Hick, 'On "Consistent" Poverty', CASEpaper 167 (Centre for the Study of Social Exclusion, London School of Economics, 2012).

[18] Nolan and Whelan, *Resources* (1996).

[19] Sweden was omitted because of the large number of missing values on deprivation measures and Croatia did not join the EU until 2013.

[20] Nolan and Whelan (n 16) 113.

[21] Hick, '"Consistent" Poverty' (2012) 9.

[22] R Hick, 'Material Poverty and Multiple Deprivation in Britain: the Distinctiveness of Multidimensional Assessment' (2016) 36 *Journal of Public Policy* 277.

[23] These dimensions were chosen because, in the language of capability theory, each represents functionings (beings and doings) that it can be assumed all respondents would avoid if they could.

C. Statistical Bias

Most official estimates of the number of people living in poverty or material deprivation are based on household surveys although many people experiencing the most extreme forms of poverty and social exclusion may not be living in households. For example, they may be homeless and living rough, living in institutions or living in refugee camps or they may be Roma or undocumented migrants who are left out of surveys. As a result, most official estimates of the number of people living in extreme poverty or experiencing multiple social deprivation, including the EU's 'at risk of poverty or social exclusion surveys',[24] are underestimates. Accurate estimates of the number of people living in extreme poverty require a bespoke sampling frame from which they are not excluded. The JRF Report 'Destitution in the UK' provides one example of how this can be achieved.

D. Destitution in the UK

In 2016, the Joseph Rowntree Foundation (JRF) published a study of destitution in the UK.[25] The study defined people as destitute *either* if they or their children lacked two or more of six essentials in the previous month, because they could not afford them, *or* because their income was so low[26] that they were unable to purchase these essentials for themselves, for example because they received them as a hand-out.[27] Thus, as proposed by Nolan and Whelan, they used a combination of low-income and material deprivation measures. The six essentials were:

- shelter (they have slept rough for one or more nights);
- food (they have had fewer than two meals a day for two or more days);
- heating their home (they have not been able to do this for five or more days);
- lighting (they have not been able to do this for five or more days);
- clothing and footwear (appropriate for weather); and
- basic toiletries (soap, shampoo, toothpaste, toothbrush).

[24] Available at https://ec.europa.eu/eurostat/statistics-explained/index.php/People_at_risk_of_poverty_or_social_exclusion.

[25] S Fitzpatrick, G Bramley, F Sosenko, J Blenkinsopp, S Johnsen, M Littlewood and B Watts, *Destitution in the UK* (York, Joseph Rowntree Foundation, 2016).

[26] An average of (i) the actual expenditure on essential items by the poorest 10% of the population, (ii) 80% of the Joseph Rowntree Foundation (JRF) minimum income standard costs for the equivalent items, and (iii) the amount members of the public thought the relevant-sized household needed to avoid destitution.

[27] Respondents were asked if this was the reason and a check was made to see whether their income was below the relevant poverty line (60% of median income after housing costs). A check was also made to ensure that they had no or negligible savings. See Fitzpatrick et al, *Destitution* (2016) 8.

Estimates of the number of destitute individuals and households in the UK were based on a survey of users of 6–8 voluntary sector crisis centres providing advice, support and material assistance[28] in each of 10 case study areas in one week in 2015.[29] 40 per cent of the estimated total of 1,250,000 people were destitute on both criteria, 49 per cent on the first criterion only, ie they said they could not afford to purchase two or more of the essential items although their incomes were above the 'extremely low' standard, and 12 per cent on the second criterion only, ie they had been able to purchase the essential items although their incomes were below the 'extremely low' standard. The most common items destitute service users lacked were food (76 per cent), clothing (71 per cent), toiletries (62 per cent), heating (53 per cent), lighting (30 per cent) and shelter (25 per cent). One quarter of the total reported that they had slept rough during the previous month. Of the total number of essential items that destitute service users lacked, 12 per cent lacked none or one, 22 per cent lacked two, 24 per cent lacked three, 22 per cent lacked four, and 21 per cent lacked five or six. In other words, two thirds of the destitute service users lacked three or more of the essential items.[30]

The three main sub-groups of destitute persons identified in the JRF Report were:

- migrants born outside the UK – 139,145 households (20.8 per cent);
- UK-born people with complex needs who had either slept rough or received money from begging or were sampled from a homelessness or complex needs service – 268,456 households (40.2 per cent);
- other UK-born people without complex needs who were destitute but did not fit into either of the above two categories – 260,145 households (39.0 per cent).[31]

Each of the sub-groups seems to have experienced a different set of problems that led to destitution. For those who were UK-born and had complex needs, delays in claiming benefit and sanctions when they were on benefit[32] were

[28] These included food banks, soup runs, homeless, complex needs and migrant services and generic advice services.

[29] On the basis of 2,009 returns, Suzanne Fitzpatrick and her colleagues estimated that the total number of service users in these 10 areas in the relevant survey week was 21,778, of whom 13,969 (64%) were destitute (using the above definition). They then estimated the number of destitute households who were in touch with voluntary sector crisis centres throughout the UK in a representative week in 2015 (184,500) and the number of destitute households who were in touch with voluntary sector crisis centres throughout the UK over the whole of 2015 (668,000). These households comprised 1,250,000 people of whom 312,000 were children.

[30] Fitzpatrick et al (n 25) 14.

[31] ibid, 19.

[32] For an account of benefit sanctions in the UK, see M Adler, 'The New Leviathan: Benefit Sanctions in the UK' (2016) 43 *Journal of Law and Society* 195, and *Cruel, Inhuman or Degrading Treatment? Benefit Sanctions in the UK* (London, Palgrave Macmillan, 2018).

particularly important trigger points, although relationship breakdown, domestic violence and getting evicted were all more strongly associated with this sub-group than with the others. Those who were UK-born but did not have complex needs tended to become destitute because they got behind with their bills, got into debt and, perhaps, borrowed money to deal with these problems thereby making them worse. Delays in claiming benefits and sanctions when they were on benefit were also important trigger points. Migrants were less likely to have experienced any of the above problems, although losing a job was a more important trigger point for them than for the other sub-groups.

It is conventional to think of social security – broadly defined here to include all forms of publicly funded financial support for those who are unable to support themselves by working or those who have additional needs due to sickness, disability, other forms of incapacity, maternity or childcare costs, that are deemed worthy of support by the community – as a social institution that prevents or ameliorates destitution. It probably is for most people most of the time. However, social security can also give rise to destitution. There are, no doubt, many reasons why this should be so but three of them can be mentioned here: the fact that some categories of people are not able to claim social security; delays in processing claims to social security and sanctions that penalise recipients of social security for failing to meet the increasingly onerous behavioural requirements that are associated with the receipt of social security benefits.

Benefit delays were the most frequently reported benefit problem, affecting 40 per cent of all destitute service users in the survey of voluntary sector crisis centres.[33] Interviewees waiting for Jobseeker's Allowance (JSA) payments to start experienced delays of up to six weeks, which presented serious problems for those moving in and out of casual or short-term work. Some interviewees claimed that repeated administrative failures in benefit processes had led to serious delays and caused considerable hardship.

Benefit sanctions, ie suspension of payment for periods ranging from four weeks (for the first offence) to three years (for the third offence) were reported by 30 per cent of destitute service users.[34] Benefit sanctions are disproportionately applied to vulnerable claimants and cause considerable hardship. They constitute the coercive component of the conditionality regime whose aim is supposedly to get those on benefit to return to work. Although the threat of being sanctioned probably does encourage some claimants to step up their job-search activities,[35] a recent study has shown that the main effect of imposing sanctions was to eject claimants from the benefits system and to distance them from the world of work. This study found that, for each 100 adverse sanction

[33] Fitzpatrick et al (n 25) 31–32.

[34] See Adler, 'The New Leviathan' (2016) and Adler *Cruel, Inhuman and Degrading Treatment?* (n. 32).

[35] According to a recent report by the National Audit Office, the DWP has little idea of how claimants respond to sanctions. See National Audit Office, *Benefit Sanctions*, HC 628, Session 2016–17, 30 November 2016.

decisions, only about 7.4 claimants moved into work whereas 35.9 claimants, ie almost five times as many, moved on to 'unknown destinations', ie 'dropped out'. The remainder returned to benefits, but many of those who were sanctioned ended up on the streets.[36]

E. The European Picture

The Europe 2020 Strategy has set the target of 'lifting at least 20 million people out of the risk of poverty and social exclusion' by 2020 as compared with 2008.[37] 2008 was selected as the baseline year for monitoring progress because it was the most recent year for which comprehensive social indicators were available. The indicator of poverty and social exclusion used by the European Commission is an aggregate of three sub-indicators: monetary poverty; multiple deprivation; and low work intensity.

1. Monetary poverty is set at 60 per cent of the national median equivalised disposable income. Although this is an arbitrary threshold, Hick has argued that it represents a rough proxy of Townsend's poverty threshold.[38] Clearly, estimates of the number of people at risk of poverty depend on where this threshold is set.
2. Severely deprived people are defined as those who cannot afford at least four[39] of the following:
   - (i) to keep up with rent or utility bills, hire purchase instalments or other loan payments;
   - (ii) a week's holiday away from home;
   - (iii) to keep their home warm;
   - (iv) to pay for unexpected expenses;
   - (v) to eat meat, fish or other protein-rich nutrition every second day;
   - (vi) to own a car;
   - (vii) to own a washing machine,
   - (viii) to own a colour TV; or
   - (ix) to own a telephone.

[36] R Loopstra, A Reeves, M McKee and D Suckler, 'Do Punitive Approaches to Unemployment Benefit Recipients Increase Welfare Exit and Unemployment: A Cross-area Analysis of UK Sanctioning Reforms', *Sociology Working Paper 2015–01* (Oxford, Department of Sociology, University of Oxford, 2015).

[37] European Commission, 'Taking Stock of the Europe 2020 Strategy for Smart, Sustainable Growth', COM(2014) 130 final (Brussels, 2014).

[38] R Hick, 'Poverty as Capability Deprivation: Conceptualising and Measuring Poverty in Contemporary Europe' (2014) 55 *European Journal of Sociology* 295–323.

[39] In an analysis of how these dimensions of multiple deprivation relate to economic stress, Hick has used a threshold of three or more of these deprivation items. See R Hick, 'The Coupling of Disadvantages: Measuring Poverty and Multiple Deprivation Before and After the Great Recession' (2016) 18 *European Journal of Social Security* 2.

3. Very low work intensity refers to the number of people aged 0–59 living in households where the adults worked less than 20 per cent of full-time during the previous year.

Lack of work drives monetary poverty and multiple deprivation. In 2013, almost 50 per cent of the unemployed were at risk of poverty after social transfers.

The EU has estimated that 122.6 million people were at risk of poverty or social exclusion in the 28 Member States in 2013. This represented 24.5 per cent of the EU population. About 40 million people, 32.6 per cent of the total, were affected by more than one dimension of poverty and 9.3 per cent were affected by all three dimensions. Those who were most affected were women, children, people in single-parent households (who were most likely to be at risk), lower educated people and migrants.

The countries with the highest proportions at risk of poverty and social exclusion were among those with the lowest GDP per head (although they included one middle-range country, Greece, and did not include some of the poorest countries in Europe, eg Croatia and Poland, while the countries with the lowest levels at risk of poverty and social exclusion were among those with the highest GDP per head (although they also included one relatively poor country, the Czech Republic). The countries with the highest proportions at risk of poverty and social exclusion were among those with the highest Gini coefficients (all except Hungary were within the range 34.5–35.5) while the countries with the lowest levels at risk of poverty and social exclusion were among those with the lowest Gini coefficients (all except France were within the range 25.1–26.2).

Some people have argued that extreme poverty only has any real meaning if it is persistent and the OECD has compared persistent poverty for a selection of countries.[40] The EU has produced data on those lacking four or more items and on a composite measure (lacking four or more items and below 60 per cent of median income in at least two of last three years).[41] There were very small proportions in the richer EU countries, eg The Netherlands and Sweden (0.0 per cent), Denmark (0.1), UK (0.2), Belgium and France (0.5) but in some of the poorer countries, e.g. Latvia (33.7 per cent), Poland (31.1), Lithuania (28.7), Hungary (20.4), the proportions were over 20 per cent.

Because the European Commission Report is very reliant on EU-SILC data,[42] which are based on households, it urges Eurostat to make its sampling frame as comprehensive as possible and proposes alternative methods for collecting data including specially targeted surveys.

[40] OECD, 'Growing Unequal? Income Distribution and Poverty in OECD Countries' (Paris, 2008) ch 6.

[41] European Commission, 'The Measurement of Extreme Poverty in the European Union' (Brussels, Directorate General for Employment, Social Affairs and Inclusion, 2011) Table 10.1.

[42] 'European Union Statistics on Income and Living Conditions' produced by Eurostat.

III. THE TOP-DOWN VIEW

A. The 'Rich' and the 'Super Rich'

As pointed out in section II, there are a number of different ways of defining who is to count as poor in a given society, each with their own advocates. However, there is probably even less agreement on defining who is to count as rich. The definitions that are most frequently used are statistical ones based on the distribution of income. Although these definitions may have little social significance, it has become conventional to define the 'rich' and the 'super-rich' as comprising those with the top x per cent of income in society.

The British social geographer, Danny Dorling, has argued that there is a real social divide in the UK between the 'super rich', defined as the richest one per cent, and the remaining 99 per cent of the population, and suggested that this is of greater significance than the divide between the 'rich', defined as the top ten per cent, and the rest.[43] He goes on to point out that, every year for the last 30 years, over 70 per cent of those who have taken part in the British Social Attitudes Survey have stated that the income gap is too large.[44] By 2012, the last year for which published data were available, that figure had risen to 82 per cent – only 14 per cent stated that the gap was about right. The time series is shown in Figure 5.1 below.

Figure 5.1 Attitudes towards inequality and redistribution, 1983–2012 (the last year for which published data were available)

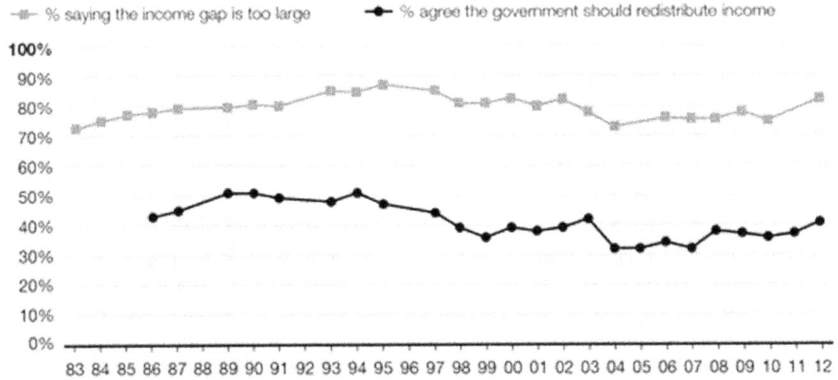

Over the past three decades, inequality among the bottom 99 per cent of the UK population has fallen – the Gini coefficient for the bottom 99 per cent has

[43] D Dorling, *Inequality and the 1%* (New York and London, Verso, 2014).

[44] N Pearce and E Taylor, 'Government Spending and Welfare' in A Park, C Bryson, E Clery, J Curtice and M Phillips (eds) *British Social Attitudes 30* (London, NatCen Social Research, 2014) 33–61, Fig 2.2.

fallen by five per cent from what it was in 1991 (when it was 0.30).[45] On the other hand, over the same period, inequality among the top one per cent, ie among the super rich has increased. Dorling also points out that, while the top one per cent of households received 9.8 per cent of national income in 1990, this increased to 15.4 per cent in 2007 before falling, after the financial crisis of 2008, to 12.7 per cent in 2012, the last year for which data were available. He goes on to argue that, although the super rich are extraordinarily rich, they often feel relatively poor. This reflects the 'financial chasm' that has grown up between them and the rest of the population – those at the bottom of the top one per cent are more likely to look up to see how poorly off they are in relation to the giants above them than look down to see how privileged they are in relation to the masses below. They compare themselves with those whose basic pay, bonuses and perks are even higher than their own.

B. The European Picture

The Luxemburg Income Study (LIS) indicates that, in terms of income, the UK is the seventh most unequal country among 30 OECD countries and the fourth most unequal in Europe. This can be seen in Figure 5.2 below, which makes it clear that the Nordic countries are among the most equal.[46]

Figure 5.2 How unequal is income in other countries?

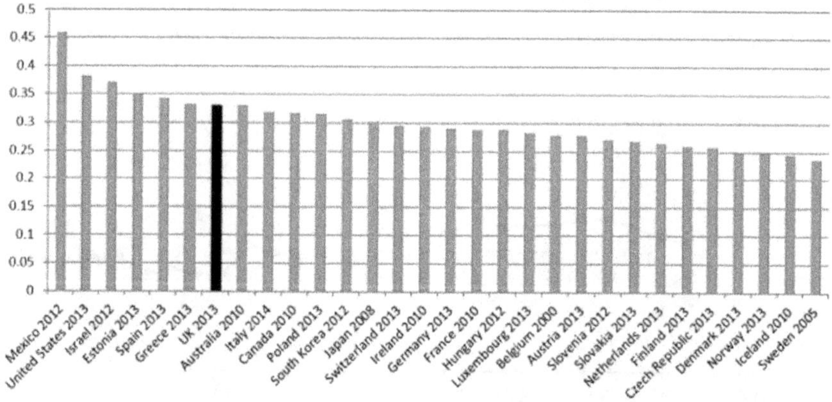

For several reasons, and notwithstanding the limitations in the data outlined above, income inequality has increased in most European countries over the last three decades. This can be seen in Figure 5.3 below.

[45] The Gini coefficient is the most commonly used measure of inequality in income and wealth. It varies between 0 (representing complete equality) and 1 (representing the most extreme inequality).

[46] The LIS data can be accessed in Equality Trust, 'The Scale of Inequality in the UK' (London, 2017), available at www.equalitytrust.org.uk/scale-economic-inequality-uk.

Figure 5.3 Changes income inequality levels in EU and OECD countries, 1980–2014

Gini coefficient of disposable income inequality in 2014 (or latest year) and mid-1980s when available, total population

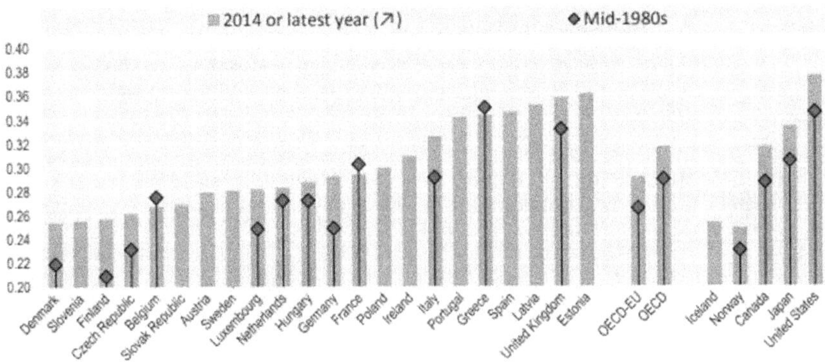

Source: OECD Income Distribution Database (http://oe.cd/idd).

The Gini coefficient for the distribution of income in Europe increased across the board from an average of 0.28 in the 1980s to an average of 0.30 in 2014. This was, in part, because tax and transfer systems became less redistributive. That said, the Gini coefficient remained stable or even declined in some countries, eg in Belgium, France and Greece (until the financial crisis of 2008). Considering these differences, it is hard to talk about a single 'European' model.

At the same time, the profiles of individuals at the bottom and those at the top of the income and wealth distributions have changed. Those at the bottom are no longer the elderly but, rather, young people and families with children. Inheritance is still very important[47] and many of those at the top have benefitted from intergenerational transfers. However, they have been joined by entrepreneurs and business executives who are rewarded with (large) bonuses on top of their (large) salaries. Although tax and transfer policies significantly reduce market inequalities, some countries manage to redistribute incomes much more effectively than others.

C. The Global Picture

The share of the world's total wealth owned by the richest one per cent of people has been on an upward path ever since the financial crisis, passing the 2000 level in 2013 and increasing every year after that. Thus global wealth inequality has not only been high but has also been rising in the post-crisis period.

[47] See P Fessler and M Schütz, 'Private Wealth across European Countries: the Role of Income, Inheritance and the Welfare State', Working Paper Series No 1847 (Frankfurt, European Central Bank, 2015).

As shown in Figure 5.4 below, 70.2 per cent of the global adult population currently owns a mere 2.7 per cent of global wealth while 8.6 per cent of the global adult population owns a massive 85.6 per cent of global wealth.

Figure 5.4 Global inequalities in wealth

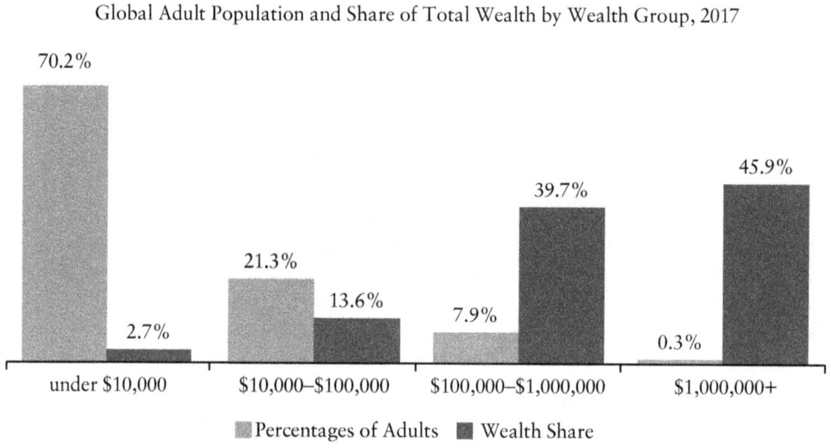

Using an updated and expanded data set published by Credit Suisse in November 2017, Oxfam has revealed that 42 people now own the same amount of wealth as the poorest half of humanity.[48]

D. Statistical Bias

It should be noted that most estimates of the income and wealth of the rich and the super rich are based on tax data and that they assume that people pay all the tax they ought to pay. In the case of the super rich, the data are taken from the Forbes World's Billionaires list.[49] Forbes uses shareholder information, company financial statements, current exchange rates and meetings with billionaires themselves to estimate individual net worth. However, because tax avoidance, tax evasion and the non-payment of tax on illegal activities like money laundering and drug-dealing are widespread among the rich and, in particular, among the super rich, this results in serious underestimates of the number of rich and, in particular, super-rich individuals. If estimates for tax avoidance and tax evasion are taken into account, the extent of inequality in all countries, but more so in countries with lax tax regimes than in others, would be even greater.[50] More accurate estimates would require a

[48] Available at www.oxfam.org/en/pressroom/pressreleases/2018.

[49] Available at www.forbes.com/billionaires/#6598210e251c.

[50] According to the National Bureau of Economic Research, an independent, non-profit think tank based in Cambridge, MA, the 'ultra rich', defined as those whose net worth is more than

more appropriate sampling frame, but what such a sampling frame would look like or how it could be constructed are far from clear.

E. The Super Rich

In the UK, the super rich, ie the richest one per cent of individuals, receive 15 per cent of national income, the same share as they received in 1937. This is much less than their counterparts in the USA (which is one of the most economically unequal countries in the world), who receive 20 per cent of national income, but much more than their counterparts in Japan, which is one of the most economically equal countries, who receive ten per cent.

The Nobel prize-winning economist Paul Krugman[51] has put forward three stylised explanations for extreme inequality. According to Krugman, it could be due to the fact that individuals vary hugely in their productivity, in their luck, or in the power wielded by the rich and the super rich, and he argues that there is some truth to each of these accounts. However, he claims that the real issue is whether income and wealth can be redistributed from the rich to the poor without undermining economic progress.

IV. THE INTEGRATED VIEW

A. Arguments For and Against Redistribution

One possible argument for not redistributing income is that high levels of inequality contribute to economic growth from which everyone, including the poor, benefits. However, the different economic circumstances of countries with similar levels of inequality (eg the USA and Mexico) and the similar economic circumstances of countries with very different levels of inequality (eg the USA and Sweden) provide little support for this view. Another Nobel prize-winning economist, Joseph Stiglitz, who used to believe that there was a trade-off between equality and economic growth, has now come to the view that greater equality and improved economic performance are complementary.[52]

While extremes of wealth and poverty coexist and the super rich live lives of unimaginable luxury at the same time as the destitute struggle to make

US $45 million, are 10 times more likely to evade taxes than the average citizen; are more likely to use offshore accounts; and hardly anyone except the ultra rich uses offshore accounts. Tax havens hold 10% of global GDP, 'offshore' wealth is shifting from Switzerland to Asia, countries with more offshore wealth also use more tax havens, and substantially increases inequality. These findings are summarized in International Consortium of Investigative Journalists, '7 Charts that Show how the Rich Hide their Cash' (2017) ICIJ Newsletter, 13 September.

[51] P Krugman, 'Is Vast Inequality Necessary?' (2016) *New York Times*, 15 January.

[52] JE Stiglitz, 'Inequality and Economic Growth' (2016) 86 *Political Quarterly* 134.

ends meet, many people (myself included) think there is a moral imperative to redistribute resources from those with the broadest shoulders to those who lead stunted lives, especially if, as appears to be the case, there are no adverse economic or social consequences. Tolerance of high levels of inequality, on the one hand, and a commitment to reduce them, on the other, reflect political choices. Of course, such political choices are not made in a vacuum and there may be all kinds of institutional and ideological factors that make it difficult to translate political choices into meaningful reform. The only point to be made here is that a transfer of resources from the rich to the poor could be effected if the political will was there.

B. The Global Picture

According to the Serbian-American economist Branko Milanović, the main reason for increases in the real incomes of the poorest people from the developing world has been economic growth in China.[53] Milanović claims that, until approximately 2000, China was the sole force for the reduction of global inequality. He argues that the main reason for the declining real incomes of working people in the developed world was globalisation, and the fact that relatively cheap labour in developing countries made them more attractive for companies as a source of labour than the traditional sources of labour in developed countries. He also argues that the main reason for increases in the real incomes of the rich, most of whom live in the developed world, was globalisation, since this provides a rationale for firms to pay enormous incomes to their senior staff, on the grounds that they need to do so to attract and retain them in a globalised economy. A second reason is the ineffectiveness of taxation in a world in which capital can migrate from one country to another and governments are either unwilling or unable to prevent this.

Slower economic growth in China following the financial crisis of 2008 has not only meant that the incomes of lower-paid workers in developed countries have continued to stagnate, but also that stagnation extended to those with higher incomes.[54] Whether the real incomes of the poorest people in the world will continue to improve depends, in large measure, on economic growth in other poor countries, particularly in other Asian countries like India, Indonesia, Bangladesh, Thailand and Vietnam. In addition, what to do about the declining real incomes of working people in the developed world remains a problem. What is clear is that some poor people, in the developed world as well as in the

[53] B Milanović, *Global Inequality: A New Approach for the Age of Globalization*, (Cambridge, MA, Belknap Press of Harvard University Press, 2016).

[54] ibid, 31.

developing world, are bound to get left behind. One conclusion of this chapter is therefore that the problem of extreme poverty is unlikely to disappear.

Twenty years ago, 19 per cent of the world's population were living in what the UN defined as 'absolute poverty', meaning living on less than US $1.90 a day. Ten years later, that number was less than nine per cent. In other words, the number of people living in absolute poverty actually fell by more than 50 per cent over a 10-year period. During this period, hundreds of millions of the poorest people in the world were raised out of absolute poverty, resulting in improvements to their living standards which, both as a proportion and as an absolute number, is an unprecedented economic achievement. Over the same period, there was a marked decline in the living standards of the less well-off in developed societies, many of whom lost their jobs and experienced a fall in their living standards.

How can these developments, with the very rich getting even richer, the relatively poor losing out while many of the very poorest were raised out of poverty, be explained? Milanović represents these three developments as a single 'elephant-shaped curve',[55] which is shaped like an elephant, rising from left to right like an elephant's tail and back, then sloping downwards as it gets towards the elephant's head, and finally rising sharply as it follows the contour of the elephant's raised trunk. The 'elephant-shaped curve' is depicted in Figure 5.5 below.

Figure 5.5 Changes in global income distribution, 1998–2008

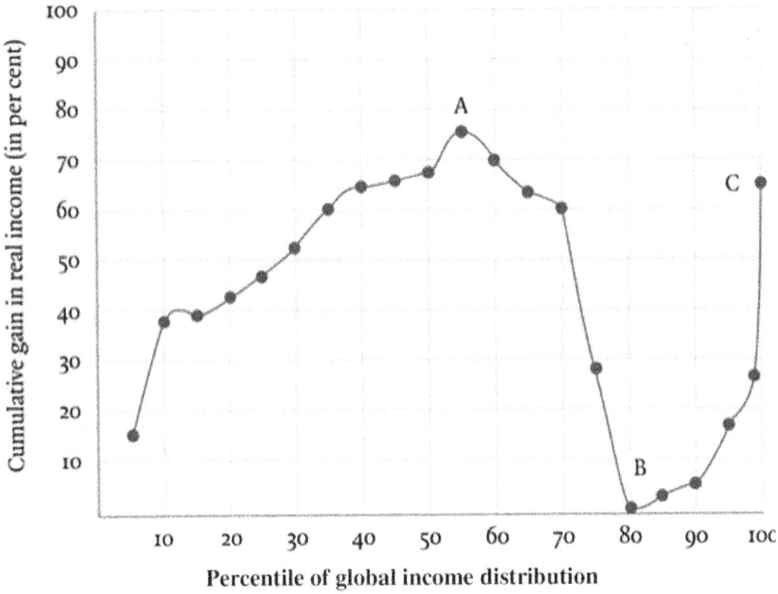

Source: Milanović, *op. cit.*, Figure 1.1: 11.

[55] ibid, 33.

Most of those to the left of Point A on the graph comprise the poor in the developing world, who experienced significant gains in real income in the 10 years after 1998. Those between points A and B are mainly those in the developed world who experienced a marked decline in their real incomes. In other words, the global poor have been getting consistently better off over the last decade while those who were most affected by globalisation, the majority of whom live in the developed world, have seen their incomes decline. At the same time, the people to the right of Point B on the graph experienced significant gains in real income during this period. This applies to the rich as a whole (the top 20 per cent of the global income distribution on the graph) but, in particular, to the very rich, in particular the top one per cent, whose incomes approached point C on the graph.

The main reason for increases in the real incomes of the poorest people in the developing world (which comprise those who appear below point A on the graph) was economic growth in China. According to Milanović, until approximately 2000, China was the sole force for the reduction of global inequality. The main reason for the declining real incomes of workers in the developed world (who comprise most of those who appear in the range A-B on the graph) was that they were squeezed between their own countries' top earners, who continued to make money out of globalisation, and developing countries' workers, whose relatively cheap labour made them more attractive for companies to employ. Milanović argues that this process is not at an end and will polarise Western societies into two groups, a very successful and rich class at the top and a much larger group of people whose jobs will entail servicing the rich class in occupations where human labour cannot be replaced by robots.[56] Finally, the main reason for increases in the real incomes of the rich, most of whom live in the developed world, was, once again, globalisation, which provides a rationale for firms to pay enormous incomes to their senior executives, on the grounds that they need to do so to attract and retain them in a globalised economy. Another important factor was the ineffectiveness of taxation in a world in which capital can migrate from one country to another and governments are either unwilling or unable to prevent this.

How changes in the worldwide pattern of inequality were affected by the financial crisis of 2008 is still unclear. According to Milanović, the absence of growth in the developed world after 2008 meant not only that the incomes of the lower middle classes in these countries continued to stagnate but also that stagnation extended to those with higher incomes.[57] As a result, the elephant's back (A to B on the graph) sloped downwards even more steeply, but its trunk

[56] ibid, 214.
[57] ibid, 31.

(to the right of B on the graph) sloped upwards less steeply. At the same time, because incomes continued to rise in China,[58] the elephant's tail (to the left of A on the graph) continued to rise.

Since 2011, economic growth in China appears to have slowed down and, Milanović argues, improvements in the real incomes of the world's poor depend on economic growth in other poor countries, particularly in other Asian countries like India, Indonesia, Bangladesh, Thailand and Vietnam. However, even if this occurs, some poor people are bound to get left behind and the problem of extreme poverty is unlikely to disappear.[59]

V. SOME NORMATIVE CONCLUSIONS

Reducing extremes of income is difficult but not impossible. Although many of the super rich have benefitted from intergenerational transfers, they have been joined by entrepreneurs and business executives who have not necessarily enjoyed these advantages. Intergenerational transfers can be limited by means of progressive inheritance taxes and a clamp-down on the use of trusts which enable the deceased to pass assets to beneficiaries without having to go through probate and pay tax.

In his last book, the economist Tony Atkinson proposed that 'Receipts of inheritance and gifts *inter-vivos* should be taxed under a progressive lifetime capital receipts tax'[60] and this, rather than the progressive global tax on capital advocated by the French economist Thomas Piketty,[61] is probably the best way forward. It would, of course, require a high level of international cooperation that, in today's political climate, is probably quite unrealistic. However, some progress may be achievable through a series of incremental steps, either by individual countries or, better still, on a collaborative basis. Globalisation undoubtedly makes it difficult for individual countries to raise taxes because capital and labour can migrate from countries with high taxes to countries with low taxes and countries with strict tax regimes to countries with lax ones. However, difficult is not the same as impossible.

Excessive pay and bonuses could be reined in through increased worker representation on boardroom pay committees and requiring companies to publish and justify their pay ratios. An assault on offshore accounts, tax havens

[58] According to Milanović (ibid) 30, the average urban income doubled between 2008 and 2011 and the average rural income increased by 80 per cent.

[59] ibid, 213.

[60] AB Atkinson, *Inequality. What Can be Done?* (Cambridge, MA, Harvard University Press, 2015) 193–96).

[61] T Piketty *Capital in the Twenty-First Century* (Cambridge, MA, Belknap Press of Harvard University Press, 2014) 515.

and shell companies would ensure that excessive incomes and bonuses are subject to tax while an increase in taxes on the highest incomes would ensure that those with the broadest shoulders make the largest contribution. The fact that extremes of income and wealth are so much greater in some countries than in others shows that something can be done about the problem. As argued above, the arguments about what to do and how to do it are political rather than economic ones.

A. The Possibility of a Social Maximum

This discussion raises the question of whether there ought to be a social maximum as well as a social minimum. The arguments for a social maximum are democratic (the rich and, in particular, the super rich exercise a degree of power and influence that is inconsistent with the egalitarian premises of democracy), utilitarian (taking a pound from a rich and, in particular, a super-rich person and giving it to a poor and, in particular, a destitute person hurts the rich person less than it helps the poor person, and so is a net gain to society) and expedient (imposing a social maximum and redistributing the excess resources of the super rich to enhance the life chances of the those living on the social minimum would be very efficient in that the excess resources of the super-rich would go a long way).

B. The Case for Redistribution

There is a strong moral case for redistributing resources from those with the broadest shoulders to those who lead stunted lives, not least because such a move is unlikely to have adverse consequences for the economy or for society as a whole. That far too many people lead stunted lives and that others lead unbelievably affluent lifestyles is clear, but whether, and if so what, should be done about it are clearly highly contested questions.

Extreme inequalities undermine solidarity and have many undesirable consequences. As Wilkinson and Pickett have demonstrated, inequality has 'pernicious effects on societies: eroding trust, increasing anxiety and illness, (and) encouraging excessive consumption'.[62] They show that, for each of 11 different health and social problems (physical health, mental health, drug abuse, education, imprisonment, obesity, social mobility, trust

[62] R Wilkinson and K Pickett, *The Spirit Level: Why Equality* (London, Penguin Books, 2011). Although Wilkinson and Pickett's conclusions have been subjected to extensive criticism, there seems to be general agreement that there is a correlation between the extent of income inequality and the incidence of health and social problems. However, it must be conceded that there is less agreement about whether income inequality causes health and social problems independently of other factors.

and community life, violence, teenage pregnancies, and child well-being), outcomes are significantly worse in more unequal countries, in both developed and developing societies and that this requires, at one and the same time, an increase in taxes on the rich and the super rich, and measures that would directly benefit those experiencing poverty, in particular those experiencing extreme poverty. Redistribution should be a two-edged sword, and the two sets of measures need to proceed in tandem.

6

Is there Common Ground for Defining a Decent Social Minimum in Europe?

TIM GOEDEMÉ, TESS PENNE, OTTO SWEDRUP, KAREL VAN DEN BOSCH AND BÉRÉNICE STORMS[1]

I. INTRODUCTION

IN AN ERA of disappointing poverty trends in Europe,[2] there is an increasingly urgent call to strengthen the social dimension of the EU in order to secure a decent minimum income for all. There have been various soft law initiatives, such as the recently proclaimed European Pillar of Social Rights (see in particular principle 14), that assess a right to adequate minimum income protection. However, the right to a decent social minimum or an adequate minimum income risks remaining a hollow phrase in absence of a pan-European consensus on its normative content. Furthermore, monitoring the adequacy of minimum income schemes at the EU level requires the translation of this theoretical concept into a monetary benchmark that is comparable in a meaningful way across countries. In Europe, usually the at-risk-of-poverty threshold is used for this purpose. This threshold defines the adequacy benchmark as 60 per cent

[1] This chapter builds on T Penne, O Swedrup, K Van den Bosch and B Storms, 'Exploring Common Ground for Defining Adequate Social Participation in 24 EU Capital Cities', CSB Working paper (Antwerp, University of Antwerp, 2019). We are very grateful to Toomas Kotkas, Frans Pennings, Ingrid Leijten and the participants of the Workshop on Specifying and Securing a Social Minimum in Oñati, Spain, 29–30 June 2017 for thoughtful comments and suggestions. In addition, we would like to thank all country teams that participated in the pilot project for the development of a common methodology on reference budgets in Europe (see T Goedemé, B Storms, T Penne and K Van den Bosch, 'The Development of a Methodology for Comparable Reference Budgets in Europe – Final Report of the Pilot Project' (Brussels, European Commission, 2015) for the full list of researchers involved in the project). Funding by the European Commission (DG Employment and Social Affairs) is gratefully acknowledged (contract no VC/2013/0554). The views expressed in this chapter are those of the authors and do not necessarily coincide with those of the funders of the underlying research. All remaining errors and shortcomings are our own.

[2] eg B Cantillon, T Goedemé and J Hills, *Decent Incomes for All. Improving Policies in Europe* (New York, Oxford University Press, 2019).

of national median equivalent disposable household income.[3] This benchmark clearly varies with average living standards across countries, but it is not clear to what extent it refers to what can be considered an adequate minimum income. On the contrary, even though the indicator certainly has its merits, the at-risk-of-poverty indicator is rather arbitrary and assumes that the minimum resources required for a decent living standard are a fixed proportion of median incomes. Consequently, it appears to refer to different levels of adequacy or decency across countries.[4] Is it possible to identify an alternative benchmark that is comparable in a more substantive sense? At least, this would require that the concept of a decent living standard could rely upon a common understanding across Europe. In this chapter, we therefore explore whether such a common understanding is likely to exist. To do so, we focus on the closely related concept of adequate social participation, connect this with recent theories of human needs and use results from a research project on the development of comparable reference budgets in the European Union.

A venerable and internationally widespread method to define a decent social minimum is the reference budget approach. In this research tradition, priced baskets of essential goods and services are constructed, reflecting a certain living standard, such as 'minimum adequate' or 'participation level' standards.[5] One of the main advantages of the approach is that it gives a clear understanding of what is perceived as an acceptable living standard in society, based on different information sources, taking into account the institutional, cultural and social context. Although most European countries have experience with developing reference budgets, the budgets are usually not comparable, as they are developed for varying purposes using a variety of methods.[6] Recently, important steps towards a comparative methodology have been taken in two related European projects,[7] funded by the European Commission and coordinated by the Herman Deleeck Centre for Social Policy (University of Antwerp). This chapter is largely based on the results coming from the 'pilot project on the development of a methodology for comparable reference budgets in Europe'.[8] In this project, we have developed a common method to construct comparable reference budgets

[3] eg AB Atkinson, B Cantillon, E Marlier and B Nolan, *Social Indicators: The EU and Social Inclusion* (Oxford, Oxford University Press, 2002).

[4] *cf* T Goedemé, T Penne, T Hufkens, A Karakitsios, A Bernát, A Franziskus, B Simonovits, EC Álvarez, E Kanavitsa, I Cussó Parcerisas, JR Romaní, L Mäkinen, M Matsaganis, M Arlotti, M Kopasz, P Szivós, V-M Ritakallio, Y Kazepov, K Van den Bosch and B Storms, 'What Does It Mean To Live on the Poverty Threshold? Lessons From Reference Budgets' in B Cantillon, T Goedemé and J Hills (eds), *Decent Incomes for All* (New York, Oxford University Press, 2019).

[5] B Storms, T Goedemé, K Van den Bosch, T Penne, N Schuerman and S Stockman, 'Review of Current State of Play on Reference Budget Practices at National, Regional, and Local Level' (Brussels, European Commission, 2014).

[6] ibid.

[7] T Goedemé, B Storms, S Stockman, T Penne and K Van den Bosch, 'Towards Cross-country Comparable Reference Budgets' in Europe: First Results of a Concerted Effort' (2015) 17 *European Journal of Social Security* 3; Goedemé et al, 'The Development of a Methodology' (2015).

[8] T Goedemé et al (n 1).

that illustrate what families need for adequate social participation across Europe. Following this methodology, comparable baskets for a healthy diet were constructed in 26 EU Member States, as well as a basket for housing, health and personal care in eight Member States.[9] In this chapter, we focus on the first step in the process: the search for a common theoretical and normative understanding of what an acceptable minimum means across Europe.

The chapter is structured as follows. First, we elaborate on the concept of adequate social participation. Subsequently, we discuss the theoretical framework that we take as a starting point for listing a number of essential needs that have to be fulfilled to enable social participation. In the next section, we rely on two different methods in order to assess empirically whether there is a common understanding of adequate social participation across Europe. We first assess 'formal' social norms as laid out by international conventions and European legal instruments pertaining to the domain of adequate social participation. Subsequently, we rely on focus group discussions in 24 EU capital cities, carried out in 2015, to explore whether citizens could arrive at a common understanding of 'adequate social participation'. To the best of our knowledge, this was the first qualitative study to assess in a comparative setting simultaneously in many European countries what 'adequate social participation' means and which needs should be fulfilled to be able to participate adequately in society. We conclude that, at least at an abstract level, there seems to be sufficient common ground across EU capital cities for a shared understanding of what adequate social participation should imply. This suggests that it makes sense to continue this line of research and to try to operationalise the concept of adequate social participation in more concrete terms to create a comparable monetary benchmark of adequate incomes in the European Union.

II. A DEFINITION OF ADEQUATE SOCIAL PARTICIPATION

We focus on the concept of adequate social participation, mainly because this concept has received quite some attention in national and international efforts to construct a comparable benchmark to assess the adequacy of income policies, and in particular reference budgets. We define adequate social participation as the ability of people to adequately play (take and make) the various social roles one should be able to play as a member of a particular society.[10] This implies

[9] ibid; K Van den Bosch, T Goedemé, N Schuerman and B Storms, 'Reference Housing Costs for Adequate Dwellings in Ten European Capitals' (2016) 3 *Critical Housing Analysis* 1; E Carrillo-Álvarez, T Penne, H Boeckx, B Storms and T Goedemé, 'Food Reference Budgets as a Potential Policy Tool to Address Food Insecurity' (2019) 16 *International Journal of Environmental Research and Public Health* 32; Goedemé et al, *What Does it Mean …?* (2019).

[10] B Storms, 'Referentiebudgetten voor Maatschappelijke Participatie', PhD thesis (Antwerp, University of Antwerp, 2012).

that the physical, psychological and social needs are fulfilled in order to take the different social positions in society in line with the dominant social expectations associated with them, as embodied by the institutions of the society in which one lives, and in such a way that it does not cause harm to one's possibilities to do so in the future. In addition, adequate social participation implies that people should be able to contribute to society not only by playing various social roles, but also by having the opportunity to redefine their social roles.

We would like to highlight briefly several important elements of this definition of adequate social participation. First, we define social roles as the social expectations attached to a position that someone in society takes.[11] For the purpose of identifying a concrete monetary benchmark, we focus on social positions defined in broad terms (eg being a mother, an employee or a citizen) which society recognises as those that its members should be able to play or should be given the opportunity to take at the minimum.

Second, we define social expectations more broadly as commonly held expectations regarding what people (are able to) think, have and do, *as embodied by the institutions of a society*. We use the concept of 'institutions' in a dual way:[12] (i) institutions as socially constructed rules; and (ii) institutions as relatively stable patterns of behaviour and interaction, which are often in close interaction with the latter socially constructed rules. As emphasised by Vrooman,[13] one can make a distinction between formal rules, and informal rules that regulate society. In this chapter we focus both on formal and informal social expectations for defining what an adequate minimum is.

Third, we recognise that society is not a fixed social entity. In fact, systems of political authority and cultural expectations may be multi-layered,[14] with some forms of political authority being worldwide, some European, some 'national' and others being rather regional or local. The same is true for dominant cultural expectations. Also, societies can be plural, that is, they can be deeply divided along cultural, religious, ethnic or other lines.[15] In other words, when identifying what could be a decent minimum income, we suggest to pay attention to the *dominant* social expectations that relate to the place where people live, including their worldwide, European, national, regional and local aspects.

Fourth, in what follows, we focus on the material needs of households, assuming that the political and institutional context is organised such that it respects and fosters essential freedoms and is conducive to adequate social participation.

[11] *cf* 'Scripts for social conduct' as in BJ Biddle, 'Recent Developments in Role Theory' (1986) 12 *Annual Review of Sociology* 67; GM Platt, 'Status and Role, Social Psychology of' in NJSB Baltes (ed), *International Encyclopedia of the Social & Behavioral Sciences* (Oxford, Pergamon, 2001).

[12] *cf* TR Voss, 'Institutions' in Baltes, *International Encyclopedia* (2001).

[13] CJ Vrooman, *Rules of Relief. Institutions of Social Security, and Their Impact* (The Hague, SCP, 2009).

[14] *cf* S Mau and R Verwiebe, *European Societies* (Bristol, The Policy Press, 2010).

[15] Eg J Nagata, 'Plural Societies' in Baltes (n 11).

Given our focus on EU Member States, we assume that these societal preconditions are in place.[16] Even so, there is (much) room for improvement, especially now that some EU Member States have weakened the democratic character of their society[17] and some reduced the quality of publicly subsidised goods and services.[18]

III. A THEORETICAL FRAMEWORK OF HUMAN NEEDS[19]

It is useful to embed our notion of adequate social participation into a broader theoretical framework on human needs. This provides a stronger basis for discussing the needs that should be fulfilled in order to be able to participate adequately in society. In addition, it provides more guidance to reflect upon the necessities for adequate social participation in terms of concrete goods and services as well as the relation between individual and household needs on the one hand, and the characteristics of the social environment on the other. In what follows, we build on different strands in the literature as represented by the works of Len Doyal and Ian Gough, Amartya Sen and Martha Nussbaum. Even though these normative frameworks cannot be fully reconciled, we consider it useful to bring some of the insights of these intellectual strands together.[20]

In several papers Amartya Sen convincingly argues that the living standard should not be understood in terms of utility (the pleasure we derive from something) or opulence (accumulated wealth) but in terms of capabilities: what a person can be or do.[21] Capabilities have to be distinguished from 'functionings'. 'Capabilities' refers to the total set of possibilities available to persons, while 'functionings' refers to the subset of realised capabilities, implying some choice. Therefore, in evaluating people's standard of living one should not rely

[16] For a discussion of societal preconditions, see, for instance, L Doyal and I Gough, *A Theory of Human Need* (Houndmills, Macmillan, 1991).

[17] eg A Ágh, 'The Decline of Democracy in East-Central Europe' (2016) 63 *Problems of Post-Communism* 277.

[18] eg F Cervero-Liceras, M McKee and H Legido-Quigley, 'The Effects of the Financial Crisis and Austerity Measures on the Spanish Health Care System' (2015) 118 *Health Policy* 100; I Keramidou and L Triantafyllopoulos, 'The Impact of the Financial Crisis and Austerity Policies on the Service Quality of Public Hospitals in Greece' (2018) 122 *Health Policy* 352.

[19] This section builds on B Storms, T Goedemé, K Van den Bosch and K Devuyst, *Towards a Common Framework for Developing Cross-nationally Comparable Reference Budgets in Europe* (Antwerp, Herman Deleeck Centre for Social Policy, University of Antwerp, 2013).

[20] The capability approach links in several ways to legal theory on socio-economic rights, which we highlight below in relation to formal social expectations. For example, David Bilchitz takes his starting point from the writings of Sen and Nussbaum when setting up a theoretical framework to analyse and discuss the justification and enforcement of socio-economic rights, see D Bilchitz, *Poverty and Fundamental Rights* (Oxford, Oxford University Press, 2007).

[21] eg A Sen, *Choice, Welfare and Measurement* (Oxford, Blackwell, 1982); A Sen, *The Standard of Living* (Cambridge, Cambridge University Press, 1987); A Sen, 'Capability and Well-being' in MC Nussbaum and A Sen (eds), *The Quality of Life* (Oxford, Clarendon Press, 1993).

on functionings, but on capabilities. In this spirit, when developing a benchmark for adequate social participation the focus should be on what people should be able to be and do, rather than on what they actually are or do. Further, another strength of the capability approach is that it takes into account the variability in the relation between the means and actual opportunities.[22] People having the same or similar personal resources can have different abilities to achieve certain functionings, for a variety of reasons. In other words, when developing a benchmark for adequate social participation, it is essential to take the individual situation and social context into account: not everyone requires the same level of financial resources (or even the same goods and services) to achieve the same living standard: this varies with personal and contextual characteristics and circumstances.

In order to determine the essential capabilities for adequate social participation, it would be helpful if one could rely on a list of 'basic capabilities', dealing with human needs and including those capabilities that are essential to live the kind of life that is 'worthy of the dignity of the human being'.[23] While Sen himself never proposed such a list, we believe that the list formulated by Martha Nussbaum[24] and the hierarchical model of human needs developed by Len Doyal and Ian Gough[25] are promising examples, which can be used in the operationalisation of the minimum acceptable way of life.[26] To give people the ability to fully participate in society (Doyal and Gough) or to live a flourishing life (Nussbaum), both put forward the same 'universal needs' or 'basic capabilities', namely physical health ('bodily integrity') and autonomy of agency ('practical reason'), which is closely matched to the need for meaningful social bonding ('affiliation'). An important difference between these theories is that Nussbaum's list consists mainly of what she calls 'combined capabilities', which include also the suitable external conditions for the exercise of functions, while Doyal and Gough make a clear distinction between universal human needs and the requisite universal societal preconditions. Given that for our purposes this distinction is very useful, we build primarily on Doyal and Gough's work.

We slightly modified Doyal and Gough's original list of intermediate needs to adapt it to the current European context and our purpose of creating reference budgets that could provide a monetary benchmark for adequate social participation.[27] Of course, such a list of needs is not sacrosanct, and could

[22] Eg A Sen, 'Poor, "Relatively Speaking"' (1983) 35 *Oxford Economic Papers* 153.
[23] M Nussbaum, *Women and Human Development* (Cambridge, Cambridge University Press, 2000).
[24] ibid.
[25] L Doyal and I Gough, *A Theory of Human Need* (Houndmills, Macmillan, 1991).
[26] Note that both texts were developed independently of each other. For a discussion of the similarities and differences, see in particular I Gough, 'Lists and Thresholds' in F Comim and MC Nussbaum (eds), *Capabilities, Gender, Equality* (Cambridge, Cambridge University Press, 2014).
[27] A brief literature review of the relevance of each of these intermediate needs can be found in Goedemé et al, 'Towards Cross-country Comparable Reference Budgets' (2015); and Goedemé et al (n 1).

be organised differently, but it has proven to serve usefully our purposes for developing reference budgets. Also, it should be stressed that most of the elements covered by this list can also be recognised in other attempts to define the minimum for adequate social participation, a life in accordance with human dignity, a 'flourishing life', or 'ends of development'.[28,29]

Our proposed list includes the following needs: To live healthily and act autonomously, people need *a balanced diet*. Food and nutrition play a decisive role in the maintenance of good health and in the prevention of various diseases. Besides healthy food, people also need *suitable clothing*. Clothes serve different purposes in European societies, for instance, offering protection against the weather elements and providing individuals with a certain identity. Like food and clothing, *adequate personal hygiene* and accessible *healthcare* are essential intermediate needs that must be fulfilled if an individual is to participate in society. Proper hygiene serves two important purposes. Primarily, it contributes to maintaining a good health by combating infectious microorganisms, both at a personal level and in relation to an individual's environment. Second, personal hygiene serves a psychological and social purpose. Without adequate personal hygiene, there is a danger of social exclusion due to a perceived failure to adhere to the social norm. A next intermediate need that must be met in order for people to be able to live healthy and autonomous lives is that of *adequate housing*. Each dwelling must fulfil three universal criteria such that the health of the occupants would not be jeopardised.[30] First, the dwelling must offer its occupants security and protection, both against the elements and against bearers of disease. Second, a dwelling must be conducive to a hygienic lifestyle. Third, it must be sufficiently spacious to allow the activities that are required for meeting the 'intermediate' needs, such as preparing and eating food, washing, maintaining social relations and rest and leisure.

Even though all 'intermediate' needs are related to both health and autonomy, the first five needs are primarily relevant for health, while the next five refer mainly to autonomy and are more culturally sensitive. To be able to act autonomously as adults, individuals must have experienced *security in childhood*. Doyal and Gough outline four more or less universal psychosocial needs that

[28] *cf* S Alkire, 'Dimensions of Human Development' (2002) 30 *World Development* 181; MC Nussbaum, *Creating Capabilities: The Human Development Approach* (Cambridge, MA, Harvard University Press, 2011).

[29] It should also be mentioned that, regardless of the views proposed in political theory and philosophy on the normative basis for a minimum, several of the needs listed below are needs that can be considered at the foundation of economic and social rights. Katharine G Young presents different approaches to defining a minimum core, 'giving content to economic and social rights'. One of the approaches described by Young is one that relies on 'the "basic needs of rights-holders as a sufficiently determinable standard for the minimum core".' KG Young, 'The Minimum Core of Economic and Social Rights: A Concept in Search of Content' (2008) 33 *Yale Journal of International Law* 114.

[30] Doyal and Gough, *A Theory* (1991) 196–97.

must be fulfilled for children and youngsters anywhere in the world to experience adequate security in childhood. According to them, all children need love. They also require new experiences in order to be able to develop cognitively, emotionally and socially. Furthermore, all children need praise, recognition and positive feedback. Finally, all children need a gradual broadening of responsibilities.[31] Beside security in childhood, people must be able to maintain *meaningful social relationships*. After all, humans are social creatures and they have a fundamental need for social connectedness. It is through daily contacts with relatives, neighbours and friends that individuals are, from their childhood, familiarised with the ideas, values and norms of the culture and society in which they live. People are also social creatures out of need. Even if individuals are adequately supported by qualitatively satisfactory provisions, they are confronted daily with all kinds of practical problems or issues that can only be resolved if they possess the necessary knowledge and skills or are able to acquire them, or by calling on help from others. Other problems may require emotional or practical support. Although the maintenance of mutual relationships primarily requires cultural capital, people also need some minimal economic resources to meet each other. Turning from the social to the cognitive component of personal autonomy, an eighth intermediate need is related to the capability of *lifelong learning*. In modern societies, both employability and active citizenship are dependent upon having adequate social competences for taking part in and contributing to economic and social life. A next intermediate need that one has to take account of in order to guarantee people full social participation is the need for *rest and leisure*. Rest allows the body and mind to recuperate and recover, while leisure contributes to physical, social, and emotional health.[32] Furthermore, to lead an autonomous life, people need a basic degree of economic and physical *security*. Finally, people need to be *mobile* to fulfil their various social roles adequately (eg to go to work, visit friends, or go shopping). As is true for the other intermediate needs, the minimal mobility requirements depend on the individual's living situation (eg health, employment) as well as on the structural societal conditions (eg availability of public transport).

IV. COMMON GROUND ACROSS EU MEMBER STATES FOR DEFINING ADEQUATE SOCIAL PARTICIPATION

In the previous section we identified a list of essential human needs based on a theoretical framework on social participation. However, if the concept of 'adequate social participation' is to be used for meaningful comparative

[31] WHO, 'Manuals on Child Mental Health and Psychosocial Development' (Geneva, WHO, 1982).

[32] Eg D Coleman and SE Isoahola, 'Leisure and Health – the Role of Social Support and Self-determination' (1993) 2 *Journal of Leisure Research* 111.

research, at the very least there should be some common understanding of what 'adequate social participation' is across EU Member States. If fundamentally different social positions and needs are associated with adequate social participation in different EU Member States, comparability risks being a hollow term. In what follows we briefly illustrate the approach that we have followed, without claiming completeness.

A. Methodological Considerations

We have validated commonalities across EU Member States on the basis of two sources: (i) formal social expectations have been assessed in terms of commitments of Member States to international conventions and European legal instruments; and (ii) informal social expectations have subsequently been assessed in three focus group discussions in each of the participating countries.

To assess formal social expectations, we turn to some relevant legal sources at the European level as a way of evaluating to what extent there is any formal common ground to be found. We are, as mentioned above, not claiming to do a full investigation into the different legal provisions highlighted below, but rather look at relevant legal sources in an explorative manner as a first step towards identifying a common ground. Obviously, formal social expectations can be stronger or weaker. For instance, some countries may sign up to international agreements, but fail to properly translate their promises into national legislation, concrete policies and law enforcement. Therefore, what we identify as common ground on the basis of a textual reading of international declarations or covenants should not be interpreted as 'having exactly the same formal social expectations'. The starting point for this exercise was the list of needs derived from Doyal and Gough's Theory of Human Need. In a first step we identified the relevant legal provisions which relate to our list of intermediate needs, as a way of pointing to the existence of a normative basis and thus some common ground between EU Member States on these issues. Similarly, we have identified a formal common ground for a core list of social positions based on a reading of relevant EU legal instruments. The connection between essential needs and the universe of social rights might be a bit more straightforward, merely judging from the exercise of assessing different social positions from the legal instruments chosen for this study.[33] However, identifying a formal common list

[33] Brinks, Gauri and Shen discuss how 'the rights language can be read to express something presumably universal about human needs', see D Brinks, V Gauri and K Shen, 'Social Rights Constitutionalism: Negotiating the Tension Between the Universal and the Particular' (2015) 11 *Annual Review of Law and Social Science* 289, 290. They focus on social rights in constitutional texts among other things to review an increased use of social rights language. In their study, they also approach and characterise the legal instruments as empirical material to study if and to what extent social rights are mentioned in domestic constitutions.

of social positions allows for a more concrete discussion on what is needed for social participation, which was used in the focus group discussions.

In order to get more insight into the informal social expectations in society, three focus groups were conducted in each of 24 EU capital cities.[34] We have opted for the focus group technique as it allows for gaining more insight into the *well-considered* views of citizens after some face-to-face discussion with others. This is important, given the rather abstract nature of the exercise and the type of common ground that we try to identify (ie the outcome of a well-reasoned debate). Since needs are socially perceived, informed discussions between different people with different experiences are necessary to stimulate a public perspective on what families minimally need. To stimulate an informed discussion, the participants were informed about the formal social expectations identified in the previous phase of the project. Given the qualitative nature of the exercise, it should be clear that the results are not necessarily representative for the views of the population in each country or capital city: a larger random sample would be required to assess their representativeness. Moreover, the outcome of focus group discussions is very context-specific and depends among others on the role of the moderator, the recruitment procedure, the group composition and the specific group dynamics. Therefore, in order to maximise comparability, the process was harmonised through a clear focus group script, containing detailed instructions on recruitment, preparation, organisation, content and analysis. The national partners recruited for each focus group five to 11 participants of active age (30–50), through a questionnaire for recruitment, ensuring a mix of different family situations, and a variety of socio-economic backgrounds. We have deliberately chosen to include people with different backgrounds in order to increase the variation of opinions and validity of the outcomes. All country teams started from a common (translated) topic list and indicated a trained moderator to conduct the focus groups according to common guidelines. The main focus of the analysis was the nature, the origin and the construction of the arguments on what is acceptable and feasible within the given socio-cultural context.

B. Formal Social Expectations

All 28 EU Member States have committed themselves to a number of international conventions and European legal instruments, which impose responsibilities on the Member States to secure certain individual social rights for its citizens, residents as well as individuals present on the territory. In line with the ambition of finding common ground and the overall aim of identifying a social minimum, our attention has turned primarily towards legal sources

[34] Some country teams organised two rather than three focus groups. The EU countries not covered by this exercise are Estonia, Ireland, Slovakia and the United Kingdom.

providing protection for social rights within the European context.[35] In absence of a common standard within EU law guaranteeing a minimum protection of social rights, we turn to the European Convention on Human Rights (hereafter 'the ECHR') well as to the European Social Charter (hereafter 'the ESC'), which were accepted by the Council of Europe.[36] The choice to focus on the ECHR and the Charter has been made in order to, as best as possible, find a common normative basis that would facilitate a comparative analysis. Since all 28 EU Member States are parties to the ECHR we have chosen to use it as a starting point. At present, the EU and its institutions are not *directly* bound by the ECHR since the EU has not acceded to the ECHR. The rights of the ECHR do apply in all Member States, but are not legally binding for the EU and its institutions. Even though the European Court of Justice applies the ECHR and the case law of the European Court of Human Rights (hereafter 'the ECtHR'), it does so indirectly.[37] The (revised) ESC, on the other hand, is not ratified by all Member States. Nevertheless, it is still an important legal instrument within the social dimension of the EU and could be seen as an already agreed upon normative platform in the area of social rights.[38]

Many, if not all, of the essential needs listed above can, at least at a minimum level, be said to be protected under provisions made by the ECHR as well as the ESC. For example, a number of the needs in the list clearly relate to core socio-economic rights protected under the ECHR. To name a few; the need for *adequate housing* (the right to respect for the home, Article 8 of the ECHR; Article 31 of the ESC)[39] and the need for *accessible healthcare* (the right to health care, Articles 2 and 3 of the ECHR; Articles 11 and 13 of the ESC providing the right to social and medical assistance) are both needs relating to core socio-economic rights which are recognized by the ECHR and the ESC.[40]

[35] In this chapter we use the term 'social rights' when referring to rights in areas of welfare, such as social assistance, education, health care, housing and more. We also, when discussing the ECHR, refer to 'core socio-economic rights' as an interchangeable term to 'social rights'. For a clarifying discussion on the terminology, see I Leijten, *Core Socio-Economic Rights and the European Court of Human Rights* (Cambridge, Cambridge University Press, 2018), 14ff. A longer discussion on social rights, human rights and the welfare state can be found in J King, *Judging Social Rights* (Cambridge, Cambridge University Press, 2012) 20ff.

[36] A Swiatkowski and M Wujczyk, 'The European Social Charter as a Basis for Defining Social Rights for EU citizens' in F Pennings and M Seeleib-Kaiser (eds), *European Citizenship and Social Rights: Entitlements and Impediments to Accessing Welfare* (Cheltenham: Edward Elgar, 2018).

[37] Council of Europe, 'Accession by the European Union to the European Convention on Human Rights: Answers to Frequently Asked Questions' (1 June 2010). Since the Treaty of Lisbon, in force since December 2009, not only EU Member States are committed to the European Convention, but also the European Union has committed to acceding to the European Convention on Human Rights. The EU is obliged under Art 6(2) of the Treaty of Lisbon to accede to the ECHR.

[38] S Stendahl and O Swedrup, 'Social Human Rights as a Legal Strategy to Enhance EU Citizenship' in F Pennings and M Seeleib-Kaiser (eds), *European Citizenship and Social Rights: Entitlements and Impediments to Accessing Welfare* (Cheltenham, Edward Elgar, 2018).

[39] See also S Stendahl and O Swedrup, 'A Legal Analysis of the Possibilities and Impediments for Citizens Seeking to Enforce their Social Rights' (2016) deliverable 6.4 of the bEUcitizen project.

[40] See also Swiatkowski and Wujczyk, *The European Social Charter* (2018) 13.

In order to specify the content of these rights and further analyse to what extent the needs listed above can be seen as covered by the scope of these rights, case law of the ECtHR should be studied.[41]

In a next step, we are interested in developing a more concrete list of social positions (defined in broad terms) related to these needs, by using the same type of approach. In the process of assessing a list of core social positions, we decided to also include the Charter of Fundamental Rights of the European Union ('the Charter') as a legal source in order to further elaborate on potential common ground. The Treaty of Lisbon ensured the entry into force of the Charter, originally drafted in 2000. Insofar as the Charter and the Convention include the same rights, the meaning and scope of those rights would be the same as those laid down by the Convention (Article 52(3) of the Charter). As we did for the identification of essential needs, we have also, but to a lesser extent, used the ESC to add to our understanding of core social positions.

As a starting point, the identification of a core list of social positions one should be able to take, and their related activities, goods and services should be such that they allow for a life in human dignity. As is stated by the Charter (Article 1): Human dignity is inviolable. It must be respected and protected.' In addition, institutions or social expectations that imply discrimination on any ground such as sex, race, colour, ethnic or social origin, genetic, features, language, religion or belief, political or any other opinion, membership of a national minority, property, birth, disability, age or sexual orientation should not affect the core list (*cf* Articles 20–23 of the Charter). In other words, to give an example, even if dominant informal social expectations would be such that women would not work, if 'doing paid work' is on the core list, it should be there for both men and women. That being said, the core list of social positions that have been identified on the basis of the sources used, can be summarised as follows:

- Being a *child, father, mother, wife or husband*: Article 12 of the ECHR ('Right to marry'); Article 9 of the Charter ('Right to marry and to find a family').
- Being an *employee* or *self-employed*: Article 16 of the ECHR ('Freedom to conduct a business'); Article 15 of the Charter ('Freedom to choose an occupation and right to engage in work').
- Being a *member* of associations of various types, including in particular trade unions: Article 11 of the ECHR ('Freedom of assembly and association'); Article 12 of the Charter ('Freedom of assembly and of association').

[41] Leijten, Core Socio-Economic Rights (2018) 233ff. Note that at the EU level there are also quite a few 'soft law' initiatives that support the idea of a common understanding of the necessities for adequate social participation (including Council decisions, resolutions by the European Parliament and policy documents by the European Commission). The most recent policy framework related to a decent social minimum in the EU is the European Pillar of Social Rights proclaimed by the

- Being a *student*: Article 2 of the First Protocol, added to the ECHR in 1952 ('Right to education'); Article 14 of the Charter ('Right to education').
- Being an *active participant* in political elections, and especially a voter: Article 3 of the First Protocol, added to the ECHR in 1952 ('Right to free elections'); Articles 39 and 40 of the Charter ('Right to vote and stand as a candidate at elections to the European Parliament' and 'Right to vote and stand as candidate at municipal elections').
- Being a *citizen*, more broadly speaking (various articles throughout the Charter).

C. Discussions in Focus Groups

The above-mentioned list of intermediate needs and social positions served as input for the focus groups in order to facilitate the discussion on what people need for adequate social participation. In each capital city, the country teams conducted three focus groups where they tested to what extent this list of social positions resonated with the 'well-considered views' of citizens in the EU.[42]

Overall, all focus groups expressed agreement with the list of social positions that was derived from legal provisions. In addition, most focus groups specified refinements of the general positions. In every focus group, the participants emphasised at least one social role related to family life, such as parent or child. For participants with children, the role of being a good parent was often said to be their most important function in life. Further, it is remarkable that nearly all focus groups agreed that everyone should be able to be an employee, and in the majority of the countries this was brought up spontaneously before showing the predefined list.

One social position that was not fully agreed upon was 'being a member of a trade union', especially in countries where trade union membership is very low. However, almost in every country 'being a member of an association' has been spontaneously identified as an essential social position, or it was agreed upon when the list was shown. Especially for children, focus group members agreed upon the essential need to belong to a social network. Further, for children as well as for adults, the position of a student was in all countries considered essential, and the use of digital media was stressed as crucial in this regard. Finally, being a voter and citizen was brought up by nearly all focus groups as crucial social positions. In many focus groups, participants argued that a more

EU Council, the Commission and the Parliament on 17 November 2017, which provides a guiding framework directly aimed at fulfilling people's essential needs and enhancing social rights for all EU citizens, including a set of 20 rights and principles.

[42] 'Well-considered' in this context means views expressed in a dialogue (discussion) with others, with some time for reflection and potential to revise one's views at the end of the discussion.

politically or socially active role should be stressed such as an active or engaged citizen, a volunteer, an activist or an opposition member.

There were also social positions that were considered essential in various focus groups, while not identified on the basis of our reading of the European Convention or the Charter:

- Being a friend and being a neighbour.
- Caring roles (caregiver as an adult for the parents, homemaker, pet-carer, patient), especially within the family context as caring and being cared for, but also as an insurance-taker or a patient within healthcare institutions.
- Several educational positions such as a (social) media user/producer, an educator/teacher (also as a parent), a classmate and a member of a parent association.
- Positions within the domain of leisure were mentioned such as a consumer of culture, a traveller, a hobbyist and a sports(wo)man.
- Being a member of local communities such as municipalities, cities and apartment councils or of bigger entities such as Europe.
- The role of a consumer or customer. It was noted that consuming is an essential part of participation in modern society.
- Being a member of a religious group or some other kind of like-minded ideological group was seen as an essential social position for one's autonomy and identity.

It would be interesting to see whether in a new round of focus group discussions participants from all EU countries would support the inclusion of these additional positions to the list of essential positions. In any case, on this ground we can tentatively conclude that at least in these focus groups there was quite some common understanding across EU capitals of a core group of social positions that people should be able to take in order to participate adequately in society.

After the discussions on essential social positions, the focus groups were asked which activities and goods and services should be provided at the minimum in order to fulfil these social positions adequately. Subsequently, these concrete items were grouped into larger categories of needs. Finally, the predefined list of essential needs was shown in all focus groups to check whether these categories were acceptable or if they should be adjusted and why. In other words, the main aim was not to draft a complete list of goods and services, but to use them as examples to derive inductively a list of more abstract needs that should be fulfilled. Again, we found that there was general agreement on the importance of all the needs listed above. The more physical needs for food, clothing, adequate housing, and personal and healthcare were seen as self-evident without evoking much of discussion. As regards clothing, focus groups in some countries argued how this is related to various informal social expectations. Also with regard to the need for mobility and security there seemed to be strong agreement in the focus groups across EU cities. It is worthwhile noting that when discussing the need for security, participants stressed the need for financial security through insurances, income, pensions and bank accounts, but also entitlement to social rights, a social safety net of friends and relatives, access to services, legal protection and employment regulation.

Besides the more physical needs, the focus groups across all countries emphasised also the importance of social relations, education, leisure time and employment, albeit with large socio-cultural differences between countries. The most important element with respect to social relations across many discussion groups was the need for communication, especially through digital (social) media. However, this provoked also lots of discussion, for example regarding whether or not a smartphone or a personal computer are minimum necessities. The need for internet and a mobile phone were also considered essential in many cases for fulfilling the need for information. The participants often pointed out that everyone should be able to inform himself or herself through television, newspaper, the library and especially by making use of the internet. Moreover, the need for communication and information, in particular through the use of digital media, was according to some focus groups (in Belgium, Greece, Germany, Denmark, Italy, Finland, Malta and Portugal) not represented well enough by the other categories of needs. Yet, only a few groups suggested creating a separate category. Also, rest and leisure is seen as an essential need in nearly all countries. In various countries people with a relatively low income as well as people with higher socio-economic positions argued that they face problems of limited time to fulfil their needs for rest and leisure, to maintain social relations, and to combine work and family life. Especially for single-parent families or for parents working full time, there is often lack of time to properly fulfil these needs. In this context, accessible and affordable childcare was indicated as an important service to which people should have sufficient access.

In all countries, focus groups agreed with the need for a safe childhood. Education was especially highlighted, and in some countries, it was even identified as a distinct need. The focus groups emphasised that in order to be a good parent one should be able to take care of children and provide them a safe, supportive environment with affordable, accessible and good-quality services such as education and childcare, but also sport clubs or youth movements, (free) public transport, healthcare and infrastructure (eg playgrounds). For instance, when public schools lack quality or when the access is limited, people need more financial means to provide an adequate educational level for their children (eg through private alternatives).

In the majority of the countries the focus group participants argued that not only children but also adults should be able to engage in a process of lifelong learning. However, in a few focus groups, the concept of lifelong learning evoked some disagreement. When it was formulated in a less formalised sense, but rather as keeping up with progress in society or learning new things, most focus groups agreed that it should be an essential need. Finally, in all countries, focus groups highlighted the need for decent work. In the list of intermediate needs based on the Theory of Human Need, employment was not identified as a distinct intermediate need. However, there seemed to be general agreement in the focus groups across countries to identify access to decent work as a separate essential need in order to stress the importance of having a job for adequate social participation. Another additional category of essential needs that came back frequently in the focus group discussions across different countries, is the need for active participation and involvement in society. This was often related to the essential social position of being an active and entitled citizen (social rights and freedoms) who needs political representation and involvement. These two additions to the list of essential needs merit more attention in the future.

V. CONCLUSION

Valid comparative assessments of the adequacy of the minimum income protection provided by European welfare states could boost efforts by policy makers to guarantee adequate incomes throughout the EU. Such assessments require a monetary benchmark that is comparable across countries. The more such a benchmark relies on a common normative understanding of what 'adequacy' means, the more convincing it will be for evaluating the adequacy of minimum income standards across the EU. In this chapter, we explored whether there is sufficient common ground for a shared normative understanding of what adequacy means in more concrete terms. To do so, we started from the concept of adequate social participation, which we defined as the ability of people to adequately play (take and make) the various social roles one should be able to play as a member of society. This notion of adequate social participation was further developed in dialogue with the Theory of Human Need and some insights from the capability theory. Essential needs that should be fulfilled for adequate social participation include access to adequate housing, clothing, an adequate diet, personal hygiene and healthcare, rest and leisure, the means for maintaining significant social relations, security in childhood, mobility, security and lifelong learning. Subsequently, we explored whether across Europe there is some common understanding of what adequate social participation means and what needs should be fulfilled in order to be able to participate adequately in society.

On the basis of a brief review of international standards as well as a series of over 65 focus group discussions in 24 EU capital cities, we conclude that at least at an abstract level, there is sufficient common ground for a European understanding of 'adequate social participation' and for defining the needs that should be fulfilled. More in particular, we found that many of these needs resonate well with 'formal social expectations' as embedded in the ECHR and the ESC. However, not all of the needs for adequate social participation are mentioned by these international legal sources. Yet, with very few exceptions the focus groups supported the relevance of each of these needs for adequate social participation. Furthermore, several discussion groups found that some needs were missing from the theoretical framework, including access to decent work and an active (political) participation and involvement in society. In addition, in quite a few countries it was stated that the importance of access to communication technologies and information should be emphasised more strongly. In addition, based on the ECHR and the ESC, we outlined a list of essential social positions that people should be able to take in the context of adequate social participation. Such a list helps to specify a common understanding of adequate social participation and to identify the required resources for adequately fulfilling the formal and informal social expectations associated with these positions (ie their social roles). Subsequently, we asked participants in discussion groups to reflect on what they consider essential social positions that people should be able to take as a member of their society. The results of these discussions suggest that there is quite some common understanding of what adequate social participation entails in these terms, even though several refinements and additions to the list of essential positions were suggested by some discussion groups.

Further research, including a new round of discussions and, preferably, involving sufficiently large random samples of respondents are required to assess to what extent these additional suggestions resonate with the well-considered views of citizens across Europe. In addition, also formal social expectations could be studied in a much more extensive form, for instance by also consulting other European legal sources, but also by exploring to what extent national legislation converges (and diverges) with regard to essential features of what can be considered adequate social participation. Such an analysis should go further than assessing which needs and social positions are essential, and analyse the formal expectations regarding the social roles that people should be able to play at a minimum as a member of society. For instance, what are the formal expectations regarding parents and citizens? What are the implications of these expectations for the goods and services to which individuals and households must have access in order to be able to live up to these expectations? Such an analysis, especially if undertaken jointly by legal scholars and social scientists in a transdisciplinary research context, would be a next fruitful step in developing well-founded reference budgets with a strong empirical basis.

We consider the findings presented in this chapter to be promising in view of developing a meaningful comparative benchmark for cross-national monitoring of income adequacy. First results of developing such a benchmark have already led to new insights (eg Carrillo et al, 2018; Goedemé et al, 2019[43]) but, clearly, the development of comparable reference budgets is still in its infancy, with quite some room for innovative research on this very challenging topic.

[43] Carrillo-Álvarez et al, 'Food Reference Budgets' (2019); Goedemé et al, 'What Does It Mean to Live on the Poverty Threshold?' (2019).

7

Poverty Measurement and Poverty Alleviation between Norm-setting and Empirical Inquiries

EBERHARD EICHENHOFER

I. INTRODUCTION

TO WIPE OUT poverty is not the only, nor the central, but a predominant aim of social policy. What, however, characterises and constitutes poverty? The chapter tries to find an answer to this question. In the context of social policy and social welfare law poverty is conceived differently. These differences can be explained by the different perspectives of both disciplines. The social policy concept of poverty refers to the interrelation between the living conditions of an individual and the average individual or a particular segment of the entire population of a given society. When determining these interrelations, empirical denominators that are built on economic indicators and open to be measured in monetary terms are identified as personal income or wealth. In social welfare law the notion of need is broad – it can be characterised as a physical, mental, social or economic deficit. In any respect, when defining the poverty threshold, a normative and an empirical dimension can be identified and discerned. Under this assumption poverty becomes a both absolute and relative concept, as it becomes, firstly, necessary to identify the living conditions which require a poverty alleviation measure as such and, second, necessary to specify the individual needs a person cannot satisfy him- or herself. Under these circumstances, comparisons are required and the concept of poverty becomes a relative and absolute one. The definition of a poverty line or a social welfare threshold has to integrate normative and empirical dimensions. Both dimensions are to be combined, as both are always involved in decisions about what constitutes poverty. Both dimensions have to be approached in an appropriate manner. The interplay between them is complex, as there are empirical facts that do not count and norms that do not convince.

II. POVERTY AS AN ISSUE OF SOCIAL POLITICS AND SOCIAL WELFARE LAW

To wipe out poverty is a predominant aim of social policy.[1] But what characterises poverty? In an interim approach, poverty is often associated with social exclusion and epitomised as a cause or consequence of a dreadful life. To qualify individual living conditions in a societal context as deplorable ones, requiring public intervention, remains provisional and vague, as long as such assessment depends on personal perceptions. It cannot be taken for granted that everyone shares the same perceptions, and for policy purposes empathy does not suffice as a basis to build on. Efforts to determine what poverty conceptually characterises and constitutes are therefore needed. They have to be directed towards qualifying poverty explicitly. When poverty has to be addressed by public policy measures, the underlying concept must be outlined in a clear and interpersonally convincing manner.

When doing this, poverty cannot adequately be conceived in substance, but as a relation between the living conditions of different persons. In a social intervention perspective poor people are to be discerned from the 'ordinary' ones. From the social welfare law perspective the poor become entitled to social benefits, whereas the non-poor do not. As poverty entitles individuals in accordance with their social deficit, this deficit makes them different from the non-poor. Such a relation between different living circumstances has to be analysed using both normative and empirical indicators. Both indicators depend on each other, as normative decisions are built upon descriptions of empirical findings.

How this interplay between the normative and the empirical should be approached shall be shown in an analytical inquiry that illustrates how social policy decisions interpret poverty when taking measures against it. Such a view is neither common, nor intends to describe specifically, how poverty should be measured. It illustrates how poverty is determined in social policy, and which criteria are applied. Such an analysis helps to understand how social policy and social welfare law work and conceive the social challenges they both address.

Social policy and social welfare law are built on different concepts of poverty. Section III discusses how the political concept of poverty differs from the legal one. This is due to differences between the normative and the empirical dimension of poverty, which, hence, demand for different reactions (section IV). These differences can be explained by the functional differences normative and empirical perspectives prevail in both social policy and social welfare law (section V). In order to come to an adequate understanding of poverty, both dimensions should be integrated in a specific manner. How this is done will be demonstrated in section VI.

[1] R Titmuss, *Social Policy. An Introduction* (London, Pantheon Press, 1974) 23 ff.

III. THE NOTION OF POVERTY IN SOCIAL POLICY AND IN SOCIAL WELFARE LAW

Poverty is a concept, not a fact,[2] as it not only describes reality but also conveys moral, ethical and political judgements.[3] When poverty is acknowledged as a social deficit that calls for social intervention, a politically chosen intervention helps to explain how the social deficit is defined.[4] Such an effort is built upon the assumption that individual self-reliance is the general social rule and social protection for individuals is limited to certain persons, if there are justifiable grounds due to their specific personal shortcomings and needs arising from the former.

When looking at the definitions in social policy and social welfare law, it becomes evident that both disciplines address poverty from different angles.[5] Social policy analyses the distribution of income and wealth in a given society. When it comes to identify the distribution of income and wealth, the various positions of individuals can be observed and imbalances between them can be made visible. Social policy reacts to overcome shortcomings of individuals from a broader societal perspective. The prevailing perspective is the entire society.

Under this perspective poor individual living conditions are identified as a social deficit. The distribution of cash benefits is regarded as the crucial indicator of poverty alleviation and, at the same time, as the central instrument to overcome poverty. This view emphasises monetary indicators, measured by metric scales. Seen from this angle, the position of an individual is identified as the relation between this person and the rest of the society as for his or her income and wealth are concerned. Poverty and social assistance are associated with the demand that a minimum of resources is a prerequisite to participate in a particular society. Under this approach all social relations are market relations, which are built upon the exchange of goods and services on the basis of money.[6]

Therefore, how much a person needs in order not to be poor depends on the society in which he or she lives.[7] The social policy concept of poverty refers to the interrelation between the living conditions of an individual and the average

[2] WJ Villmez, 'Poverty' in EF Borgattol and RJV Montgomery (eds) *Encyclopedia of Sociology*, 2nd edn, Vol 3 (New York, Macmillan Reference USA, 2000) 2209.

[3] ibid.

[4] ibid, 2210.

[5] G Kockheimer, *Methoden der Armutsmessung* (Berlin, Logos, 2012); B Becker and B Mentel, 'Aspekte Regionaler Arbeitsmarktmessung in Deutschland' (2010) *Wirtschaft und Statistik* 383; Bundesministerium für Arbeit und Soziales, *Lebenslagen in Deutschland der Fünfte Armuts- und Reichtumsbericht der Bundesregierung* (Berlin, Bundesministerium, 2017) 98ff.

[6] R Hauser, 'Das Maß der Armut: Armutsgrenzen im Sozialstaatlichen Kontext. Der Sozialstaatliche Diskurs' in E-U Huster, J Boeckh and H Mogge-Gutjahn (eds), *Handbuch Armut und soziale Ausgrenzung* (Wiesbaden, Springer VS, 2008) 94.

[7] AB Atkinson, *Poverty in Europe* (Oxford, Blackwell, 1998) 24; TM Smedding, 'Poverty Measurement' in D Brady and L Burton (eds), *The Oxford Handbook of the Social Science of Poverty* (Oxford, Oxford University Press, 2016) 21, 27.

individual or another segment of the entire population of a given society. How these interrelations are to be determined depends on empirical denominators that are normally built upon economic indicators and, hence, open to be measured as personal income or wealth in monetary terms.[8] They can be translated into varying amounts of money, which are translated as the necessary help as due and, thus, to be transferred to the person in need. Social policy approaches to poverty are therefore built upon disposable returns to be expressed in individual differences of disposable money. Irrespective of the definition of poverty in relative or absolute terms, each approach creates a distributive distinction, which shows that poverty has many different faces.[9]

Income as central perspective on poverty was criticised by Amartya Sen's capability approach,[10] which underlines that the needs of individuals are different. So, to meet these needs by social action, different amounts and types of resources are required. But this criticism is directed towards the prevailing mindset in social policy.

In social welfare law the concept of poverty is associated with individual's needs. A need can stem from a lack of money, but this is neither imperative nor the starting point of welfare law. A physical impairment creates a handicap; if this leads – due to social barriers and prejudice – to disabilities, social reactions under the UN Convention on the Rights of Persons with Disabilities are to be taken. The social benefit is directed towards overcoming the handicap by rendering a service in kind, eg a medical treatment, a drug or a place of shelter, etc. Social welfare law makes social work committed to help poor people. The individual hardship constitutes the personal need and sets rather the starting point and gives a justification for social intervention. The need is to be assessed and the intervention is conceived as being justified as such – due to the need's existence. Therefore, in social welfare law, the need of a person constitutes his or her poverty. To identify needs, a metric scale is not decisive and it is not necessary to give poverty a scalar expression.

In this understanding of social welfare law, poverty is not the same deficit that raises concerns in social policy. In social welfare law the notion of need is vast – it can be characterised as a physical, mental, social or economic deficit. From a historical perspective, to compensate such deficits by paying benefits in cash is to be regarded as a new form of social help. Traditionally, social work stands for meeting needs by giving physically and directly the goods or services the

[8] PG Rosner, *The Economics of Social Policy* (Cheltenham, Edward Elgar, 2003) 285.

[9] T Roberts, 'Poverty' in G River and JM Ryan, *The Concise Encyclopedia of Sociology* (Oxford, Blackwell, 2011) 463.

[10] A Sen, 'Equality of What?' in S McMurrin, *Tanner Lectures on Human Values*, Vol I, (Cambridge, Cambridge University Press, 1980); R Hick and T Burchhardt, 'Capability Deprivation' in D Brady and L Burton (eds), *The Oxford Handbook of the Social Science of Poverty* (Oxford, Oxford University Press, 2016) 75ff.

individual deserves. This is done by rendering benefits in kind. This concurs with the long tradition of institutional relief, in which social welfare is concentrated on institutions like hospitals, poorhouses, asylums or workhouses. Also, in the more modern version of open welfare, social work treats social deficits specifically directly and as such: the individual should receive a proper treatment that meets his or her specific individual needs in an adequate manner. It is necessary to find the appropriate instrument for curing the corresponding deficit. Social work individualises each help so that it addresses the specific needs of specific person in need.

A view of poverty which is driven by the perspective of the institutions of poverty alleviation might seem unorthodox or even circular, but it helps to better understand how institutions work and how they matter for poor people's living circumstances. Therefore, such a perspective is appreciated as a new approach to social intervention[11] as it helps to clarify which role policy and institutions play in dealing with poverty. The normative aim of this help is to enable poor people to live as 'ordinary' persons. This means, for example, in cases of sickness or need for long-term care, giving the poor a treatment comparable to the treatment of those who are able to afford it. In a social welfare law perspective, some deficits – primarily medical impairments and physical handicaps – are dealt with as if they were subjective ones, whereas comparative views seem to become irrelevant.

IV. WHAT JUSTIFIES THE DIFFERENCES BETWEEN THE APPROACHES?

A. Different and Interrelated Approaches

The differences, outlined above, in the way in which the two disciplines analyse and administer social interventions can be explained by the different underlying approaches to determine poverty. Social policy tends to identify poverty as a social phenomenon and elaborates strategies to overcome it. Social welfare law, on the other hand, is about administrating poor relief and making sure that the help provided for the individual brings about a decent life for the entitled individual. The first approach is oriented towards the deficit; the second, however, to the proper remedy for the individual. Social welfare law treats poverty as an individual phenomenon; social policy, in contrast, as a social challenge and concern. Traditionally, poverty had been conceived in absolute terms. The idea that to overcome poverty, a fixed bundle of goods would be required and should

[11] D Brady, A Blume and H Kleider, 'How Politics and Institutions Shape Poverty and Inequality' in D Brady and L Burton (eds), *The Oxford Handbook of the Social Science of Poverty* (Oxford, Oxford University Press, 2016) 115ff; MR Rank, 'Toward a New Paradigm for Understanding Poverty' (2006) 20 *Journal of Law and Policy* 866.

be given to the person in need,[12] was the starting point of poor law. Mollie Orshasky, who was working in the US Social Security Administration, defined in 1965 the poverty line as the 'cost of food sufficient for an adequate nutritional level on the assumption that persons must spend one third of their after tax income on food'.[13] This effort requires, hence, a convincing understanding about which items are required to meet the basic needs – irrespective of personal preferences, tastes or options, individual living conditions and impairments and, finally, the potential to produce goods and services without any transfer of money. However, it is open for discussion why one third of one's personal income should be spent on food and not less or more.

It is important to underline that poverty alleviation has an absolute dimension. This dimension becomes evident when looking at the alternative to poverty alleviation, ie lack of any support. All the descriptions of poverty through concepts like social exclusion or fundamental inequality[14] emphasise that poverty means dreadful living circumstances and conditions. The argument according to which poverty alleviation has to safeguard human dignity emphasises this view.

But when the support to be given requires an explicit definition, a comparative view prevails. The help must be adjusted to the social deficit. This requires not only an appropriate reaction to overcome the deficit, but it should also be justifiable in relation to the members of the society who are expected to make the help feasible. Therefore, it would be a misconception to think that both the absolute and the relative dimension of poverty allow each discipline to neglect the perspective of the other one. The interrelation of two disciplines is never a master-and-servant one. For strategies to combat poverty, the potential, restrictions and achievements of social welfare law also becomes decisive for social policy. But, vice versa, social welfare law cannot restrict itself to only finding its own approach to wipe out poverty. This becomes obvious when dealing with benefits in cash for needy persons.

To administer monetary benefits is central for social assistance law. But it is not enough to determine the amount of money the state can afford in comparison with other necessary public expenditures. Parliamentary decisions not only determine how much the state will pay for the needy persons, as they also need to reflect the beneficiaries' demands. This means that parliaments have to consider whether the remedy expected can be responsive to poor people's needs and enable them to withstand situations of economic crisis.[15] Such decisions are

[12] Atkinson, *Poverty* (1998) 26; Smedding, *Poverty Measurement* (2016) 27; Rosner, *Economics* (2003) 279ff; G Bäcker, G Naegele, R Bispinck, K Hofmann and JNeubauer, *Sozialpolitik und Soziale Lage in Deutschland* (Wiesbaden, Springer VS, 2008) Vol 1, 95.

[13] WJ Villmez, 'Poverty' in EF Borgattol and RJV Montgomery (eds) *Encyclopedia of Sociology*, 2nd edn, Vol 3 (New York, Macmillan Reference USA, 2000) 2213.

[14] Roberts, *Poverty* (2011) 464.

[15] Roberts (n 9) 464.

not a matter of simple and personal discretion or preferences, but the decisions should be built upon two indicators: consumption and wages.[16]

Both indicators determine the role of the poor in a society that is governed by market rules. As social assistance is about facilitating a fair consumption for needy people in a market society, it is to be examined what level of consumption is necessary to safeguard decency. The second indicator is wages. Due to the 'less eligibility' principle, social assistance payments should be lower than the earnings acquired by taking part in the labour market even by the least qualified members of the working class. This principle dates back to the English Poor Law of 1834 and since then it has been recognised as a good practice worldwide.

This rule that social assistance should be lower than the lowest wages shall prevent work from not being sufficiently attractive. Sufficient minimum wage guarantees are established to safeguard a wage that allows decent living and to keep the wage level higher than the social assistance threshold. Therefore, the determination of the benefits in social assistance law is much more than just establishing a certain sum of money by a political choice. Each responsible decision depends on empirical data as to the consumption and the wages of the population. In this context the problem emerges whether the mean or the median income is the better indicator;[17] the latter is preferred due to its ability to address the distribution of income, which the first one does not take into account.

The topic of how to determine the poverty line shows how social policy and social welfare law are confronted with similar questions. To fix a poverty line that allows the measurement of poverty by analysing the distribution of income and wealth is a key task for social policy analysis. The task of fixing the relevant amount for determining social assistance payments confronts public policy with similar questions. The answers given by both disciplines have more common features than there are differences between them.

B. Consumption

Patterns of consumption – normally available in statistical data – create the empirical basis by which a poverty threshold can be determined and legislation on the amount of social assistance built on. When this was done in Germany, the first step was to identify the relevant income group whose consumption should be regarded as comparable for the social assistance recipients in general. Initially, the lowest fifth of the population was taken as the relevant group. In a more recent approach, the lowest 15 per cent of the income-earners became the group of reference.

This lowering of the percentage for determining the income group for comparison was driven by an intention to lower social expenditure. When it

[16] Rosner (n 8) 279ff.

[17] Atkinson, *Poverty* (1998) 14; Rosner (n 8) 282.

comes to establishing social assistance payments on an empirical basis, an accompanying act of norm-setting always takes place, which allows politics a wide range of discretion[18] – irrespective of the prevailing method of measuring it. If one takes a basket of commodities that are essential for living in dignity, the composition of this basket is a matter of discretion; but also in statistical models, not factual but normative parameters prevail, when it comes to decide, which group's expenditure is relevant and which items and categories of expenditure are to be taken as relevant. Normative decisions are needed and they become decisive for the outcome.

In this context a further question emerges as to which goods and services are to be taken into account when determining the average consumption of the entire population. Does politics tolerate empirically relevant consumption of the target population or does it tend to disregard some consumption because it is conceived as socially or morally inacceptable? Some years ago, this problem became a political issue in Germany when a recalculation of social assistance payments was made.

The former Minister of Labour and Social Affairs – a medical doctor who in contrast to her predecessors neither smoked nor drank a drop of alcohol – raised the question of whether or not the expenditure for alcohol and cigarettes should be taken into account when defining the level of social assistance payments. She argued that smoking and drinking had detrimental effects for consumers' health. These costs had been identified empirically as an important part in the consumption of the poorest. The Minister succeeded with her proposal to exclude these expenses. Consequently, the average expenses for beer were replaced by the cost of a comparable quantity of water. The example illustrates how acts of norm-setting and social experience interact when defining social assistance rates on the basis of empirical findings of average consumption patterns.

If a comparison of expenses is made, the goods and services should not be assessed as to whether they are morally tolerable or not. Each omission of a category of goods violates the principle according to which the consumption patterns to be secured are to be defined by the consumption which actually exists. A norm-setting built upon the distinction between acceptable and non-acceptable goods disregards that the consumption patterns are treated as a social fact, based on social experience. In addition, an assessment of personal consumption needs that are built on average expenditure is only a vague indicator for the de facto expenses of the various individuals. Also in this respect, it would be a fallacy to deduct from the average consumption individual's consumption need. Such an approach that disregards empirical findings on consumption and tries to replace them with moral arguments confuses empirical with normative arguments. A law that bans – with moral arguments – cigarettes and alcohol as illegitimate consumption alters the methods of

[18] G Cremer, *Armut in Deutschland* (München, CH Beck, 2016) 68ff.

identifying needs. Such identification is regularly not based on facts that are to be verified empirically in the social reality. As no social assistance recipient is hindered in buying cigarettes and alcohol, and there is no legal limitation for such acquisitions, such deduction against empirical evidence intentionally disregards relevant expenses merely because of moral doubts about their necessity. When the average expenditure for these items is disregarded in the normative rules on the determination of social help, the procedure infringes the rules on which the calculation is established – to look at reality and not at fiction – even if it reckons on acceptable moral demands.

C. Production

A further task in assessing poverty rates is to determine the relation between a social assistance payment and wages. This endeavour encounters a series of unsolved problems. The first stems from growing income differences within societies. Disparities in income distribution grow worldwide. Despite being smaller in traditional welfare states than in other societies, they can also be observed in developed welfare states, irrespective of whether they are in good or bad economic conditions.[19] Inequality of income has increased hitherto in good times and has also continued to increase in bad times.[20] Inequality grew within the working population,[21] whereas at the same time inequality between countries decreased.[22] The emergence of non-standard work and income growth in highly competitive fields of activities has led to a job polarisation.[23] Today, a concentration of wealth among the richest can be seen,[24] whereas at the same time, private indebtedness grows and in some countries it grows substantially.[25]

If the groups of the very rich and the very poor grow in a society and correspondingly the middle class declines, the average income will lose its role as an indicator and benchmark for the typical and representative and characteristic of a conventional lifestyle. Average income becomes more and more a fictional or artificial figure which lacks any social relevance, whether a mean or median is used as an indicator for poverty. The OECD suggests a policy of increasing women's participation in work and the provisions of good-quality jobs in order to improve fairness, investment and growth as appropriate means for fighting against these developments.[26]

[19] OECD, 'In It Together. Why Less Inequality Benefits all, Overview of Inequality Trends, Key Findings and Policy (Paris, OECD Publishing, 2015) 21–22.

[20] OECD, 'Together' (2015) 23.

[21] ibid 24–26.

[22] F Bourguignon, *Die Globalisierung der Ungleichheit* (Hamburg, ÖGB Verlag, 2013) 27, 29.

[23] OECD (n 20) 29.

[24] ibid 35.

[25] ibid 35.

[26] ibid 39.

The second problem stems from the family orientation of the social assistance system. If an individual is entitled to social assistance, the payments are not defined by the entitled person's need only but by the income and expenses of their entire household. If there are other persons living in the household, it becomes an issue of how social assistance deals with these persons. If they are needy as well, the payments to the entitled person have to reflect the needs of the household's other members, at least if they belong to the entitled person's family. Under this assumption the needs of a family member is to be assessed. If they are children, the question arises whether the children's needs can be expressed as a proportional share (ie a certain percentage), which stands in relation to the needs of an adult. In the economics of scale, shared costs of living are lower, as one can live more cheaply together than as individuals. As not all live in a family with others, the single-person household counts as the common household for measuring person's needs.[27] Therefore, the effect of a joint use of goods and services in a household is to be assessed and figured out as an economic advantage – and because of this, it should be taken into account as a negative indicator for determining the relevant payment.

The third problem results from the fact that when the average income is empirically assessed, social assistance payments represent a substantial part of the income, especially if the relevant segment of income earners is the lowest quintile or 15 per cent of the population. If such a 'semi-relative'[28] approach is adopted, the definition of the adequate social assistance on the empirical basis of available income depends to a great extent on the outcomes of the preliminary norm-setting in social assistance law and other branches of social protection. This also means that the ideal to keep the poverty line in conformity of the living conditions of the entire population is abandoned.

Under the very realistic assumption that if a substantial part of the disposable income among the low-income population stems from the social assistance, then the norm-setting becomes circular because it is based on empirical findings. The pre-existing social expenditure is translated into individual transfers of cash or services to a specific extent; they set data for income of a substantial part of the population, particularly among those with small incomes. Consequently, this method tends to reproduce the income structure created directly by social policy norm-setting in the field of social assistance.

D. Periodical Rate and Atypical or Irregular Needs

The last problem concerns the benefit structure of social assistance. Normally, the debate is focused on determining a rate – which is periodically paid – in order to sustain the needy person. However, social work is, in practice, confronted

[27] Smedding, *Poverty Measurement* (2016) 31.
[28] ibid 29.

with needs that do not fit into the scheme of periodical payments that is based on empirical findings on regular spending of the low-income population. This underlines the fact that personal needs are difficult to standardise. In other words, social work is confronted with the expenses that are not measured on ordinal, but only on cardinal scales.

What about persons with special needs due to poor health or pregnancy? What about needs emerging from moving house, costs after childbirth or when children enter school and need a uniform? What about the needs caused by celebrating a wedding and organising a celebration, or enabling children to take part in school excursions? Under all these circumstances lies the question of how to deal with atypical or irregular needs.

According to a holistic view, poverty is visualised as a status of social dependency that has to do with the contingencies of life and the fact that a person is not able to cope with and master it. These circumstances are not to be standardised and, therefore, they are not to be restricted to a descriptivist indicator or to a situation which takes place only periodically.

V. WHY BOTH THE NORMATIVE AND THE EMPIRICAL DIMENSION ARE IMPORTANT

A. Poverty and Equality

The debate on poverty is always about equality and the degree to which a society should tolerate differences between people's needs or try to overcome them. Also, international comparisons and cross-country analyses depend on a relative concept of poverty.[29] The welfare state gained momentum from the criticism against unjustifiable privileges. All social utopians based their proposals on an egalitarian view of the society. Thomas More sketched Utopia as a society where each has an equal share of the jointly produced goods and services. Edward Bellamy pleaded to give everyone a social dividend or social credit – a minimum income sufficient for survival. Aristotle regarded justice and harmony, balance and proportionality, virtues and equality as more or less the same. Gracchus Babeuf stated that a fair society has to be established beyond richness and poverty: 'In a true society there should be neither rich nor poor; the rich who will not give up their superfluity to help the needy are the enemies of the people'.[30] TH Marshall portrayed the welfare state as some 'kind of basic human equality, associated with full community membership, which is not inconsistent with a superstructure of economic inequality'[31] and stated, 'Equalisation is not so

[29] ibid 28.

[30] F-N Babeuf and S Marechal, 'The Manifesto of Equality' in LP Pojman and R Westmoreland (eds), *Equality* (Oxford, OUP, 1997) 45, 51.

[31] TH Marshall, 'Citizenship and Social Class (1950)' in TH Marshall and T Bottomore (eds), *Citizenship and Social Class* (London, Pluto Press, 1992) 45.

much between classes as between individuals within a population which is now treated for this purpose as though it was one class. Equality of status is much more important than equality of income'.[32] This requires inequality at least insofar as markets are built on competition.

The welfare state seeks to create a fair society. But this society is based on a contradiction in that it draws from economic differences its central momentum and mobilises all driving forces for its development and, on the other hand, it secures equal rights. As such, equality is not absolute in character, but has a relative meaning. The demands of equal rights, chances or equal pay for equal work are relative, because equality depends on circumstances outside of itself! Equality describes a relationship between persons, things or states of affair. Aristotle's demand to attribute to each one according to her or his personal circumstances ('*suum cuique*!') remains blank and vague as long as one does not define the key characteristics of the individual.

B. Equality as an Ambiguous Concept

Equality is ambiguous as it does not absolutely require treating persons, things or states of affair as being alike to each other when they differ in substance. Thus, these differences matter when it comes to guaranteeing equality. 'The practice of doing justice signals the need, the rights and deserts of particular subjects'.[33] 'Equal' distributions of merits or needs presumes differences in existing merits or needs. Michael Walzer states that equality is complex because when determining the specific measures, different objects of possible distribution and the various impacts of attributions are to be taken into account. According to him, a liberal society is defined by different spheres of freedom that constitute a society on the basis of spheres of liberties[34] – the public and the private sphere, the religious, academic, political, economic and social spheres come into existence. 'The demand of equality can take various forms, and a certain amount of plurality of concern is inescapable of basal equity itself'.[35] For individuals it might be possible to adhere to the different spheres of a society differently.

C. Equality and Decency of Life

Has egalitarianism an intrinsic moral value, so that equality is to be achieved for its own sake? One criticism could be that the misery of those living a

[32] ibid.
[33] CL Carr, 'The Concept of Formal Justice' (1981) 39 *Philosophical Studies: an International Journal for Philosophy in the Analytical Tradition* 224.
[34] M Walzer, 'Liberalism and the Art of Separation' (1984) 12*Political Theory* 315.
[35] A Sen, *Inequality Reexamined* (Oxford, Oxford University Press, 1992) 131.

dreadful life is not sufficiently explained by the fact that others have a better life; the misery simply stems from the fact that a dreadful life is dreadful (Harry Frankfurt). In a similar vein, Avishai Margalit[36] states that inequalities violate justice and fairness because they disregard the discriminated persons by annihilating their status as human beings. So, equality is deeply linked with rules, human rights and dignity. It guarantees that rules are administered universally. 'Formal justice becomes ... the particular virtue of the rule governed activities'.[37] Despite justice being built upon rules, it demands more than just respecting rules. Any idea of justice requires substantial principles which cannot be deducted from equality. Equality as personal chances touches not only upon morality but also on economic outcome, as it allows and fosters competition and pursues efficiency.[38]

Equality requires impartiality. Is it realistic, however, to assume that individuals will abstain from personal interests and preferences when assessing what equality demands under specific circumstances?[39] Equality cannot and shall not level out good or bad luck or individual differences in ability or thrift. The results of the natural lottery society can and shall not be corrected by the society at large.[40] 'Educating individuals to the limits of their capacity is a legitimate aim, and social inequality, generated in the pursuant of a legitimate aim is not unjust, if natural differences among the persons are its primary cause'.[41] Furthermore, to help the victims of cultural, ethnic, social or sexual discrimination requires acknowledging a whole range of cultural, ethnic, social or sexual differences. Equality means respecting inequalities as determining factors of the human species and to establish rules based upon the different characteristics of human beings. In other words, overcoming historical discriminations does not require equality but rules based on and intended to emphasise inequality.[42] Social security directs towards equal social rights, but the content of these rights can strongly differ because of the varying lives and living conditions of the beneficiaries.

Finally, when poverty is defined as a state of relative disadvantage, it leads to the paradoxical consequence of perpetuating poverty, as long as differences in income and living conditions prevail. Under this assumption there will always be a segment of the population that is considered poor, regardless of actual levels of wealth.[43] Thus, equality cannot and should not be the leading value upon

[36] A Margalit, *The Decent Society* (Harvard, Harvard University Press, 1991).

[37] Carr, *Formal Justice* (1981) 222.

[38] W Galston, 'A Liberal Defense of Equal Opportunity' in L Pojmann and R Westmoreland (eds), *Equality* (Oxford, Oxford University Press, 1997) 170ff.

[39] T Nagel, *Eine Abhandlung über Gleichheit und Parteilichkeit und andere Schriften zur Politischen Philosophie* (Paderborn, Schöningh Paderborn, 1994).

[40] T Nagel, 'Justice and Nature' (1997) 17 *Oxford Journal of Legal Studies* 303.

[41] ibid.

[42] Sen, *Inequality* (1992) 2.

[43] Roberts (n 9) 464.

which social policy is to be built. The imperatives and motives of today's social policy are neither to disregard nor to discriminate against others in order not to exclude individuals from society.

These imperatives are meaningful as individual rights and freedoms, and not as a demand for equality! From this it follows that the empirical evidence of differences in life chances and living conditions is not, as such, sufficient to identify a social deficit which gives rise to social benefits. There is always an additional normative decision to be taken as to which degree differences must or should be tolerated. Such a decision has to be justified by political decisions that need both an empirical and a normative foundation. When under a less eligibility rule the benchmark for poverty is determined, an empirical comparison between different living conditions is necessary, but this will be done with the intention of identifying the difference between poor and non-poor persons. Also, the principle of progressive realisation shows that each effort for poverty alleviation depends on space and time, which makes it relative. The help offered by the society is, finally, embedded in a social relationship which is built upon reciprocity, which explains why the poor are not only entitled to help, but by the same token obliged to overcome their own neediness by means of their own efforts.

VI. HOW TO ACHIEVE POVERTY MEASUREMENT TO BECOME THE RESULT OF A COMBINATION OF THE NORMATIVE AND THE EMPIRICAL

A. Norm-setting

In the context of social policy intervention the first decision to be made when determining poverty is whether it is to be conceived as a status of exemption or not. If not, poverty is dealt with as a regular condition. Ideas on the creation of a Basic Income[44] for each are associated with this assumption. If poverty is, however, regarded as an irregular condition in a world built upon self-reliance, a needs-oriented approach prevails. Under this assumption poverty becomes a relative concept, as it becomes necessary to specify the individual needs a person cannot satisfy him or herself. Under these circumstances, comparisons are required, and the concept of poverty becomes a relative one and not an absolute one. This view goes back to the first writers on poverty of the eighteenth century, according to whom the concept of poverty or deprivation describes a shortcoming of the poor in relation to the average population. So, the average living conditions set the benchmark for the status of poverty. In addition, as public policy measures to alleviate poverty realise in a defined social benefit, in

[44] K Widerquist, J Nogera, Y Vanderborght and J De Wispelare (eds), *Basic Income. An Anthology of Contemporary Research* (Oxford, Blackwell, 2013).

each act of norm-setting lies an implicit definition of poverty. This definition has to envisage the paradox that the more generous a benefit is, the more beneficiaries are acknowledged and, hence, the higher the poverty rate becomes.

B. Empirical Evidence

In order to deal with these challenges by political measures, empirical evidence is necessary to identify the shortcomings that define a situation as poverty. This implies that a decision which describes differences of the physical, mental or economic situation of a given situation identifies a specific standard of living and consumption potential in relation to the living conditions of the rest of the population and characterises that situation as a hardship. Such a circular reasoning is misleading: the poverty level should not essentially be determined by the level of social assistance paid to the low-income population. Instead, a comparison should be made between the population living without public support and the one being supported. In this respect, one must rely on idealised and rough normative concepts of equality so that small differences in income can bring about salient differences in social rights. The widely accepted poverty threshold of 60 per cent of the average income is built on such reasoning.

C. Legal Outcomes: Norm-setting Built on Empirical Findings

Both methodological and normative arguments reflect the observation that the identification of poverty should be a joint effort to combine normative decisions with empirical findings. In order to identify a social deficit, it is necessary to make a contrast between the poor and the non-poor. The poverty line describes a difference between the first and the latter, which is to be established on the basis of a common denominator that lays the ground for the comparison.

For the sick/healthy divide this operation is clear – even if there are borderline cases that are difficult to assess. In regard to a comparison of the economic conditions of living, the division has to be made according to the same principle, ie defining the difference in income and wealth between those who are able to sustain themselves and those who are not. When the average living conditions no longer stand for typical living conditions – in regard to both earnings and consumption – the norm-setting efforts lack empirical evidence, which makes it more difficult to find a convincing standard to be stablished.

The definition of a poverty line or a social welfare threshold has to integrate normative and empirical components because they are always involved in decisions about what constitutes poverty. Both elements have to be used in an appropriate manner. As noted above, the interplay between them is complex because there are empirical facts that do not count and normative reasons that do not convince.

Part 3

Securing a Social Minimum: Obligations for States and Individuals

8

Territorial and Extraterritorial Obligations to Ensure a Decent Social Minimum

ELENA PRIBYTKOVA[1]

I. INTRODUCTION

HUMAN RIGHTS OBLIGATIONS relating to a decent social minimum constitute a theoretical and practical lacuna. This chapter intends to shed light on some controversial issues that are at the centre of today's interdisciplinary debates: What territorial and extraterritorial duties correspond to basic human rights indispensable for a decent social minimum? What is the nature, status, content, and scope of these obligations? What entities are responsible for securing access to a decent social minimum nationally and universally? Who is entitled to claim safeguarding a decent social minimum? Before offering my answers to these questions, I will briefly address two more general issues: What is a decent social minimum? And how does it relate to the principles of social and global justice?

The chapter provides a concise preliminary outline of a conception of territorial and extraterritorial obligations relating to a decent social minimum, rather than explicating it in detail. It also presents a general overview of various types of these obligations. A rigorous analysis of human rights obligations to secure a decent social minimum as well as the formulation of rules for their allocation to particular duty-bearers is beyond the scope of this chapter.[2]

[1] The research was supported by the SNSF Ambizione grant (No 142547) and a grant of the Research Fund of the University of Basel. I am very grateful to the organisers of the workshop 'Specifying and Securing a Social Minimum' at Oñati International Institute for the Sociology of Law and the working conference 'The Battle against Poverty: Specifying and Securing a Social Minimum' at Gothenburg University for their invitation and to all participants of the workshop and the conference for their significant comments.

[2] I analyse the topic of territorial and extraterritorial obligations to secure a social minimum in more detail in my Habilitation monograph, *A Decent Social Minimum in the Language of Human Rights* (forthcoming).

The chapter approaches obligations to secure access to a decent social minimum from several sides: it examines their interpretations in moral, legal, and political philosophy, in human rights instruments, as well as in the practice of international, regional, and national monitoring and accountability bodies. While combining philosophical and legal analysis, I intend to demonstrate how theories of social and global justice can contribute to justifying, conceptualising and allocating territorial and extraterritorial human rights obligations to guarantee a decent social minimum. At the same time, I will explore to what extent contemporary human rights theory and practice are capable of finding solutions to the most urgent and complex issues surrounding a decent social minimum.

This chapter has the following structure. Following the Introduction, Section II investigates a definition and the major ideas underlying a decent social minimum. Section III explores its relation to principles of basic equality, relational and distributive justice. Section IV analyses territorial and extraterritorial obligations relating to a decent social minimum. Section V deals with two types of extraterritorial obligations, remedial extraterritorial obligations and global obligations, and their interrelation. Section VI focuses on right-holders and bearers of human rights obligations to ensure a decent social minimum nationally and universally.

II. TOWARDS A DEFINITION OF A DECENT SOCIAL MINIMUM

A decent social minimum is a multidimensional concept, which involves several interrelated meanings. It is often determined as: (i) a certain level of well-being which should be secured for all members of society to protect them against poverty;[3] (ii) a cross-cultural standard of a decent life;[4] (iii) a body of basic human rights;[5] and/or (iv) a fundamental idea of social and global justice.[6] All these interpretations are correct and describe various aspects of a complex and multi-level concept of a social minimum. I suggest the following definition of a decent social minimum which integrates these aspects: it is a set of territorial and extraterritorial human rights guarantees, which represent an intercultural core of social and global justice and are aimed at protecting persons from

[3] See, for instance: J Waldron, 'Rawls and the Social Minimum' in J Waldron, *Liberal Rights. Collected Papers 1981–1991* (Cambridge, Cambridge University Press, 1993) 250; A Sen, 'Capability and Well-Being' in M Nussbaum and A Sen, *The Quality of Life* (Oxford, Clarendon Press, 1993) 41; T Pogge, *World Poverty and Human Rights*, 2nd edn (Cambridge, Polity Press, 2008) ch. 1.

[4] See: J Rawls, *Justice as Fairness: A Restatement* (Cambridge, MA, Harvard University Press, 2001) 127f; M Nussbaum, *Woman and Human Development. The Capabilities Approach* (Cambridge, Cambridge University Press, 2000) 5–6.

[5] H Shue, *Basic Rights: Subsistence, Affluence and U.S. Foreign Policy*, 2nd edn (Princeton, NJ, Princeton University Press, 1996) 19; D Miller, *National Responsibility and Global Justice* (Oxford, Oxford University Press, 2007) ch. 7.

[6] Pogge, *World Poverty* (2008) ch 1, 4; Miller, *National Responsibility* (2007) ch 7.

extreme poverty; enabling them to lead a decent life; ensuring their involvement in society and access to shared material and intellectual values; and providing an opportunity for their moral and intellectual flourishing.

Legal and political philosophers appeal to various criteria to arrive at a definition of a decent social minimum, such as primary goods (John Rawls),[7] basic needs (David Miller),[8] basic income (Philippe Van Parijs),[9] recourses (Stuart White),[10] human capabilities (Amartya Sen, Martha Nussbaum),[11] and human flourishing (Thomas Pogge).[12] There is also a long tradition, expressed in both legal and philosophical doctrines,[13] human rights instruments[14] and the

[7] While Rawls', *A Theory of Justice* (1971) upholds the principle of the greatest benefit for the worst-off (the 'maximin principle') which does not guarantee a minimally decent life, his *Justice as Fairness* (2001) recognises the necessity to ensure a social minimum. Rawls acknowledges the influence of Jeremy Waldron's critique that in the original position people would prefer a social minimum to the maximin principle. See: J Rawls, *A Theory of Justice*, rev edn (Cambridge, MA, Harvard University Press, 1999) § 46; Rawls, *Justice as Fairness* (2001) 127f; Waldron, 'Rawls' (1993) 262.

[8] Miller (n 5) ch 7.

[9] P Van Parijs, *Real Freedom for All: What (If Anything) Can Justify Capitalism?* (Oxford, Oxford University Press, 1995). See also: P Van Parijs and Y Vanderborght, *Basic Income: A Radical Proposal for a Free Society and a Sane Economy* (Cambridge, Mass, Harvard University Press, 2017).

[10] Stuart White defines a social minimum as a 'bundle of resources which suffices in the circumstances of a given society to enable someone to lead a minimally decent life'. S White, 'Social Minimum' in *Stanford Encyclopedia of Philosophy*, available at plato.stanford.edu/entries/social-minimum. See also: J King, *Judging Social Rights* (Cambridge, Cambridge University Press, 2012) 17.

[11] A social minimum refers to what Sen defines as basic capabilities, ie individuals' ability 'to do certain basic things' and 'satisfy certain crucially important functionings up to certain minimally adequate levels', such as 'the ability to meet one's nutritional requirements, the wherewithal to be clothed and sheltered, the power to participate in the social life of the community'. Below this 'minimally acceptable levels of certain basic capabilities […] people count as being "scandalously deprived"'. See Sen, 'Capability and Well-Being' (1993) 41; A Sen, 'Equality of What?' The Tanner Lecture on Human Values Delivered at Stanford University (22 May 1979) 218–19, available at www.ophi.org.uk/wp-content/uploads/Sen-1979_Equality-of-What.pdf. See also Martha Nussbaum's approach to defining a 'threshold level of each capability' as well as 'a list of central capabilities' which provides 'the basis for determining a decent social minimum in a variety of areas'. Nussbaum, *Woman and Human Development* (2000) 5–6, 75, 78–80.

[12] Pogge (n 3) ch 1. For Cécile Fabre's concept of minimally flourishing life, see: C Fabre, *Whose Body is it Anyway?: Justice and the Integrity of the Person* (Oxford, Clarendon Press, 2006) 34f.

[13] The principle of human dignity was the starting point for the justification of the human right to a dignified existence by various, and even competing, approaches. See: E Pribytkova, 'The Human Right to a Dignified Existence: The Ethical Foundations of the Contemporary Legal Order' in W Brugger and S Kirste (eds), *Human Dignity as a Foundation of Law* (Archiv für Rechts- und Sozialphilosophie, 137, 2013) 117–29. See also: S Liebenberg, 'The Value of Human Dignity in Interpreting Socio-Economic Rights' (2005) 21 *South African Journal of Human Rights* 1.

[14] According to the common Preamble to the International Covenant on Civil and Political Rights (ICCPR) and the International Covenant on Economic, Social and Cultural Rights (ICESCR), fundamental human rights 'derive from the inherent dignity of the human person'. General Comments of the UN Committee on Economic, Social and Cultural Rights (CESCR) reaffirm that basic elements of the right to an adequate standard of living – the rights to adequate food, water, sanitation, housing, and health – are 'indivisibly linked to the inherent dignity' of a person and 'indispensable for leading a life in human dignity'. See CESCR General Comment No 4, para 7; General Comment No 12, para 4; General Comment No 14, paras 1, 25; General Comment No 15, paras. 1, 11, 29.

judicial practice at regional and national levels,[15] to employ human dignity as a normative basis for the human rights guarantees of a decent social minimum. It is interesting that although the above-mentioned scholars use various criteria for determining a social minimum, some of them, at the same time, resort to the concept of human dignity as an essential idea of a decent social minimum.[16] This chapter is not an exception.

I develop an idea that three fundamental entitlements of a person to a special moral and legal status, basic equality and membership in humanity, which are embedded in the International Bill of Human Rights compose a justificatory basis for the human rights guarantees of a decent social minimum. Article 1 of the Universal Declaration of Human Rights (UDHR) proclaims that 'all human beings are born free and equal in dignity and rights'. This globally accepted norm contains three essential sub-norms: first, each individual is a bearer of inalienable dignity and human rights, ie, possesses a *special moral and legal status*; second, people are equal in a certain fundamental sense, as holders of dignity and human rights, and should be treated and regarded as equals (*basic equality* or *equality of status*); and third, dignity and human rights belong to a person not because of his or her political connection with the state, but because he or she is a member of a human society (*membership in humanity*). These fundamental entitlements in their correlation underlie the principle of human-centricity, which considers an individual to be an absolute value and the ultimate unit of both moral and legal concern.[17]

[15] For example, the European Court of Human Rights (ECtHR) protects the guarantees of a freedom from poverty 'granted to individuals on account of the dignity attached to the human being' (*VM and Others v Belgium*, Second Section, No 60125/11, 7 July 2015 §160). The Inter-American Court of Human Rights (IACtHR) interprets the fundamental right to life as the right not to be 'prevented from having access to the conditions that guarantee a dignified existence' (the *'Street Children' (Villagrán Morales and others) v Guatemala*, Merits, 19 December 1999 §144). According to the African Commission on Human and Peoples' Rights (ACHPR), 'without access to economic, social and cultural rights, the dignity of the individual and of peoples is threatened' (Guidelines and Principles on Economic, Social and Cultural Rights in the African Charter on Human and Peoples' Rights, Preamble). This position was also expressed in cases *Social and Economic Rights Action Center (SERAC) and Center for Economic and Social Rights (CESR) v Nigeria* (155/96, 27 October 2001 § 65) and *Sudan Human Rights Organisation & Centre on Housing Rights and Evictions) v Sudan* (279/03-296/05, 13–27 May 2009 §146). The German Constitutional Court recognised the state's duties to secure the 'minimum conditions for a dignified existence' (BVerfGE 40, 121, 18 June 1975), while the Swiss Federal Supreme Court shaped an unwritten basic right to protection from an 'undignified begging existence' (BGE 121 I 367, 1995 S373). An excellent analysis of diverse judicial definitions of human dignity can be found in C McCrudden, 'Human Dignity and Judicial Interpretation of Human Rights' (2008) 19 *European Journal of International Law* 655.

[16] See, for instance: Rawls, *A Theory of Justice* (1999) § 67; Nussbaum (n 4) 5; M Nussbaum, 'Human Dignity and Political Entitlements' in *Human Dignity and Bioethics: Essays Commissioned by the President's Council on Bioethics* (The President's Council on Bioethics, Washington, DC, 2008), available at https://bioethicsarchive.georgetown.edu/pcbc/reports/ human_dignity/chapter14.html; T Pogge, 'Dignity and Global Justice' in M Düwell, J Braarvig, R Brownsword and D Mieth (eds), *The Cambridge Handbook of Human Dignity* (Cambridge, Cambridge University Press, 2014) ch 52.

[17] This position is rooted in the philosophy of Kant, who justified a prohibition of the instrumentalisation of individuals and demanded treating a person never merely as a means to an end, but

These three fundamental entitlements of a person underpin a decent social minimum. In this sense, territorial and extraterritorial obligations to ensure a decent social minimum are aimed at enabling individuals to enjoy a special moral and legal status, basic equality and membership in humanity and eliminating obstacles which prevent this. *Special moral and legal status* of a person is incompatible with extreme poverty and inequality, which are characterised by severe socio-economic deprivation, oppression, disempowerment, social exclusion, marginalisation and stigmatisation, and, therefore, calls for human rights guarantees of freedom from poverty and secure access to a decent standard of living. The entitlement to *basic equality*, aimed at preventing the divide into first-class and second-class humans both within and across national borders, serves as a normative foundation for relational and distributive human rights guarantees of a decent social minimum. *Membership in humanity* gives rise to a claim-right to a just global order, in which a decent social minimum is ensured, and to corresponding shared obligations of members of the international community to create and maintain this global institutional order.[18]

Elsewhere, I demonstrated that the idea of a high moral and legal status of a person expressed by the concept of human dignity underlies the basic human rights indispensable for the enjoyment of a dignified existence, to which obligations of home states and other members of the international community correspond.[19] The following two sections of this chapter specify which obligations stem from the fundamental entitlements of basic equality and membership in humanity.

III. A DECENT SOCIAL MINIMUM AS A CORE OF SOCIAL AND GLOBAL JUSTICE

As maintained in the previous section, a fundamental entitlement to equality of status (or basic equality) underpins human rights obligations to guarantee a decent social minimum. Basic equality represents what Fyodor Dostoevsky characterised as equality in 'moral worth'.[20] According to Jeremy Waldron's

at the same time always as an end (the formula of the end in itself of the categorical imperative). I Kant, *The Metaphysics of Morals* (Cambridge, Cambridge University Press, 1996) 29. Thomas Pogge and Kok-Chor Tan see a person as an 'ultimate unit of moral concern'. T Pogge, 'Cosmopolitanism and Sovereignty' (1992) 103 *Ethics* 48; Pogge (n 3) 175; K-C Tan, *Justice Without Borders: Cosmopolitanism, Nationalism and Patriotism* (Cambridge, Cambridge University Press, 2004) 35ff. I intend to underscore that an individual is a possessor of a high moral and legal status. It is important to note that the principle of human-centricity does not exclude the recognition of worth of the other species.

[18] For more details see E Pribytkova, 'Global Human Rights Obligations Relating to a Decent Standard of Living', JSD Dissertation (New York, Columbia Law School, 2019).

[19] See Pribytkova, 'The Human Right to a Dignified Existence' (2013) 117–29.

[20] F Dostoevsky, *A Writer's Diary* (Evantston, IL, Northwestern University Press, 2009) 512. This idea grounded the justification of the right to a dignified existence in Russia proposed by Dostoevsky's friend and follower, Vladimir Solov'ev. See Pribytkova (n 13) 119–22.

compelling opinion, the principal premise of basic equality is that 'fundamentally there is just one sort of human being, just one rank of humanity'.[21] John Rawls considered 'equality as it applies to the respect which is owed to persons irrespective of their social position' to have a priority over other types of equality.[22] Ronald Dworkin justified a fundamental entitlement to equality of status as a basic 'right to treatment as an equal', which he opposed to a derivative 'right to equal treatment'.[23]

The demand for equality of status represents a minimum core of both *distributive justice*, which calls for a fair allocation of social goods or recourses essential for leading a decent life, and *relational justice*, that requires treating and regarding individuals as equals, ie with, as Dworkin specifies, 'equal concern and respect in the design and administration of the political institutions that govern them' at local and global levels.[24] Basic equality does not request an equal distribution of resources, wealth or income neither among states nor between individuals, but rather protecting from poverty and extreme inequality as well as securing access to a decent life. Local and global orders embodying the principle of basic equality should ensure individuals' full-fledged and meaningful participation in all key institutions and practices, including significant decision-making processes, regardless of their economic and social position, place of origin, or citizenship.[25]

Being rooted in the internationally recognised principle of basic equality, a decent social minimum itself is at the heart of social and global justice. It comprises territorial and extraterritorial human rights guarantees indispensable for securing very basic conditions in domains of distributive and relational justice: distributive justice guarantees aimed at ensuring *minimum socio-economic conditions of a decent life* or a decent standard of living;[26] and relational justice guarantees directed to ensure *minimum political conditions of a decent life* as well as to promote *non-discrimination and non-dominance* (equal membership in human society). What exactly are these basic minimum conditions of a decent life?

[21] J Waldron, *One Another's Equals: The Basis of Human Equality* (Cambridge, Mass, Harvard University Press, 2017) 6. Other conceptions of basic equality, see D Miller, 'Equality and Justice' (1997) X *Ratio* 222–37; RJ Arneson 'Egalitarianism' in EN Zalta (ed), *The Stanford Encyclopedia of Philosophy* (2013) available at plato.stanford.edu/entries/egalitarianism.

[22] Rawls (n 7) 511. E Pribytkova, 'A Decent Social Minimum as a Matter of Justice' in HP Gaisbauer, G Schweiger and C Sedmak (eds), *Ethical Issues in Poverty Alleviation* (Dordrecht, Springer, 2016) 43–56.

[23] R Dworkin, *Taking Rights Seriously* (Cambridge, Mass, Harvard University Press, 1977) 273.

[24] ibid 218; R Dworkin, *Sovereign Virtue: The Theory and Practice of Equality* (Cambridge, Mass, Harvard University Press, 2000) 411.

[25] For more details on the classification of global obligations of distributive justice and relational justice see Pribytkova, 'Global Human Rights Obligations' (2019).

[26] Since the guarantees of a decent standard of living represent only one kind of a social minimum guarantee, the substitution of the concept of a decent social minimum with the concept of a decent standard of living is incorrect.

In the midst of *minimum socio-economic conditions of a decent life* is the internationally recognised human right to an adequate, or decent, standard of living.[27] The UDHR states that 'everyone has the right to a standard of living adequate for the health and well-being of himself and of his family, including food, clothing, housing and medical care and necessary social services' (Article 25, para 1). The ICESCR acknowledges universal human rights of every person to 'an adequate standard of living for himself and his family, including adequate food, clothing and housing, and to the continuous improvement of living conditions' (Article 11, para 1) and 'the enjoyment of the highest attainable standard of physical and mental health' (Article 12, para 1).[28] International human rights instruments consider human rights to adequate food,[29] water,[30] sanitation,[31] housing,[32] clothing[33] and health[34] to be key components of the composite human right to a decent standard of living. As additional components of the right one often determines the human rights to transportation, energy, communications technology,[35] social services,[36] and the improvement of living conditions.[37] Along with the right to an adequate standard of living, the other basic socio-economic rights necessary for the enjoyment of a decent life – such as the rights to social security, work, decent working conditions, rest and leisure, just and favourable remuneration, and minimum wage, to form and to join trade unions, education, participation in cultural life, and to enjoy the benefits of scientific progress[38] – constitute an important precondition for a decent social minimum.

Minimum political conditions of a decent life presume individuals' enjoyment of basic civil and political rights necessary for their active, full-fledged and meaningful participation 'at all stages of the design, implementation and

[27] This chapter treats the right to a decent standard of living and the right to an adequate standard of living as synonyms.

[28] Components of the right an adequate standard of living are enshrined in the other international – the Convention on the Rights of the Child (CRC, Arts 24, 27), the Convention on the Rights of Persons with Disabilities (CRPD, Art 28) and the Convention on the Elimination of all Forms of Discrimination Against Women (CEDAW, Art 14) – and regional – the African Charter on Human and Peoples' Rights (Art 16), the European Social Charter (Arts 4, 13), the Charter of Fundamental Rights of the European Union (Art 34), the Additional Protocol to the American Convention on Human Rights in the Area of Economic, Social and Cultural Rights (Arts 6, 7, 9, 12, 15) – human rights instruments.

[29] UDHR, Art 25, para 1; ICESCR, Art 11, para 1; CRC, Art 27 para 3; CRPD, Art 28 para 1.

[30] CRPD, Art 28, para. 2; CEDAW, Art 14, para 2.

[31] CEDAW, Art 14, para 2.

[32] UDHR, Art 25, para 1; ICESCR, Art 11 para 1; CRC Art 27 para 3; CRPD Art 28 para 1; CEDAW Art 14 para 2.

[33] UDHR, Art 25, para 1; ICESCR, Art 11 para 1; CRC, Art 27 para 3; CRPD, Art 28 para 1.

[34] UDHR, Art 25, para 1; ICESCR, Art 12 para 1; CRC, Art 24 para 1; CRPD, Art 25; CEDAW, Art 12 para 1.

[35] CEDAW, Art 14, para 2.

[36] UDHR, Art 25, para 1; CRPD, Art 28, para 2.

[37] ICESCR, Art 11; CRPD, Art 28, para 1.

[38] See UDHR, Arts 22–27; ICESCR, Arts 6–10, 13–15; CRC, Arts 26, 28–29, 31–32; CRPD, Arts 24, 27, 30; CEDAW, Arts 10–11, 13–14.

evaluation of policies that affect them',[39] including the rights to take part in the conduct of political and public affairs,[40] freedom of thought, conscience and religion,[41] freedom of speech and expression,[42] freedom of assembly and association,[43] as well as the right to access to justice and effective and affordable remedies.[44] Minimum political conditions of a decent life include also guarantees of individuals' participation in the design and administration of core global institutions. Individuals' home state and global civil society serve as two major 'channels' for representing interests and protecting human rights of individuals in the global domain. In this respect, basic equality imperative calls for two interrelated measures. On the one hand, it requires correcting the asymmetries in international decision-making processes through ensuring active and meaningful participation of developing states as equal members of the international community and taking into account human rights of people they are representing, in particular the most vulnerable, disadvantaged and marginalised individuals and social groups.[45] On the other hand, basic equality demands promoting individuals' abilities to assert and defend their rights directly and through their (global) social networks (see section VI).

An essential relational condition of a decent social minimum is also the guarantees of *non-discrimination and non-domination* which are foundational for human rights law. The UDHR proclaims that all individuals 'are equal before the law and are entitled without any discrimination to equal protection of the law' (Article 7). The International Covenant on Civil and Political Rights (ICCPR) at Article 26 enunciates that

> the law shall prohibit any discrimination and guarantee to all persons equal and effective protection against discrimination on any ground such as race, colour, sex, language, religion, political or other opinion, national or social origin, property, birth or other status.

As the Committee on Economic, Social and Cultural Rights (CESCR) amplifies, the principle of non-discrimination also involves a prohibition of discrimination on account of poverty: 'individuals and groups of individuals must not be arbitrarily treated on account of belonging to a certain economic or social group or strata within society'.[46] Essential relational guarantees complementing the

[39] M Sepúlveda Carmona, ‚Report of the Special Rapporteur on Extreme Poverty and Human Rights on the Right to Participation of People Living in Poverty', A/HRC/23/36, 2013, para 17.
[40] UDHR, Art 21; ICCPR, Art 25; CRPD, Art 29; CEDAW, Art 7.
[41] UDHR, Art 18; ICCPR, Art 18; CRC, Art 14.
[42] UDHR, Art 19; ICCPR, Art 19; CRC, Arts 12–13; CRPD, Art 21.
[43] UDHR, Art 20; ICCPR, Art 21–22; CRC, Art 15; CRPD, Art 29; CEDAW, Art 7.
[44] UDHR, Art 8; ICCPR, Art 2; CRPD, Art 13; CEDAW, Art 15.
[45] See OHCHR, ‚Principles and Guidelines for a Human Rights Approach to Poverty Reduction Strategies', para 104(c).
[46] CESCR, General Comment No 20, para 35.

principle of non-discrimination are those limiting unfair domination of powerful actors on both local and global levels.[47]

Hence, basic distributive and relational human rights obligations to ensure a decent life correspond to the fundamental entitlement to equality of status underlying a decent social minimum. The next section specifies territorial and extraterritorial aspects of these obligations.

IV. TERRITORIAL AND EXTRATERRITORIAL OBLIGATIONS TO SECURE A DECENT SOCIAL MINIMUM

International human rights law has created a two-level model of human rights obligations relating to a decent social minimum: the national (territorial) and international (extraterritorial) obligations. For instance, the ICESCR at Article 2, para 1 enshrines states' obligations

> to take steps, *individually and through international assistance and co-operation*, especially economic and technical, to the maximum of its available resources, with a view to achieving progressively the full realization of the rights recognized in the present Covenant by all appropriate means [emphasis added].

The ICESCR also acknowledges that the right to an adequate standard of living gives rise to the corresponding obligations of the state to 'take appropriate steps to ensure the realization of this right, recognizing to this effect the essential importance of international co-operation based on free consent' (Article 11 para 1).[48] In this respect, basic socio-economic rights indispensable for the enjoyment of a decent life ground both territorial obligations of states and shared extraterritorial obligations of members of the international community.[49]

In comparison to the ICCPR (Article 2, para 1), the ICESCR does not contain a jurisdictional clause. However, the Optional Protocol to the ICESCR, which permits individuals to bring claims to the consideration of the CESCR, uses the criterion of jurisdiction (Article 2). According to the case law of UN treaty bodies, states' jurisdiction extends outside their territory in situations when they exercise effective territorial and personal control abroad as well as when there is a causal link between their activity and human rights impacts beyond

[47] For an analysis of guarantees of non-domination, see: Pribytkova, 'A Decent Social Minimum' (2016).

[48] The ICESCR also enshrines extraterritorial obligations to cooperate for the realisation of 'the fundamental right of everyone to be free from hunger' as the core element of the right to an adequate food, in particular, obligations to 'ensure an equitable distribution of world food supplies in relation to need' (Art 11 para 2).

[49] CESCR Comments specify global obligations to cooperate and assist corresponding to the rights to adequate food, water, sanitation, housing, and health. See: General Comment No 4, paras 10, 13, 19; General Comment No 12, para 36, 38, 40; General Comment No 14, para 38, 40, 45, 63; General Comment No 15, paras 30–38.

their borders.[50] Article 2 of the ICESCR also implies that states' jurisdiction embraces situations when they act for the realisation of socio-economic rights universally. UN Treaty-based bodies, the CESCR, the Committee on the Rights of the Child (UN CRC), and the Committee on the Elimination of Discrimination against Women (CEDAW) demand that states do not only respect, but also protect and fulfill socio-economic rights abroad.[51] Though a binding human rights instrument regulating states' extraterritorial obligations is still lacking, the Maastricht Principles on Extraterritorial Obligations in the Area of Economic, Social and Cultural Rights[52] (the Maastricht Principles) and commentaries to them provide a systematic explication of states' extraterritorial obligations in the area of socio-economic rights.[53]

Territorial and extraterritorial human rights obligations to ensure a decent social minimum include both *interactional obligations* that shape the conduct of multiple local and global actors and *institutional obligations* that apply to a national and international institutional structure. These human rights obligations are based on two essential entitlements enshrined in the UDHR: first, the entitlement of a person 'to *realization, through national effort and international co-operation* and in accordance with the organization and resources of each State, *of the economic, social and cultural rights* indispensable for his dignity and the free development of his personality' (Article 22, emphasis added); and second, the entitlement 'to a *social and international order* in which the rights and freedoms set forth in this Declaration can be fully realized' (Article 28,

[50] In concluding observations on Israel, the CESCR asserted that jurisdiction extends to all territories and populations under states' effective control. CESCR, 'Report on the Eighteenth and Nineteenth Sessions', E/1999/22, E/C.12/1998/26, 1999, para 234. According to the Human Rights Committee (HRC), which considers individual complaints for violations of human rights recognised in the ICCPR, jurisdiction concerns the relationship between individuals and states in relation to a violation of human rights, 'wherever they occurred'. HRC, *Delia Saldias de Lopez v Uruguay*, Communication No 52/1979, 1984, para 12.2. See also HRC, General comment No 36, paras 26, 66. In the interpretation suggested by the Maastricht Principles, 'a State has obligations to respect, protect and fulfil economic, social and cultural rights in […] situations over which State acts or omissions bring about foreseeable effects on the enjoyment of economic, social and cultural rights, whether within or outside its territory' (Principle 9).

[51] See, eg CESCR, 'Concluding Observations on the Second and Third Periodic Reports of Switzerland', E/C.12/CHE/CO/2-3, 26.11.2010, paras 24–25; 'Concluding Observations on the Sixth Periodic Report of Germany', E/C.12/DEU/CO/6, 12 October 2018, paras 8–9, 12–15, 20–21; UN CRC, 'Combined Fourth and Fifth Reports Submitted to the CRC by Singapore under Article 44 of the Convention', CRC/C/SGP/4-5, 3 November 2017, para 29; 'Combined Fifth and Sixth Periodic Reports Submitted to the CRC by Australia under Article 44 of the Convention', CRC/C/AUS/5-6, 15 January 2018, paras 41–43; 'Combined Fifth and Sixth Periodic Reports Submitted to the CRC by Italy under Article 44 of the Convention', CRC/C/ITA/5-6, 05.06.2017, paras 24–27; CEDAW, 'Concluding Observations on the Combined Eighth and Ninth Periodic Reports of Canada', UN CEDAW/C/CAN/CO/8-9, 18 November 2016, paras 18–19; 'Concluding Observations on the Ninth Periodic Report of Norway', CEDAW/C/NOR/CO/9, 17 November 2017, paras 14–15.

[52] The Maastricht Principles is a non-binding international expert opinion created on 28 September 2011, by 40 outstanding human rights scholars and practitioners.

[53] For an analysis of some gaps in the Maastricht Principles, see Pribytkova (n 18).

emphasis added). The latter entitlement stipulates the institutional aspect of the former and they both reveal the dual nature of human rights obligations relating to a decent social minimum. Hence, a decent social minimum contains interactional obligations to implement minimum human rights guarantees of a decent life and institutional obligations to create and maintain a just local and global order indispensable for enjoying a decent social minimum nationally and universally.

Territorial and extraterritorial obligations are closely interrelated. Home states are not always able to protect human rights of its citizens and residents from violations of other members of the international community, often participate themselves (willingly or unwillingly) in human rights abuses and even initiate them, while engaging global actors. The inability or unwillingness of the state to ensure a secure access to a decent social minimum for its population gives rise for obligations of the international community to cooperate and provide assistance. Let us consider some cases demonstrating the interrelation between territorial and extraterritorial obligations to ensure a decent social minimum.

In the case *Catan and Others v the Republic of Moldova and Russia* (Nos 43370/04, 8252/05 and 18454/06, 19 October 2012), children and parents from the Moldovan community in Transdnistria (Pridnestrovian Moldavian Republic) claimed violation of the right to education as a result of the forced closure of the schools, a language policy forbidding the use of the Latin alphabet in schools, and systematic acts of harassment and intimidation undertaken by the officials. The ECtHR found that since Russia exercised effective control over the Moldovan Republic of Transdnistria, through 'continued military, economic and political support', the case fell within Russia's jurisdiction. Hence, while giving a direct protection to the cultural right to education,[54] the ECtHR recognised extraterritorial responsibility of a foreign state, Russia, for violation of the right to education.[55] Though the ECtHR found that the human rights violations fell also within the jurisdiction of Moldova, it concluded that the latter was not responsible for them.

[54] Human rights enshrined in the European Convention on Human Rights are predominantly civil and political rights. The first Protocol includes the only socio-economic right – the right to education (Art 2). That is why objects of other socio-economic rights most often receive indirect protection in the ECtHR. For details see: E Pribytkova, 'Protection from Extreme Poverty in the European Court of Human Rights' in HP Gaisbauer, G Schweiger and C Sedmak (eds), *Absolute Poverty in Europe: Interdisciplinary Perspectives on a Hidden Phenomenon* (Bristol, Policy Press, 2019) 335–59.

[55] The ECtHR has come a long way from the famous case *Bankovic and Others v Belgium and 16 Other States* (No 52207/99, 12 December 2001), where it did not see any jurisdictional link between the victims of NATO bombing in Belgrade and 17 NATO Member States, to later cases, where it recognised that states' jurisdiction spreads beyond their territory in situations of effective territorial and personal control abroad, as well as states' acts and omissions producing effects outside their own territory (*Issa and Others v Turkey* (No 31821/96, 16 November 2004), *Al-Jedda v the United Kingdom* (No 27021/08, 7 July 2011), *Chiragov and Others v Armenia* (No 13216/05, 16 June 2015)).

Another resonance case refers to the construction of the Chixoy Dam in Guatemala in 1975–1983, during which more than 10,000 Maya Achi Indians were displaced or injured.[56] Guatemalan security forces committed rapes and killings, and massacred hundreds of Maya Achi, including women and children. The serious violations of human rights of Maya Achi people, including basic socio-economic rights, and the lack of access to land and natural resources, led to severe poverty and hunger of those who survived. The Commission for Historical Clarification found that the government of Guatemala holds 'undeniable responsibility for human rights violations and infringements of international humanitarian law' as well as 'acts of genocide against groups of Mayan people'.[57] The Inter-American Court of Human Rights (IACtHR) also declared the international responsibility of Guatemala authorities for multiple and severe violations of human rights of Maya Achi communities.[58] The World Bank and Inter-American Development Bank financed and supervised the project as part of their obligations of development assistance. The forced removal of Maya Achi communities from their land was a foreseeable result of the 'development' project. The banks took part in major decision-making processes concerning the dam, had access to but ignored information about the genocide and abuses of human rights of Maya Achi people, and continued funding the project. Despite of this, both banks denied any responsibility. Since the jurisdiction of the IACtHR does not extend to intergovernmental organisations (IGOs) and the latter enjoy immunity from the jurisdiction of domestic accountability mechanisms, the banks were never held accountable.[59]

[56] Indian Law Resource Center, 'Indigenous Survivors of Chixoy Dam Take Case to UN', available at https://indianlaw.org/content/indigenous-survivors-chixoy-dam-take-case-un. The Guatemalan Civil War (1960–1996) resulted in more than 200,000 murders and the disappearance of more than 45,000 civilians, including 5,000 children. 'Guatemala: Laying a mother to rest after 31 years', www.undp.org/content/undp/en/home/ourwork/ourstories/guatemala-laying-a-mother-to-rest-after-31-years.html.

[57] 'Guatemala. Memory of Silence. Report of the Commission for Historical Clarification Conclusions and Recommendations', paras 122, 126.

[58] In the case of the *Río Negro Massacres v Guatemala* (4 September 2012), the IACtHR found that Guatemala is responsible for numerous violations of human rights, predominantly civil and political, in particular the rights to life (Art 4), human treatment (Art 5), judicial personality (Art 3), personal liberty (Art 7), privacy (Art 11), fair trial (Art 8), judicial protection (Art 25), rights of the family (Art 17) and rights of the child (Art 19), freedom from slavery (Art 6), freedom of conscience and religion (Art 12), freedom of movement and residence (Art 22), and obligation to respect human rights (Art 1) recognised in the Inter-American Convention on Human Rights; obligation to prevent, investigate, and punish violence (Art 7) acknowledged in the Inter-American Convention on the Prevention, Punishment and Eradication of Violence Against Women; obligations to prevent and punish torture (Art 1), take effective measures and punish torture and cruel, inhuman, and degrading treatment (Art 6), and investigate and prosecute (Art 8) enshrined in the Inter-American Convention to Prevent and Punish Torture; as well as obligations not to practice, permit or tolerate forced disappearance of persons and to punish those committing these crimes (Art 1) presupposed by the Inter-American Convention on Forced Disappearance of Persons.

[59] For a legal analysis of the *Chixoy Dam* case, see F Coomans and R Künnemann, *Cases and Concepts on Extraterritorial Obligations in the Area of Economic, Social and Cultural Rights* (Cambridge, Intersentia, 2012) 201–08; The Chixoy Dam case: 'Need for full World Bank and Inter-American Development Bank Accountability', available at www.gi-escr.org/latest-news/chixoy-dam.

The third example concerns oil exploitation in Nigeria undertaken by transnational corporation, Shell Petroleum Development Company (a Nigerian subsidiary of Royal Dutch Shell), and the state-owned enterprise, Nigerian National Petroleum Corporation. Accompanied with frequent oil spills and gas flaring, it caused serious environmental damage, heavily polluted air, water, and soil, negatively affected almost all aspects of the indigenous Ogoni communities' life and violated their fundamental rights indispensable for leading a decent life, including the rights to food, water, sanitation, housing, and health, while increasing their poverty, marginalisation, and disempowerment. The Ogoni protests against these violations were brutally suppressed by the Nigerian authorities acting on request of and sponsored by Shell.[60] Activists of the Movement for the Survival of the Ogoni people and their supporters were prosecuted, tortured, raped and murdered.[61] For several decades, Ogoni people have been seeking justice in national, regional and foreign courts, quasi-judicial and non-judicial bodies. For instance, in the case of the *SERAC and CESR v Nigeria* (2001), the ACHPR recognised that the Nigerian Government was responsible for numerous human rights violations of Ogoni.[62] Since holding Shell Corporation accountable is beyond the ACHPR's jurisdiction, Ogoni people and NGOs representing them have undertaken many attempts (with varying degrees of success) to bring Shell to justice in courts and non-judicial bodies in Nigeria, the US, the UK and the Netherlands.[63] Hence, Shell is still

This is just one case of more than 500 dam construction projects in 92 countries funded by the World Bank, which caused severe human rights abuses, especially of the most vulnerable individuals and groups, as well as negative environmental impacts. See ‚Dams & the World Bank', available at www.whirledbank.org/ environment/dams.html.

[60] Amnesty International provided a documented proof of Shell's complicity in murders, rapes and acts of torture through the encouragement and financial support of the Nigerian military's measures to silence the protests of the Ogoni communities against Shell's harmful activities in their land. See Amnesty International, 'Nigeria: A Criminal Enterprise? Shell's Involvement in Human Rights Violations in Nigeria in the 1990s' (2017), available at www.amnesty.org/en/documents/AFR44/7393/2017/en.

[61] In 1995, nine leading Ogoni activists ('Ogoni 9') were arbitrary accused of murder and publicly executed. More than 3,000 Ogoni people were forced to leave their land. See: C Ryerson, 'Shell in Nigeria: The Case for New Legal Strategies for Corporate Accountability' (2018), available at https://legaldesign.org/calblog/2018/7/5/shell-in-nigeria-the-case-for-new-legal-strategies-for-corporate-accountability.

[62] In particular, the Nigeria violated the right to freedom from discrimination (Art 2), rights to life (Art 4), property (Art 14), health (Art 16), protection of family (Art 18.1), wealth and natural recourses (Art 21), and clean environment (Art 24) recognised in the ACHPR.

[63] For instance, *Ken Wiwa et al v Royal Dutch Petroleum Co et al* (No 96 Civ 8386, SDNY 2009), *Ken Wiwa et al v Brian Anderson* (No 01 Civ 1909, SDNY 2009), and *Ken Wiwa v Shell Petroleum Development Co of Nigeria Ltd* (No 04 Civ. 2665, SDNY 2009) – out-of-court settlement for $15.5 million; *Kiobel v Royal Dutch Petroleum Co* (569 US 108 2013) – dismissed for lack of subject-matter jurisdiction; *Bodo Community and Others v Shell Petroleum Development Company of Nigeria Ltd* ([2014] EWHC 1973 (TCC), 20 June 2014) – out-of-court settlement for £55 million. On 1 May 2019, the District Court of The Hague decided that the lawsuit brought by four widows of the Ogoni 9 against Shell (No C /09/540872/ HA ZA 17-1048) is within its jurisdiction. In 2011, Amnesty International and Friends of the Earth International submitted a 'Complaint to the UK and Dutch National Contact Points under the Specific Instance Procedure of the OECD Guidelines for Multinational Enterprises' which, however, did not bring much result. For an analysis, see Ryerson, 'Shell in Nigeria' (2018); SH Cleveland, 'After Kiobel' (2014) 12 *Journal of International Criminal Justice* 551.

not held accountable for many human rights violations committed against the Ogoni communities and the victims of these violations are still waiting for adequate remedies.

These three examples not only stress the interrelation between territorial obligations of home states and extraterritorial obligations of global actors, but also reveal the lack of appropriate mechanisms for holding IGOs and non-state entities, including transnational corporations, accountable for breaches of their extraterritorial obligations.

Extraterritorial obligations are often believed to be (i) secondary, (ii) conditional, and (ii) consequent obligations. This view is incorrect, since it proceeds from a false understanding of various types of extraterritorial obligations. To demonstrate this, I should turn to the classification of extraterritorial obligations.

V. CLASSIFICATION OF EXTRATERRITORIAL OBLIGATIONS

There is a tradition to distinguish between *remedial extraterritorial responsibilities* for a negative effect on the enjoyment of human rights and *global obligations*, which arise when human rights deprivations cannot be attributed to any particular actors or institutions. A criterion used for this classification is the possibility to establish a causal link between acts or omissions of certain actors and human rights abuses. Thus, the Maastricht Principles classify '*obligations relating to the acts and omissions* of a State, within or beyond its territory, that have effects on the enjoyment of human rights outside of that State's territory' and '*obligations of a global character* that are set out in the Charter of the United Nations and human rights instruments to take action, separately, and jointly through international cooperation, to realize human rights universally' (Principle 8, emphases added).

Remedial extraterritorial obligations and global obligations are simultaneous and frequently overlap.[64] Simultaneity of these obligations means that they cannot be mutually discharged: a compensation for the caused harm does not relieve actors of their global obligations and, vice versa, the fulfillment of global obligations (for instance, cooperation for a just and sustainable global order or assistance to the global poor) does not exempt actors from their remedial responsibilities for extraterritorial human rights violations they caused. Extraterritorial obligations of one type may arise from the non-fulfilment of an obligation of the other type. For example, a failure to fulfil global obligations

[64] See: O De Schutter, A Eide, A Khalfan, M Orellana, M Salomon and I Seiderman, 'Commentary to the Maastricht Principles. Commentary to the Maastricht Principles on Extraterritorial Obligations of States in the Area of Economic, Social and Cultural Rights' (2012) 34 *Human Rights Quarterly* 1101.

may be a basis for an obligation to compensate the injured individuals (see the Chixoy Dam case discussed in section IV) and/or other actors who have provided assistance to the former; and a failure of responsible actors to compensate for harm caused by them, in turn, may ground other actors' shared global obligations to act for the realisation of human rights of the affected individuals and communities to protect them or provide assistance (for instance, to Maya Achi, Ogoni, or Moldovan communities).

Despite the close interrelation of the two types of extraterritorial obligations, remedial responsibilities should not be substituted with global obligations, ie the caused harm should not be compensated under the mask of 'assistance'.[65] Only in certain cases – when urgent help to the victims of human rights violations is necessary; or responsible actors are unable to provide (full) compensation – violators' remedial responsibilities may be superseded by obligations of global assistance performed by third parties, with the consequent reimbursement of the costs of assistance. It is also necessary to stress that the victims have the right to the truth about violations of their human rights, which should be guaranteed not only territorially, but also extraterritorially.[66] Hence, the recognition and realisation of extraterritorial remedial obligations is essential for the protection of victims, holding violators accountable and preventing further human rights abuses.

Global obligations represent the least investigated and the most unfulfilled type of extraterritorial obligations. It is possible to classify *global obligations of result* focused on achievements and outcomes of actors' activities and *global obligations of conduct* relating to actors' efforts to achieve a certain goal. The former include institutional obligations to create and maintain a just global order through which a decent social minimum may be ensured worldwide and interactional obligations to realise human rights indispensable for enjoying a decent life universally (see section IV). Global obligations of conduct embrace obligations to cooperate and obligations to assist those in poverty. Obligations to cooperate are recognized in the Charter of the United Nations ('UN Charter'), the UDHR as well as some other international human rights instruments, such as the CRC and the Declaration on the Right to Development (DRD).[67] International human rights instruments often explicitly or implicitly integrate obligations to assist into obligations to cooperate.[68] Even if it is not explicitly

[65] See, for example, T Pogge, '"Assisting" the Global Poor' (2007) 13 *The Proceedings of the Twenty-First World Congress of Philosophy* 189–215. I address this issue in Pribytkova (n 18).

[66] According to the Maastricht Principles, 'victims have the right to truth about the facts and circumstances surrounding the violations, which should also be disclosed to the public, provided that it causes no further harm to the victim' (Principle 38).

[67] See the UN Charter (Art 1 para 3, Arts 55–56), UDHR (Art 22), CRC (Art 4), DRD (Art 3 para 3, Art 4 para 2, Art 6 para 1).

[68] For example, the CRPD states that obligations of international cooperation involve duties of technical and economic assistance (Art 32 para 1). See also De Schutter et al 'Commentary to the Maastricht Principles' (2012) 1104.

stated in the ICESCR and the CRC, the CESCR and the UN CRC treat obligations to assist as part of obligations to cooperate.[69]

The scope of remedial responsibilities is determined by the harm caused to the victims of territorial and extraterritorial human rights violations. The latter have the right to effective and affordable remedies and adequate (full and effective) reparation, covering 'all injuries suffered by victims' and including 'measures of restitution, compensation, rehabilitation, and satisfaction', as well as 'guarantees of non-repetition'.[70]

I suggest that the scope of territorial and extraterritorial obligations to ensure a decent social minimum should be determined by the *principles of sufficiency* and a *decent minimum sacrifice*.[71] The principle of sufficiency implies conditions necessary for a decent social existence of a person, ie, his or her active, full-fledged and meaningful participation in all core social, economic, political and cultural institutions and practices in local and global domains, including important decision-making processes, as well as access to shared material and intellectual values, and an opportunity for his or her moral and intellectual flourishing. The principle of a decent minimum sacrifice requires the burdens of (global) obligations to be compatible with fundamental interests, rights and duties of actors. In this respect, individuals should be able to enjoy a decent life,[72] while collective (global) actors should not be imposed upon to sacrifice their goals and other (territorial/extraterritorial) human rights obligations.[73] Harmonising these principles is possible through a fair distribution of shared (global) obligations among members of the (international) community that would limit their individual burdens.[74] Experts argue that global poverty is avoidable at relatively low costs for individual actors under condition that global obligations are distributed fairly.[75]

[69] See, for example, CESCR General Comment No 3, paras 13–14; General Comment No 4, para 19; General Comment No 12, para 38; General Comment No 14, para 38; General Comment No 15, para 30; UN CRC General Comment No 15, para 88.

[70] See the UN Principles and Guidelines on the Right to a Remedy and Reparation (Arts 18–23), the UN Set of Principles for the Protection and Promotion of Human Rights through action to Combat Impunity (Principle 34), and the Maastricht Principles (Principle 38).

[71] For an analysis of these principles, see Pribytkova (n 18).

[72] See also Cécile Fabre's argument that better-off bear duties to assist 'if, and only if, they would not jeopardize their own prospects for a minimally flourishing life', Fabre (n 12) ch 1.

[73] D Bilchitz, 'Do Corporations Have Positive Fundamental Rights Obligations?' (2010) 57 *Theoria: A Journal of Social and Political Theory* 25.

[74] For instance, an attempt to quantify the scope of global obligations to assist and to bring it in accordance with the principles of a decent minimum sacrifice and the principle of sufficiency, has resulted in the formulation of the UN target for Official Development Assistance (ODA), which currently amounts 0.7% of gross national income (GNI) and is proposed to be increased to the target to 1% of GNI.

[75] J Sachs, *The End of Poverty: Economic Possibilities for Our Time* (New York, Penguin Press, 2005) ch 15; JD Sachs, V Fajans-Turner, T Smith, C Kennedy-Cuomo, T Parejo and SS Loni, *Closing the SDG Budget Gap* (New York, Move Humanity, 2018); Paul Collier, *The Bottom Billion: why the Poorest Countries are Failing and What can be Done about it* (Oxford, Oxford University Press, 2007) ch 11; Oxfam International, 'Public Good or Private Wealth?' briefing paper (2019) 60–71, available at

Understanding the difference between the two types of extraterritorial obligations gives us the ground for responding to the question asked in section IV on the interrelation between territorial and extraterritorial obligations. The thesis that the extraterritorial obligations are always secondary, conditional, and consequent obligations means that global actors or the international community as a whole are considered to be responsible for the realisation of human rights only: (i) if the home state is unable to do this independently; (ii) under conditions that the home state has used maximum resources available to it; and (iii) after the global actors (especially foreign states) have fulfilled their territorial obligations to the full extent. I argue that this thesis is incorrect.[76] Since remedial responsibilities do not depend on whether the harm is caused within the state's territory or abroad, remedial extraterritorial responsibilities are primary, unconditional and simultaneous with territorial remedial responsibilities.[77] Global institutional obligations to create and maintain a just global order (recognized in the Article 28 of the UDHR) aimed at the realisation of individuals' fundamental entitlement to *membership in humanity* are also primary, unconditional, and simultaneous. Being simultaneous to territorial obligations,[78] interactional global obligations are secondary and may be conditional on individuals' inability to obtain social support of their state, whereas global obligations of emergency assistance are unconditional in this respect.[79]

VI. RIGHT-HOLDERS AND DUTY-BEARERS

Whereas territorial legal relations of states towards its residents may be characterised as vertical and international legal relations between states and other members of the international community as horizontal, extraterritorial legal relations are diagonal by their nature. In this sense, obligations of global actors (foreign states, IGOs, and non-state entities) correspond to human rights of

https://oxfamilibrary.openrepository.com/bitstream/handle/10546/620599/bp-public-good-or-private-wealth-210119-en.pdf.

[76] Experts correctly claim that obligations to assist 'would be close to meaningless' if global actors enjoy 'absolute discretion to prioritise territorial obligations over extraterritorial' ones. A Khalfan, 'Division of Responsibility between States' in M Langford, W Vandenhole, M Scheinin and W van Genugten (eds), *Global Justice, State Duties: The Extraterritorial Scope of Economic, Social, and Cultural Rights in International Law* (Cambridge, Cambridge University Press, 2013) 329. See also P Alston and G Quinn, 'The Nature and Scope of States Parties' Obligations under the International Covenant on Economic, Social and Cultural Rights' (1987) 9 *Human Rights Quarterly* 179.

[77] See also Pogge (n 3).

[78] It seems the CESCR also takes the position that territorial obligations of social support and global interactional obligations to assist are simultaneous, since it encourages states to provide international assistance even if the latter lack sufficient recourses to fulfill their territorial obligations. See, eg, the CESCR's recommendation to Spain to reach the international standard of the official development assistance (0.7% of GDP) despite the state's austerity measures. The CESCR Concluding observations on the fifth periodic report of Spain (E/C.12/ESP/5, 2012), para 10.

[79] For more details, see Pribytkova (n 18).

individuals. In Thomas Gammeltoft-Hansen's apt expression, legal theory and practice should make a 'quantum leap', in order to develop an adequate toolkit for investigating and regulating the reality that does not fit into the usual framework of horizontal and vertical relations.[80] This 'quantum leap' calls for two ground-breaking reforms aimed at shifting from the Westphalian state-centered paradigm to a human-centered world order.[81]

First, individuals proclaimed as major possessors of human rights by international human rights law must be recognised as independent full-fledged subjects of extraterritorial legal relations capable directly, ie without the mandatory mediation of the state, to demand the realisation of their human rights from global actors and to hold the latter accountable for human rights violations and non-fulfillment of their extraterritorial human rights obligations. This includes ensuring individuals' participation in key decision-making, norm-setting and institution-designing processes that concern their human rights, including ex ante and ex post human rights impact assessments and human rights due diligence, as well as providing their direct access to effective and affordable remedies at international, regional and national levels.

Second, extraterritorial obligations should be allocated not only to states, but to all global actors: IGOs, non-state entities and individuals.[82] This measure is justified by two interrelated reasons. On the one hand, the role of non-state entities, in particular IGOs, NGOs, transnational corporations and global civil society, in framing global discourse, norms, institutions and practices and influencing the enjoyment of human rights universally has been substantially increased. Many global actors have undoubtedly superior capacities than average states. For example, in 2016, 71 out of the 100 major world economies were transnational corporations, and only 29 states.[83] The fifth largest global economy is formed by approximately. 10 million contemporary local and global NGOs receiving support from one-third of the world population and involving a quarter of the population as volunteers.[84] Decisions of IGOs, especially UN agencies, the Bretton Woods Institutions, and WTO frame

[80] T Gammeltoft-Hansen, 'Growing Barriers: International Refugee Law' in M Gibney and S Skogly (eds) *Universal Human Rights and Extraterritorial Obligations* (Philadelphia, University of Pennsylvania Press, 2010) 80–81.

[81] On the necessity of this paradigm shift see: A Clapham, *Human Rights Obligations of Non-State Actors* (Oxford, Oxford University Press, 2006) 1f; M Salomon, *Global Responsibility for Human Rights: World Poverty and the Development of International Law* (Oxford, Oxford University Press, 2007) 115f.

[82] See Salomon, *Global Responsibility for Human Rights* (2007) 45–46; W Vandenhole (ed) *Challenging Territoriality in Human Rights Law: Building Blocks for a Plural and Diverse Duty-Bearer Regime* (Oxon–New York, Routledge, 2015); A Vandenbogaerde, *Towards Shared Accountability in International Human Rights Law. Law, Procedures and Principles* (Cambridge, Intersentia, 2016) Part III; S Deva and D Bilchitz (eds) *Building a Treaty on Business and Human Rights: Context and Contours* (Cambridge, Cambridge University Press, 2017).

[83] See https://oxfamblogs.org/fp2p/of-the-worlds-top-100-economic-entities-29-are-states-71-are-corporates.

[84] See '25 Facts and Stats about NGOs Worldwide', available at techreport.ngo/previous/2017/facts-and-stats-about-ngos-worldwide.html.

not only the global order, but have significant impact on political and socio-economic systems throughout the world.[85] Extraterritorial obligations of global actors should correspond to the vast capacities and freedoms they enjoy. On the other hand, as the three examples in section IV demonstrated, states are not always able to act as primary actors of justice, respect, protect and fulfil the rights of their residents. In Onora O'Neill's convincing opinion, the realisation of human rights should not be 'endlessly postponed until more competent and just States emerge'.[86]

Key international human rights instruments provide a normative foundation for allocating institutional and interactional extraterritorial human rights obligations to IGOs, non-state actors and individuals. Thus, the UDHR underscores that not just states, but 'every individual and every organ of society' should strive to promote respect for human rights and to 'secure their universal and effective recognition and observance' through national and international measures.[87] Though the ICESCR and the CRC regulate obligations of states, the CESCR[88] and the UN CRC[89] clarify that socio-economic rights bind also other members of the international community. Although customary international law still remains state-focused it also provides a certain legal basis for extraterritorial obligations of multiple actors.[90]

[85] See, for instance, T Pogge, *Politics as Usual: What Lies Behind the Pro-Poor Rhetoric* (Cambridge, Polity Press, 2010); T Stichelmans, 'How International Financial Institutions and Donors Influence Economic Policies in Developing Countries', A Eurodad discussion paper (2016), available at www.eurodad.org/files/pdf/57f4f4163d760.pdf.

[86] While criticising statist approaches to global justice, O'Neill also asserts that it is too naive to expect that states, being by their nature anti-cosmopolitan institutions, will take leading positions in implementing duties of global justice. O O'Neill, 'Cosmopolitan Rights and State Obligations' in O O'Neill, *Justice Across Boundaries: Whose Obligations?* (Cambridge, Cambridge University Press, 2016) 160, 176.

[87] In accordance with it, the Vienna Declaration and Programme of Action stresses obligations of 'States and international organizations, in cooperation with non-governmental organizations, to create favourable conditions at the national, regional and international levels to ensure the full and effective enjoyment of human rights' (Art 13). The Declaration on the Right and Responsibility of Individuals, Groups and Organs of Society to Promote and Protect Universally Recognized Human Rights and Fundamental Freedoms recognises a significant role and obligations of individuals, social groups, institutions and NGOs 'in contributing, as appropriate, to the promotion of the right of everyone to a social and international order' in which universal human rights are fulfilled (Art 18.3). See also the CRPD (Art 32 para 1).

[88] See CESCR, General Comment No 12, paras 36, 38, 40; General Comment No 14, paras 45, 63; General Comment No 15, para 38; General Comment No 17, paras 61, 82; General Comment No 18, para 53; General Comment 19, para 61. See also the Limburg Principles on the Implementation of the International Covenant on Economic, Social and Cultural Rights (Limburg Principles), Principle 34.

[89] See UN CRC, General Comment No 5, sections I and J; UN CRC General Comment No 15, paras 75–89; UN CRC General Comment No 16, para 47–48; UN CRC, Concluding observations on the Third and Fourth Periodic report of Sri Lanka, CRC/C/LKA/3-4, 1.10.2010, paras 18–19; UN CRC, Concluding observations on the combined third to sixth periodic reports of Guinea, CRC/C/GIN/CO/3-6, 28.02.2019, paras 14–15.

[90] See Clapham, *Human Rights Obligations* (2006) 86–87; P Alston, 'Ships Passing in the Night: The Current State of the Human Rights and Development Debate Seen through the Lens of the Millennium Development Goals' (2005) 27 *Human Rights Quarterly* 778; Pribytkova (n 18).

Hence, the recognition of individuals as independent subjects of extraterritorial relations and all members of the international community as bearers of extraterritorial obligations is essential for the shift from a state-centered to human-centered global order. This shift does not mean the decline of the state, but rather rethinking its role. The state, along with a (global) civil society, should remain an important instrument for representing the interests and protecting the human rights of individuals in the global domain.

VII. CONCLUSIONS

In this chapter, I argued that territorial and extraterritorial guarantees of a decent social minimum are aimed at enabling individuals to enjoy their three fundamental entitlements – a special moral and legal status, basic equality and membership in humanity – which underlie an idea of human-centricity and are embedded in the International Bill of Human Rights. A decent social minimum comprises important territorial and extraterritorial human rights guarantees that derive from equality of status: the minimum socio-economic (distributive) guarantees of a decent life or a decent standard of living; and minimum political (relational) guarantees of a decent life (equal membership in human society as well as non-dominance and non-discrimination). Within extraterritorial obligations relating to a decent social minimum one can distinguish remedial extraterritorial responsibilities for a negative effect on the enjoyment of basic human rights indispensable for leading a decent life and global obligations to realise a decent social minimum universally. Though these obligations are closely interrelated, they should not substitute one another. The chapter asserted that individuals must be recognised as independent full-fledged subjects of extraterritorial legal relations capable of claiming the realisation of their human rights directly from global actors and of holding the latter to account. At the same time, all members of the international community – states, IGOs, non-state entities and individuals – should be acknowledged as important agents of social and global justice and bearers of extraterritorial obligations to respect, protect and fulfill socio-economic rights indispensable for the implementation of a decent social minimum.

9

Ending Poverty: Human Rights and Responsibilities

DAVID PIACHAUD

I. INTRODUCTION

In 1948, the United Nations' Universal Declaration of Human Rights began with recognition that

> disregard and contempt for human rights have resulted in barbarous acts which have outraged the conscience of mankind' and a statement that 'the equal and inalienable rights of all members of the human family is the foundation of freedom, justice and peace in the world.[1]

The Declaration was a remarkable act of accord and hope that was drawn up by a Committee chaired by Eleanor Roosevelt with leading roles played by members from Canada, China, France, Lebanon and the Soviet Union.[2] The Declaration was adopted by the UN General Assembly in 1948 with 48 nations in favour, eight abstentions and none opposed.

The Declaration set out in 30 Articles, beginning with Article 1 – 'All human beings are born free and equal in dignity and rights' – a set of civil, political and social rights. Most relevant to ending poverty and ensuring a social minimum for all was Article 25, which prescribed:

> The right to a standard of living adequate for the health and well-being of himself and his family, including food, clothing, housing and medical care and necessary social services, and the right to security in the event of unemployment, sickness, disability, widowhood, old age or other lack of livelihood in circumstances beyond his control.[3]

Yet a statement of a right is not the same as its realisation. Sadly, many of the rights set out remain a long way from 'universal and effective recognition and

[1] United Nations, 'Universal Declaration of Human Rights' (New York, United Nations, 1948).
[2] MA Glendon, *A World Made New* (New York, Random House, 2001) 45.
[3] United Nations, 'Universal Declaration' (1948).

observance'. On the latest figures for 2015, the World Bank estimate that over 700 million people are living below the international poverty line of US $1.90 a day.[4]

Nearly 70 years after the Declaration of Human Rights, in 2015 the United Nations adopted 17 Sustainable Development Goals to be achieved by 2030, many of which reiterate the Rights in the 1948 Declaration. The first Goal is to 'End poverty in all its forms everywhere'.

The UN has, then, not been short of fine words and noble aspirations. But are they more than that? What implications do they have for policy? These are some of the questions that this chapter discusses. In the next section rights and the concept of a social minimum are briefly discussed. Then the relationship between rights and responsibilities is explored. In the following two sections, policy for achieving a social minimum and ending poverty is discussed, first, in the context of advanced economies and, second, in relation to global poverty. Finally, some conclusions are drawn.

II. RIGHTS AND A SOCIAL MINIMUM

The idea of human rights in general, and social rights in particular, has been extensively discussed elsewhere and raises many questions. As the *Stanford Encyclopedia of Philosophy* puts it: 'questions about the existence, content, nature, universality, justification, and legal status of human rights'.[5] Here only a few of these questions are touched on.

Rights in the 1948 Declaration can be divided into several categories: rights relating to life, liberty and personal security, civil, political and social rights. Of the latter, TH Marshall wrote:

> The civil element is composed of the rights necessary for individual freedom – liberty of the person, freedom of speech, thought and faith, the right to own property, and to conclude valid contracts, and the right to justice … By the political element I mean the right to participate in the exercise of political power … By the social element I mean the whole range from the right to a modicum of economic welfare and security, to the right to share to the full in the social heritage and to live civilised life according to the standards prevailing in society.[6]

In this chapter the emphasis is on social rights, but it should be recognised that social, civil and political rights are often interdependent. For example, all social rights should apply without distinction by race, sex or religion as a civil right;

[4] World Bank, 'Poverty Overview' (2018), available at www.worldbank.org/en/topic/poverty/overview.

[5] J Nickel, 'Human Rights' in EN Zalta (ed), *The Stanford Encyclopedia of Philosophy* (2017), available at plato.stanford.edu/archives/spr2017/entries/rights-human.

[6] TH Marshall, 'Citizenship and Class' in TH Marshall and T Bottomore, *Citizenship and Social Class* (London, Pluto Press, 1992) 8.

yet this has been a matter of contention in many countries. Again, the right to freedom of opinion and expression is fundamental to the right to education. Equally, civil and political rights depend on social rights; a person who is starving to death gains little from the knowledge that they have freedom of expression. As Maslow's hierarchy of needs implies, without the maintenance of health then there is no prospect of human happiness; without education there is little likelihood of involvement in the political process.[7] Thus, civil and political rights depend on social rights.

Signing up to the UN Declaration did not commit signatories to anything, and some nations have shown little regard to civil, political or social rights. But perhaps there is more attention to social rights than in the past; as Polly Vizard wrote:

> Poverty and other aspects of socio-economic deprivation such as hunger, starvation, lack of access to healthcare and education, and exploitative working conditions, were downgraded and neglected as human rights concerns for much of the second half of the twentieth century. However, there is now substantially more international recognition and acceptance of a broader characterization of human rights incorporating social, economic, and cultural rights as well as civil and political rights; and positive as well as negative duties.[8]

Many regard a social minimum as a basic human right, without which all other rights have little meaning. Yet defining a social minimum presents many problems and the achievement of that social minimum raises many contentious issues.

A social minimum income is often conceived of as an income adequate to keep an individual or household out of poverty – ending poverty and achieving a social minimum are treated here as equivalent. It is widely recognised that a social minimum is essential for a just society and that in developed economies the law and public policy have a central role to play in ensuring such a social minimum. While this chapter concentrates on a social minimum this is, of course, not the only goal of a just society. Concerns about inequalities of wealth, of power, and of opportunities are legitimate and real concerns, as are issues of recognition and discrimination.

Many have argued that a social minimum cannot and should not be conceived solely in terms of income but must encompass access to clean air and water, education and much else that cannot be directly purchased. As Sen wrote:

> Policy debates have indeed been distorted by over-emphasis on income poverty and income inequality, to the neglect of deprivations that relate to other variables, such as unemployment, ill health, lack of education, and social exclusion.[9]

[7] A Maslow, *Motivation and Personality* (New York, Harper, 1954).

[8] P Vizard, 'The Human Rights and Equalities Agenda' in D Hartley and P Lucinda (eds), *Social Advantage and Disadvantage* (Oxford, University Press, 2016) 42.

[9] A Sen, *Development as Freedom* (Oxford, University Press, 1999) 108.

Nevertheless, for simplicity, the emphasis here is on income poverty and how a social minimum can be achieved.

What level a poverty line or social minimum should be set at has been the subject of a substantial literature, summarised by Atkinson[10] and Alcock.[11] What is clear is that any social minimum must reflect context and circumstances. Context matters in that what is seen as a social minimum varies with prevailing living standards and norms; in other words, poverty is a relative concept. In one society, warm clothing and housing may be essential to survival; in many societies a mobile phone is now a necessity for economic and social participation. Circumstances matter since people have very different capabilities and needs and they live in differing family structures and locations. It is clear that a social minimum income needs to take account of family composition, of special needs such as extra costs due to disability, and of housing costs, which can differ greatly depending on type of tenure and location.

A social minimum that is very simple is unlikely to be fair, because of all the many variations in needs. If a social minimum is much more complex, then policy to achieve it is inevitably more complex. There is, in short, no simple policy to achieve a just social minimum for all.

III. RIGHTS AND RESPONSIBILITIES

Rights cannot be separated from responsibilities.

The term 'responsibility' is used here, but other terms such as 'duty' and 'obligation' could be used instead. Further, if conditions are attached to receipt of a social benefit then this is, in effect, a responsibility or obligation attached to the benefit.

The importance of responsibilities can be seen by imagining a world in which no one accepted any responsibilities; in such a world the assertion of any human rights would count for nothing. If no rights of any sort existed, it would be a world in which life was indeed nasty, brutish and short.

Yet responsibilities have been given far less attention than rights. As Onora O'Neill argued:

> In the text of the Universal Declaration of Human Rights of 1948, … nations, peoples, states, societies and countries are variously gestured to as agents against whom individuals have rights. Little is said about any differences between these varying types of agents, or about their capacities and vulnerabilities, and there is no systematic allocation of obligations of different sorts to agents and agencies of specific types … It may seem a scandal that the Universal Declaration is so cavalier about identifying agents of justice … The Declaration approaches justice by proclaiming rights. It proclaims

[10] A Atkinson, *Poverty and Social Security* (Brighton, Harvester Press, 1989).
[11] P Alcock, *Understanding Poverty* (Basingstoke, Palgrave, 2006).

> what is to be received, what entitlements everyone is to have; but it says very little about which agents and agencies must do what if these rights are to be secured.[12]

Questions which are then fundamental to social rights are:

- Who bears the responsibility that goes with the right? Should it be placed on government, on communities, on families or individuals, or some combination of these?
- What responsibilities are just and socially beneficial?

Many see responsibilities as falling principally on states. Vizard wrote:

> It has become increasingly accepted that all human rights – civil, political, economic, social, and cultural – give rise to positive duties on states to protect and promote human rights as well as negative duties on states to refrain from undermining human rights.[13]

It has been common to think of social responsibilities as falling on the state, and influential studies such as Titmuss's *Social Division of Welfare*[14] put most of the emphasis on the state. Yet the responsibilities the state can take on depend on the resources the state can deploy, which depend crucially on the willingness of the public to pay taxes. States can pass laws but they cannot legislate resources into existence nor ordain behaviour that the public is unwilling to undertake.

This is most obvious in relation to children. Infants are not capable of providing for themselves; therefore, unless they are cared for collectively, parents must be responsible. As the UN Convention on the Rights of the Child states: 'The parent(s) or others responsible for the child have the primary responsibility to secure, within their abilities and financial capacities, the conditions of living necessary for the child's development.'[15]

Similarly, the right to freedom from discrimination may be enacted in law, but it is individuals, groups and communities in their attitudes and behaviour that are most likely to discriminate; unless their behaviour is non-discriminatory then the right will not have been realised.

Some see responsibilities on individuals as obligations of being a citizen, but this depends on the concept of citizenship. Plant distinguished two concepts of citizenship:

> The first sees citizenship as a status that is not fundamentally altered by the virtue (or lack of it) of the individual … You should thus be able, as a citizen, to claim benefits even if you are not discharging what others may regard as your proper obligations to

[12] O O'Neill, 'Agents of Justice' in T Pogge, (ed) *Global Justice* (Oxford, Blackwell, 2001) 190–91.

[13] Vizard, 'The Human Rights' (2016) 44.

[14] R Titmuss, 'The Social Division of Welfare' in *Essays on the Welfare State* (London, George Allen and Unwin, 1958).

[15] United Nations, 'United Nations Convention on the Rights of a Child', Art 27(2) (New York, United Nations, 1989).

> society ... The second and alternative view, places much less emphasis on rights, and focuses instead on obligation, virtue and contribution. ... The idea of reciprocity and contribution are at the heart of this concept of citizenship: individuals do not and cannot have a right to resources of society unless they contribute to the development of that society through work or other socially valued activities, if they are in a position to do so.[16]

If social rights are to be a reality, it is hard to see how this can be achieved if citizens fail to undertake some social obligations – whether to respect the rights of others, to pay taxes or to treat others without discrimination. The question then is what should be the extent of such obligations or responsibilities?

This conclusion was supported by Marshall who went further and included an obligation to work; as Peter Dwyer put it:

> Marshall saw citizenship as a status that entailed both rights and duties ... Compulsory duties, the duty to pay tax and national insurance contributions, to accept compulsory education and the now defunct military service, are seen as relatively unproblematic and it is taken for granted that if the citizen wishes to claim their rights then they must accept such attendant duties. Paramount importance is attached to the duty to work. Marshall's emphasis on this 'essential duty' and more importantly 'to put one's heart into one's job' clearly indicates that the individual citizen has a duty wherever possible to recognise a responsibility for themselves and the wider communities that they inhabit.[17]

Dwyer argues that in Britain in the last 25 years both the New Right and New Labour have promoted Plant's second concept of citizenship, even though they come from different philosophical traditions:

> A new welfare orthodoxy that stresses reduced access to public welfare provision, a stronger link between rights and responsibilities, and an increasingly moral agenda is now dominant ... The social component is essentially undergoing a redefinition, in which certain welfare rights are increasingly conditional upon citizens first agreeing to conform to appropriate patterns of behaviour as defined by the state or other provider of welfare.[18]

This emphasis on responsibilities was evident in the New Labour Government's approach to the welfare system:

> The welfare system is a proud creation. But reform is essential if we are to realise our vision of a modern nation and a decent and fair society. Through our proposals we aim to break the cycle of dependency and insecurity and empower all citizens to lead a dignified and fulfilling life. We need a new 'contract' between citizen and state, with rights matched by responsibilities. We will rebuild the welfare state around a work ethic; work for those who can; security for those who cannot ... Our ambition is

[16] R Plant, 'So you Want to be a Citizen?', *New Statesman*, 6 February, 1998, 30.
[17] P Dwyer, *Welfare Rights and Responsibilities* (Bristol, Policy Press, 2000) 57.
[18] Dwyer, *Welfare Rights* (2000) 95.

> nothing less than a change of culture among benefit claimants, employers and public servants – with rights and responsibilities on all sides.[19]

In Britain, the trend towards greater emphasis on personal responsibility and conditionality has continued, indeed accelerated, after the New Labour Government was replaced first by a coalition then by a wholly Conservative government.

Special issues concerning rights and responsibilities arise in relation to children. When, as stated earlier, the UN Convention on the Rights of a Child places primary responsibility for the welfare of children on parents this was not without difficulties.

First, families may break down; parents may separate, one or both may die, one or both parents may disclaim responsibility for a child, or they may be abusive. Second, even with adequate income – which many families do not have – this does not mean that enough is necessarily spent on the child(ren); alcohol, drugs or gambling may take precedence. What then protects child rights? The sad answer is that, in many cases, little does: the extended family may provide support or, in extreme cases, child protection authorities may take a child into care – a drastic step with wide-ranging effects on the child.

What governments in most developed economies do is assist families to have an adequate income through child benefit schemes. Children not only incur costs of food, clothing, heating, holidays, phones, computers and much else; they also incur time costs in caring for them, which inevitably reduce earnings. The time costs of children are reduced by compulsory schooling – although longer half-terms and training days for teachers impose greater time costs on parents. The widespread development of childcare and greater public subsidy for it, as shown by Ludovica Gambaro and others,[20] does allow more time for parents to take paid work. For the child, high-quality childcare assists socialisation and preparation for schooling, but poor-quality childcare, sometimes likened to warehousing, may harm rather than benefit the child.

The reliance on parents for maintaining children's rights assumes competent parenting. In many cases preparation for parenting has, however, been seriously inadequate. One explanation for poor parenting is that, as families have become smaller, living more isolated, less communal lives, children have less opportunity to observe and serve an informal apprenticeship in parenting – which on any reckoning is a most challenging occupation. The British education system spends more time teaching children how to solve quadratic equations than about parenting. Since the rights of children depend on their parents' capacity to be parents, this is a puzzling situation.

For the rights of a child to be successfully realised, parents must have developed the skills needed to act as responsible parents, or at least some of them, and

[19] Department of Social Security, 'New Ambitions for our Country: A New Contract for Welfare' (London, HMSO, 1998) 1, 24.

[20] L Gambaro, K Stewart and J Waldfogel, *An Equal Start?* (Bristol, Policy Press, 2014).

have the income necessary to support their children. Both these are fundamental to ensuring a social minimum for children.

IV. POVERTY AND POLICY IN ADVANCED ECONOMIES

The right to an income adequate for health and wellbeing – in effect a social minimum income – is a key right in the UN Declaration of Human Rights. How is it to be achieved in advanced economies? And how does it relate to other rights that are relevant to income such as the right to employment and the right to social security?

What is fundamental, and brings these questions together, is the extent and nature of the responsibility of the individual and of the state in ensuring a social minimum.

To simplify, a social minimum for all can be ensured in one of two ways:

- Path A – The social minimum is paid by the Government to all citizens regardless of their circumstances, financed by taxation on other income.
- Path B – Employment is provided for all those able to work, paid at the level of the social minimum or above, while those who cannot work receive the social minimum through the social security system.

Under Path A, the primary responsibility lies with the Government, but all have responsibility to pay taxes to pay for the social minimum. Under Path B, those who can have a responsibility to take paid work while the Government has responsibility to ensure employment for all who can work and to provide social security for those who cannot.

In effect, Paths A and B are both capable of ensuring a social minimum and both rely on rights set out in the UN's Declaration – but different rights.

The reason these different paths have been set out is because they relate to one of the central current debates concerning the future of social policy. Path A broadly corresponds to the idea of introducing a Universal Basic Income. Path B relies on an enhanced labour market with a revived social security system.

The attraction of Path A is that all would automatically receive the social minimum. The major problem is that this minimum would be paid to everyone and would therefore be far more expensive than existing social security, and this would create a responsibility on all to pay much higher tax rates. Further, many would not support paying the social minimum to everyone without any test of age, disability or willingness to work. On the other hand, some foresee a drastic decline in employment with the spread of digital technology and robots, so that requiring people to work may be pointless.

The attraction of Path B is that state support is focused on those unable to work due to illness or disability or being over pension age. Those now unemployed and unable to find work would, if the state guaranteed employment, be able and required to work. The cost of Path B would be far lower than for Path A.

Discussion of a Universal Basic Income is, however, more complicated than the simplified comparison of two paths to a social minimum presented here.

First, proposals for a Universal Basic Income vary greatly. Some are for a full basic income that could replace most of social security. Other proposals are for a partial basic income that would operate alongside social security. If a basic income replaced social security and the poorest were not to be made worse off, providing an adequate basic income to everyone would be extremely expensive and would involve massive increases in tax rates. A basic income at a level that is only adequate in combination with social security would be less costly, but it would not achieve the goal of meeting the right to an adequate income through a basic income alone. Whether a basic income was full or partial, if it were universal it would be paid to all, including those who are not remotely poor; inevitably, in terms of tackling poverty, a universal basic income would be economically inefficient.

Second, some envisage a universal basic income operating alongside existing social services. For others the attraction of a social minimum defined solely in terms of money income is that one minimum might in effect discharge all the state's obligations: the American neoconservative Charles Murray[21] sees a minimum income as replacing existing social services and leaving individuals to provide for their own and their family's education and health; it is intended to roll back the state and encourage or impose private choice and personal responsibility. Critics of Murray recognise that leaving children entirely to the responsibility, or irresponsibility, of parents would not of course mean that all children would be worse off, but it would certainly expose many to severe deprivation in childhood and throughout life. Thus thinking about a social minimum cannot be reduced to achieving a certain money income but must involve many dimensions – reduced here to money income, education and health.

Necessarily, retaining social security, as Path B entails, involves conditions or responsibilities and these may be oppressive and unjust. Stuart White[22] explained the issues clearly: if the Government makes welfare benefits conditional on taking any job offered, then avoiding exploitative or abusive jobs is hard; if a parent ignores a work-conditionality rule then the cost will be borne not only by the parent but also by his or her children; if work-conditionality is appropriate what about the wealthy who can live comfortably without any need to work?

It is claimed that a basic income could avoid invidious conditions, but this is at a price. Why should someone with an interesting, well-paid job be free to give it up and get a social minimum income while making no contribution to the economy or society? Why should someone with an uninteresting, poorly paid

[21] C Murray, *Guaranteed Income as a Replacement for the Welfare State* (Oxford, Foundation for Law, Justice and Society, 2006).

[22] S White, 'Social Minimum' in EN Zalta (ed), *The Stanford Encyclopedia of Philosophy* (2015), available at plato.stanford.edu/archives/win2015/entries/social-minimum.

job be required to pay tax to support such a lifestyle of someone with better opportunities than they have? Such inherent injustices of a full universal basic income cast grave doubt on whether taxpayers would be willing to meet the cost.

There are of course threats and uncertainties about future job prospects. In the medium-to-long term the potential impact of robots is perhaps the biggest concern. Some, including several who have made colossal fortunes in Silicon Valley, see no prospect of future full employment and regard a basic income as a means of supporting those not wanted as productive workers. Yet this is a prescription for a two-class world of, first, citizens who own or operate the robots and, second, those who are pensioned off as soon as they leave school – such second-class citizens, unemployed and unemployable, were graphically described as 'the useless class' by Harari.[23]

The right to work remains a crucial, if neglected, right. The goal of genuine full employment was once central to government policies, but in many advanced economies it has now in effect been set aside. Yet without full employment, the right to work is purely notional. As argued here, the *right* to work with, in appropriate cases, an associated *responsibility* to work, is essential if a social minimum is to be achieved.

V. GLOBAL POVERTY AND POLICY

Human rights are, in principle, for all humans. The goals in the 1948 UN Declaration, extended in the UN's Sustainable Development Goals in 2015,[24] not only included the ending of poverty but also zero hunger, good health and well-being, quality education, gender equality, clean water and sanitation, and decent work. Whether in terms of rights or development goals, it is clear that human aspirations transcend national borders and on a global scale far exceed achievement.

Poverty in developing countries is, first, the responsibility of their own governments. The policies they have pursued for good and ill are, however, far beyond the scope of this chapter. Here the focus is on the role of advanced nations with respect to global poverty.

Poverty in advanced economies can potentially be ended by redistribution from those better-off to those who fall below a social minimum. In much of the world, however, a large proportion of the population is below or close to a social minimum and it is not feasible to end poverty through internal redistribution alone. For global poverty to be ended there must, as the UN description of the Sustainable Development Goals puts it, be economic growth that is inclusive to provide sustainable jobs and greater equality. This requires investment in

[23] YN Harari, 'The New Opium of the Masses', *The Guardian*, 8 May 2017.
[24] United Nations, 'Sustainable Development Goals Reports' (New York, United Nations, 2016).

education and health, improved infrastructure and opportunities to trade, as well as stable and just governments.

The question arises of what are the responsibilities of advanced economies and their governments to assist the end of global poverty and ensure a right for all in the world to a social minimum. This section discusses these responsibilities.

David Miller, in his book on *National Responsibility and Global Justice*, outlines two concepts of responsibility:

> Remedial responsibility starts with patients – people who are deprived or suffering – and asks who should shoulder the burden of helping them .... We are vulnerable creatures whose lives may not be worth living unless others are willing to come to our aid and supply us with resources.
>
> Outcome responsibility starts with agents ... human beings are choosing agents able to control their actions and to take responsibility for the results. For such agency to exist they must be willing to bear losses and enjoy gains.[25]

The first of these concepts – remedial responsibility – is well illustrated with a parallel drawn by Peter Singer; he wrote:

> I begin with the assumption that suffering and death from lack of food, shelter and medical care are bad ... if it is in our power to prevent something bad from happening, without thereby sacrificing anything of comparable moral importance, we ought, morally to do it. An application of this principle would be as follows: if I am walking past a shallow pond and see a child drowning in it, I ought to wade in and pull the child out. This will mean getting my clothes muddy, but this is insignificant, while the death of a child would presumably be a very bad thing.[26]

Miller has concerns about Singer's argument and applies his distinction between outcome and remedial responsibility:

> First, Singer asks no questions about outcome responsibility for global poverty: he does not ask why so many are poor, whether responsibility lies with rich nations, with the governments of poor nations, etc. – he treats poverty as if it were a natural phenomenon like an earthquake. Second, Singer has an implicit theory of remedial responsibility, namely that we are each remedially responsible for all the suffering we can prevent without sacrificing anything of comparable importance. The mere capacity to prevent suffering is by itself sufficient to assign responsibility.[27]

Whether we all should have a remedial responsibility and redistribute privately via charities or collectively via overseas aid, the fact is that such redistribution is very limited. Overseas aid in most western countries amounts to less than the target level of 0.7 per cent of national income, and much of it is

[25] D Miller, *National Responsibility and Global Justice* (Oxford, University Press, 2007) 108.
[26] P Singer, 'Famine, Affluence and Morality' (1972) 1 *Philosophy and Public Affairs* 231.
[27] Miller, *National Responsibility* (2007) 237.

distributed to achieve goals far removed from tackling poverty. Private support for poverty relief is closely linked to specific events – famines, natural disasters and wars – and is in most cases a small fraction of government overseas aid. There seems little likelihood of a major expansion of overseas aid and the prospect of an international tax system paying for a global social minimum seems a utopian dream.

A further concern about international humanitarian relief – the equivalent of accepting remedial responsibility – is the ability of aid agencies, however well-intentioned, and the ability of poverty-stricken states to handle poverty relief. As Alan Ryan has written:

> Humanitarian intervention will surely continue to be one of the great unresolved issues both in international ethics and in state practice. The duty to save the innocent from ill-usage gives the moral upper hand to interventionists, while the difficulty of intervening intelligently gives the prudential upper hand to their opponents.[28]

The past record of overseas aid is not unquestioned. William Easterly reviewed the record of western nations' attempts to end world poverty in his book, *The White Man's Burden*, which he sub-titled 'Why the West's efforts to aid the rest have done so much ill and so little good'. He wrote:

> Aid won't make poverty history, which Western aid efforts cannot possibly do. Only the self-reliant efforts of poor people and poor societies themselves can end poverty, borrowing ideas and institutions from the West when it suits them to do so.[29]

What then of outcome responsibility? Are advanced economies responsible for the poverty of nations?

Robert Nozick in his influential work, *Anarchy, State and Utopia*,[30] argued that if goods were justly acquired, without force or fraud, then the present distribution is just, no matter how unequal it is. His work is cited by many neoconservatives who argue that only the most minimal state intervention is justified. Taxation, he argued, is effectively theft, since it deprives individuals of property that they are entitled to, providing they have been obtained by free and fair exchange. Given much less attention is what Nozick wrote about unjust acquisition. If past or present acquisitions were unjust – involving stealing, fraud, enslavement or forcibly excluding some people from exchanges – then, Nozick argued, a principle of rectification is necessary. Unfortunately, he did not explain with any precision the circumstances in which acquisition could be judged unjust.

It can be argued, and many historians do so, that much global poverty is attributable to the impact of slavery and colonialism, particularly on African

[28] A Ryan, *On Politics* (London, Allen Lane, 2012) 1006.
[29] W Easterly, *The White Man's Burden* (Oxford, University Press, 2006) 334.
[30] R Nozick, *Anarchy, State and Utopia* (New York, Basic Books, 1971).

and Asian nations. There is, on this view, an outcome responsibility on those in advanced nations whose current prosperity is based on past acquisitions gained by force or fraud. For examples: the wealth of Jardine Matheson in Hong Kong was based on the illegal trade in opium backed by the British Government; Cecil Rhodes' fortune was based on manipulation and British military force in southern Africa; King Leopold's power and wealth in the Congo were based on subjugation and slavery – indeed the Congo has been successively or simultaneously exploited for ivory, rubber, diamonds, gold, copper, cobalt and, most recently, coltan for use in electronics devices. Have such activities been 'legal' and just? Have they fostered economic growth and contributed to ending poverty?

Past actions have created outcomes for which some degree of responsibility surely rests on advanced nations. But rectification for past actions presents many problems. How, for example, can the Aboriginal population of Tasmania be compensated when that population was wiped out? It is perhaps easier to focus on the present and focus on outcome responsibilities when current actions jeopardise human rights and make ending poverty a more distant goal.

Some assume that almost all current political and economic relationships are beneficial to all, including the poorest. Others point to ways in which advanced nations and their corporations do not respect human rights and contribute to continuing poverty. For example:

- selling goods through corrupt practices, undermining corporate and government probity;
- selling dangerous goods, including unhealthy drugs and weapons;
- polluting air and water in production of goods for consumption in advanced nations;
- dispossessing poor farmers of their land, for example to produce beef for advanced nations;
- condoning tax havens that undermine government tax-collection and provide resorts for fraudulent politicians to amass secret fortunes;
- contributing to climate change that most seriously endangers the poorest and least mobile; and
- recruiting highly skilled professionals, such as doctors and scientists, with no compensation to their country of origin and training.

All these activities, which are all-too common, have outcomes that contribute to global poverty. Yet advanced economies rarely take responsibility for the outcomes of such policies and the losses they cause. When, for example, bribery is condoned – even when it is contrary to national laws and notions of corporate responsibility – undermining good governance and contributing to poverty at the bottom of the power structure, the 'rationale' is often offered that, since others do it, we must do it too – an ethically indefensible argument.

Insofar as current political and economic relations, and the policies that underlie these relations, contribute to global poverty, this creates an outcome responsibility to remedy the poverty created – or, at the very least, stop the activities that damage the poorest nations. Most advanced economies and corporations have yet to acknowledge that responsibility and take it on fully, if at all. When it is, there will be a much-improved prospect of ending poverty and ensuring a social minimum for all.

VI. CONCLUSIONS

The assertion of human rights is, quite literally, wishful thinking. Yet wishes drive human behaviour. For some prominent world leaders, those wishes are for wealth beyond the dreams of avarice, personal aggrandisement and control of others. Others wish for a world in which all can enjoy clean water, all children can be educated and everyone can have at least a social minimum level of living – wishes that have been expressed as human rights. To move from the assertion of human rights to their realisation involves, as this chapter has stressed, responsibilities – whether we call these duties, obligations or the satisfaction of conditions. These responsibilities may rest on the state, on citizens as members of communities, on parents and on individuals. Only if these associated responsibilities are met, can rights be achieved.

This chapter has attempted to show how different routes towards the goal of ending poverty involve different distributions of responsibilities and have different prospects of success in realising the goal of ending poverty and the right for all to have a social minimum. That right will, however, remain merely wishful thinking unless its importance for people's lives is widely understood and there is a just distribution of responsibilities for that right.

Within nations, it has been argued that responsibilities should not only fall on the state but should also be borne by those who can and should bear individual, family or community responsibility. Rather than suggesting that everyone should be provided with a universal basic income, as some have proposed, the right to an adequate income for all is better achieved by ensuring for most the opportunity to work in a decent job for a decent income with decent childcare facilities, and the responsibility on individuals to do that work; for those who cannot work and those with extra needs what is necessary is a fair social security system. These are rights specified in the UN's Declaration and Sustainable Development Goals, but they are far from universally available.

Global poverty may to some degree be alleviated by redistribution from richer to poorer nations motivated by humanitarian responsibility, but this is unlikely to be sufficient to end global poverty. What is likely to have a more substantial global impact is the promotion of sustainable economic growth and better governance with governments and corporations from rich as well as poor countries taking responsibility for the outcomes of many of their activities that at present are responsible for, and sustain, poverty.

The right of all individuals, adults and children, to survive is the most fundamental of human rights. Without it, no other rights have any real meaning. Survival depends on ensuring a social minimum for all. While human rights and the distribution of responsibilities for them are not straightforward, unless they are thought about clearly they are unlikely to be realised. Failure to end poverty and realise a social minimum for all will undermine not only the justice but also the stability of all human societies.

10

The Legal Status of Recipients of Public Assistance

FRANS PENNINGS

I. INTRODUCTION

THE PREVIOUS CHAPTERS discussed the concepts and methods for defining a social minimum. In this chapter the legally enforceable social minimum benefit – *public assistance benefit* – is discussed. Of interest for us is the legal status of the benefit recipients, by which is meant the overall character of the rights, duties and responsibilities of a person. Since the level of this type of benefit and conditions for eligibility and for continuing to receive this benefit vary extremely from country to country, we will not describe these here. However, what interests us is whether there are specific characteristics of these right and duties that can be said to be linked to the position of recipient of a public assistance benefit. Such recipients are, after all, in a special position: on the one hand, they receive the benefit on the basis of solidarity from society, in other words it is not based on contributions; on the other, it is a safety net benefit, ie if it is refused then there is 'nothing else'.

This chapter will focus on developments in Western European countries, where public assistance provisions were introduced, in one way or another, centuries ago, and have since developed into a tight legal framework. This has led, in principle, to legal certainty for benefit recipients. Such a system can, however, also impose very strict conditions that can lead to sanctions if the conditions are not observed. This can seriously impact on the legal status of benefit recipients. I will go into the theoretical background of benefit conditions for minimum income recipients in section II. After this I will take the Dutch situation as a case study. In this country the legal certainty for public assistance recipients has increased over time. However, the conditions for public assistance have also been tightened in recent years and heavy sanctions can be imposed in case of particular behaviours. An analysis of this interaction in the case study gives a good insight into the legal status of public assistance recipients, the various dimensions of conditionality, and how conditionality can be controlled by criteria developed in case law. Indeed, the role of the judiciary was the reason for employing the Netherlands as a case study.

The chapter is construed as follows. It begins by discussing the relationship between conditionality and a minimum income. Section III describes how over time the legal status of public assistance claimants changed from pure dependency without any rights to a position with legally enforceable rights. Section IV introduces the case study: it describes the development of an enforceable right to social assistance in the Netherlands. Section V describes how in the Netherlands conditionality has been given a 'modern' meaning by requiring counteractivities from public assistance recipients. This form of conditionality is typical for subsistence benefits and can have a significant impact on the legal position of the benefit recipients. Section VI concerns a second aspect of conditionality, ie the sanctions in cases where benefit recipients have not followed the rules. Section VII will draw conclusions from this analysis and we will come back to the notions of section II. Section VIII provides some conclusions.

II. THE RELATIONSHIP BETWEEN CONDITIONALITY AND PUBLIC ASSISTANCE

Conditionality is a phenomenon, since it is more than the sum of the conditions for a particular benefit. After all, no benefits are completely unconditional; a citizens' basic income[1] can be considered as such, but this is still in the stage of experiments and defining objectives. However, the crux of conditionality is that conditions can have the intention of pushing a person in a certain direction. In that sense, conditions of aid to developing countries by the IMF or conditions related to access of new Member States to the EU have been discussed and criticised for having a significant impact on applicants.

An interesting discussion on the relationship between conditionality and minimum incomes can be found in the work of Stuart White.[2] White discusses conditionality as imposing requirements on the behaviour of the recipients. Conditions on behaviour are of a special kind, since there is a risk that persons are forced to do work of a very low character and or that their dignity is infringed. White starts by discussing the statement that if a minimum income is a social right, it must be unconditional. He rejects this statement, however, and clarifies that a right to a minimum income does not mean a right to be *given*

[1] https://citizensincome.org.

[2] S White, 'Should a Minimum Income be Unconditional?' in S Civitarese Matteuci and S Halliday (eds), *Social Rights in an Age of austerity* (London, Routledge, 2018).

a minimum income, but a right of *reasonable access* to a minimum income.[3] From a legal standpoint, this is a remarkable distinction. After all, as noted above, most, if not all, rights to benefits are conditional. Also for the right to unemployment benefit, for example, it is generally required, inter alia, that one is not voluntarily unemployed, that one has not refused work and that one is looking for work. So conditions do not take away the character of the right to benefit. The term 'reasonable access' is a problematic from a legal perspective, since it may give room to the benefit administration to grant benefits or not. In other words, the legal character itself does not mean that there are no conditions for the right, but it means that if these conditions are fulfilled, there is a legally enforceable right to this benefit. However, the exact character of the conditions is relevant and conditionality in public assistance may become controversial, in particular, when its character differs from that of other types of benefit. This is the so-called conditionality creep, ie the risk that by broadening the conditions for benefit, the legal position of benefit recipients is seriously undermined.[4]

White continues by discussing the justifications for conditionality and which limits can be set to conditions. This makes it very interesting for our purpose. One ground for conditionality he mentions is paternalism; the other is fairness.

The paternalistic ground is that conditionality is justified since it is good for the welfare recipient. For instance, requiring them to work is good for one's well-being. The fairness argument dictates that the required behaviour is fair to other members of the society. The other members may expect that the benefit recipient tries to avoid benefit dependency (ie is 'self-sufficient'). Another, different, argument for fairness is *reciprocity*: as a matter of fairness, persons owe society a reasonable productive contribution in return for minimum income.

White mentions some conditions for conditionality. His first condition is that reciprocity-based work obligations must be applied consistently (for everybody receiving the benefit) and equitably (this requires due process and protection from unreasonable requirements). 'Those subject to conditionality must have adequate rights to challenge decisions made about their eligibility and not stand at the mercy of bureaucratic judgment.'[5]

It might, however be, White argues, that, when such conditions on conditionality are not satisfied, and conditionality is therefore unjust, that the disputed condition can still be justified by paternalistic reasons: doing this work is good

[3] White, 'Minimum Income' (2018) 182.

[4] See also G Vonk, 'Repressive Welfare State, the Spiral of Obligations and Sanctions' (2014) 16 *European Journal of Social Security* 188. Vonk refers to P Dwyer, 'Creeping Conditionality in the UK: From Welfare Rights to Conditional Entitlements?' (2004) 29 *Canadian Journal of Sociology* 265.

[5] White (n 2) 185.

for them. However, such justification has to be examined very critically. After the discussion of the Dutch developments later in this chapter I will come back to these concepts.

III. THE DEVELOPMENT OF AN ENFORCEABLE RIGHT TO PUBLIC ASSISTANCE

A. A Short Overview of the Period before the Second World War

Probably the earliest official policy principles regarding poor relief were developed in Great Britain, where a Poor Law Commission was established by the Government to investigate the situation of providing relief to the poor, including persons with a low income. The findings of this research were published in the famous Poor Law Report of 1834.[6] The Poor Law Commission concluded that, since the lowest wages lay below the poverty rates under the Poor Law at that time, many people preferred to remain out of work. As a response to this the Commission introduced the infamous 'less eligibility' principle: the situation of an applicant for relief should not be made 'really or apparently as eligible' (in the terms of the report) as that of the independent labourer of the lowest class.[7] From now on public assistance should only be available for those whose neediness was proved by their willingness to accept the harsh regime of the workhouse. In the workhouse the circumstances had to be less eligible than in the lowest-paid jobs. This was to be realised by rules stipulating that residents wear special clothes, that members of a family were separated from each other, that visitors were not allowed, and that smoking and drinking were prohibited. A stay in the workhouse was to be as unpleasant as possible. It was not intended to reduce poverty, but to deter pauperism.[8] Thus the history of public social assistance started with an outspoken view on conditionality for its claimants.

Although the British populace was heavily opposed to these proposals and there were several demonstrations against the Act – in pamphlets the workhouses were nicknamed Bastilles[9] – the Poor Law Amendment Act of 1834 was modelled on the less eligibility principle.

However, in practice, the eligibility principle could not be applied as consistently as intended, for the Act met both problems of principle and practice. This was due to the fact that temporary unemployment was almost inevitable for the working class. The Act was in any case inappropriate for industrial areas, since there were simply too many unemployed to place them all in workhouses.

[6] See, on the research method and its critics, SG and EOA Checkland (eds), *The Poor Law Report of 1834* (Harmondsworth, Penguin, 1974).

[7] Note that this principle does not regard the question of whether a claimant is eligible, but of whether the conditions for assistance are attractive to the claimant.

[8] D Fraser, *The Evolution of the British Welfare State* (London, Palgrave, 1973) 43.

[9] M Bruce, *The Coming of the Welfare State* (London, Batsford, 1973) 39.

For this reason, soon after the introduction of the amended Act, assistance was also provided outside the workhouse.[10] In order to test the eligibility for those who could not be placed in a workhouse, a labour test was applied: assistance was only given to participants in work projects. It fits well in the ideological approach to relief that these projects had to be less eligible than the lowest-paid work in the labour market.

Also in other West-European countries, eg the Netherlands and Germany, relief recipients were regarded with suspicion in the nineteenth and first half of the twentieth century. They were often required to work in a workhouse if they were able-bodied or in special work projects, the work often being meaningless, meant only to keep them away from idleness and to make sure they really saw no alternative to asking for relief.[11]

It is not the objective of this section to give a full overview of the history of public assistance, but to show that recipients of this benefits were treated in a specific way. They were deterred from claiming support by being obliged to work, even if there was no real work available for them.

B. Developments in Views on Conditionality

Gradually, in the course of the nineteenth century, the poor and workhouse approaches disappeared. It took some time, however, before states began to acknowledge that providing assistance was a public obligation. In the Netherlands, for instance, poor relief was primarily seen as a task for private organisations, such as churches and charities. In such a system, the decision to actually provide relief depended on the discretion of volunteers working for such organisations. In order to assess whether the applicants really deserved the relief, these volunteers often investigated the private situation of applicants and examined how clean the house was, how the children were educated, whether alcohol was used, etc. If they came to the conclusion that the applicant was an 'undeserving poor person' (ie a poor person not deserving relief) there were no legal ways to challenge the rejection of the relief application.

In particular, the harsh economic crisis in the 1930s made politicians and economists aware that economic developments were decisive in relation to the existence and extent of unemployment and poverty.[12] The attitude to poverty

[10] In 1854 84% of the received assistance outside the workhouse; Fraser, *Evolution* (1973) 48.

[11] See for Germany, B Klees, *Arbeitslosigkeit und Recht, ein Handbuch zur Gegenwehr* (Frankfurt/M, Nachrichten-Verlags-Gesellschaft, 1984) 101; A Faust, 'Der Staat und die Arbeitslosigkeit in Deutschland 1890–1918; 'Arbeitsvermittlung, Arbeitsbeschaffung und Arbeitslosenversicherung' in W Mommsen and W Mock, *Die Entstehung des Wohlfahrtsstaates in Großbritannien und Deutschland 1850–1950* (Stuttgart, Klett-Cotta, 1982). For the Netherlands, see P de Rooy, *Werklozenzorg en werkloosheidsbestrijding 1917–1940. Landelijk en Amsterdams Beleid* (Amsterdam, Van Gennep, 1979).

[12] This was, for instance, the case in the UK, W Beveridge, *Unemployment: a Problem of Industry* (London, Longmans, 1909 and 1930), but also in the Netherlands.

changed, and several schemes were introduced to keep people out of social assistance. Insurance schemes for the risks of old age, surviving the breadwinner, unemployment, sickness and disability were developed, and these were important for keeping people out of poverty and poverty relief.

Insurance benefits fitted into the prevailing ideology that people have to help themselves by their own efforts. The right to benefit, based on previous contributions of the individual, was regarded as a contractual right[13] and contributions were seen as an instrument to select the genuine unemployed. 'Armed with (the) double weapon of a maximum limit to benefit and of a minimum contribution, the operation of the scheme itself will automatically exclude the loafer.'[14]

The contributory principle was seen as an instrument by means of which benefit were only payable to persons who had been regularly employed, as only they would be able to satisfy the contribution conditions. By means of the contributory principle, a distinction was made between the 'truly unemployed' and those in casual work.

Such instrument does, by definition, not exist for public assistance. Therefore it is hard to prevent populists from demanding a paternalistic and minimalistic treatment of public assistance recipients, even if such treatment does not really solve the (poverty) problem. The history of inadequate treatment of persons hit by the severe and long crisis in the 1930s led to an ambition, which flourished during the Second World War, to have a better society, and public assistance gradually came be seen as an indispensable part of the welfare state, a safety net for those for whom there were no other means.

IV. THE DEVELOPMENT OF THE LEGAL CHARACTER OF THE DUTCH PUBLIC ASSISTANCE BENEFIT

In the Netherlands, the confirmation of a legal right to public assistance was for the first time realised in the Public Assistance Act of 1965. Initially this Act did not grant a right to benefit, but imposed an obligation on the municipality where the person lived to pay benefit if the conditions set out in the Act were fulfilled. A decision by the municipality on a claim could be appealed by the claimant to a higher administrative body (ie not a formal court). In practice this meant that there was a legal right to this benefit if the conditions were fulfilled.

In the Dutch Constitution of 1983 (Article 20) it was laid down that persons of Dutch nationally who cannot provide for their own subsistence costs

[13] AI Ogus, 'Great Britain' in P Köhler and H Zacher (ed), *The Evolution of Social Insurance 1881–1981* (London, etc, Frances Pinter, 1982) 183.

[14] Quoted in W Beveridge, *Unemployment: a Problem of Industry* (London, Longmans, 1909 and 1930) 265.

have a right to public assistance according to the rules laid down in an Act. Subsequently, the Public Assistance Act of 1995 was revised so that:

> Each person of Dutch nationality who in the Netherlands is in such circumstances, or threatens to become in such circumstances, that he or she does not have the means for providing in the necessary costs of living is entitled to public assistance.[15]

In this way an enforceable right was now fully acknowledged. If an application for benefit is rejected or a decision is made that a claimant wants to challenge, he or she can, after having followed a review procedure in the municipality, appeal to a court of first instance; the applicant can appeal from that lower court's decision to a higher court, the *Centrale Raad van Beroep* (Central Appeals Court), which is for most issues in the social security field the highest court. The procedural rules are those of the *Algemene wet bestuursrecht* (General Act on Administrative Law), being the same for all types of social security and other areas of administrative law.

The Dutch Public Assistance Act provides that one is eligible for public assistance if one does not have the means for the necessary costs of living. This suggests that in any individual case an assessment is made. However, since 1974 the Public Assistance Act (or decrees based on this Act) prescribes the applicable benefit rates for defined types of households. Moreover, the applicable public assistance rate for a couple (married or not) was connected to that of the statutory minimum wage. One can conclude that the idea of 'less eligibility' was completely left in this regard. Although it was in later times disputed whether this connection with the minimum wage was to be maintained, because it made accepting work at minimum wage level less attractive, the connection has survived and is frequently referred to as a 'a principle of civilisation'. In order to encourage taking up work, the solution was found in giving tax cuts for persons in work, thus creating differences in net income between persons in work and benefit recipients.

The objective of these rules on the benefit levels is to create legal certainty. The Public Assistance Act or Regulations based on the Act mention detailed rules for when the standard rates can be increased in individual situations (eg in case of extra costs) or lowered (eg if a benefit recipient has lower costs because of living with other persons). The Act also gives detailed rules on the means test on income and capital and specifies the obligations to seek work, which resemble to a large extent those of unemployment benefit.

This statutory framework for eligibility and conditions for access to public assistance has meant that the legal character of this benefit is regulated in a way that is to a very large extent comparable to that of other social security benefits.

Although much more can be said about the development and application of the Dutch public assistance rules, we can be clear that in the 1970s in the

[15] Act on the revision of the Public Assistance Act, Art 7.

Netherlands public assistance became part of a legal regime, in which there is a legal right to public assistance when conditions are fulfilled. Concepts undermining the legal status of the public assistance recipients, such as 'less eligibility', work tests and discretionary powers for the benefit authorities, have disappeared or have to a large extent been reduced, and are subject to judicial control.

V. THE INCREASED CONDITIONALITY BY REQUIRING COUNTERACTIVITIES

A. The Introduction of Obligations to Perform Unpaid Work

Even though the legal character of public assistance has approached that of social security benefits to a large extent, every now and then attempts can be seen to treat beneficiaries differently from other benefit recipients. Before discussing these attempts, it has to be acknowledged that for a considerable group of public assistance recipients it is very hard to enter or re-enter he labour market. Lack of qualifications, physical or psychological problems and/or their private situation make it difficult for them to take up work. For these persons sheltered workplaces and work experience schemes were established in the twentieth century. Under such schemes participants had an employment relationship with corresponding labour rights, including a statutory minimum wage (or higher than that minimum if provided so in collective labour agreements).[16] However, in the 1990s these work experience schemes were terminated. The idea behind the schemes was that as a result of the work experience obtained in subsidised jobs participants acquire abilities and experiences useful for the regular labour market. When it appeared that very few of the participants actually found work in the regular (ie non-subsidised) market, these subsidised work schemes were seen as a failure and abolished. Since then, all benefit recipients, regardless of their position, have to do their best to find work in the regular labour market. However, for a considerable group of benefit recipients there are no real prospects of finding work, because they are or feel incapacitated for work or are not employable in the regular labour market.[17]

Instead of re-introducing the sheltered work and subsidised job schemes, the Dutch Government found it 'unacceptable' that benefit recipients remained 'idle' for a long time. It introduced the rule that they have to show their active participation in society and do something in return for their benefit. This approach

[16] See F Pennings, *Benefits of Doubt. A Comparative Study of the Legal Aspects of Employment and Unemployment Schemes in Great-Britain, Germany, France and the Netherlands* (Deventer, Kluwer Law International, 1990).

[17] In 2013 only 7.3% of the social assistance recipients found a job (https://joop.vara.nl/nieuws/bijstand-steeds-vaker-uitzichtloos). Currently, the economic situation is much better, but still it is hard for them to find work.

was expressed by the new name of the Public Assistance Act: *Participatiewet* (Participation Act), introduced in 2003.

The required activities can have two forms.

(a) One is the so-called *participation job*. The participation job is meant for persons who cannot be placed in a real job. It requires them to do, for a maximum period of two years, unpaid work, and this is supposed to help them to acquire work experience. Participation jobs must be additional to the regular labour market jobs, and must not substitute paid work. Those who refuse to cooperate can be subject to a sanction, which entails that they receive a lower benefit for a certain period.

Municipalities appear to have problems with finding work that can be done in a participation job. In order to create opportunities, a considerable number of municipalities[18] have made arrangements with private companies, so posting benefit recipients to regular employers. Participants remain in receipt of public assistance benefit while doing this work and receive an additional payment of two euros per hour.[19] The company pays compensation to the municipalities for the benefit recipients. For the municipality this cooperation is attractive, since its expenses for benefits are to a large extent compensated. The companies that post the workers are paid for this and employers have cheap labour. An example of such jobs are those in a mail distribution centre. It is obvious that these are not really outside the regular labour market; in other words, substitution of regular jobs is still a danger.[20]

Also under the old rules of the Public Assistance Act benefit recipients were required to extend their availability to any work they can do, but the new development is that the work is (almost) unpaid. Another problem is that since doing the job is supposed to increase work experience, the quality of work is important. However, not all the work that is provided has such quality, as it is often unskilled work. A third problem is that such work is often done on the regular labour market, which means that there may be a serious substitution problem.

(b) The second is that recipients of public assistance can be required to perform *unpaid work* that is not done in a job, but has a particular value for society. An example is accompanying elderly persons on shopping trips or visiting the theatre, or cleaning the buildings of amateur sports clubs. These measures are based on the view that public assistance recipients have to do something in return for their benefit. If they refuse to do this 'voluntary'

[18] A Eleveld, 'Flextensie en de Kwalificatie van de (Meerpartijen) Overeenkomst met de Re-integrerende Bijstandsgerechtigde', 2017 *Tra* no 38, mentions 50 municipalities working with this private company (in 2016).

[19] See further Eleveld (ibid) on the practices of this type of participation job.

[20] www.fnv.nl/sector-en-cao/alle-sectoren/publiek-belang/post-en-pakketten/postnl/nieuws/Wegwerpwerknemers-PostNL-hebben-recht-op-echte-baan-en-gelijk-loon (accessed 11 May 2017).

work, their benefit can be reduced.[21] Since this societal work does not have the form of a job and the work is unpaid, it may seriously affect the legal position of public assistance recipients. The requirement to do this work arose after the Second World War, and is different from the well-accepted conditions that they have to actively seek and accept suitable work.

B. Tests by the Courts

The question was raised before the Dutch courts whether the new obligations were consistent with the prohibition to subject persons to forced labour (inter alia in the European Convention for the Protection of Human Rights and Fundamental Freedoms (ECHR)). A first case concerned a public assistance recipient who, following academic study, remained unemployed and was obliged to participate in a programme of a municipality to perform work (type (a), discussed above).[22] He had to sign a work experience agreement to undertake, at his choice, either weeding and hoeing parks or packing boxes. He signed the agreement, but after a disagreement with his case manager, refused to continue to perform the activities, after which his benefit was reduced by 40 per cent during one month.

The court decided that the municipality had, by its the decision to reduce the benefit, not infringed Article 4 ECHR (forced labour). The following question was whether this was compulsory labour, also prohibited by Article 4 ECHR. The fact that the activities were not voluntarily done did not mean that this question was answered in the affirmative, since, the court argued, public assistance is a safety net that presumes a return to paid work as soon as possible. Within this framework a benefit recipient can be required to do unpaid work in order to obtain work experience and/or qualifications. However, the court added, this does not exclude the possibility that in some circumstances such first work projects infringe Article 4 ECHR. In this case the court considered that at the particular moment when the participant refused to continue his work, the activities had not yet constituted such a disproportional or excessive burden that they could for this reason already be considered compulsory labour in the sense of Article 4. However, such activities could become such a burden if a person has to perform work under the threat of benefit reduction and *it is completely clear that the activities do not have any positive impact on his reintegration in the regular labour market* [italics added for emphasis].

In another case, the Central Appeals Court (the court of second instance and highest court on social security issues, introduced in section III) further developed the limits within which public assistance recipients can be required

[21] Article 9(1)(c) Participatiewet.
[22] Court Arnhem 8 October 2008, ECLI:NL:RBARN:2008:BF7284.

to do work under the *Participatiewet*.[23] It considered that in this case the prohibition of slavery in the sense of Article 4(1) ECHR was not at stake.[24] Nor can it be called forced labour. In respect of the ECHR the question is therefore only whether the prohibition of compulsory labour is infringed. The Court considered that also an assessment of the possibilities of reintegration into work falls within the scope of compulsory work. A test whether a reintegration scheme is consistent with Article 4(2) ECHR has to take all the circumstances of the case into account, including essential parts of international law, and its interpretation by experts and the practice of the Member States. In this assessment the following four points are relevant:

(1) the nature, place, duration and working times of the activities to be performed under the scheme in relation to the possibilities, work experience, education and family situation of the person concerned;
(2) the duration of the unemployment of the person concerned;
(3) if and how the provision can contribute to the reintegration into work of the person concerned; and
(4) the level of the sanction in case of non-cooperation.

The court then considered that:

> Only if it can, in view of all the circumstances, not be required (anymore) from a candidate of a scheme to do the activities that are part of the scheme because of the excessive or disproportional character of these activities and/or a total lack of perspective for reintegration into work could there be a situation of compulsory work and could this be in conflict with Article 4 ECHR.

From this decision it follows that an individual approach is required when particular return activities under the scheme are required; general conditions cannot be applied. However, if work programmes do not have a clear reintegration objective, they are not allowed; moreover sanctions in case of non-cooperation must not be excessive.

In a later case, before a court of the first instance, a return activity for benefit was disputed. The court considered that from the Explanatory Memorandum of the Participation Act[25] it appeared that the activity has to be unpaid and useful to society. It does not have to be directly aimed at reintegration into work. The activity must not hinder reintegration into work, since reintegration into work has, in line with the Act, priority. The municipality has to decide in the individual case and in view of the available unpaid societal useful activities the nature, duration and extent of the activity. The extent of the activities and the duration have to have a fixed timeframe. In this case the objective of the scheme

[23] Central Appeals Court 8 February 2010, ECLI:NL:CRVB:2010:BL1093.
[24] The Court referred to the *Siliadin* judgment of the European Court of Human Rights (ECHR 26 July 2005, no 73316/01) to support this argument.
[25] Parliamentary papers 2011–212, 33.161, in force as from 1 January 2015.

was to acquire work experience and the activities had to be carried out for 32 hours a week for one year. Therefore, this scheme exceeded the conditions that can follow from a return activity that can be required, since this is no longer a limited activity. Moreover, the individual activities of the participants have to be taken into account. The municipality argued that the person was not restricted in his possibilities to do work, and therefore had to attend this project. However, the court decided that this approach was not individual enough. Therefore, the age, education, work experience and other relevant personal circumstances had to be taken into account. Moreover, the work experience scheme had not defined the work activities to be undertaken at all. For this reason the Court did not uphold the sanction imposed on the person concerned.[26]

This case law is helpful in setting limits to the requirements and thus protects the legal status of public assistance recipients. It has, however, certainly not diminished the effects of the new conditions on the legal position of benefit recipients fully, since only extreme cases have been redressed so far.

VI. THE INCREASED SANCTIONS IMPOSED ON BENEFIT RECIPIENTS UNDER DUTCH LAW

A second dimension concerns the sanctions that are applicable to benefit recipients.[27] In 1996 in the Netherlands, an Act was adopted on fines, measures and recovery of social security benefits. This act was meant to reinforce the sanction system and to force the benefit administration to require reimbursement of benefits in case of undue payment and to oblige them to impose a sanction in case benefit rules were not observed. The objective and system of the Act was that the rules were to be very strictly enforced.

The rules were tightened to a considerable degree in 2013 by the Act called Tightening and Enforcement of Public Assistance Sanctions. The Act introduced draconian sanctions in situations where beneficiaries had not given the relevant information that their circumstances had changed, such information having the potential to affect their benefit entitlement. Until that time, the maximum fine in case of fraud was 2,219 euros; under the new Act the fine became 100 per cent of the benefit sum that was involved. In other words, the fine is the gross amount of benefit that was unduly paid following a failure to make a declaration. For instance, if the person did not notify the benefit administration that he or she was no longer not eligible for child benefit since the child had found work, which led to undue payment of, say, 1,000 euros, not only does this undue benefit have to be reimbursed, but in addition a fine of 1,000 euros is imposed.

[26] Court Zeeland-West-Brabant 25 February 2013, ECLI:NL:RBZWB:2013:BZ5171.

[27] See, more generally on sanctions, M Adler, *Cruel, Inhuman or Degrading Treatment? Benefit Sanctions in the UK* (London, Palgrave, 2018).

Fines can be very high, particularly if a benefit has been unduly paid over several years. In case of a repeated infringement of the obligation to inform the benefit administration, the fine is 150 per cent of the amount of the undue benefit.[28]

Decisions following these new rules were disputed and were brought before Court. Again, the Central Appeals Court made a major correction to the rules.[29] The Court did not accept the basic rule that the fine must always be as high as the amount of the benefit that was unduly paid. Instead, the court ruled that the fine has to be adjusted to the individual situation of the public assistance recipient. It argued that since the sanctions were set so high, the Court must more strictly test whether the level of the fine is proportional to the rule that is not observed. This test is based on Article 6 ECHR, which has direct effect in the Dutch legal system.

The Court ruled that a standard sanction of 100 per cent is not consistent with the proportionality test. Instead, the individual situation of the person concerned has to be taken into account. A fine of 100 per cent can be imposed only if it can be shown by the municipality that the person concerned intentionally acted in order to receive a higher benefit by not giving the correct information. In case of gross negligence the fine can be 75 per cent. It is up to the municipality to demonstrate intentional act or gross negligence.

In case of 'normal' culpability the fine can only be 50 per cent. A lower fine (25 per cent) is possible in case of reduced culpability. It is up to the municipality to consider whether in the case concerned there is reduced culpability.

In the cases in which the Court developed its approach, it decided that in two cases the benefit recipients had the intention to get a higher benefit. They had consciously not informed the benefit administration that they had taken up work since they knew that this would affect their benefit. In these cases a fine of 100 per cent was allowed. In the third case the person concerned had not informed the benefit administration of his change of address. The municipality had, however, not demonstrated that the person had neglected this obligation on purpose. Therefore the Court reduced the fine to 50 per cent. In the fourth case the claimant had grown six hemp plants and not reported this. The fine was 100 per cent of the possible financial income from these plants, but it was reduced to 50 per cent by the Court. It took into account that the number of plants was relatively low, there had not been a criminal prosecution, and the claimant had consistently argued that the plants were for his personal use only and he had not harvested plants yet.

In this way the court made important changes to rules on the fines to be imposed and it took in its decision the individual situation into account. The legislature accepted this approach and codified it; it amended the law in

[28] Initially the Government even intended to exclude the beneficiary, in case of recidivism, for a period of five years. After a negative advice by the Council of State, the fine was set at 150%.

[29] Decision of 23 June 2015, ECLI:NL:CRVB:2015:1801.

order to implement the case law. The sanctions are still high, but the court decisions have considerably reduced them.

VII. ANALYSIS IN THE LIGHT OF THE CONDITIONS ON CONDITIONALITY

In the Dutch case the requirement of doing voluntary work was presented as 'giving something back to society'. In other words, it was based on the idea of reciprocity. However, this condition does not satisfy the requirement mentioned by White that it is applied equally to everybody. White argues that conditionality is justified if the conditions apply to everybody in society. Thus persons not working but living off the revenues of their assets have to be subject to this condition. Even if we consider this requirement to be too extreme (can all these groups compared in all respects?), we may expect this equal treatment as regards other benefit recipients, for instance of unemployment benefit. And even if that is not the case, we can expect that it is applied to all other public assistance recipients. However, all these expectations are not fulfilled. It appears that many municipalities do not enforce this obligation of doing voluntary work.[30]

White gives, in that situation, room for the paternalistic argument.

The requirement to do this 'voluntary work' is new, in any case since the Second World War, and is different from the well-accepted conditions that they have to actively seek and accept suitable work.

It appears from research that certainly not all participants are unhappy with their volunteer work. They receive more attention and more appreciation than when staying at home. In this respect, it is 'good for them'. However, it can mean, in the longer term, that both the volunteer organisation and the volunteers themselves want to continue the situation as the organisation needs the 'workers', and for the volunteer it is safe. As a result the distance to the labour market becomes even larger.[31] So the argument of what is good for them is at least ambiguous.

The other form of conditionality is that of working in an unpaid job. Also here the equal treatment condition is not satisfied. There appear to be big differences between municipalities. Secondly, the equitability principle is infringed. Persons can be put to meaningless work and for a long period, and large sanctions can be imposed if they refuse to accept this. Here the relevance of the judiciary control, described in the Dutch case, becomes clear. In any case, the courts have set some limits to this type of conditionality. The case law ensured

[30] www.binnenlandsbestuur.nl/sociaal/nieuws/szw-participatiewet-in-veel-gemeenten-niet.9570821.lynkx (accessed 31 January 2019).

[31] T Kampen, *Verplicht Vrijwilligerswerk. De Evaringen van Bijstandscliënten met een Tegenprestatie voor hun Uitkering*, dissertation (Amsterdam, University of Amsterdam, 2014).

a due process, control of the sanctions and examination of the work is not absolutely senseless. However, it is also clear that not all negative aspects of conditionality can be taken away by courts. Therefore, the criteria developed here should first and foremost be used by the legislature when defining the conditions for benefit.

The second dimension of conditionality described in the Dutch case study is that of the high sanctions in case of particular behaviours. These sanctions are much higher than in criminal law for comparable or even much more serious offences. If fines are imposed that are very much higher than the fines that would be imposed in criminal law, and if the difference between criminal and public assistance fines can be a factor of 10,000 or more, benefit recipients do not have the same protection as other groups in society and this seriously undermines their legal position. Moreover, the fines can lead to such high debts that the individual will never be able to honour them, which will lead to even more social exclusion. So the equality condition is not satisfied. The courts set clear limits to these, and reinforced a due process, by expressly stating that now that the sanctions were set so high, the Court must more strictly test whether the level of the fine is proportional to the rule that is not observed.

We can also see that the international conventions (the prohibition of compulsory labour, the right to a due process and the proportionality principle) are important to set conditions to the application of conditionality. Still, as Kotkas argues in chapter twelve, the test by courts is necessarily a formal one, so it remains to the legislature to elaborate its own criteria to justify conditionality. The criteria discussed here, derived from White, can be useful for this purpose.

In addition, it is desirable to place this within a broader perspective. As was discussed in section V A, in the Netherlands there are no longer subsidised jobs for those out of work. The rationale is that everybody should find work in the regular labour market. However, it appears that for some categories of recipients this is very difficult (in fact impossible) to have access to the labour market given, inter alia, their lack of employability, education and adjustment to the labour market and labour discipline. Most likely, in an ever more competitive world where automatisation and robotisation threaten many low-skilled jobs, this problem will even become larger.

One can object to such analysis, since it means that some individuals are given up for the labour market. However, the alternative is the present pressure on benefit recipients or, in other words, the increased conditionality. Therefore subsidised jobs that are suitable for the persons concerned, with a regular labour law position and wage, have important advantages and are a serious alternative for public assistance recipients. Since, after all, public assistance is under pressure because it is seen as a safety net only for those who cannot find work on the labour market, it is very well defensible that the solution has to be found in the labour market.

VIII. CONCLUSIONS

The 'less eligibility' principle was an important concept in the early predecessors of the present public assistance laws. Even if this principle was not mentioned as such in poor laws at the time, the idea was always that asking for relief was to be made very unattractive. This was an extreme form of conditionality, simply making receiving poor relief unattractive. Gradually, public assistance moved into the legal sphere and claimants were given a legally enforceable right. The obligation to seek and accept work is inherent to this benefit, in any case for those who can work, and in this it is not different from unemployment benefit. However, there are also forms of conditionality in the Netherlands that are typical for public assistance. It is more problematic for the legislature to give a justification for this than in the 'less eligibility' times; the enforcement is also more problematic. Is it to acquire work experience? Or to integrate in society? Or to give something back to society?

In any case, these forms of conditionality can mean that persons have to do meaningless work or volunteer work that does not help at all to enter or re-enter the labour market. Fighting idleness and/or requiring gratitude are objectives that are not connected with other benefit schemes, and if these are the justification for conditionality, they need very serious justifications (if they can be found). Otherwise they principally undermine the legal position of public assistance recipients.

Part 4

Securing a Social Minimum: The Role of Courts and Supervisory Bodies

11

Giving Legal Substance to the Social Minimum

COLM O'CINNEIDE

I. AN INTRODUCTORY NOTE – SETTING THE SCENE

THE CURRENT POLITICAL crisis which has engulfed the neoliberal political/economic orthodoxy of the last few decades has reopened serious debate about the social ordering of contemporary societies. Long-term socio-economic trends are also influencing this debate, especially factors related to the environment, globalisation and technological development. It is increasingly clear that the current socio-economic status quo in western liberal democracies is unsustainable – an insight which is generating some rich discussions across a variety of fields of intellectual activity.[1]

Law is no exception. Fifteen years ago, a tiny minority of legal scholars were interested in the relationship between political economy, social rights/equality claims, and the interlocking structures of public and private law regulation. That has changed – dramatically. Now, there exists intense debate about in particular the status and function of socio-economic rights (hereafter 'SER'), their relationship with other national and international legal standards, and whether and how legal protection of such rights can secure better social protection in liberal democracies.[2]

Despite all this intellectual activity, sceptical questions can be asked as to the desirability of legal rights featuring prominently in debates about how to secure the 'social minimum' (which, in common with other chapters in this book, is understood to refer to the floor of socio-economic protection that states should put into place to show adequate respect for the human dignity and equal status of their inhabitants). It could be argued that it is better for debates about social protection and the role of the state in securing the socio-economic well-being

[1] For a flavour of the rich and wide-ranging nature of these debates, see ch 5 (Adler) and ch 9 (Piachaud) in this volume.

[2] See eg ch 2 (Bilchitz), ch 16 (Boyle) and ch 13 (Warwick) in this volume.

of its inhabitants not to be contaminated with 'rights talk', given what Moyn has described as its 'individualistic and anti-statist' ethos.[3] The post-war European welfare states, which provided a floor of social protection arguably unmatched elsewhere in human history, were constructed with scant reference to the conceptual language of rights.[4] Is this language of rights – especially as articulated through an inevitably constrained and constricting legal vocabulary – really of any particular use when it comes to discussing ways of reimagining the concept of a social minimum for our marketised, fragmented, increasingly technology-disrupted society?[5]

It certainly would be foolish to place too much faith in the potential of legal rights discourse in particular to be a major weapon in the fight to secure a decent social minimum for all. The conceptual structure of legal human rights, which is predominantly focused on the dignity and status of individuals as understood through the lens of social contract theory, lacks the capacity to give full expression to the egalitarian, solidaristic and redistributionist values that in the final analysis provide the only stable foundation for a comprehensive system of social protection.[6] Furthermore, law tends to be an inefficient tool for achieving radical social change – which, as Adler and Piachaud emphasise in their contributions to this volume, is sorely needed. Legal actors are predominantly focused on maintaining stability and consistency within the functioning of the legal system rather than acting as agents of social transformation, while the rigidity and comparatively closed structure of the legal process makes it a poor vehicle for engaging with issues of social protection and economic redistribution.[7]

However, it would also be foolish to ignore the potency of rights discourse.[8] At both the political and legal levels, it can lend significant normative weight to moral claims that might otherwise be relegated to the status of 'politics as usual'. If effective ways could be found of bringing this normative weight to bear in the context of debates about the 'social minimum', this could bring

[3] S Moyn, *Not Enough? Human Rights in an Unequal World* (Cambridge, MA, Harvard University Press, 2018).

[4] See ch 12 by Kotkas in this volume; also, by the same author, 'The Short and Insignificant History of Social Rights Discourse in the Nordic Welfare States' in T Kotkas and K Veitch, *Social Rights in the Welfare State: Origins and Transformations* (London, Routledge, 2017) 15–34. However, note also by way of contrast, the interesting discussion in MR Madsen, 'Between the Law-State and the Welfare State: The Structural Limits of Legal-Political Liberalism in the Danish Welfare State', forthcoming in M Feeley and M Langford, *The Limits of the Legal Complex: Nordic Lawyers and Political Liberalism* (2019).

[5] In the workshops held to discuss first drafts of the chapters in this volume, in July 2017 in Oñati and September 2018 in Gothenburg, the usefulness or otherwise of legal rights discourse in structuring and giving effect to the social minimum was a source of considerable debate – which greatly assisted the writing of this chapter. Interestingly, at both events, legal experts were often more sceptical of the usefulness of law than their counterparts in the wider social sciences: the former tended to emphasise the limits of legal mechanisms, while the latter were more positive about their potential.

[6] F Atria, 'Social Rights, Social Contract, Socialism' (2015) 24 *Social & Legal Studies* 598.

[7] See further ch 12 (Kotkas) in this volume.

[8] See further ch 16 (Boyle) and ch 9 (Piachaud) in this volume.

new justificatory pressure to bear on government (in)action in the field of social protection that might otherwise be largely insulated against political or legal challenges. It could also push back against the dominant influence of neoliberal orthodoxy which has shaped debates about the social minimum for decades now, by using the potent language of rights to frame the importance of access to education, healthcare and other forms of basic social provision to human flourishing.[9] This could have particular impact when it comes to interpreting the legislative framework that regulates access to social entitlements, which as Frans Pennings notes in chapter ten of this volume, has become increasingly restrictive in many European states.

Finding effective ways of protecting SER through law has particular potential in this regard. Political claims about the importance of SER, such as the right to social security or to healthcare, can be easy to ignore – but legal claims are less so, if they have a solid basis in national and/or international law. Legal action compels some sort of state response: it can thus be effective in opening up aspects of state functioning to challenge, which might otherwise be fairly impervious to other forms of external pressure. In particular, as Gauri and Brinks have argued, giving legal protection to SER has the potential in particular to open up avenues for members of marginalised social groups to challenge failures in social provision – and thereby to introduce new forms of accountability for how the social minimum is designed and implemented in practice.[10]

However, achieving this potential is not an easy or straightforward matter. There are complex design issues to be addressed before the legal protection of SER can play a meaningful role in supplementing other policy levers in securing adequate access to the social minimum. If such legal protection is purely tokenistic in character, or lacks credibility and/or effectiveness, then it may have counter-productive effects.[11] This chapter focuses on one specific, if key, design challenge – namely how to ensure that legal tests designed to identify breaches of SER are sufficiently clear, determinate and demanding to play a useful role in protecting access to the social minimum.

II. THE CHALLENGES OF GIVING LEGAL EFFECT TO SER

As concepts, SERs serve several different functions. In particular, they give expression (via the potent language of rights discourse) to the normative obligations of states to take adequate steps to secure the socio-economic wellbeing of their inhabitants. They are also supposed to serve as legal and political benchmarks to assess whether states are living up to their commitments. In other

[9] See, in general, A Sen, *The Idea of Justice* (Cambridge, MA, Harvard University Press, 2009).

[10] V Gauri and DM Brinks, 'Human Rights as Demands for Communicative Action' (2012) 20 *Journal of Political Philosophy* 407.

[11] See ch 2 (Bilchitz) in this volume.

words, they play both a symbolic and a legal/regulatory role: they set out the objectives of state action in the socio-economic field, and are also supposed to serve as measuring tools in monitoring and regulating state progress towards achieving those particular objectives.[12]

Such social rights commitments receive plenty of lip service in official rhetoric. The majority of national constitutions contain provisions that rhetorically affirm the fundamental character of one or more SER.[13] Furthermore, almost all liberal democratic states have agreed to be bound by international human rights treaties containing SER provisions, with the International Covenant on Social, Economic and Cultural Rights (ICESCR), the European Social Charter (ESC) and the ILO 'core standards' framework being the most prominent examples.

However, in actuality, SER are widely regarded as having little if any real substance – either at the symbolic/political level, or as a matter of law. As Alston has recently argued, rhetoric endorsement of such rights should not be confused with real commitment.[14] National governments often treat their SER obligations under ICESCR and other human rights treaties as amounting to little more than vague expressions of good faith. Even in states whose constitutions affirm the existence of such rights, or who directly incorporate the provisions of international treaty instruments such as ICESCR into domestic law, such rights are often viewed as amounting to little more than abstract 'maxims of political morality'.[15] In other words, states are willing to acknowledge the importance of SER as abstract objectives to be realised in the long term – but are extremely reluctant to subject themselves to SER compliance requirements.

This reflects the marginal and contested status of SER within liberal democratic constitutional theory, as well as human rights discourse more generally. Plenty of scepticism exists as to whether SER really qualify as substantive 'rights', in the sense of being imperative claims that impose binding obligations upon state institutions. In particular, SER are regarded as being highly indeterminate. They are widely assumed to lack specific content, and therefore are incapable of giving rise to legally cognisable 'rights' which impose corresponding Hohfeldian duties upon the state and/or other private actors.[16]

This perception that SER are at best 'imperfect obligations', and at worst pure exercises in well-meaning rhetoric, casts a shadow over all promotional or enforcement activity intended to secure better respect for such rights. It fuels

[12] Gauri and Brinks, 'Human Rights as Demands' (2012).

[13] R Hirschl, 'From Comparative Constitutional Law to Comparative Constitutional Studies' (2013) 11 *International Journal of Constitutional Law* 1, 8–9.

[14] P Alston, 'The Populist Challenge to Human Rights' (2017) 9 *Journal of Human Rights Practice* 1.

[15] This phrase is associated with Dicey's criticisms of the deployment of abstract guiding norms within the tradition of French constitutionalism: see AV Dicey, *Introduction to the Study of the Law of the Constitution* (London, Macmillan, 1st edn 1885; 10th edn, 1959) App I.

[16] See eg M Cranston, 'Rights: Real and Supposed' in DD Raphael (ed), *Political Theory and the Rights of Man* (Bloomington, Indiana University Press, 1967) 43–51; O O'Neill, 'The Dark Side of Human Rights' (2005) 81 *International Affairs* 427.

the widely held belief that they amount to little more than social justice claims dressed up in a thin veneer of 'rights talk' and lacking much in the way of real normative force.

This 'indeterminacy' critique of SER also feeds into and reinforces the widely held assumption that any self-respecting democracy must leave important issues of social and economic policy to be resolved by democratically accountable politicians, especially when such issues generate complex and 'polycentric' considerations relating to resource allocation. The apparently insubstantial nature of SER is used as a justification for classifying them as matters of 'policy' rather than 'principle', to use Dworkin's classification:[17] they are usually viewed as matters best left to be regulated by the free flow of political debate and bureaucratic control, rather than benefiting from the special legal and political status according to 'real' human rights.[18] This generates resistance to any attempts to take SER more seriously: it even encourages national and international courts and other key actors to develop 'containment doctrines' designed to prevent existing forms of rights protection spilling over into the socio-economic realm.[19]

The apparent indeterminacy of SER can also hinder their impact, even in contexts where political and/or legal actors are favourably disposed towards recognising them as 'real' human rights. National and international human rights bodies frequently talk about the importance of SER, but rarely focus in on any specific alleged infringements of such rights – often because considerable uncertainty exists as to what qualifies as a breach of any given SER.[20] At national level, it is commonplace for governments to be accused of breaching social rights: however, such accusations often have little impact, given the lack of consensus that exists about the substantive content of such rights. Even well-meaning public servants struggle to get to grips with what they can see as the highly open-ended and uncertain norms set out in international SER instruments.[21]

Enthusiasts for SER[22] tend to get impatient with this indeterminacy critique. They often argue that SER are intrinsically no more indeterminate than civil and political rights (CPR) such as freedom of speech, fair trial or equality and non-discrimination: both SER and their civil and political counterparts protect the core of human dignity, and the only substantive distinction between the two

[17] R Dworkin, *Taking Rights Seriously* (Cambridge, MA, Harvard University Press, 1978).

[18] G Liu, 'Rethinking Constitutional Welfare Rights' (2008) 61 *Stanford Law Review* 203.

[19] C O'Cinneide, 'The Problematic of Social Rights – Uniformity and Diversity in the Development of Social Rights Review' in L Lazarus, C McCrudden and N Bowles (eds), *Reasoning Rights: Comparative Judicial Engagement* (Oxford, Oxford University Press, 2014) 297–315.

[20] See ch 13 (Warwick) in this volume.

[21] A UK civil servant once confessed to the author of this chapter that she had tried to apply the relevant standards from ICESCR and other SER instruments as set out in the Scottish National Action Plan for Human Rights (prepared by the Scottish Human Rights Commission – accessible online at www.snaprights.info) to public housing allocation decisions, and had found them to be lacking sufficient substance to be of much practical use to her.

[22] The term 'enthusiasts for SER' is not meant in a pejorative sense: I am one myself.

categories of rights is that an overlapping political/legal consensus has not yet emerged as to the substantive content of SERs as opposed to free speech and the other 'better established' CPR. They also tend to highlight the uncertain penumbra of well-established civil and political rights such as fair trial, and by extension suggest that the process of defining the scope and substance of SER poses no inherent difficulties that are not also present in case of civil and political rights.[23]

Moving away from the conceptual level, SER enthusiasts also argue that interpretative tools exist that are capable of giving clear definition to these rights. They highlight in particular the legal techniques used by expert human rights bodies such as the Committee on Economic, Social and Cultural Rights (CESCR) to flesh out the abstract guarantees set out in instruments such as ICESCR, and the way in which judicial organs such as the South African Constitutional Court have similarly interpreted and applied national constitutional SER guarantees. According to the enthusiasts, the interpretative methods used by such bodies provide clear evidence that SER can be read as imposing specific and tangible duties upon particular state actors – and therefore cannot be dismissed as empty maxims. They also argue that these methods show that SER can be interpreted and applied in a way that does not unduly constrain democratic choice, while still ensuring effective protection for the social minimum that should be available to all within a given society.[24]

This debate has turned on the spotlight on how the legal protection of SER has developed in practice. Existing legal mechanisms for interpreting and applying SERs have been analysed in detail, with a view to assessing the effectiveness and feasibility of adjudicating SER. There is now an extensive literature on this topic, which is impossible to summarise in detail. However, it is possible to identify certain trends and practices, which give some indication of how the legal protection of SER might be designed so as to enhance its capacity to make a positive contribution to the maintenance of a decent social minimum in contemporary societies.

III. ADJUDICATING SER – TRENDS AND PRACTICES

The first attempts made to inject a substantive SER dimension into the functioning of national constitutional systems tried to make use of the role of constitutions as 'mission statements', ie affirmations of the values and principles that are supposed to guide state conduct.[25] Social rights provisions were

[23] See eg N Jheelan, 'The Enforceability of Socio-Economic Rights' (2007) 2 *European Human Rights Law Review* 146.

[24] For this debate, see in general C Gearty and V Mantouvalou, *Debating Social Rights* (Oxford, Hart, 2010).

[25] J King, 'Constitutions as Mission Statements' in D J Galligan and M Versteeg (eds), *Social and Political Foundations of Constitutions* (Cambridge, Cambridge University Press, 2013) 73–103.

inserted into the text of the Mexican Constitution of 1917, the Constitution of the Weimar Republic in 1919, and subsequently into many other constitutional texts drawn up in the aftermath of the two world wars and the decolonisation process. These constitutional provisions were intended to assert the fundamental importance of SER, and to orientate the exercise of state power by the executive, judicial and, in particular, the legislative branches of government towards socially positive goals.[26]

These ambitions attracted controversy from the outset. Many legal scholars viewed the inclusion of social rights provisions within constitutional texts as an exercise in empty rhetoric, while conservative critics attacked their inclusion on the basis that they constituted an attempt to close down political debate about the orientation of public policy. However, the inclusion of 'orientating' or 'directive' SER provisions in national constitutional texts proved to be a popular option. It proved to have particular appeal in continental Europe in the wake of WWII, as it provided constitutional backbone for the establishment of the post-war national welfare states.[27] It also appealed to the drafters of many Latin American and African constitutions, both in the post-war era of decolonisation and the era of post-Cold War democratisation that begin in the late 1980s.[28] As a result, many nation's constitutions now expressly affirm that they are 'social states'[29] and/or contain lists of fundamental social rights or directive principles setting out social goals to which state policy should strive to give effect.[30]

These provisions are generally viewed as establishing objective constitutional norms that are supposed to provide a normative steer for the exercise of public power by the executive, legislative and judicial branches. In some states, these objective norms have acquired a degree of legal substance – in the sense that they are treated as part of the background framework of constitutional principles that courts must take into account in reviewing the actions of public authorities and interpreting and applying other legal norms.[31] In other states, they take effect solely within the symbolic/political plane.

[26] Hirschl, 'From Comparative Constitutional Law' (2013).

[27] See eg Art 23 of the Constitution of Belgium, Arts 19, 20 and 22 of the Constitution of the Netherlands; Arts 21 and 22 of the Constitution of Greece; Arts 56, 59, 63–72, 108–109, 167, 216 of the Constitution of Portugal.

[28] See eg Title V of the Constitution of Costa Rica 1949; Ch VI of the Constitution of the Republic of Ghana 1992; Ch II of the Constitution of the Federal Republic of Nigeria 1999.

[29] See eg Art 1(1) of the Constitution of Spain; Art 2 of the Constitution of Portugal; Art 2 of the Constitution of Slovenia; Art 20 of the German Basic Law.

[30] Directive Principles India/Ireland; ss 26 and 27 of the South African Constitution 1996.

[31] Thus, in Germany, primary and secondary legislation may be interpreted by reference to the requirements of the 'social state' (*Sozialstaat*) principle, which is one of the primary elements of the constitutional order which has a textual anchor in Art 20 of the German Basic Law providing that the 'Federal Republic of Germany is a democratic and social federal state' [author's italics]: see HM Heinig, 'The Political and the Basic Law's Sozialstaat Principle – Perspectives from Constitutional Law and Theory' (2011) 12 *German Law Journal* 1879–886. See also G Katrougalos, 'The Implementation of Social Rights in Europe' (1996) 292 *Columbia Journal of European Law* 277–312.

However, this attempt to embed SER 'mission statements' in national constitutions has had limited impact. The normative steer provided by constitutional social rights provisions or directive principles generally takes effect only within the interstices of the liberal constitutional framework of values. This means they do not usually disturb existing assumptions about separation of powers, and it is generally assumed that the legislative and executive should play the dominant role in defining the scope and content of SER. As a result, it is often unclear what will constitute a failure by the political branches of government to give them effect.[32] Furthermore, such SER provisions are often couched in such general terms as to lack any clear normative substance. This dilutes their impact at both the legal and political levels, and ensures they remain overshadowed by the indeterminacy issue. By and large, they resemble rhetorical gestures rather than concrete commitments.[33]

Similar issues arise with the SER instruments developed within the framework of the UN, ILO, Council of Europe and other international organisations. These instruments – ICESCR, the European Social Charter (ESC), the various ILO Conventions and Recommendations and so on – set out binding international SER standards, with a view to establishing a common floor of transnational protection for social rights. Their provisions have played an important role in shaping debates about SER, and have exerted a certain degree of influence over the development of national law and policy – in particular in the area of labour market regulation. However, once again, indeterminacy has limited their impact, along with the lack of strong enforcement and monitoring mechanisms: states have considerable wriggle room under these instruments, and for the most part face little justificatory pressure to enhance the level of social protection they provide.[34]

These limitations of SER provisions at both national and international level has prompted many scholars and activists to argue that courts and other monitoring/enforcement bodies should take a more active role in interpreting and securing compliance with these provisions. Supporters of this approach argue that, just as judicial interpretation has helped to give greater shape and definition to civil and political rights, so too could it help to combat the indeterminacy problems with SER – thereby in turn generating more justificatory pressure on governments and legislatures to comply with these standards.[35]

These arguments have struck a chord in many different legal systems. Giving courts and other enforcement bodies greater authority to interpret and apply

[32] C O'Cinneide, 'Austerity and the Faded Dream of a Social Europe' in A Nolan (ed) *Economic and Social Rights after the Global Financial Crisis* (Cambridge, Cambridge University Press, 2014) 169–201.

[33] ibid.

[34] ibid.

[35] M Langford, 'The Justiciability of Social Rights: From Practice to Theory' in M Langford (ed) *Social Rights Jurisprudence: Emerging Trends in International and Comparative Law* (Cambridge, Cambridge University Press, 2012) 3–45.

SER standards is increasingly viewed as a way of putting flesh on the bones of existing constitutional and international human rights treaty commitments, and thereby of opening up new avenues for disadvantaged individuals and groups to challenge state inertia in giving effect to these standards.[36] It is now possible to speak of the existence of a 'social rights problematic', whereby the lack of a SER adjudicatory mechanism is increasingly viewed as constituting a defect or lacuna within a national constitutional order.[37]

Indeed, the shift in the discourse that surrounds SER has been so marked that Tushnet in 2013 claimed that 'debate has ended over whether constitutions should include such rights and whether, if included, those rights should be judicially enforceable ... [n]ot "whether," but "how" is the question now on the table among serious scholars and judges'.[38] This is a (deliberately?) exaggerated argument: deep scepticism still persists in many jurisdictions about the feasibility and desirability of giving/allowing courts to play an active role in interpreting and secure respect for SER. But it has resulted in the emergence of SER rights review in multiple different jurisdictions around the world, ranging from India, Brazil and Colombia to certain US state jurisdictions and even within the framework of EU law via the provisions of the EU Charter of Fundamental Rights and Freedoms. It has also led to steps being taken at international level to reinforce the status and interpretative authority of SER monitoring bodies, such as the CESCR and the European Committee on Social Rights (ECSR) – as exemplified by the addition of an Optional Protocol providing for an individual complaints mechanism to ICESCR,[39] and a 'collective complaints' mechanism to the ESC.[40]

However, the jury remains out as to the legitimacy and effectiveness of such forms of SER review. To establish themselves as meaningful forms of rights adjudication, they need to meet certain challenges. For example, they must be able to cope with the complexity of state administrative structures, and function in a way that minimises any unwanted and unplanned negative consequences for social protection in the states where they take effect.[41] SER review must also be conducted in a manner that takes the fact of political

[36] See ch 16 (Boyle) in this volume.

[37] O'Cinneide, 'Austerity and the Faded Dream' (2014).

[38] M Tushnet, 'A Response to David Landau', Opinio Juris Blog, 23 January 2012, available at http://opiniojuris.org/2012/01/23/hilj_tushnet-responds-to-landau.

[39] For analysis, see M Langford, B Porter, R Brown and J Rossi (eds), *The Optional Protocol to the International Covenant on Economic, Social and Cultural Rights: A Commentary* (Pretoria, Pretoria University Press, 2016).

[40] R Churchill and U Khaliq, 'The Collective Complaints System of the European Social Charter: An Effective Mechanism for Ensuring Compliance with Economic and Social Rights?' (2004) 15 *European Journal of International Law* 417.

[41] R Stacey, 'Dynamic Regulatory Constitutionalism: Taking Legislation Seriously in the Judicial Enforcement of Economic and Social Rights' (2017) 31 *Notre Dame Journal of Law, Ethics and Public Policy* 85–128. See also J King, *Judging Social Rights* (Cambridge, Cambridge University Press, 2012).

disagreement seriously: it must leave ample room for electoral contestation and popular mobilisation to shape the general direction of socio-economic policy, while also opening up new avenues for marginalised segments of society to participate in this process of collective self-determination.[42] And, in particular, it must engage with the problem of indeterminacy: the practice of SER review must give real substance to the scope and content of these rights, while simultaneously respecting the need for all forms of constitutional rights adjudication to conform to rule of law values such as clarity, consistency and internal coherence.[43]

In other words, SER review by courts and similar institutions must avoid the Scylla of under-enforcement (which is linked to indeterminacy) on the one hand and the Charybdis of judicial overreach on the other – or, as Michelman put it, adjudicators engaged in SER review need to avoid the dangers of either illegitimately 'usurping' the functions of other branches of government or of 'abdicating' their responsibility to protect social rights.[44] Without careful navigation of this treacherous passage, the legal protection of SER is unlikely to contribute much to securing an adequate social minimum. Even if SER adjudication manages to walk this tightrope, other hurdles exist: governments may prove unresponsive to the its conclusions, background socio-economic or political circumstances may make SER decisions unenforceable, or potential litigants may be unwilling or unable to access the legal process to trigger SER claims in the first place. But, unless legal protection of SER is capable (as a first step) of giving these rights some tangible content in a way that does not fall foul of the 'usurpation'/'abdication' tension, it will have nothing to offer wider debates about securing the social minimum.

IV. EVADING THE 'MINIMUM' – WHY SER ENTHUSIASTS ARE OFTEN RELUCTANT TO ENGAGE WITH THE SUBSTANTIVE CORE OF SER

Negotiating this 'usurpation'/'abdication' tension will inevitably be a difficult process. Many leading commentators have suggested that this tension can be managed through the use of 'weak-form', 'experimental', 'catalytic' and other 'dialogical' modes of judicial review, whereby courts enter into deliberative-dialogical relationships with other constitutional actors to address violations of SER.[45] Others have focused on the potential of court-supervised participative

[42] A Pillay, 'Towards Effective Social and Economic Rights Adjudication: The Role of Meaningful Engagement' (2012) *10 International Journal of Constitutional Law* 732.

[43] S Liebenberg, 'Needs, Rights and Transformation: Adjudicating Social Rights in South Africa' (2006) 17 *Stellenbosch Law Review* 5.

[44] F Michelman, 'Socioeconomic Rights in Constitutional Law: Explaining America Away' (2008) 6 *International Journal of Comparative Constitutional Law* 663.

[45] M Tushnet, *Weak Courts, Strong Rights: Judicial Review and Social Welfare Rights in Comparative Constitutional Law* (Princeton NJ, Princeton University Press, 2008); K Young, *Constituting*

processes, which can bring public authorities and socio-economically disadvantaged groups together in a process of 'meaningful engagement'.[46]

All these dialogical/catalytical techniques may help courts and other bodies manage the process of SER adjudication, by providing them with useful ways of navigating a feasible path between judicial overreach on one hand and under-protection of SERs on the other. But the extent to which the literature on SER review has focused on these managerial techniques is striking – and concerning. These modes of adjudication can help to alleviate some of the tensions associated with SER review, but ultimately by themselves provide little if any answer to the problem of indeterminacy. They fail to provide any meaningful guidance as to when courts and enforcement bodies are justified in finding particular forms of state (in)action to be a violation of the relevant provisions of national and/or international human rights law relating to SER. As such, they focus on process rather than substance.

In part, this reflects the existence of considerable scepticism in some of the leading academic commentary on SER rights review as to the desirability of trying to define the content of such rights. Katie Young and others have argued that attempts to identify the basic needs that should be guaranteed by SER are conceptually flawed.[47] In their view, such needs vary from individual to individual and/or can only be defined by reference to a 'thick' contextual account of relevant circumstances that lie beyond the expertise or capacity of courts and other enforcement bodies to formulate. As such, they argue that any form of SER review that is focused on identifying the content of such rights will inevitably either overreach (as arguably took place in the early years of the Brazilian jurisprudence)[48] or degenerate into a highly attenuated and minimalistic form of legal protection which will cover little more than bare survival needs. Instead, they argue that the focus of SER review should be on benchmarking whether state action is enhancing or undermining existing methods of protecting such rights. In other words, courts and other enforcement bodies in monitoring compliance with SER standards should direct their energies towards

Social Rights (Oxford, Oxford University Press, 2012); R Dixon, 'Creating Dialogue about Socio-Economic Rights: Strong-Form versus Weak-Form Judicial Review Revisited' (2007) 5 *International Journal of Comparative Constitutional Law* 391; O Gerstenberg, 'The Justiciability of Socio-economic rights, European Solidarity, and the Role of the Court of Justice of the EU' (2014) 33 *Yearbook of European Law* 245.

[46] Pillay, 'Meaningful Engagement' (2012); S Liebenberg and K Young, 'Adjudicating Social and Economic Rights: Can Democratic Experimentalism Help?' in H Garcia, K Klare and L Williams (eds) *Social and Economic Rights in Theory and Practice, Critical Inquiries* (London, Routledge, 2015) 237–58.

[47] Young, *Constituting Social Rights* (2012); also X Contiades and A Fotiadou, 'Social Rights in the Age of Proportionality: Global Economic Crisis and Constitutional Litigation' (2012) 10 *International Journal of Constitutional Law* 660.

[48] O Ferraz, 'Brazil: Health Inequalities, Rights and Courts' in AE Yamin and S Gloppen (eds) *Litigating Health Rights: Can Courts Bring More Justice to Health?* (Cambridge, MA, Harvard University Press, 2011) 76–102.

assessing the reasonableness or proportionality of government measures which affect existing levels of social rights protection, with the dialogical/catalytical adjudicatory techniques discussed above serving as a way of opening up this process to previously marginalised perspectives.[49] The emphasis should be on scrutinising the justifiability of state action that has a negative impact on the social minimum, rather than attempting to define the scope and substance of SER as such.

This approach mirrors key elements of the techniques used by CESCR to monitor state compliance with their obligations under ICESCR. In interpreting the obligations imposed on state parties by Article 2 ICESCR to 'take steps … to the maximum of its available resources, with a view to achieving progressively the full realization of the rights recognized in the present Covenant', CESCR places considerable reliance upon the concepts of 'reasonable progression' and (to a lesser extent) 'non-regression' in assessing state compliance with their SER obligations.[50] In other words, the Committee primarily monitors state performance with reference to the extent to which they are progressing towards, or deviating from, the ideal state of SER protection that the Committee outlines in its General Comments and other interpretative statements. In contrast, the Committee places less emphasis on delineating the minimum core of ICESCR rights and assessing whether states have given effect to this core: it is interpreted as only including a residual quantity of bare needs, and both CESCR and assorted academic commentators have expressed concern that compliance with this minimum core should not be taken to constitute conformity with a state's overall obligations under ICESCR.[51]

An analogous approach has been adopted in South Africa, with the Constitutional Court there reviewing the reasonableness of state (in)action which affects progress towards giving effect to SER: questions of the core content of such rights are relevant to such reasonableness review, but are not central to its functioning.[52] A similar approach appears to underlie the application of proportionality analysis in the context of judicial review of state measures affecting social rights entitlements in certain European states.[53]

Thus, as advocated by Young and others, the focus in many of the most prominent systems of SER review is on reviewing the reasonableness or proportionality of state measures, with reference to the manner in which they alter existing forms of social provision. The question as to what forms of social

[49] Liebenberg and Young, 'Adjudicating Social and Economic Rights' (2015).

[50] UN CESCR, General Comment No 3: The nature of States parties obligations (Art 2, para 1 of the Covenant), UN Doc. E/1991/23 (1990).

[51] K Young, 'The Minimum Core of Economic and Social Rights: A Concept in Search of Content' (2008) 33 *Yale Journal of International Law* 113.

[52] See in general S Liebenberg, *Socio-Economic Rights: Adjudication under a Transformative Constitution* (Claremont, Juta, 2010).

[53] Contiades and Fotiadou, 'Age of Proportionality' (2012).

support individuals are entitled to 'as of right' – ie what 'social minimum' is the state required to provide – is relegated to the margins.[54]

V. ENGAGING THE SOCIAL MINIMUM – GIVING SUBSTANCE TO SER

This attractiveness of this benchmarking approach lies in how it avoids the need to define the basic social obligations of the state towards the inhabitants of its territory: it leaves such issues to the political process, and confines itself to assessing the reasonableness or proportionality of measures that adjust the established floor of social protection. It patrols respect for the social minimum, rather than seeking to define it – which could be viewed as showing proper respect to the politicians and experts that define its content, and as adhering to traditional legal methodology by reviewing the procedural logic of decision-making processes rather than their substance as such.[55]

However, there are problems with this approach. Concepts such as 'reasonableness', 'non-regression', 'reasonable progression' and 'proportionality' are inherently vague and open-ended. As Bilchitz has argued in respect of the use of proportionality analysis in this context, such an adjudicative device 'cannot conceptually provide content to rights and, rather, requires … supplementation by a doctrine of content'.[56] Without such a doctrine specifying the scope and content of social rights, or at least the outline of such a doctrine, there is a risk that wide-ranging reasonableness review may generate seriously inconsistent or incoherent case law.[57] In other words, patrolling respect for the social minimum may appear to adhere to orthodox judicial review methodology – but it will be difficult to decide on a consistent and rigorous basis when public authorities have failed to show respect for the minimum, if there is no clear idea of what respecting the minimum entails as a matter of substance.

The concern of Young and others that a focus on defining the scope and substance of SER will generate a 'lowest common denominator' jurisprudence is legitimate: mapping out what states must provide as a minimum does risk that floor becoming a ceiling. However, the alternative – side-stepping the issue of content, and trying to evade the indeterminacy problem of SER through the

[54] See further ch 12 (Kotkas) in this volume.

[55] See further ch 14 (Leijten) in this volume.

[56] D Bilchitz, 'Socio-economic Rights, Economic Crisis, and Legal Doctrine' (2014) 12 *International Journal of Constitutional Law* 710–39, and also his chapter in this volume. Contiades and Fotiadou in replying to Bilchitz's argument have argued that the use of proportionality analysis by the Italian and Portuguese courts amongst others during the austerity crisis has shown that no such 'doctrine of content' is required to generate a coherent and substantive case law: X Contiades and A Fotiadou, 'A Reply to David Bilchitz' (2014) 12 *International Journal of Constitutional Law* 740. I do not share their unqualified enthusiasm for this case law.

[57] For general discussion of this point, see J King, *Judging Social Rights* (Oxford, Oxford University Press, 2012).

use of benchmarking strategies – brings its own problems: any jurisprudence established on this basis will be built on unstable foundations, and may struggle to attain coherence and genuine substance.

In contrast, for all the dangers of a substantive approach degenerating into a 'bare minimum' analysis, it has the advantage of focusing attention on the positive entitlements of individuals. It also arguably can provide courts and other enforcement bodies with a clearer normative steer as to how they should exercise their review functions, and give more definition to open-ended tests such as reasonableness or proportionality.[58] It also would parallel the type of reasoning deployed in civil and political rights adjudication, which is structured around assessing the legitimacy of government interference with a defined set of prima facie entitlements – perhaps acquiring more legitimacy as a consequence.

Conceptual tools also exist which can be brought to bear to delineate the core content of SER in a way that does not reduce it to the lowest common denominator. Existing established human rights standards, relating to both SER and their civil and political counterparts, can be extended incrementally through standard legal/analogical reasoning.[59] The content of this social minimum can also be derived in part from the various statutory and administrative guidelines that specify the baseline forms of social support to be provided in general to citizens of the state:[60] such guidelines can provide courts and other enforcement bodies with a point of reference in determining the substance of a state's SER obligations more generally.[61] Social science research on the necessary scope and substance of a social minimum, such as that outlined by Eichenhofer and Goedemé et al in their contributions to this volume, can also be a useful reservoir of expertise – subject to the limited capacity of judges and other legal actors to integrate expert perspectives from other disciplines into the specialist framework of legal discourse. Furthermore, as the philosophical debate about SER has mushroomed over the last decade or so, the crude 'basic needs' approach to determining the core content of SER has increasingly given way to more robust forms of analysis, which focus on defining SER in terms of the minimum respectful treatment that should be enjoyed on an equal basis by all inhabitants of a shared social space.[62]

Such a greater focus on defining the substance of SER could be integrated within existing modes of rights review in this context: what is being argued for

[58] Bilchitz, 'Socio-economic Rights' (2014).

[59] King, *Judging* (2012).

[60] See ch 10 (Pennings) in this volume.

[61] A careful analogy could be drawn here to developments in India: see M Khosla, 'Making Social Rights Conditional: Lessons from India' (2010) 8 *International Journal of Constitutional Law* 739.

[62] S Meckled-Garcia, 'Giving up the Goods: Rethinking the Human Right to Subsistence, Institutional Justice, and Imperfect Duties (2013) 30 *Journal of Applied Philosophy* 73–87. Morales has suggested that the substance of the social minimum should be defined by reference to what is necessary to enable citizens to participate effectively in the shaping of their society: see L Morales, 'The Discontent of Social and Economic Rights' (2017) *Res Publica* 257.

here is not an abandonment of catalytic approaches and their like, but their enhancement. Indeed, trace elements of such a substantive approach can be detected in the jurisprudence of most SER adjudicatory mechanisms. This is particularly pronounced in the India and Colombian systems – but the case can be made that even SER review in states like South Africa that are wedded to a reasonableness approach tends to be most effective in situations where: (i) the core content of the right in question can be readily identified, or (ii) where an analogy can be drawn with established norms relating to the enjoyment of core civil and political rights such as equality, privacy or even property.[63]

Templates also exist at both national and international level that serve as potential models as to how a more substantive engagement with the content of SER can be woven into the jurisprudence of courts and other enforcement bodies interpreting such rights – and which are fully compatible with dialogical/catalytical adjudicatory approaches.[64]

For example, the 2010 German Federal Constitutional Court (FCC) judgment in the *Hartz IV* case confirmed that the principle of human dignity set out in Article 1 of the Basic Law requires that persons in need be provided with sufficient material support to enable them to maintain a dignified existence and to participate in the social, cultural and political life of their society, and reviewed the manner in which benefit levels had been fixed by the German federal legislature by reference to this core requirement. Similarly, the FCC ruled in the case of *Asylum Seekers Benefits* that the amount of cash benefit paid to asylum-seekers waiting processing of their claims was incompatible with the substantive socio-economic requirements of the human dignity principle, and required the legislature to reconsider the amount of benefits available to this vulnerable group. Both judgments gave a certain amount of discretion to the legislature to set appropriate levels of social support, but nevertheless set out certain parameters within which this discretion had to operate – which were based upon the Court's interpretation of the substantive socio-economic content of the human dignity principle.[65]

Similarly, the jurisprudence of the European Committee on Social Rights in interpreting the ESC is built around a 'substantive content' model. The Committee makes use of both conceptual analysis and also established practice across Europe, together with authoritative points of reference such as Eurostat poverty levels, to help identify the extent of social protection that states are obliged

[63] See eg the judgment of the *South African Constitutional Court in City of Johannesburg v Blue Moonlight* [2011] ZACC 33 (CC).

[64] The jurisprudence of the European Court of Human Rights may also have some relevance here: see ch 15 (Kagiaros) and ch 14 (Leijten) in this volume.

[65] C Bittner, 'Human Dignity as a Matter of Legislative Consistency in an Ideal World: The Fundamental Right to Guarantee a Subsistence Minimum in the German Federal Constitutional Court's Judgment of 9 February 2010' (2011) 12 *German Law Journal* 1941; S Egidy, 'The Fundamental Right to the Guarantee of a Subsistence Minimum in the Hartz IV Case of the German Federal Constitutional Court' (2011) 12 *German Law Journal* 961.

to provide to individuals under provisions such as the Article 12 ESC right to social security or the Article 13 ESC right to social assistance. These thresholds are often attacked by states as being too demanding,[66] but they do establish concrete baseline standards. The Committee's jurisprudence is not binding on state parties to the ESC (who include all the EU states, as well as the vast majority of the membership of the Council of Europe): however, their interpretation of the rights set out in the Social Charter is authoritative, meaning that national authorities should take this jurisprudence into account in framing national law and policy (even if this obligation is frequently ignored in practice).[67] Given the status of this jurisprudence, and the way it frames SER standards in substantive rather than purely procedural terms, the Social Charter has much to offer as a potential template for the future development of a fully fleshed-out SER jurisprudence.

VI. CONCLUSION

The indeterminacy critique of SER needs to be taken seriously. If they are to have real bite, social minimum standards framed with reference to SER need to acquire a substantive, tangible dimension. For this to happen, activists and litigators need to focus on establishing how an alleged breach of a SER falls foul of constitutional standards, judges need to define the scope and content of such rights in such a manner that ensures that they provide genuine protection to individuals, and academics and other commentators need to reflect critically on what specific forms of state (in)action are incompatible with a socially engaged understanding of constitutionalism. Ways exist of identifying the content of a meaningful social minimum that individuals are entitled to as of right, and for courts to enforce compliance with this norm through strong or weak methods of review or some combination of the two – as demonstrated by the German Constitutional Court's approach in *Hartz IV* and *Asylum Seeker Benefits*.

Having said that, an important point of qualification has to be entered here. As Van der Walt has argued, any SER jurisprudence will develop against the backdrop of conventional assumptions about separation of powers and the dominant political views of the day about the regulation of market economies and the appropriate level of social protection. As a result, any legal mode of SER rights protection will inevitably be orientated towards identifying the

[66] O'Cinneide (n 32). Complaint 48/2008, *European Roma Rights Centre (ERRC) v Bulgaria*, Decision on the Merits of 18 February 2009: instead of ruling that Bulgarian legislation which barred individuals unemployed for more than six months from receiving unemployment relief was a retrogressive step, the ECSR concluded that the legislation breached Bulgaria's baseline obligation to provide a floor of social assistance to everyone in need imposed by Art 13§1 ESC.

[67] C O'Cinneide, 'The European Social Charter and the UK: Why it Matters' (2018) 29 *King's Law Journal* 275.

'worst acceptable governmental practice' that will pass muster, as tends to be the case in other areas of constitutional rights review more generally – and this will impose inevitable constraints upon its transformative potential, irrespective of the particular model of social rights review one adopts.[68] In this respect, Samuel Moyn's recent argument that human rights discourse in general is limited by its orientation towards a sufficiency approach is worth noting: despite the protests of some of his critics, this is probably true in the SER field as it is in other contexts.[69]

The legal language of rights and constitutional controls thus cannot give comprehensive expression to concepts of social justice, and should not be expected to do so. Political pressure and legislative reform will ultimately be the driver of any real change in this regard – as is normatively and practicably desirable.[70] However, a substantive approach to legal SER review as outlined here has the potential to add value to rights discourse and the wider project of securing adequate access to a decent social minimum, by sharpening the effectiveness of existing SER legal mechanisms at national or international level.

Emilios Christodoulidis argues that social rights constitutionalism, ie a commitment to making SER enforceable in law, has an 'antinomic significance' which injects 'productive tension' into contemporary constitutional discourse, not least because it disturbs 'attempts to accommodate the continuity of civil, political, and social rights in the face of the contradictory articulation of social democracy and capitalism'.[71] It is suggested that the approach suggested here to the definition and adjudication of SER through law will give more legal substance to the idea of a social minimum, and thus has the potential to amplify this 'antinomic' effect.[72]

[68] See J van der Walt, 'Delegitimation by Constitution? Liberal Democratic Experimentalism and the Question of Socioeconomic Rights' (2015) 3 *Critical Quarterly on Legislation and Law* 303.

[69] Moyn, *Not Enough* (2018). See also O Ferraz, 'Poverty and Human Rights' (2008) 28 *Oxford Journal of Legal Studies* 585.

[70] On this point, see Ferraz (ibid).

[71] E Christodoulidis, 'Social Rights Constitutionalism: An Antagonistic Endorsement' (2017) 44 *Journal of Law & Society* 123.

[72] As such, it has the potential to contribute to the wider transformative project outlined in ch 5 (Adler) and ch 9 (Piachaud) in this volume.

12

Legal Strategies and the Question of the Social Minimum: A Systems-Theoretical Approach

TOOMAS KOTKAS

I. INTRODUCTION

THE QUESTION ABOUT the social minimum is a complex one. To begin with, one should first have to decide which aspects of individuals' *social* life are to be included in the notion of social minimum. Although the 'social' has many dimensions, most of us would agree that at least income security, health and the possibility of participating in everyday social and societal activities all constitute something that one would normally define as elements of social life. Secondly, the question becomes more difficult when we are to determine the *minimum*. What is a sufficient level of income in a given society? How healthy, and with what cost, do we expect people to be? What are everyday social activities? Thirdly, what kinds of institutional or organisational arrangements should be used to secure the social minimum: pecuniary benefits, services, or both? And further, even if we could reach an agreement on these issues, we are still faced with enormous social and moral philosophical questions. Why would the social minimum need to be guaranteed in the first place? Who should guarantee (and pay) for it? Who are to be included in the system that secures the social minimum? What can be expected in return?[1]

All these questions are present, in one way or another, when political and legal decisions on the social minimum are made. Some of the questions are perhaps more political than legal in nature, like for instance the question about the institutional and organisational arrangements. Some of the questions, in turn, may just as well end up in courts to be decided – regardless of legislator's antecedent political decisions or because of them. Today, the majority of

[1] See eg S White, 'Social Minimum' in EN Zalta (ed), *The Stanford Encyclopedia of Philosophy*, Winter 2015 edn, available at plato.stanford.edu/archives/win2015/entries/social-minimum.

constitutional and human rights scholars seem to agree that there is no categorical difference between social rights, on the one hand, and civil and political rights, on the other.[2] However, some still insist that social rights should not be promoted through courts. Instead, their value 'lies principally in the political arena'.[3]

Even though cases concerning constitutional social rights and social human rights – like the right to a social minimum – are from time to time addressed in courts, ie within the legal system, this does not necessarily mean that the questions about the social minimum would be addressed in the same manner and after the same logic as they are addressed in the political system. In fact, in this chapter I will argue that the legal system tends to deal with the question of social minimum differently from the political system. In the legal system, the question about the social minimum is often translated or 'programmed' into a different, juridical, question. Rather than independently defining a precise pecuniary minimum limit for social security benefits, the legal system – courts in particular – adheres to juridical strategies that include legal syllogism, the proportionality principle and the principle of equality.

In order to validate my argument, I will analyse three particular cases. All three cases are, in fact, statements given by the Constitutional Law Committee of the Finnish Parliament on questions relating to the social minimum. According to Section 74 of the Constitution of Finland, 'The Constitutional Law Committee shall issue statements on the constitutionality of draft law and other matters brought for its consideration, as well as on their relation to international human rights treaties.' In this regard, the duties of the Constitutional Law Committee resemble the duties of any constitutional court that exercises ex ante constitutional review.[4] The Committee has been characterised as a quasi-judicial body because it is composed of Members of the Parliament but advised by constitutional experts whose opinions in practice determine the outcome of the statements of the Committee.[5]

[2] See eg M Langford, 'The Justiciability of Social Rights: From Practice to Theory' in M Langford (ed), *Social Rights Jurisprudence: Emerging Trends in International and Comparative Law* (Cambridge, Cambridge University Press, 2008) 30–31; C Geartey and V Mantouvalou, *Debating Social Rights* (Oxford, Hart, 2010) 17; D Barak-Erez and AM Gross, 'Introduction: Do We Need Social rights? Questions in the Era of Globalisation, Privatisation, and the Diminished Welfare State' in D Barak-Erez and AM Gross (eds), *Exploring Social Rights: Between Theory and Practice* (Oxford, Hart, 2011) 8; J King, *Judging Social Rights* (Cambridge, Cambridge University Press, 2012) 1; D Garland, 'On the Concept of "Social Rights"' (2016) 24 *Social and Legal Studies* 622, 625; see also ch 14 (Leijten) and ch 15 (Kagiaros) in this volume.

[3] Gearty and Mantouvalou, *Debating* (2010) 1; see also F Atria, 'Social Rights, Social Contract, Socialism' (2016) 24 *Social and Legal Studies* 598.

[4] The ex ante constitutional review differs from ex post review that takes place in courts. The ex post review primarily focuses on individual cases and their circumstances. Of course, the ex post constitutional review also often brings about a need for legislative reform.

[5] K Tuori, 'Judicial Constitutional Review as a Last Resort' in T Campbell, KD Ewing and A Tomkins (eds), *The Legal Protection of Human Rights: Sceptical Essays* (Oxford, Oxford University Press, 2011) 365.

Two objections could be raised here. First, if the Constitutional Law Committee is comprised of politicians, can it be paralleled with a constitutional court? If we assume a systems-theoretical perspective, the answer is affirmative. From the point of view of the systems theory, the institutional and organisational framework of constitutional review – be it ex ante or ex post facto – does not matter. What only matters, according to Niklas Luhmann, is the code according to which the constitutional review carried out, ie the binary code of legal/illegal.[6] The constitutional review that takes place in the Constitutional Law Committee adheres to this binary code. Second, why Finland? Apart from the obvious reason relating to the nationality of the author, it can also be claimed that Finland serves as good as an example as any other European constitutional welfare state that has had, during the past few decades, to adjust its social policy to the challenges brought by economic stagnation and the increased influx of immigrants – refugees in particular. These factors have had a clear impact on social policy and social security legislation in Finland like in other European countries.

Indeed, Niklas Luhmann's systems-theoretical approach to law will serve as an interpretative framework for the analysis of the three statements of the Constitutional Law Committee. The choice of theoretical framework indicates that this chapter dissociates itself from all normative claims concerning the question about the justiciability of (constitutional) social rights and the right to a social minimum in particular, ie whether courts should decide on the social minimum or not. As this chapter shows, legal systems do address questions concerning the social minimum. As already said, in this chapter the focus is on *how* the legal system deals with these complex questions. It will be argued that rather than defining absolute pecuniary limits for the social minimum, the legal system uses 'legal programmes' through which the question of the social minimum takes different forms.

In conclusion, I will also explain – in Luhmannian terms – why this is so. From the point of view of Luhmannian social theory, legal programming is indispensable for the maintaining of the functional differentiation of social subsystems. Without legal programming the systemic demarcation between law and politics would be in danger of blurring. This, in turn, would weaken the ability of the legal system to stabilise normative expectations and to produce predictability in modern complex societies. It is important to scrutinise the question of the right to a social minimum also from the perspective of social theory because this contextualises the whole issue and reminds us that constitutional and human rights adjudication also entails potential risks and downsides. We should not too readily assume a straightforward view according to which constitutional and human rights adjudication is automatically the best way to promote the right to a social minimum. The role of courts and adjudication depends on the

[6] N Luhmann, *Law as a Social System* (Oxford, Oxford University Press, 2004) 369–70.

current status of a given society. I will come back to this question in the conclusions of this chapter.

II. LUHMANN ON LAW

According to Luhmann's well-known claim, all societal subsystems – including the legal system – are operatively closed systems, which produce and reproduce their unity internally. The legal system is an autopoietic system that produces its structures by its own operations. Through these self-referential operations the legal system draws a distinction between itself and its environment. There are no causal relations between the legal system and other subsystems. Other subsystems merely provide 'irritations' for the legal system but the legal system decides independently whether they are juridically relevant and how they should be dealt with from the legal system.[7]

The operative closure of the legal system is based on a distinct binary code, which all legal communication follows. The binary code of law, ie legal/illegal, distinguishes law from other functional subsystems such as politics and economy. In order for communication to be legal communication, it must follow this code. What the legal system – courts in particular – basically does, is decide whether a particular action, deed or behaviour is legal or illegal. However, the code itself cannot, of course, provide criteria for deciding between legal and illegal. Therefore programmes, ie legislation and legal rules, are required. While the binary code of law stays the same, the legal programmes/rules change over time. The change of law is constant.[8]

Although law, like all societal subsystems, is operatively closed, it is connected with its environment through 'structural couplings'. Luhmann names the constitution as an example of a structural coupling between the legal system and the political system. Through the constitution – and legislation in general – the political system channels its power in order to produce collectively binding decisions. Respectively, viewed from the point of view of the legal system, the constitution sets restraints to the use of political power. Structural couplings allow systems to co-evolve simultaneously.[9]

The function of law is to stabilise normative expectations and thus produce predictability in the (increasing) complexity of the society. The success of law as an autopoietic and differentiated system depends on its ability to fulfil this function.[10] In order to be able to perform its function, the legal system and legal argumentation in particular must process and reduce information. Not all

[7] Luhmann, *Law* (2004) 76–141.

[8] Luhmann (n 6) 173–210.

[9] Luhmann (n 6) 403–12; R Nobles and D Schiff, *Observing Law Through Systems Theory* (Oxford, Hart, 2013) 164–95.

[10] Luhmann (n 6) 142–72.

information in the outside environment is relevant for the legal system. The legal system operates with the help of 'redundancies', ie condensed legal information such as legal concepts, principles and doctrines. In routine cases the appropriateness of these redundancies is not called into question. In hard cases the new information with which the environment irritates the legal system is reduced into new redundancies – new concepts, principles, doctrines – in the legal system.[11]

It is not possible here to try to give a comprehensive and detailed account of Luhmann's systems-theoretical approach to law. I have only provided the basics for those readers who might not be familiar with Luhmann's systems-theory. In what follows, I hope to elaborate the theory a bit further by analysing the three statements of the Constitutional Law Committee of the Parliament. As said, the Committee is considered here, first and foremost, a quasi-judicial body because it operates according to the binary logic of the legal system, ie legal/illegal – or to be more specific, in this case, constitutional/unconstitutional. So, what will be said of the strategies that the Committee has adhered to, applies to courts in any Western legal systems.

III. THREE LEGAL PROGRAMMES TO ADDRESS THE QUESTION OF SOCIAL MINIMUM

A. Programme 1: Applying a Preset Limit (Syllogism)

The social minimum is probably never defined in constitutions in a precise way. Most constitutional rights provisions are abstractly formulated in order to stand the test of time. This is also the case with the Constitution of Finland. Section 19(2) of the Constitution prescribes that 'Everyone shall be guaranteed by legislation the right to basic subsistence in the event of unemployment, illness, and disability and during old age as well as at the birth of a child or the loss of a provider.' The *travaux préparatoires* of this particular provision do not give us any more guidance on the correct level of 'basic subsistence'. It was simply stated in the Government Bill that when evaluating the sufficiency of the basic subsistence, attention should be paid to the social security benefit system and a person's circumstances, like his or her family status, as a whole.[12]

By contrast, social minimum benefits are usually precisely defined in social security legislation. For instance, the amount of minimum unemployment benefit in Finland, called 'labour market subsidy', was roughly 697 euros per month in 2019. Labour market subsidy is a benefit designed for unemployed job-seekers who enter the labour market for the first time, have no recent work experience,

[11] Luhmann (n 6) 313–22; M King and C Thornhill, *Niklas Luhmann's Theory of Politics and Law* (Hampshire, Palgrave MacMillan, 2003) 48–52.

[12] HE 309/1993, p 70.

or have exhausted their eligibility for the basic or earnings-related unemployment allowance.[13] It is a means-tested benefit. The purpose of the labour market subsidy is to guarantee a person's basic subsistence during the period of unemployment.

From time to time, the Constitutional Law Committee of the Finnish Parliament has had to evaluate the constitutionality of proposed retrenchments in the social security system and particular social security benefits. For instance, in 2003, the Finnish unemployment security legislation was reformed. During the reform, the constitutionality of the 'partial labour market subsidy', which had been in use already prior to the reform, came under scrutiny. The partial labour market subsidy was 60 per cent of the full amount and it was paid to unemployed persons who still lived with their parents, ie mainly youth.

In regard to the proposal to retain the partial labour market subsidy in the social security legislation, the Constitutional Law Committee of the Parliament stated that such a rigid criterion, ie living with one's parents, was not appropriate because it did not pay attention to the economic situation of the parents. Furthermore, the Committee held that the partial labour market subsidy reduced by 40 per cent would have clearly been below the minimum standard set in the ILO Convention 168 on Employment Promotion and Protection against Unemployment.[14] According to the Article 15(1b) of the Convention, periodically paid unemployment benefits that are not based on contributions or previous earnings

> shall be fixed at not less than 50 per cent of the statutory minimum wage or of the wage of an ordinary labourer, or at a level which provides the minimum essential for basic living expenses, whichever is the highest.

The end result was that the labour market subsidy was transformed entirely into a means-tested benefit.

The 'legal programming' applied by the Constitutional Law Committee was in this case a rather straightforward one. Because the partial labour market subsidy would have remained below a preset limit, it was easy for the Committee to declare it illegal, ie unconstitutional. In other words, there was no need for the Committee to engage in complex considerations about the *actual* sufficiency of the proposed partial benefit. It should be mentioned that the Committee altered its earlier view from 1993 when it still had considered partial labour market subsidy as constitutional.[15] What had changed since then, however, was that the constitutional rights reform had been carried out in 1995. In that reform constitutional social rights were included in the (then) Constitution of 1919.

[13] The other minimum unemployment benefit is basic unemployment allowance. It is paid to an unemployed who meets the 'work requirement', ie one must have been employed for at least 26 weeks during the 28 months preceding the unemployment, one must have worked at least 18 hours per week and one's pay must have complied with the terms of the relevant collective agreement or been at least 1,187 euros per month.

[14] PeVL 46/2002 vp, p 5.

[15] PeVL 32/1993 vp, p 3.

There are, of course, principled problems related to preset limits of a social minimum. Unlike the ILO, the UN Committee on Economic, Social and Cultural Rights has been reluctant to define minimum essential levels of different social security benefits. A predefined percentage of average wages is a poor indicator if the average wages in a given country are too low to begin with. Instead of such universal indicators, the Committee has invited state parties to develop appropriate national benchmarks.[16] However, from the point of view of the legal system, any preset level – be it international or national – enables the legal system to decide on the social minimum without paying too much (if any) attention to the current economic and societal circumstances of a given society. The preset limit is an example of *conditional programming* that is characteristic of law and legal systems. In this particular case the conditional programme can be formulated as follows: *if* the unemployment benefit remains below 50 per cent of the statutory minimum wage, *then* it is illegal/unconstitutional. In other words, we are dealing with a case of juridical syllogism. In applying conditional programming, the legal system allows other systems, eg the political system, to apply purpose-oriented programmes. The desirable level of a social minimum can be changed and agreed within the political system. As Luhmann has argued, the legal system 'offers only conditional certainties'.[17]

B. Programme 2: Applying the Proportionality Principle

There are many ways to execute retrenchments of the social security system. Besides lowering the level of benefits, as in the above example, costs of the social security system can also be cut down by freezing index increments of particular benefits. This means was resorted to in Finland in 1996 when the Government proposed in a Bill a freezing of index increments of the labour market subsidy as well as the basic unemployment allowance and its child increments for the following year. The aim was to reduce the costs of unemployment by 440 million Finnish marks.[18] The country was still recovering from the economic recession of the early 1990s that is considered the most severe in the post-war Finnish history.

The Government Bill was referred to the Constitutional Law Committee of the Parliament. The Committee stated that in regard to the basic social security benefits that are directly funded by the State, it is reasonable to expect that the current state of the national and public economy could be taken into consideration when deciding on the level of these benefits. However, the Committee

[16] CESCR, General Comment No 19: The right to social security (art 9), 4 February 2008, E/C.12/GC/19, paras 75–76.
[17] Luhmann (n 6) 196–203.
[18] HE 88/1996 vp. The sum equals to about 100 million euros in today's rates and currency.

argued that all retrenchment that would mean a 'substantial interference' in the level of basic income security would not meet the requirement set by the Section 19(2) of the Constitution. The Committee did not specify in detail what the 'substantial interference' would mean in practice. It only stated that the level of benefits securing basic subsistence could not be lower than what is demanded by Section 19(1) of the Constitution that enshrines to everyone the right to an indispensable subsistence (ie the so-called 'existence minimum'). In practice, the proposed freezing of index increments together with the already implemented retrenchment measures would have meant that the unemployment benefits in question would have remained the same while the general income level had increased by 10 per cent during the same period. As a conclusion, the Constitutional Law Committee did not find this a 'substantial interference' in the constitutional right to basic subsistence in case of unemployment.[19] The Bill was therefore passed by the Parliament.

Even though the Constitutional Law Committee did not explicitly refer to the general principle of proportionality, it can be argued that it applied this principle. The legal issue at stake was whether the proposed retrenchment measure was acceptable in proportion to the aspired-to goals – especially from the point of view of the constitutional right to basic subsistence. By addressing the whole issue as a question of proportionality, the Committee avoided the essential question whether the frozen basic unemployment allowance and the labour market subsidy were high enough for unemployed people to get economically by in the contemporary Finnish society. The Committee did not engage in considerations about the *absolute* adequate level of basic unemployment benefits. Instead, it only scrutinised them *relatively*; 10 per cent difference was not considered as a substantial interference. The political question about the social minimum was thus transformed into a juridical question of proportionality.

C. Programme 3: Applying the Equality Principle

Should the social minimum be the same for everyone residing within the same jurisdiction? Even though most of us would intuitively answer this question affirmatively, the issue does not seem to be so black and white. For instance, unemployment security legislation in many countries includes provisions that allow the authorities to reduce the level of unemployment benefits if the recipient has neglected his or her responsibilities to seek a job or to participate in services that promote employment. During the recent years, the question about the relationship between the social minimum and equality has also emerged in another context, ie the right of immigrants to social security benefits.

[19] PeVL 88/1996 vp.

In 2016, the Finnish Government issued a Bill in which it was proposed that the labour market subsidy paid to unemployed immigrants who had been granted a residence permit would have been temporarily renamed as 'integration benefit' that would have amounted to 90 per cent of the full labour market subsidy. The Bill was justified with a need to make Finland a less appealing country of destination for immigrants, on the one hand, and to help all admitted immigrants to better (!) integrate in the Finnish society, on the other hand. Thirdly, the aim was also to cut down costs of immigration.[20]

The Government Bill was referred to the Constitutional Law Committee of the Parliament for review. The Committee stated that the Government failed to provide constitutionally acceptable arguments for the reduced labour market subsidy, ie the integration benefit. The Committee held that the Bill was discriminatory because it placed immigrants in a less favourable position in regard to nationals based only on their immigrant status, ie their origin. The Bill therefore violated Section 6(2) of the Constitution of Finland, which includes a ban on discrimination based on sex, age, origin, language, religion, etc.[21]

For Luhmann, the principle of equality is 'the most abstract preference of the [legal] system, the final criterion for attribution of conflicts as legal and illegal.'[22] Indeed, equality as a *form* guarantees the operative closure of the legal system because equality does not refer to any normative concept outside the legal system. Equality is simply a form that is applicable to every imaginable contingency of the environment that causes irritation for the legal system. Everything can be regarded as equal or as unequal. However, equality as a form does not predetermine who or what things are to be treated equally. It needs to be transformed into norms through legal programming. To claim that some or some things are equal thus needs justifications, ie *why* some or some things are to be treated equally and others not.[23]

In its statement the Constitutional Law Committee did not find the Government's justifications legally acceptable. The purpose of the Bill to make Finland a less appealing country of destination was questionable in regard to Section 22 of the Constitution, which imposes a duty for the public authorities to guarantee the observance of constitutional and human rights. Furthermore, the Committee did not find the need for retrenchment a legitimate ground for differential treatment of nationals and immigrants. Thirdly, the Committee did not find it convincing an argument that the reduced labour market subsidy would have promoted the integration of immigrants into the Finnish society.[24] In addressing the Government Bill as a question concerning equality, the Constitutional Law

[20] HE 169/2016 vp.
[21] PeVL 55/2016 vp, pp 4–5.
[22] Luhmann (n 6) 132.
[23] Luhmann (n 6) 131–36, 217–18; King and Thornhill, *Niklas Luhmann's* (2003) 63–68.
[24] PeVL 55/2016 vp, pp 4–5.

Committee did not need to engage in complex argumentation about the social minimum, ie would the reduced integration benefit have secured the subsistence of immigrants or not. Instead, the Committee argued that whatever the social minimum may be, it must be the same for unemployed nationals and unemployed immigrants.

IV. CONCLUSIONS

In this concluding section of the chapter I will explain from the point of view of the Luhmannian systems-theoretical approach to law why the legal system – courts and quasi-judicial – transforms the question of the social minimum into a question of juridical syllogism (ie applying a preset limit), of the proportionality principle, or the principle of equality. One could, of course, try to find an explanation that would relate to the particular jurisdiction, which has provided us with the examples. Finland is typically categorised as a Nordic welfare state. Nordic welfare states have been said to form a distinct group of welfare states traditionally based on four common principles, ie the universality of social rights/benefits, emphasis on public/governmental responsibility, income and gender equality, and the full employment target.[25]

Nordic welfare states have also been characterised, first and foremost, as political projects. In other words, Nordic welfare states were not built on constitutional social rights. There has traditionally existed certain scepticism amongst the courts and the judiciary towards judicial activism in cases relating to social rights.[26] In fact, constitutional social rights provisions are a rather recent phenomenon in the Nordic countries, with the exception of Denmark. The right to receive public assistance was included already in the Constitution of 1849 but its practical significance has remained low until recent years. The Danish Constitution does not include other social rights provisions. In Finland, comprehensive social rights provisions were included in the Finnish Constitution only in 1995. In Norway, a provision on a right to subsistence was included in the Constitution only in 2014. The Norwegian Constitution lacks a

[25] See eg M Kautto, J Fritzell, B Hvinden, J Kvist and H Uusitalo, 'Introduction: How Distinct are the Nordic Welfare States?' in J Fritzell, B Hvinden, M Kautto, J Kvist and H Uusitalo (eds), *Nordic Welfare States in the European Context* (London and New York, Routledge, 2001) 1–13; P Kosonen, 'Globalization and the Nordic Welfare States' in R Sykes, B Palier and P M Prior (eds), *Globalization and the European Welfare States: Challenges and Change* (Hampshire, Palgrave, 2001) 153, 155.

[26] See S Hänninen, 'Pohjoismaisen Hyvinvoinnin Poliittinen Eetos' (2001) 26 *Tiede & Edistys* 19; K Ketscher, *Socialret: Almindelige Principper, Retssikkerhed og Administration, Grundværdier* (København, Forlaget Thomson, 2002) 239; L Vahlne Westerhäll, 'Om Sociala Rättigheters Funktion och Konstruktion' in G Regner, M Eliason and H-H Vogel (eds), *Fetskrift till Hans Ragnemalm* (Lund, Juristförlaget i Lund, 2005); T Kotkas, 'The Short and Insignificant History of Social Rights Discourse in the Nordic Welfare States' in T Kotkas and K Veitch (eds), *Social Rights in the Welfare State: Origins and Transformations* (Abingdon, Routledge, 2016) 15.

provision on the right to social security. The Constitution of Sweden still to date does not include provisions on justiciable constitutional social rights.[27]

In jurisdictions where constitutional social rights and social human rights discourse has traditionally been faint and courts have been reluctant to take an active role in general it is not surprising that courts have also been careful in not taking on the question of the social minimum. Of course, one should bear in mind that there has not necessarily been a need for it either. As Malcolm Langford has pointed out, the judicial receptivity to social rights adjudication depends, along with both judicial and general societal stance towards constitutional and human rights, on the degree of the *political* achievement of social rights.[28] In international comparison, the political achievement of social rights has certainly been high in the Nordic welfare states.

There is an aspect in Langford's argument that points, in fact, to Luhmannian systems theory. Indeed, if we approach the question – why courts are reluctant to define the social minimum – from the point of view of Luhmannian systems theory, we need to pay attention to the 'developmental stage' of the particular society we happen to be discussing. The key question that Luhmann tries to answer with his systems theory is why modern complex societies exist in the first place. What keeps the economy, the social sphere or the legal system from being subsumed into and determined by politics? As already indicated, the answer to this question is the fact that societal subsystems are operationally closed systems. Subsystems structure themselves and their operations autonomously. They also decide themselves how to deal with irritations coming from the environment, ie other subsystems and the society in general.

Viewed from the perspective of Luhmannian systems theory, the unwillingness of the legal system – and courts in particular – to directly define the social minimum has to do with maintaining the difference between subsystems, law and politics in particular. If the legal system would take an active role in defining the social minimum, it would blur the systemic demarcation between law and politics. This, in turn, would weaken the ability of the legal system to stabilise normative expectations and to produce predictability in modern complex societies. Luhmann has argued that the emergence of post-war welfare states entailed an increased risk of the blurring of the boundaries between politics and law. In the welfare states the conceptions of the meaning and function of constitutional rights have been changing increasingly in the direction of general programmes of values, ie guidelines for politics. In 1993, Luhmann wrote that 'Constitutional courts are intervening more and more frequently in politics with instructions on how conflicts ought to be resolved and are dictating spending, for instance, when

[27] On Norway see A Kjønstad and A Syse, 'Grunnlovsreform og Velferdsretten' (2014) *Jussens Venner* 340; on Denmark, K Ketscher, 'Retten til Eksistensminimum – og Retten til Ikke at Blive Diskrimineret' (2012) *Juristen* 177; on Sweden, A-S Lind, *Sociala Rättigheter i Förändring. En Konstitutionellrättslig Studie* (Uppsala, Uppsala Universitet, 2009).

[28] Langford, 'The Justiciability' (2008) 9–11.

thrift is advisable.'[29] This kind of inflatory and ideological use of constitutional social rights and social human rights poses a threat to the differentiation of societal subsystems.[30]

When the legal system – courts – shows restraint and applies legal programmes that deal with the question of the social minimum in its own terms, ie without entering into political or economic considerations of what is enough for people to get by in a given social and economic reality, it is simply ensuring the differentiation of societal subsystems. By approaching the question of the social minimum as a question of syllogism, of proportionality or of equality, among others, the legal system is maintaining its own operational closure in relation to other societal subsystems. This is crucial for the primary function of the legal system, ie the function of stabilising normative expectations and producing predictability in the complex reality of modern societies. From the point of view of social theory, the political doctrine of the separation of state powers translates into a broader question of the very existence and viability of modern societies.

We need to bear in mind, though, that Luhmann's theory is a theory of modern complex societies. In modern advanced societies – like the Nordic welfare states – where the right to a social minimum has been established through the political system, there is seldom a need for the courts to secure it through adjudication. In less advanced or transitional societies where there is not (yet) an operational democratic political system in place, however, the courts may be 'forced' to be more active and to create the right to a social minimum through adjudication because the political system is not yet functioning properly. In such societies an active judiciary does not pose such a big risk to the overall functionality of the society. Where there is not yet an operational democratic political system in place, active judiciary does not pose a threat to the society. On the contrary, an active judiciary can be a necessary component in its construction. I do not mean to say that in advanced modern societies the question about the right to a social minimum does not surface from time to time. Of course, also in advanced societies there occasionally arises a need for the courts to take an active role in defending the right to a social minimum. This typically happens in times of crisis like, for instance, recently during large scale humanitarian immigration. But when it happens, the right to a social minimum is likely to be translated into legal programmes that, for their part, secure the overall functioning of the society.

[29] Luhmann (n 6) 412.
[30] Luhmann (n 6) 485.

13

Social Minima at the UN Treaty Bodies: Minimal Consistency?

BEN TC WARWICK

I. INTRODUCTION

THE AMBITIONS OF social rights are substantial, ie to progressively get to a position of an array of rights – to health, housing, food, social security and more – being fully enjoyed by all. However, while the ambition is great, the realities of working with reluctant states and limited institutions often force the attention of human rights advocates to the opposite end of ambition, ie to secure, in even the most challenging contexts, a minimum band of essential entitlements. To do so, the international human rights system has worked with a range of minimum concepts more or less intensively. The tensions between desiring something much more ambitious and the need to lock in at least some minimal standards often leads to a patchwork of minimum standards.

This chapter surveys the practices of the United Nations' primary human rights bodies (the human rights treaty bodies). It does so through an interrogation of a cache of more than 10,000 documents, including documents produced by the UN treaty bodies ('Concluding Observations on State Examinations, General Comments or General Recommendations') and those submitted to those bodies by civil society organisations (shadow or parallel reports). The chapter examines patterns in this work and discusses the development of various concepts of a social minimum in the work of these committees. A number of terms are used to express similar ideas. This collection addresses the 'social minimum', although this is not a term indigent to the UN system, which instead uses the terms 'minimum core' obligation, the 'minimum essential level' of a right, or somewhat more distinctively, a 'social protection floor'.

The following section addresses the history of these terms at the UN bodies, noting the backdrop to the use of each phrase. After this, a section is dedicated to mapping the current practice of the treaty bodies in both their outputs that set out the normative position under each treaty and in their work, which examines states' progress in realising rights within their jurisdictions. With this grounding in the origins of the terms and their use, the penultimate section analyses how these terms interact on a more conceptual level and attempts to find a degree of commonality between them. A final section offers conclusions.

II. ORIGINS AND EVOLUTION AT THE COMMITTEE ON ECONOMIC, SOCIAL AND CULTURAL RIGHTS

The term 'social minimum' does not appear in the work of the UN treaty bodies, but cognisant terms have been introduced and occasionally used.[1] Originally entering into the treaty body vernacular were the terms 'minimum core' and 'minimum essential level'. These were introduced in the early stages of the existence of the Committee on Economic, Social and Cultural Rights (CESCR), which was eventually established in 1987 after a period of ineffective monitoring by its predecessor.[2] One of the first moves made by this new body was to clarify the norms of the International Covenant on Economic, Social and Cultural Rights (ICESCR). In General Comment 3, the Committee addressed the obligations of non-discrimination, international assistance, progressive realisation, non-retrogression, and a minimum core. On the obligation to ensure a minimum core it wrote:

> On the basis of the extensive experience gained by the Committee, as well as by the body that preceded it, over a period of more than a decade of examining States parties' reports the Committee is of the view that a minimum core obligation to ensure the satisfaction of, at the very least, minimum essential levels of each of the rights is incumbent upon every State party.[3]

As well as the desire to draw upon the CESCR's collective experience,[4] it is likely that the so-called Limburg Principles influenced the decision to articulate a social minimum for the ICESCR.[5] The Limburg Principles were an influential

[1] Indeed, it is only used very infrequently by NGOs submitting their own reports to the committees; Netherlands Institute for Human Rights, 'Written Contribution To the Pre-Sessional Working Group of the 59th Session of the Committee on Economic, Social and Cultural Rights' (2016) Doc no INT/CESCR/IFL/NLD/25072/E 17–18; My Right, 'The Alternative Report On Implementation In Bosnia And Herzegovina Of The United Nations Convention On The Rights Of Persons With Disabilities', Doc no INT/CRPD/ICO/BIH/24824/E 29.

[2] CESCR, 'Report on the First Session', UN Doc E/1987/28; P Alston and B Simma, 'First Session of the UN Committee on Economic, Social and Cultural Rights' (1987) 81 *The American Journal of International Law* 747, 748–49.

[3] CESCR, General Comment 3: The Nature of States Parties Obligations (Art 2(1) of the Covenant), UN Doc E/1991/23 1990, para 10.

[4] Also discussed in CESCR, 'Report on the Second Session' (1988) UN Doc E/1988/14, 168–69.

[5] One author notes that the CESCR was 'inspired' by the Limburg principles in its early years; F Gómez Isa, 'The Reversibility of Economic Social and Cultural Rights in Crisis Contexts' in E Muniategi Azkona and L Klemkaite (eds), *Local Initiatives to the Global Financial Crisis: Looking for Alternatives to the Current Socio-Economic Scenario* (Deusto, Universidad de Deusto, 2012) 35.

statement of the norms contained in the Covenant that resulted from an expert meeting held in 1986.[6] The Limburg Principles included statements that:

> States parties are obligated, regardless of the level of economic development, to ensure respect for minimum subsistence rights for all.[7]
>
> A State party will be in violation of the Covenant, inter alia, if ... it wilfully fails to meet a generally accepted international minimum standard of achievement, which is within its powers to meet ...[8]

This term of the Limburg Principles – 'minimum subsistence' – was not ever directly taken up by the CESCR,[9] and instead the Committee opted for the term 'minimum core'. The manner in which the Committee did so, however, gave rise to the additional term 'minimum essential level'. It appears that, while the intention was to use the latter term to describe what a minimum core obligation entailed, it has taken on something of a life of its own.

The extent of the minimum core obligation entailed in the ICESCR (consisting of a duty to provide at least the minimum essential level of each right) is not self-evident (ie there is not an inherent or pre-stated level of the rights which can be identified as the minimum essential content). Instead, the CESCR has had to undertake the task of setting out the core content on a right-by-right basis (a task which it only really began engaging with in its twelfth General Comment in 1999). Some rights (the rights relating to trade unions and family)[10] have not been addressed in General Comments and therefore there remains no detail about the constituent elements of the minimum core for those rights.

Where the CESCR has addressed the content of the minimum core, it has done so with a degree of variation. In the eight General Comments issued after establishing the existence of a minimum core obligation, the Committee failed to mention the obligation or gave an elaboration of its meaning. This has proved especially limiting in relation to the rights to housing and to primary education which had General Comments issued during this period, but which had no minimum core content elaborated for them.[11]

When the minimum core experienced a renaissance in the CESCR's work in 1999, there was an initial tentativeness. The core content of the right to food was outlined briefly as an obligation to 'mitigate and alleviate hunger'.[12]

[6] 'The Limburg Principles on the Implementation of the International Covenant on Economic, Social and Cultural Rights' (1987) UN Doc E/CN.4/1987/17.

[7] ibid, Principle 25.

[8] ibid, Principle 72.

[9] Only ever being used (one assumes accidentally) in a single Concluding Observation in 2013; CESCR, 'Concluding Observations: Japan' (UN Doc E/C12/JPN/CO/3 2013), para 18.

[10] International Covenant on Economic, Social and Cultural Rights 1966 (993 UNTS 3) Arts 8 and 14 (respectively).

[11] CESCR, General Comment 4: The Right to Adequate Housing (Art 11(1) of the Covenant), UN Doc E/1992/23 1991, para 11.

[12] CESCR, General Comment 12: The Right to Adequate Food (Art 11(2) of the Covenant), UN Doc E/C12/1999/5 1999), para 6.

This was a close paraphrasing of the text of the ICESCR itself, which provided in especially strong terms that it was the '*fundamental* right of everyone to be free from hunger'.[13] The following General Comment on education, while more forthcoming, kept to the same theme of a close connection to the treaty text and mainly consisted of defining the minimum core in terms of cross references to the Covenant.[14]

This pattern was broken by the CESCR's normative guidance on the right to health, where a detailed (and bold) minimum core content was set out.[15] For example, the core content was specified to include the provision of essential drugs, including a reference to the list of drugs defined by the WHO Action Programme on Essential Drugs.[16] The core content was also defined in an interdependent fashion to include the basics of food, housing, sanitation and water. The Committee has broadly continued this level attention to the minimum core in subsequent General Comments that are centred on a single substantive right.[17] In its formulations it has, however, lapsed into a vagueness that would make it difficult to determine with clarity what is expected under the minimum core obligation. For example, the core obligation to 'respect existing social security schemes and protect them from unreasonable interference'.[18]

In introducing the minimum core obligation, the CESCR noted that demands of the duty extended to the provision of the minimum essential level of each right.[19] At the same time it provided examples of when the core obligation would be violated; when 'any significant number of individuals is deprived of essential foodstuffs, of essential primary health care, of basic shelter and housing, or of the most basic forms of education'.[20] Of course, these examples – demanding 'essential', 'basic', or 'most basic' elements of rights – add little to the search for meaning for the 'minimum essential level' of a right.

[13] ICESCR Art 11(2) (emphasis added).

[14] CESCR, General Comment 13: The Right to Education (Art 13 of the Covenant), UN Doc E/C12/1999/10 1999, para 57.

[15] CESCR, General Comment 14: The Right to the Highest Attainable Standard of Health (Art 12 of the Covenant), UN Doc E/C12/2000/4 2000, para 43.

[16] The current list of over 400 is available at; World Health Organization, 'WHO Model List of Essential Medicines (20th List)' (2017), available at www.who.int/medicines/publications/essentialmedicines/20th_EML2017.pdf?ua=1.

[17] CESCR, General Comment 15: The Right to Water (Arts 11 and 12 of the Covenant), UN Doc E/C12/2002/11 2002, para 37; General Comment 17: The Right of Everyone to Benefit from the Protection of the Moral and Material Interests Resulting from Any Scientific, Literary or Artistic Production of Which He or She Is the Author (Art 15(1)(c) of the Covenant), UN Doc E/C12/GC/17 2006, para 39; General Comment 18: The Right to Work (Art 6 of the Covenant), UN Doc E/C12/GC/18 2005, para 31; General Comment 19: The Right to Social Security (Art 9 of the Covenant), UN Doc E/C12/GC/19 2007), para 39; General Comment 21: Right of Everyone to Take Part in Cultural Life (Art 15(1)(a) of the Covenant), UN Doc E/C12/GC/21 2001, para 55; General Comment 22: The Right to Sexual and Reproductive Health (Art 12 of the Covenant), UN Doc E/C12/GC/22 2016, para 49; General Comment 23: The Right to Just and Favourable Conditions of Work (Art 7. of the Covenant), UN Doc E/C12/GC/23 2016 para 65.

[18] CESCR, General Comment 19 (n 17) para 39.

[19] CESCR, General Comment 3 (n 3) para 10.

[20] ibid.

There is a significant difficulty in understanding the sense in which an aspect of a right is essential in the Committee's view.

The CESCR dwells on the legal position of the minimum core within the ICESCR, suggesting perhaps that providing for the core is a legal baseline more than anything else.[21] The CESCR also repeatedly notes the value of the minimum core concept in facilitating domestic justiciability of the ICESCR (impliedly by showing up clear violations that can be assessed).[22] The core obligation is further used by the CESCR to circumscribe the 'international assistance and cooperation' duties that extend to states. On multiple occasions, the CESCR notes that those 'in a position to assist' should help 'developing countries' to meet the core obligations.[23] Finally, the CESCR has given the minimum core obligation an immediacy[24] and a non-derogability,[25] both of which make it an instrumentally valuable tool for advocates. Together, these roles that the CESCR assigns to the minimum core seem to indicate a functional purpose for the obligation, intended to leverage the action of states, courts and the international community.

Nowhere in its normative guidance does the CESCR focus on moral imperatives for the provision of a minimum core, nor does it stipulate a particular connection between the core content and dignity, nor does it address the practical reasons why some aspects of the rights are 'essential', while others are not. While some guidance from the Committee on the principles that guide it in elaborating the content of the minimum core would be useful, it is somewhat understandable that the CESCR has not gone too far in this direction. For example, a strong statement that the core constituted the aspects of the rights essential to dignity would have an implication for how the rest of the right was to be viewed. Likewise, to commit to a view of the minimum core as the provision needed in order to survive or exist would undermine claims that other quite basic parts of the rights are essential in this regard.

A comparison of all of the CESCR's statements on the minimum core in its General Comments yields nine themes that are from time-to-time included as part of the core:

- the essential or basic content of the right;
- non-discrimination in provision of the right;

[21] The existence of a minimum core obligation is noted as essential to the *raison d'être* of the ICESCR, which is elsewhere defined as 'to establish clear obligations for States parties in respect of the full realization of the rights in question'; ibid paras 9, 10.

[22] CESCR, General Comment 12 (n 12) para 33; General Comment 14 (n 15) para 60; General Comment 15 (n 17) para 57.

[23] CESCR, General Comment 14 (n 15) para 45; General Comment 15 (n 17) para 38; General Comment 19 (n 17) para 61; see earlier General Comment 8: The Relationship between Economic Sanctions and Respect for Economic, Social and Cultural Rights, UN Doc E/C12/1997/8 1997, para 7.

[24] CESCR, General Comment 3 (n 3) para 10.

[25] CESCR, Statement Adopted By The Committee On Economic, Social And Cultural Rights (Poverty Eradication), UN Doc E/C12/2001/10 2001 para 18.

- an aspect of the right needed to access other rights (interdependency);
- equitable distribution or access to the content of the right;
- a national plan or strategy for the realisation of the right;
- monitoring the (non-)implementation of the right;
- low-cost measures or targeted programmes;
- legislative measures to ensure provision of the right;
- some specified content unique to the right.

There is, however, little consistency in the use of these themes in different General Comments that would allow a generic picture of the core content to be derived. The only aspect that is seen throughout the General Comments is the specification of some right-dependent content. These include concerns to prohibit workplace harassment,[26] to ensure reasonable waiting times for water,[27] and to allow a free choice of education.[28]

Beyond these specifics, there are only two aspects that appear in over half of the General Comments: that states should formulate a national strategy for the right, and that there should be no discrimination in the enjoyment of the right.[29] The other aspects listed above appear irregularly, in anywhere from two (eg monitor access) to five (equitable access) General Comments. This inconsistency gives rise to three issues regarding the CESCR's development of a minimum core: the substance of the obligation, its overlap with other obligations, and the demandingness of the obligation.

With a complete lack of persistently applied aspects of the core and little consistency in its substance, the purpose of the minimum core obligation as a part of the CESCR's toolkit becomes unclear. As was explored above, it is possible from the various rationales given by the Committee, that the core is intended as a legally useful and readily instrumentalisable obligation. The idea of a minimum core (and a social minimum more generally) allows the designation of a container of issue as more important and as requiring priority. However, while the CESCR has added concerns to the minimum core 'container', it has not done so with a logic, rationale or consistency that would support the claim that these issues worthy of priority. In other words, by capriciously changing its view of what is a priority in different General Comments, the CESCR undermines its prioritisation claim. It is difficult to see in this light why states, domestic courts, or the international community would take the contents of the minimum core *as such* significantly more seriously than the obligations of the Covenant at large.

[26] CESCR, General Comment 23 (n 17) para 65.
[27] CESCR, General Comment 15 (n 17) para 37.
[28] CESCR, General Comment 13 (n 14) para 57.
[29] Each of these appear in seven of the 11 relevant General Comments.

Two of the key aspects of the minimum core are non-discrimination and the duty to formulate a national action plan. Both of these are free-standing and immediate obligations under the Covenant.[30] This indicates a high degree of overlap between the content of the core and the other immediate obligations of the ICESCR. While overlap is not necessarily problematic (indeed if the minimum core is a prioritisation device, it is inevitable), it raises the question of what the added value is from designating non-discrimination and national action plans as core obligations. As they are already immediate obligations, there is be no additional (legal) urgency added by the core concept. Yet, the CESCR's vision of the core is to provide exactly such legal importance.

There are many other aspects of the minimum core which do benefit from designation in this manner, and which would not otherwise be immediate or clear priorities for states or domestic courts. These, however, do not form part of the core's prioritisation exercise.

III. SURVEYING MINIMA PRACTICE AT THE TREATY BODIES

While the idea of a social minimum or a minimum core obligation has been predominantly developed by the CESCR, other treaty bodies have engaged with the terminology, or the idea, or both. The obligation has sometimes been key to understanding how the obligations across treaties are related. For example, in a joint meeting of the CESCR and the Human Rights Committee (CCPR) members of both committees emphasised the role of the minimum core in underscoring the indivisibility of the two traditionally separated treaties. Cleveland (of the CCPR) noted the minimum core as an important conceptual clarification in the ICESCR which has made it easier to see the commonalities between the Covenants.[31] De Schutter (a member of the CESCR) noted in the same meeting that the immediacy of the minimum core obligation was important in helping to 'overcome the divide' between the two Covenants.[32]

This section will address the patterns of engagement with three ideas most connected to the concept of a social minimum in the work of the treaty bodies: a minimum core, a minimum essential level, and a social protection floor.[33] In particular, the practices of five committees will be examined; the CESCR, the CCPR, the Committee on the Rights of the Child (CRC), the Committee on the Rights of Persons with Disabilities (CRPD), and the Committee for the

[30] CESCR, 'Statement on Public Debt, Austerity Measures and the ICESCR', UN Doc E/C12/2016/1 2016 para 4.

[31] CCPR and CESCR, 'Summary Record of the Joint Meeting of the Human Rights Committee and the Committee on Economic, Social and Cultural Rights', UN Doc CCPR/C/SR3273–E/C12/2016/SR48 2016) para 5.

[32] ibid para 9.

[33] The differences between these concepts will be unpacked in section IV below.

Elimination of Discrimination Against Women (CEDAW). While not the only committees that form part of the international human right machinery, these have been selected for examination dues to their broad ratification and their direct relevance to the social minimum concept. As these variants of the social minimum are used differently in the process of state examinations than it is in the normative (General Comment/Recommendation) work of the committees, these two types of work will be handled in separate sub-sections.

A. Normative Guidance

The CESCR has frequently addressed the normative content of a social minimum, predominantly relying on the terms 'minimum core' and 'minimum essential' content. In more recent work, the concept of a Social Protection Floor has prominently entered the CESCR's repertoire.

The CESCR has used the concepts of a minimum core and a minimum essential level in different types of output, including in General Comments, statements and a letter. It has used both terms a roughly equal number of times, but they do not always occur in the same documents. The CESCR has used the term 'minimum essential level' around two-thirds of the time without mentioning the minimum core, and around two-thirds of the use of the 'minimum core' do not co-exist in the same document with the 'minimum essential level' concept. There is little pattern to these uses, indicating a scattered rather than deliberate approach to the terms. However, a highly tentative trend might be identified in the greater use of the term 'minimum core' in statements and letters, with 'minimum essential level' being mentioned more consistently in General Comments.

The use of the idea of a Social Protection Floor has arisen in clear response by the CESCR to the International Labour Organization's (ILO) work. The term entered the CESCR's normative work in two letters issued in 2012 with a full and highly substantive statement on Social Protection Floors being issued in 2015. This timeline is closely mapped to the ILO's recommendation on National Floors of Social Protection, which was issued in 2012.[34] However, neither General Comment 22 nor 23, both of which came after the Committee's statement, make a mention of Social Protection Floors.

Perhaps unsurprisingly, given the Committee's quite different remit, the CCPR makes no mention of any of these three social minimum variants in its normative work. There would be potential, especially in light of the ILO recommendation on Social Protection Floors, for the CCPR to discuss the

[34] ILO, 'Recommendation Concerning National Floors of Social Protection' (Recommendation No 202 2012).

overlap between the rights of freedom of association and to form and join a trade union[35] and the content of a Social Protection Floor. The ILO recommendation notes that collective bargaining and freedom of association for workers should be given full respect by states.[36] There is an overlap between these norms that might have been highlighted in the CCPR's work.

The CRPD, CEDAW and CRC committee all supervise treaties which have socio-economic rights contained within them. As such, they might be expected to engage with the concept of a social minimum more readily. None of the Committees has done so with any regularity, however. The CEDAW committee has never used the concepts of a minimum core, minimum essential level, or a Social Protection Floor. The CRPD committee has only used the minimum core/minimum essential terminology on one occasion in its General Comment 4.[37] There the Committee closely paraphrased the CESCR to emphasise that 'progressive realisation' did not nullify the immediacy of other obligations. The CRPD committee also recognises the potential of Social Protection Floors in aiding their monitoring work, requesting that states provide details of these when undertaking their periodic reporting.[38]

The CRC committee has had marginally more normative engagement with the idea of a social minimum. In its General Comment 21, it uses the terms 'minimum core', 'minimum essential', and 'social protection'.[39] The 'minimum core' term also appears in General Comment 19.[40] The CRC's engagement with minimum core has some substance. The Committee links its work to that of the CESCR, but adds its own content. In the CRC context, for example, the core is seen as part of the Article 4 duty to take all appropriate measures (in distinction to the CESCR's positioning of the core as implied generally by the ICESCR[41]).[42] The CRC is also explicit (in similar ways to the CESCR) that retrogressive (backwards) measures are not permitted to encroach upon the core content of the rights.[43]

[35] 'International Covenant on Civil and Political Rights' (adopted 16 December 1966, entered into force 23 March 1976, 999 UNTS 171 1966) Art 22(1).

[36] ILO, 'National Floors of Social Protection' para 3(q).

[37] CRPD, General Comment 4: The Right to Inclusive Education, UN Doc CRPD/C/GC/4 2016 para 4.

[38] CommRPD, Guidelines on Periodic Reporting to the Committee on the Rights of Persons with Disabilities, Including under the Simplified Reporting Procedures, UN Doc CRPD/C/3 2016, paras 199, 200.

[39] CommRC, General Comment 21: Children in Street Situations, UN Doc CRC/C/GC/21 2017 paras 8, 34.

[40] CommRC, General Comment 19: Public Budgeting for the Realization of Children's Rights (Art 4), UN Doc CRC/C/GC/19 2016 para 31.

[41] CESCR, General Comment 3 (n3) para 10.

[42] CommRC, General Comment 21 (n 39) para 34.

[43] CommRC, General Comment 19 (n 40) para 31; CommRC, General Comment 21 (n 39) para 34.

B. Concluding Observations

The practice of the human rights treaty bodies in their Concluding Observations varies even more markedly. The bulk of the engagement with minimum concepts comes from the CESCR, with other committees either failing to engage or engaging in quite limited respects.

The CESCR has swapped fluidly between the minimum core, minimum essential level, and social protection floor terms. Each of the terms has been used in roughly equal numbers. These uses cluster around the topic of austerity, where the Committee emphasises the immediacy of states' core obligations.[44]

While the outputs of the CESCR use the terms without expressing a clear preference, civil society organisations in their shadow reports on state examination clearly favour the minimum essential level concept. It is also notable that despite its shorter history, the social protection floor concept has emerged strongly in the CESCR's work (indeed, more strongly than in civil society work). States, perhaps unsurprisingly, do not mention their minimum obligations often at all, with there being only four occasions in the sample where a state invoked any of the three terms.[45]

It is also worth noting, as an indicator of the slipperiness of the terminology, the occasional use of the phrase 'minimum obligations' by the CESCR and civil society groups (an issue that also occurs in reporting to the CRPD committee[46]).[47]

The CCPR, again, makes no reference to minimum concepts in its Concluding Observations. As the Committee has not established a normative minimum in its General Comments, this is not unexpected. However, the potential for such engagement has been repeatedly highlighted by the Center for Reproductive Rights[48] and Amnesty International[49] in their shadow reports which highlight important social rights/civil rights overlaps (such as in the rights to health and life).

[44] CESCR, 'Statement on Public Debt, Austerity Measures and the ICESCR', UN Doc E/C12/2016/1 2016, para 4.

[45] For example, CESCR, 'Concluding Observations: Sri Lanka', UN Doc E/C12/LKA/5 2015, para 97.

[46] National Council of Organization of People with Disabilities, 'Polio Plus, Helsinki Committee in Macedonia, Health Education and Research Association, and Open the Windows. Submission for the Consideration of the Republic of Macedonia at the 20th Session of the UN Committee on the Rights of Persons with Disabilities' (2018) Doc no INT/CRPD/CSS/MKD/31979/E 13.

[47] For example, CESCR, 'Concluding Observations: Tajikistan', UN Doc E/2007/22 2006 para 450.

[48] For example, Center for Reproductive Rights and Great Lakes Initiative for Human Rights and Development, 'Supplementary Information for the Adoption of List of Issues on Rwanda Scheduled for Review by the Human Rights Committee During Its 116th Session', Doc No INT/CCPR/ICO/RWA/20243/E 2015.

[49] Amnesty International, 'Progress, Stagnation, Regression? The State of Human Rights in the Philippines under Aquino', Doc No INT/CCPR/NGO/PHL/104/9908/E.

Given the non-engagement with minima in its normative work, it is notable that there is some degree of engagement from the CEDAW committee in its Concluding Observations. These references all occur within the context of socio-economic rights and mainly rely upon the social protection floor term.[50]

The CRC committee makes limited use of any of the terms, and when it does it is the social protection floor that it engages with most. This engagement is, however, disappointing as it takes the form of a copy-and-paste recommendation that states: 'partner with UNICEF and others to create a nationally defined social protection floor for access to basic services for children, as part of the Social Protection Floor initiative of the United Nations'.[51] The CRC committee's partial use of the terms comes against a backdrop of very little civil society reporting to the committee that invokes minimum concepts.

Finally, and similarly, the CRPD committee's use of the terms in its Concluding Observations has also been limited. When the 'minimum core' term has been used by that Committee, it has done so in the context of the civil and political right to a fair trial. The Committee's engagement with the social protection floor has been somewhat broader, but still far from substantive or frequent.

IV. CONSISTENCY AND FUTURE DIRECTIONS

This scattered practice of the treaty bodies is a challenge to make sense of, either on its own terms or in relation to the bigger picture, of the protection of human rights minima. On its own terms, there is very limited consistency within individual treaty bodies or across the different bodies that are within the same system of monitoring. This can be explained, however, by the context of a highly constrained system of human rights monitoring, with little time for monitoring, institutional architecture for ensuring such consistency, or time for normative reflection.

For example, the few hours afforded to each committee to examine the progress of states on a whole range of rights over the previous five or more years, is clearly inadequate. This inevitably causes committee experts and secretariat staff to reach for those issues most clearly presented in civil society submissions, and which are most fully developed in previous practice. For committees such as the CRC, this means that limited civil society reporting on social minima will filter into a limited consideration of these issues in Concluding Observations. For other committees with a more established view of social minima, such as the CESCR, it is a lack of consistency that emerges most strongly, with limited

[50] For example, CommEDAW, 'Concluding Observations: Guinea', UN Doc CEDAW/C/GIN/CO/7-8 2014 para 46.

[51] For example, CommRC, 'Concluding Observations: Timor-Leste', UN Doc CRC/C/TLS/CO/2-3 2015 para 53.

time and a lack of institutional continuity feeding a shifting use of terminology and concepts around the social minimum. The problem is contributed to by limited normative guidance emerging from the committees on the matter, which feeds civil society deficits of understanding on social minimum use at the UN treaty bodies. In this respect, the statement of the CESCR on the ILO's Social Protection Floor that includes some discussion of how the Social Protection Floor is tied to the CESCR's original minimum core concept, is an important development.[52]

Another important way of thinking about the practices around social minimum concepts in the treaty bodies' work is to consider at what stage in their development they are. In other terms; are some of the social minimum concepts at the beginning or the end of their life course? The clearest answer here is that the Social Protection Floor concept is in its ascendancy. However, it remains unclear whether the longer-standing minimum core and minimum essential levels concepts will be retired as a result. It seems unlikely that they will disappear entirely from the work of the treaty bodies for a number of reasons. First, that the CESCR has most strongly tied the Social Protection Floor to the right to social security[53] and General Comment 19.[54] This means there will remain a role for the minimum core in relation to other social rights. Second, and as alluded to above, the committees are responsive to the submissions of civil society and therefore any retirement of the 'core' and 'minimum essential' concepts would likely need to be marked and explicit before they would fall out of civil society vocabularies and submissions. Third, the degree of cross-fertilisation between the committees, and especially in this regard from the CESCR to the other treaty bodies, produces a latency between the normative reforms of the CESCR and changes developing in other treaty bodies' work.

The final piece of the jigsaw for the future of social minimum concepts at the treaty bodies, is the reconciliation one. If several concepts are to be carried forward, or one is to emerge as the unifying standard, how is this to be achieved? Each social minimum concept has been described in distinct terms and carries its own conceptual baggage. In some cases, these normative approaches are well established and have been developed over a period of many years. Unpicking their bases, in order to combine or eliminate redundancy is a significant task that the treaty bodies have so far seemed unwilling to undertake.

In the following sections, these key pieces of context to the treaty bodies' operation will be fed through a number of different approaches that might be taken. First, considering the utility across different concepts, before turning to how such a reconciliation between the concepts might be operationalised.

[52] CESCR, 'Statement on Social Protection Floors: An Essential Element of the Right to Social Security and of the Sustainable Development Goals', UN Doc E/C12/2015/1 2015.

[53] ibid para 4.

[54] CESCR, General Comment 19 (n 17).

A. Terms and Conceptualisations

The utility of the minima in the UN system has itself been subject to question and the minimum core obligation is credited with varying degrees of importance. Saiz, for example, noted during the 2008 economic crisis that it could be useful in requiring that states ring-fence resources,[55] thus providing an important counter to neoliberal austerity policies.[56] Others, addressing the obligation's focus on minima, have dismissed it as a 'not a very useful yardstick' in Australia[57] or indeed in Western welfare states more generally.[58] The corollary of such criticisms, according to an early account by Craven, may be that 'the Committee will primarily direct its attention to the actions of developing States'.[59] Other perspectives on the utility of the obligation focus its potential for justiciability. The CESCR itself has noted on several occasions that the domestic legal protection of the core would be an important first step towards full justiciability.[60] Likewise, early debates on an individual complaints mechanism for the ICESCR canvassed the possibility of a very limited Optional Protocol which dealt only with core obligations.[61]

However, the core has the benefit of being an immediate obligation, intended to contrast to the progressivity of the main Article 2(1) obligation.[62] The CESCR has endorsed and used this characterisation itself.[63] This means that in addition to providing a minimum benchmark for states, the obligation is also actionable for civil society actors wishing to use it as an accountability mechanism. This longstanding utility has been boosted by the attention and support of the ILO to Social Protection Floors.

The content of the ILO's Social Protection Floor is largely complementary to the ICESCR obligations, including – amongst much else – a focus on availability, accessibility, acceptability and quality[64] (which is also seen in the CESCR's work[65]). However, there are also a number of partial translations that mean

[55] I Saiz, 'Rights in Recession? Challenges for Economic and Social Rights Enforcement in Times of Crisis' (2009) 1 *Journal of Human Rights Practice* 277, 282.

[56] JJ Wills and BTC Warwick, 'Contesting Austerity: The Potential and Pitfalls of Socioeconomic Rights Discourse' (2016) 23 *Indiana Journal of Global Legal Studies* 664.

[57] D Otto and D Wiseman, 'In Search of "Effective Remedies": Applying the International Covenant on Economic, Social and Cultural Rights in Australia' (2001) 7 *Australian Journal of Human Rights* 5, 18.

[58] IE Koch, 'The Justiciability of Indivisible Rights' (2003) 72 *Nordic Journal of International Law* 3, 20.

[59] M Craven, *The International Covenant on Economic, Social and Cultural Rights: A Perspective on Its Development* (doctoral thesis, University of Nottingham 1992) 107.

[60] CESCR, General Comment 12 (n 12) para 33; General Comment 14 (n 15) para 60.

[61] B Porter, 'The Reasonableness of Article 8(4) – Adjudicating Claims from the Margins' (2009) 27 *Nordic Journal of Human Rights* 39, 44.

[62] ICESCR Art 2(1).

[63] See, for example, CESCR, General Comment 15 (n 17) para 37.

[64] ILO (n 34) para 5(a).

[65] CESCR, General Comment 14 (n 15) para 35.

subtle divergences between the work of the Committee and the ILO appear. For example, the ILO's Social Protection Floor is subject to progressive realisation.[66] However, this is a position that the CESCR has explicitly moved away from: 'the minimum core content would not be subject to the notions of progressive realization and resource availability'.[67] A further, though less fundamental, tension arises as the ILO requires states to set their own national social protection floor, while the CESCR has taken a more centralised approach and prefers to set the conditions under which the minimum will be met.

More challenging, however, is the way the ILO's approach is framed. The social protection floor is required to directly guarantee healthcare, but all other entitlements covered by the ILO's Recommendation 202 are to be accessed through 'basic income security'.[68] This means that the ILO relies on basic income and the market, to ensure that individuals can access everything from food, to water, sanitation, care and education.[69] While this use of basic income plus the market to realise human rights is widespread, including in the work of the treaty bodies, the human rights committees have reserved a space for state provision of rights where market mechanisms are ineffective. For example, in times of famine or in particularly rural areas, markets may effectively fail and leave even those beneficiaries of the ILO's 'basic income security' without a means for accessing their rights. The treaty bodies have long understood, that the state will have a more active role in providing the right in such circumstances,[70] and more recently have expressed concerns about the role in general for markets in education.[71]

Yet for all of these potential downsides of the ILO's approach (and of the treaty bodies fully adopting it) there is a clear benefit in making use of a standard with the buy-in and enthusiasm of an organisation as large and as complex as the ILO. This level of engagement with the ILO standard contrasts to at least the CESCR's previous engagements with agendas external to it, which has ordinarily been symbolic.[72] The effects of importing this enthusiasm into the treaty body system is already visible in the uptick of attention to social minimum ideas since 2012.

B. Reconciliation

If the use of social minima in the work of the treaty bodies is to continue, it would be beneficial for an exercise of rationalisation to take place. With the

[66] ILO (n 34) para 3(g).

[67] CESCR, 'Report on the Eighteenth and Nineteenth Sessions', UN Doc E/1999/22 para 499(b).

[68] ILO (n 34) para 4.

[69] ibid para 5.

[70] See, for example, CESCR, General Comment 12 (n 12) para 15.

[71] CommEDAW, 'Concluding Observations: Ghana' (UN Doc CEDAW/C/GHA/CO/6-7 2014) para 32(e); CESCR, 'Concluding Observations: Uganda' (UN Doc E/C12/UGA/CO/1 2015) para 36(c).

[72] B Warwick, 'Debt, Austerity and the Structural Responses of Social Rights' in I Bantekas and C Lumina (eds), *Sovereign Debt and Human Rights* (Oxford, Oxford University Press, 2018) 386.

handful of competing terms and concepts in play surrounding the social minimum (not to mention the range of other social rights obligations), there is a danger of creating confusion. There are, very broadly, two approaches that could be taken. First, the retirement of several of the minimum obligations and, second, the reconciliation or merging of several of the obligations.

The first approach would require some level of agreement about the appropriate terms and set of concepts – minimum essential level, minimum core, social protection floor, or social minimum – that should be pursued. In each case, the loss of a term would entail the loss of a range of associated benefits. For example, losing the minimum core or minimum essential level would lose a track record and establishment in the work of a number of the treaty bodies would sacrifice a doctrine specific to the treaty body system and would damage the work of civil society actors and courts which have attached themselves to this strand of the human rights system. On the other hand, retiring the Social Protection Floor from the treaty bodies' vocabulary would put at risk the enthusiasm and backing that has been generated by association with the ILO agenda.

The second approach does not come with many fewer difficulties. Reconciling the social minimum concepts, with their different elucidations and origins is a challenge that would require an elision of some of the distinctions. The market-based solutions of the Social Protection Floor would need to be supplemented by the fuller conception of the minimum core. And the treaty bodies may have to permit a greater role for states in setting themselves targets and in defining their own minimum standards. However, besides these substantive tasks that would accompany an attempt at reconciling the different terms, there would be tactical choices to be made. The treaty bodies would at least partially attach themselves to an initiative of a different international body with a different membership. This would surrender a degree of control over the future direction of the social minimum and would also raise questions about the legal basis for such an approach. Further, the extent of the treaty bodies' attachment to the ILO's floor would be a matter of contention. Too much editing of the Social Protection Floor Recommendation and the benefits of a unified standard and shared agenda would be diminished, while acceding to the ILO standard too fully would import a range of defects that could cause friction with the remainder of social rights obligations.

V. CONCLUSIONS

Some 30 years since the concept of a minimum core entered the imagination of the CESCR, the use of social minimum concepts across the UN treaty bodies remains extraordinarily limited. This neglect of the obligations by the monitoring bodies is only matched in the civil society reporting to the committees, which has also been slow to engage with minima, even in the most challenging of contexts. These limitations are a function of both general constraints upon the workings of the treaty bodies (including limited time to review states and develop normative frameworks), and of minimum-specific objections and complexities. The existence of these limitations, and the rather partial use of minimum concepts by the treaty bodies, should not however be taken as a comment on the potential of the idea to benefit human rights advocacy or adjudication. But the extent of the practical limitations demonstrates the challenge that lies ahead for proponents of a properly functioning social minima in the international human rights system.

This weight of practical difficulties might, quite serendipitously, be overcome by the ILO's engagement with the area of social minimum. The introduction of the Recommendation on Social Protection Floors in 2012 has given a new lease of life to minimum thinking in the treaty bodies and has generated a new normative statement by the CESCR. However, while the ILO standard brings practical benefits, there remain significant substantive differences between social protection floors and the treaty body concept of a minimum core or minimum essential level of rights protection. This creates a risk of the treaty bodies' work being diluted by the ILO approach, or the ILO standard being partly or inconsistently applied by the committees. This risk is all the more pronounced when the patchy practice across the treaty bodies is seen. There are clear barriers to cross-committee working, and these will inevitably affect whatever path is taken to reform or reinvigorate work around the social minimum.

As a whole, the story of the social minimum at the UN treaty bodies is not a classic narrative of either total success or total failure. Rather, it is a tale of multiple ideas and inconsistent practice. Attempts to secure a legal baseline for social rights have been frustrated by overlapping terms and agendas. It is ironic, then, that one of those overlapping agendas – the ILO's Social Protection Floor – might provide a way forward that can help focus attention on the crucial aspects of the treaty bodies' conception of a minimum and the associated tactical benefits of the different approaches. The 'moment' surrounding the Social Protection Floor should be enthusiastically captured by the treaty bodies, either as an irritant that paves the way for a more consistent minimum in social rights norms or, more likely, as a mechanism for consolidating and unifying a standard that has a history of patchy practice.

14

Potential and Pitfalls of Indivisible Judicial Protection of a Social Minimum: From Inflation to Procedural Protection?

INGRID LEIJTEN

I. INTRODUCTION

SOCIAL RIGHTS ARE justiciable not only on the basis of socio-economic rights norms, but also on the basis of norms guaranteeing human dignity, the right to life, or property protection. The idea that human rights are indivisible, interconnected and interdependent has travelled from the legal philosophical and political sphere to the sphere of rights adjudication.[1] Most likely to be protected under civil rights norms is some kind of social *minimum*. A focus on minimum protection is narrow enough to avoid allegations of activism while targeting protection of the most vulnerable. That such indivisible, minimum protection is feasible can be seen, for example, in Colombian and German constitutional law.[2] In the case law of the European Court of Human Rights (ECtHR; 'the Court'), social rights are to some extent guaranteed as well.[3] The

[1] This idea is generally linked to the UN stance on human rights protection, see, for instance, UN General Assembly, 'Preparation of two Draft International Covenants on Human Rights', 5 February 1952, UN Doc A/RES/453 (IV). For a more philosophical notion of indivisibility, see, eg A Sen, 'The Standard of Living: Lives and Capabilities' in G Hawthorn (ed), *The Standard of Living* (Cambridge, Cambridge University Press, 1987) 20–38, at 36–38; M Nussbaum, *Creating Capabilities: The Human Development Approach* (Oxford, Oxford University Press, 2011).

[2] See, the right to a 'vital minimum' in Colombian constitutional jurisprudence (*cf* David Landau, 'The promise of a minimum core approach: the Colombian model for judicial review of austerity measures' in A Nolan (ed), *Economic and Social Rights after the Global Crisis* (Cambridge, Cambridge University Press, 2015) 276–98), as well as the individual right to a subsistence minimum as it is recognised by the German *Bundesverfassungsgericht* on the basis of the guarantee of human dignity and the social state principle (BVerfGE 125, 175, 1 BvL 1/09 of 9 February 2010 (*Hartz IV*)). See, also on the constitutional guarantee of a social minimum, ch 16 (Boyle).

[3] *cf* IE Koch, *Human Rights as Indivisible Rights: The Protection of Socio-Economic Demands under the European Convention on Human Rights* (Leiden, Martinus Nijhoff Publishers, 2009);

ECtHR has recognised at an early stage that there is no water-tight distinction between socio-economic rights and the sphere protected by the Convention.[4] The right to respect for private life as enshrined in Article 8 ECHR, but also the protection of property in Article 1 of the First Protocol to the ECHR, and even the prohibition of inhuman and degrading treatment (Article 3 ECHR), have proven fruitful avenues for socio-economic complaints.

Protection of socio-economic rights on the basis of classic rights norms holds great promise. Fundamental rights deserve a generous, purposive interpretation that provides sufficient room for effective protection.[5] Besides, the growing importance and acceptance of economic and social rights qua individual justiciable rights supports their indivisible protection.[6] To this we can add the acceptance of positive obligations: today, most rights are understood to require the state to refrain from interfering in individuals' personal sphere as well as actively engage in the realisation of their rights.[7] Positive rights are justiciable, even though, just as with negative rights, the remedies available differ from one legal context to the other. Another thing that speaks for social protection on the basis of classical rights norms, is the fact that even though social rights norms are 'catching up', rights enshrined in socio-economic rights covenants and the like are still often perceived as second-rank. Binding legal judgments are more likely to be found in the context of civil rights, especially where international human rights obligations are concerned. This means that relying on civil rights norms may seem the smarter strategy in case of a complaint about (minimum) social rights.

The protection offered in the Council of Europe by the ECHR and its socio-economic counterpart – the (Revised) European Social Charter ((R)ESC) – is a case in point. Due to the binding character of the ECtHR's judgments, it may seem more promising to phrase a complaint in terms of the Convention rather than as an alleged violation of the (R)ESC.[8] An illuminating example is the so called 'bed, bath and bread' issue that has occupied legal and political minds in the Netherlands for quite some years now. In 2014 the European Committee of Social Rights held that the Netherlands had violated

I Leijten, *Core Socio-Economic Rights and the European Court of Human Rights* (Cambridge, Cambridge University Press 2018). *cf* also ch 15 (Kagiaros).

[4] *Airey v Ireland*, ECtHR 9 October 1979, 6289/73, para 26.

[5] A Barak, *Proportionality: Constitutional Rights and Their Limitations* (Cambridge, Cambridge University Press, 2012).

[6] Consider for example the Optional Protocol to the International Covenant on Economic, Social and Cultural Rights (UN General Assembly, 5 March 2009, A/RES/63/117, entered into force 5 May 2013), with a possibility for individual communications.

[7] For an early example from the case law of the ECtHR, *cf Marckx v Belgium*, ECtHR 13 June 1979, 6833/74, para 31; *Case Relating to Certain Aspects of the Laws on the Use of Languages in Education in Belgium*, ECtHR 23 July 1968, 1474/62, 1677/62, 1691/62, 1769/63, 1994/63 and 2126/64. An exception is the US legal order, in which positive obligations are not recognised (*cf Deshaney v Winnebago County Department of Social Services*, 489 US 189 (1989)).

[8] Only collective complaints can be reviewed for compliance with the (R)ESC.

Articles 13(4) and 31(2) of the (R)ESC by not securing minimum social protection for undocumented migrants whose asylum applications had been rejected.[9] Only if these migrants cooperated with the authorities to organise their return would they be eligible for basic shelter, food and clothing. Yet the Dutch Government was unwilling to attach much weight to the decision of the ECSR. In 2015, the Committee of Ministers concurred the reluctance of the political authorities,[10] while Dutch courts affirmed that a right to minimum subsistence need not be unconditional.[11] At the same time, hopes were rising that the ECtHR would corroborate the view of the ECSR by holding that the Dutch situation violated Article 3 of the Convention (the prohibition of inhuman and degrading treatment). After all, the case law of the Court is binding for the parties to the case,[12] while the ECHR norms including their interpretation – different to those of the (R)ESC – have direct effect in the Dutch legal order.[13] Yet in 2016 the ECtHR in *Hunde v the Netherlands* concluded that the complaint of an undocumented migrant under Article 3 ECHR was manifestly ill-founded.[14] Since then, more or less ad hoc solutions have been provided, mostly by local governments, for those in desperate need, and even now that there finally is a new state policy, an unconditional human right to minimum subsistence is still not explicitly recognised.

Regardless of the fact that reliance on civil rights norms is attractive, the bed, bath and bread issue also helps to show that there are limits to the protection the ECHR can offer. Arguably, the facts of the *Hunde* case weren't severe enough to potentially trigger the absolute protection of Article 3. Yet even if the applicant would not have had any means of subsistence, it is unlikely that the ECtHR would have straightforwardly held that there is an unconditional right to a subsistence minimum under the Convention.[15] The ECtHR's mandate is tied to the 'civil and political' wording of the Convention. This means that the social protection this Convention can offer is inherently limited. In line with this, the sensitive position of the ECtHR may lead to particular caution in this field. This is even more so when the topic dealt with is a politically sensitive one, such as immigration, and budgetary issues are involved. Both legal and political considerations, thus, make that the indivisible protection of a social minimum is not necessarily straightforward.

In this chapter, I aim to do three things. First, I will illustrate the indivisible protection of social rights at the same time showing that there is an inherent bias

[9] Decision on the merits, *European Committee of Social Rights, Conference of European Churches (CEC) v the Netherlands*, Complaint No 90/2013.

[10] Resolution adopted by the Committee of Ministers on 15 April 2015 (CM/ResChS(2015)5).

[11] ABRvS 26 November 2015, ECLI:NL:RVS:2015:3415 and CRvB 26 November 2016, ECLI:NL:CRVB:2015:3803.

[12] Article 46 ECHR.

[13] Articles 93 and 94 of the Dutch Constitution.

[14] *Hunde v the Netherlands*, ECtHR 5 July 2016 (dec), 17931/16. See more recently *Said Good v the Netherlands*, ECtHR 23 January 2018 (dec), 50613/12.

[15] See section II below.

against social protection when civil rights provisions are adjudicated (section II). Here I draw from the case law of the ECtHR, whose failure to clarify the prima facie social content of the ECHR rights implies overall 'balancing' tests that focus disproportionally on the interests of the state. In section III, I will explore what seems to be a way for courts like the ECtHR – as well as several constitutional courts – to nevertheless contribute to the protection of robust social rights. This is a resort to procedural review of social rights cases, which arguably helps secure what could be understood as a (substantive) social minimum. With the help of procedural review, a middle way can seemingly be found between the Scylla of determining and enforcing a detailed right to such a minimum and the Charybdis of a too deferential approach. Thirdly, regardless of its promise, I will argue that procedural review is not entirely unproblematic either (section IV). Amongst other things, the way in which it features in the ECtHR's case law suggests maybe a too individualistic approach creating conflicts with other constitutional values.

Before getting started, a few things on terminology. What I mean here by 'social minimum' is not so much a specified and fixed set of resources. Rather, when arguing that a court protects a social minimum, I mean that it guarantees (some of) the things needed for leading a minimally decent life, eg some form of (adequate) housing, healthcare, or benefits that ensure a subsistence minimum. The discussion of what a 'social minimum' exactly includes apart from particular (adjudicative) contexts, I leave to other chapters in this book.[16] The term 'procedural review' can be subject to different understandings as well.[17] What I mean by it is a form of judicial review that, rather than looking at the outcome (output) of law and (administrative and judicial) decision-making, is concerned with the way in which decisions were made and motivated. The question is then what was the input, ie what procedures were followed and which information was taken into account, and whether this leads to a violation of fundamental rights. Procedural review, in my understanding, is thus not limited to the procedural safeguards available to the complainant, such as fair trial and participation rights, albeit these may form part of this review. I will expand on this further below.

II. RIGHTS INFLATION AND BIAS

In order to understand the possibilities for, as well as the bias against (minimum) social rights protection under the ECHR, we must say something on the structure of rights and their adjudication. Fundamental rights adjudication is

[16] See ch 6 (Goedemé et al).

[17] With regard to the ECtHR, see, on the different types of procedural review, J Gerards, 'Procedural Review by the ECtHR: A Typology' in J Gerards and E Brems (eds), *Procedural Review in European Fundamental Rights Cases* (Cambridge, Cambridge University Press, 2017) 127–60.

characterised by two stages. The first is the determination of the scope of a right, and the second concerns the review of the justification adduced for interfering with this right.[18] The two stages tie in with the structure of fundamental rights, ie, with a distinction between prima facie and definitive protection. This means that there may be a prima facie right to something – say feeding birds – under a particular rights norm, but whether such right is actually protected depends on the other legal and factual circumstances.[19] A two-stage approach to rights adjudication has a number of practical advantages as well. It clarifies what claims individuals have and demarcates a court's jurisdiction. The latter is especially important where supra- or international human rights protection is concerned. Before a court like the ECtHR renders a binding judgment on a conflict between individual and general interests, it first must explain why its competence covers the issue at hand. Interpreting a right before moving to the review stage, moreover allows a court to engage with the right's content. In order for it to balance the individual right at stake against the general interest, after all, some tangible idea of what this right entails is needed.

The two stages of rights adjudication may be considered 'elementary, standard propositions which should not need stating because they are such as everyone would assent to in principle'.[20] Still, when socio-economic rights are concerned, a clear distinction is not always visible. The content of individual socio-economic rights is difficult determine and hence this step is often neglected. Instead, it seems more feasible to ask whether the Government's action or omission was reasonable.[21] In the socio-economic case law of the ECtHR, too, this court frequently refrains from determining whether and why the individual interest falls within the scope of the invoked norm. It is hesitant to link a request for (minimum) social rights protection to the 'civil and political' norms enshrined in the Convention in the sense that fails to determine what social protection prima facie may be demanded under the Convention. More precisely, the ECtHR regularly 'proceeds on the assumption' that the Convention is applicable. This was the case for example in *Sali v Sweden*, which concerned the domestic authorities' refusal to grant an unemployment benefit evaluated in the light of the protection of property.[22] In *Maggio and Others v Italy*, an applicant complained about the fact that his pension turned out lower

[18] *cf* R Alexy, *A Theory of Constitutional Rights*, transl J Rivers (Oxford, Oxford University Press, 2002) 196ff. (also 84–86, 178ff); Barak, *Proportionality* (2012).

[19] *cf* Alexy, *A Theory* (ibid) 17, 47–48.

[20] Judge Fitzmaurice' dissenting opinion in *Marckx v.Belgium*, ECtHR 13 June 1979, 6833/74.

[21] KG Young, 'Proportionality, Reasonableness, and Socio-Economic Rights' in V Jackson and M Tushnet (eds) *Proportionality: New Frontiers, New Challenges* (Cambridge, Cambridge University Press, 2017) 227–41. *cf* the South African Constitutional Court's unwillingness to recognise the minimum core content of socio-economic rights, eg *Government of the Republic of South Africa v Grootboom & Others* 2001 (1) SA 46 (CC). See, on the indeterminacy problem, also ch 11 (O'Cinneide).

[22] *Sali v Sweden*, ECtHR 10 January 2006 (dec), 67070/01.

than expected, while the Court did 'not consider it necessary … to determine whether [he] had a possession within the meaning of the Protocol No. 1'.[23] In *Berger-Krall v Slovenia*, the Court did not consider it necessary to determine whether a specially protected tenancy fell within the scope of this Protocol.[24] Clarity on prima facie rights and obligations is moreover absent where the Court in socio-economic cases holds that there *may* be positive obligations involved. This it does in cases concerning requests for adequate housing, care, or other accommodations.[25] The Court, for example, has stated that 'there may be positive obligations inherent in the effective respect for private or family life' in relation to the provision of expensive health measures.[26] Also, it 'does not rule out that, in principle, Article 8 could impose a positive obligation on the authorities to provide accommodation for a homeless gypsy which is such that it facilitates their "gypsy way of life"'.[27] This is then reason to review the issue.

Giving a broad scope to individual fundamental rights is sometimes referred to as 'rights inflation'.[28] The result that most conflicts between individual and general interests can be phrased in terms of human or constitutional rights. This need not mean that eventually, the individual interest prevails. Prima facie rights are generally rendered definitive with the help of a proportionality or balancing test. At this second stage, it is determined whether the interference with the right is justified. Because a balancing test takes into account the weight of the interests on both sides of the scale, rights inflation seems unproblematic. When more marginal or 'less fundamental' interests are included in the scope of fundamental rights, they are simply less likely to outbalance the reasons given for an alleged violation.

Nevertheless, what we see in the socio-economic case law of the ECtHR, is that if a broad interpretation results in opaque prima facie rights and obligations, or if the interpretation stage is skipped altogether, this may result in a bias against positive, socio-economic protection. That is, when the Court 'assumes' that the Convention applies, it follows that a violation will not be found. That there 'may be' positive obligations in a certain field, is too abstract a statement to guide the Court's review towards the protection of a social minimum. If the Court elaborates on this, it does so by stating that there is *no* general positive obligation to provide for a subsistence minimum. The Convention 'does

[23] *Maggio and Others v Italy*, ECtHR 31 May 2011, 46286/09 52851/08 53727/08 54486/08 56001/08, para 59. *cf* also *Valkov and Others v Bulgaria*, ECtHR 25 October 2011, 2033/04, 19125/04, 19475/04, 19490/04, 19495/04, 19497/04, 24729/04, 171/05 and 2041/05.

[24] *Berger-Krall and Others v Slovenial*, ECtHR 12 June 2014, 14717/04.

[25] *Marzari v Italy*, ECtHR 4 May 1999 (dec), 36448/97, referring to *Botta v Italy*, ECtHR 24 February 1998, 21439/93, paras 33–34.

[26] *Sentges v the Netherlands*, ECtHR 8 July 2003 (dec), 27677/02.

[27] *Codona v the UK*, 7 February 2006 (dec), 485/05 (where the complaint of a Roma person who was offered bricks and mortar accommodation instead of another site for her caravan was held inadmissible).

[28] *cf* K Möller, *The Global Model of Constitutional Rights* (Oxford, Oxford University Press, 2012).

not guarantee, as such, socio-economic rights'.[29] For example, the Court has held that 'no positive obligation for the local authorities can be inferred from Article 8 to provide the applicant with a specific apartment';[30] that 'the scope of any positive obligation to house the homeless must be limited',[31] and that Article 1 P1 'does not place Contracting Parties under a positive obligation to support a given individual's chosen lifestyle out of funds which are entrusted to them as agents of the public weal', thereby substantiating the conclusion that the legislative change had not resulted in an 'individual and excessive burden'.[32] Moreover, the Court grants the state a wide margin of appreciation in the context of general measures of economic and social strategy.[33] Due to a lack of clarity on what is required in the first place, the focus in the balancing analysis lies on the interests of the state, and this margin is then hard to overcome.[34]

According to Young, proportionality review in combination with a degree of deference, or margin of appreciation, is not very promising for ensuring social rights protection.[35] On the basis of the ECtHR's case law, it can be argued that this is even more so when these rights are dealt with on the basis of civil rights norms, and no clear interpretative statements are made regarding the prima facie protection of (minimum) social rights.

Besides, in the context of relative rights, also in relation to an absolute right such as the prohibition of inhuman and degrading treatment (Article 3), the Court is hesitant to recognise even minimum social rights. It cautiously holds that in case of 'serious deprivation or want incompatible with human dignity', a responsibility for the State *could* arise.[36] At the same time, it underlines that 'Article 3 does not place an obligation on the contracting states to alleviate the disparities between the levels of healthcare available in various countries',[37] or 'entail any general obligation to give refugees financial assistance to enable them to maintain a certain standard of living'.[38] In the case of health issues the Article 3 threshold is a high one, 'because the alleged harm emanates not from acts or omissions of the authorities but from the illness itself'.[39] Regardless of the absolute character of this provision that sits uneasily with a balancing of

[29] *Bulgakova v Russia*, ECtHR 18 January 2007, 69524/01.

[30] *Marzari v Italy*, ECtHR 4 May 1999 (dec), 36448/97.

[31] *O'Rourke v the UK*, ECtHR 26 June 2001 (dec), 39022/97.

[32] *Goudswaard-Van der Lans v the Netherlands*, ECtHR 22 September 2005 (dec), 75255/01.

[33] See, eg *Stec and Others v the UK*, ECtHR (GC) 12 April 2006, 65731/01 and 65900/01, para 52; *Stummer v Austria*, ECtHR (GC) 7 July 2011, 37452/02, para 89; *Taskin and Others v Turkey*, ECtHR 10 November 2004, 46117/99, paras 116–17; *Fadeyeva v Russia*, ECtHR 9 June 2005, 55723/00, para 104.

[34] eg *Sentges v the Netherlands*, ECtHR 8 July 2003 (dec), 27677/02 (on the request for a robotic arm).

[35] Young, *Proportionality* (2017).

[36] *MSS v Belgium and Greece*, ECtHR (GC) 21 January 2011, 30696/09, para 253.

[37] Hristosov *and Others* v Bulgaria, ECtHR 13 November 2012, 30909/06, para 111.

[38] MSS v Belgium and Greece, ECtHR (GC) 21 January 2011, 30696/09, para 249.

[39] *N v the UK*, ECtHR (GC) 27 May 2008, 26565/05.

interests or a margin of appreciation, thus, also here a bias against social protection can be identified.

III. PROCEDURAL REVIEW AS A SOLUTION

I argue elsewhere that more attention for the interpretation stage may enable a court like the ECtHR to provide more robust minimum social protection.[40] Indeed, this is a matter of giving content to what social rights are and require, and is particularly important where there is a need for demarcating judicial competences and a content-infused reasonableness test is not a feasible option. The ECtHR need not be overly cautious in this regard as different from social rights generally, a right to a social minimum can convincingly be linked to the Convention. I will not delve more deeply into the issue of interpretation here. Instead I will show how the ECtHR now seems to be partly overcoming the bias against social rights review describe above. While it is hesitant to define prima facie social rights and recognise specific social obligations, and generally grants a wide margin of appreciation in social rights cases, the court has resorted to procedural review which enables it to guarantee a kind of minimum social protection. Procedural guarantees in the socio-economic field form part of a broader trend towards 'dematerialisation', ie, a shift away from the question whether the protection provided – the output of a decision-making or judicial process – is substantially sufficient for complying with the Convention. Instead it is asked whether the procedure for reaching the decision complained about meets certain requirements.

A procedural approach can be found in the Court's case law on social security. An example concerning the right to protection of property (Article 1 P1) is the case of *Moskal v Poland*.[41] Here the Court relied on the principle of 'good governance' for concluding that no fair balance had been struck between the demands of the general interest and the protection of the individual's social security rights. Moskal was erroneously granted an early retirement pension and the effects of the relatively late withdrawal of an erroneously granted benefit and the fact that it took three years before she received a replacement, made the case turn out in Moskal's favour. The principle of good governance, according to the Court, 'requires that where an issue in the general interest is at stake it is incumbent on the public authorities to act in good time, in an appropriate manner and with utmost consistency'.[42] The judgment can be seen as suggesting that a revocation of minimum means of subsistence – even when lawful – requires the national authorities to scrutinise the individual hardship that might thereby be

[40] Leijten, *Core Socio-Economic* Rights (2018). See also ch 11 (Cinneide).
[41] *Moskal v Poland*, ECtHR 15 September 2009, 10373/05, paras 68–76.
[42] ibid, para 51.

caused and act accordingly. A more recent example is *Čakarević v Croatia*.[43] In this case a woman complained about the fact that she had to pay back a benefit that had been paid to her for too many years. According to the Court, given that the mistake was entirely the Government's and that it had not acted in good time, appropriately and consistently, the Convention was violated. Important, though not decisive, was moreover that the benefit guaranteed the applicant's subsistence minimum. Without holding that such a minimum is required under the Convention, thus, the ECtHR indirectly protected it by means of 'good governance' requirements the decision-making by the competent authorities must fulfil.

In the sphere of housing rights, a procedural approach is clearly visible in cases concerning Roma housing. Mostly these concern evictions of groups of Roma from land occupied unlawfully, while the underlying issue is that of the lack of alternative, suitable accommodation. In earlier cases, the Court relied on a wide margin and was unwilling to find a violation as soon as the procedural safeguards available to complainants appeared sufficient.[44] In *Yordanova and Others v Bulgaria* (2012) and *Winterstein and Others v France* (2013), however, its procedural approach was given a 'positive twist'.[45] In *Yordanova*, the Court held that: i) in spheres involving the application of social or economic policies the margin is wide, as is the case in the planning context; but ii) the margin might be narrower whenever what is at stake for the applicant 'is crucial to the individual's effective enjoyment of key rights'. Further, iii) procedural safeguards are 'especially material', so that iv) any person at risk of losing his home, which the Court considers the most extreme form of interference with one's right to respect for the home,

> should in principle be able to have the proportionality and reasonableness of the measure determined by an independent tribunal in the light of the relevant principles under Article 8, … This means, among other things, that where relevant arguments concerning the proportionality of the interference have been raised by the applicant in domestic legal proceedings, the domestic courts should examine them in detail and provide adequate reasons.

And finally, v):

> Where the national authorities, in their decisions ordering and upholding the applicant's eviction, have not given any explanation or put forward any arguments demonstrating that the applicant's eviction was necessary, the Court may draw the inference that the State's legitimate interest in being able to control its property should come second to the applicant's right to respect for his home.[46]

[43] Čakarević v Croatia, ECtHR 20 April 2018, 48921/13.

[44] *cf Chapman v the UK*, ECtHR (GC) 18 January 2001, 27238/95, para 114.

[45] *Yordanova and Others v Bulgaria*, ECtHR 24 April 2012, 25446/06; *Winterstein and Others v France*, ECtHR 17 October 2013, 27013/07.

[46] *Yordanova and Others v Bulgaria*, ECtHR 24 April 2012, 25446/06, para 118.

On the basis of this, the Court concluded that the prospective removal of the applicants was not justified under Article 8. This approach was confirmed in *Winterstein and Others v France*.[47] Here, the Court held that there had not only been a (procedural) violation in regard to the planned eviction, but also concerning the provision of alternative accommodation. The fact that their vulnerability and needs had not sufficiently been taken into account was reason for finding a breach of the Convention. Overall, it seems that the procedural requirements not merely determine the width of the margin, but that because key – or minimum – social rights are at stake,[48] procedural requirements must be strictly complied with and can be decisive for concluding that there had been a violation. Again here, without explicitly holding that certain minimum protection is required under the Convention, it is obvious that the Court's approach indirectly condemns a failure to provide minimum housing rights. Another example is the recent case of *Yevgeniy Zakharov v Russia*.[49] After the death of his partner, Zakharov was evicted from the room in a communal flat he had shared with her for 10 years. Although he was registered elsewhere, he had no other place to stay, and the eviction thus interfered with his right to respect for his home. The fact that the Regional Court, in reviewing the measure, had not taken the applicant's housing needs into account, was 'sufficient to enable the Court to conclude that the interference complained of was not "necessary in a democratic society"'.[50] A procedural violation thus, but one that emphasises the applicant's substantive minimum needs. In this way, the Court ensures a minimum socio-economic standard without unduly interfering with the state's social policies.

Procedural review is applied in environmental health cases dealt with under Article 8 as well.[51] And even when the absolute protection under Article 3 in relation to expulsion and health issues is involved, the Court's approach seemingly takes a procedural turn. In 1997, the ECtHR in *D v the United Kingdom* concluded that there would be violation of Article 3 if the UK were to remove the applicant, an AIDS patient who was in 'the advanced stages of a terminal and incurable illness', to St Kitts.[52] That these were 'exceptional circumstances' was later confirmed in *N v the United Kingdom*.[53] Taking a more deferential stance, the Grand Chamber there held that

> Article 3 does not place an obligation on the Contracting State to alleviate such disparities through the provision of free and unlimited health care to all aliens

[47] *Winterstein and Others v France*, ECtHR 17 October 2013, 27013/07.

[48] *Yordanova and Others v Bulgaria*, ECtHR 24 April 2012, 25446/06, para 118; *Winterstein and Others v France*, ECtHR 17 October 2013, 27013/07, para 148.

[49] *Yevgeniy Zakharov v Russia*, ECtHR 14 March 2017, 66610/10.

[50] ibid, para 37.

[51] *cf*, eg, *Taskin and Others v Turkey*, ECtHR 10 November 2004, 46117/99, para 115; *Giacomelli v Italy*, ECtHR 2 November 2006, 59909/00.

[52] *D v the UK*, ECtHR 2 May 1997, 30240/96.

[53] *N v the UK*, ECtHR (GC) 27 May 2008, 26565/05.

> without a right to stay within its jurisdiction. A finding to the contrary would place too great a burden on the Contracting States.[54]

In brief, because N was not 'at the present time critically ill', the Court held that removal would not amount to a violation of Article 3. The dissenters in *N* criticised the majority's remarks that 'Although many of the rights it contains have implications of a social or economic nature, the Convention is essentially directed at the protection of civil and political rights', and that 'inherent in the whole of the Convention is a search for a fair balance between the demands of the general interest of the community and the requirements of the protection of the individual's fundamental rights'.[55] The absolute character of Article 3, also when minimum social rights are concerned was, however, restored in *Paposhvili v Belgium*, with the help of procedural requirements. The Court here held that the 'other very exceptional circumstances' referred to in *N*,

> should be understood to refer to situations involving the removal of a seriously ill person in which substantial grounds have been shown for believing that he or she, although not at imminent risk of dying, would face a real risk, on account of the absence of appropriate treatment in the receiving country or the lack of access to such treatment, of being exposed to a serious, rapid and irreversible decline in his or her State of health resulting in intense suffering to or a significant reduction in life expectancy. The Court points out that these situations correspond to a high threshold for the application of Article 3 of the Convention in cases concerning the removal of aliens suffering from serious illness.[56]

It then set out in detail the authorities' obligation to protect the integrity of the persons concerned primarily through appropriate procedures. When someone adduces evidence that he would be exposed to a real risk of being subjected to treatment contrary to Article 3 in relation to his state of health, it is for the authorities of the returning state to assess this risk. More precisely, they 'must verify on a case-by-case basis whether the care generally available in the receiving State is sufficient and appropriate in practice for the treatment of the applicant's illness'.[57] *Paposhvili* concerned the order of removal to Georgia of a man suffering from chronic lymphocytic leukemia. Since in the proceedings the opinions issued regarding his state of health had not been examined from the perspective of Article 3, the authorities could not conclude that the applicant, if returned, would not have run a real and concrete risk of treatment contrary to Article 3.

All in all, without explicitly saying so, the Court's procedural turn in cases involving social rights forms a step towards the protection of a social minimum under the Convention. Meeting the procedural requirements set, appears incompatible with a state's refraining from providing minimum social protection.

[54] ibid, para 44.
[55] ibid.
[56] *Paposhvili v Belgium*, ECtHR 13 December 2016, 41738/10, para 183.
[57] ibid, para 189.

IV. POTENTIAL PITFALLS OF PROCEDURAL REVIEW

The ECtHR is not the only court resorting to procedural review to secure a social minimum under what are primarily civil rights norms. The German Federal Constitutional Court (FCC), for example, has set procedural requirements the legislature must meet in order to comply with the individual right to an *Existenzminimum*. This right has been recognised under the guarantee of human dignity (Article 1(1) of the German Basic Law (BL)) in conjunction with the social State principle (Article 20(1) BL).[58] A procedural approach here means that the specification of this minimum social right is left to the democratically legitimised authorities, yet the requirements set (of consistency, rationality, using sufficient data, etc) guide these authorities in the right direction. Procedural requirements form a promising alternative to substantive proportionality review, especially when the latter entails a bias against social rights. Regardless of its deference in terms of minimum social content, however, the FCC does explicitly recognise that an individual right to a social minimum exists. This is thus far lacking in the case law of the ECtHR, and as mentioned before, more explicit attention for the social rights content of the Convention would be desirable. This would help it target the protection of those in most desperate need and clarify which important individual interests should be taken into account in the national decision-making process.

There is more to say about why procedural review is at most an incomplete answer to the challenge of indivisible social rights protection by human rights courts, even apart from concerns about the variety of modes of procedural review and the Court's 'pick and choose' approach to these.[59] Although, for now, it provides an interesting alternative, procedural review comes with certain downsides as well.[60] I will use this final section to present a selection of these, while being aware of the fact that they would deserve a much more thorough examination.[61] First, procedural review may require serious adjustments in national procedures, so that these can, eg, accommodate taking into account

[58] BVerfGE 125, 175, 1 BvL 1/09 of 9 February 2010 (*Hartz IV*). *cf* I Leijten, 'The German Right to an *Existenzminimum*, Human Dignity, and the Possibility of Minimum Core Socioeconomic Rights Protection' (2015) 16 *German Law Journal* 23. See, on the constitutional guarantee of a social minimum, also ch 16 (Boyle).

[59] Gerards, *Procedural Review* (2017).

[60] See, eg, A Sathanapally, 'The Modest Promise of Procedural Review in Fundamental Rights Cases' in Gerards and Brems, *Procedural Review* (2017) 40–76; A Nussberger, 'Procedural Review by the ECtHR: View from the Court' in Gerards and Brems (n 17) 161–76.

[61] See, eg Gerards and Brems (n 17). O Mjöll Arnardóttir, 'The "Procedural Turn" Under the European Convention on Human Rights and Presumptions of Convention Compliance' (2017) 15 *International Journal of Constitutional Law* 9–35; E Brems, 'Procedural Protection: An Examination of Procedural Safeguards Read into Substantive Convention Rights' in E Brems and JH Gerards (eds), *Shaping Rights in the ECHR: The Role of the European Court of Human Rights in Determining the Scope of Human Rights* (Cambridge, Cambridge University Press, 2014) 137–61; P Popelier and C Van de Heyning, 'Subsidiarity Post-Brighton: Procedural Rationality as Answer' (2017) 30 *Leiden Journal of International Law* 5.

individual social concerns. This involves multiple resources such as time, money and personnel, and could for that reason lead to criticism on the part of states. A state's legitimate wish to retain enough sovereign space to devise procedures and policies, signals a more principled objection: to what extent is a (supranational) court competent to interfere with national procedures – is this in any way less problematic than its interference with substantive policies?[62] Procedural requirements at first glance appear 'neutral', yet say a lot about how powers are divided between the state and individuals, as well as about the relationship between rules and exceptions, to which I will get back in a second.

Second, while procedural requirements appear harmless, they cannot be applied to every thinkable complaint. When talking about human rights review, it should be ensured that a human right is involved *before* review – of any kind – is appropriate. This ties in with what was mentioned before about the need for interpretation and giving content to fundamental rights norms.[63] For a social security complaint to be reviewed under Article 1 P1 of the Conventions, for example, it must first be clear that there is a 'possession', that moreover has been interfered with. Indeed, this provision does not, as such, include a positive right to a social minimum.[64]

Third, of course, 'procedurally sound' is something other than 'human rights proof', ie adequate procedural safeguards cannot entirely guarantee that someone is treated fairly or that minimum rights protection is provided. Procedural review should not encourage mere procedural window-dressing. In this regard, the Court retains its judicial responsibility, which means that it should find a violation in exceptional circumstances even if the procedural test has been passed.[65] Compare the protection of a subsistence minimum by the FCC: although setting procedural requirements that leave the determination of this minimum to the elected bodies, it will still interfere once what is provided is 'evidently insufficient'. A similar possibility seems needed for the ECtHR to prevent states from misusing the leeway offered and taking seriously its role a fundamental rights guarantor in the Council of Europe.

[62] ibid. A Nussberger, 'Procedural Review by the ECtHR: View from the Court' in Gerards and Brems (n 17) 161–76. This issue has to do with the subsidiary role of the Court. See, on the intricate relationship between procedural review and subsidiarity, L Huijbers, 'The European Court of Human Rights' Procedural Approach in the Age of Subsidiarity' (2017) 6 *Cambridge Journal of International Law* 177; T Kleinlein, 'The Procedural Approach of the European Court of Human Rights: between Subsidiarity and Dynamic Evolution' (2019) 68 *International and Comparative Law Quarterly* 91.

[63] Section II above and ch 11 (O'Cinneide).

[64] *Béláné Nagy v Hungary*, ECtHR (GC) 13 December 2016, 53080/13 (*cf* also the dissenting opinion of Judges Nussberger, Hirvelä, Bianku, Yudkivska, Møse, Lemmens, and O'Leary, and the critical concurring opinion of Judge Wojtyczek). I would argue that this case, even though it can be seen to involve a lack of a social minimum, should not have been dealt with under Art 1P1, but instead under Art 3 or Art 8. See, on the social security protection under Art 1 P1 also I Leijten, 'From *Stec* to *Valkov.* Possessions and Margins in the Social Security Case Law of the European Court of Human Rights' (2013) 13 *Human Rights Law Review* 309.

[65] See Mjöll Arnardóttir, *Procedural Turn* (2017) 35.

Finally, although a procedural approach is sometimes criticised for focusing on structural rather than on individual justice, in the way it is used by the ECtHR in socio-economic cases, the opposite may also be true. Different from the FCC's protection of a subsistence minimum, the ECtHR's procedural review in socio-economic cases mostly is directed at the processes of executive authorities (and national courts) rather than the legislature. When it comes to 'general socio-economic policies', after all, the ECtHR is particularly cautious and still grants a wide margin. Yet the requirement of a decision-making process that takes into account the (minimum) social needs of the individual(s) concerned, may demand ad hoc rather than rule-based decision making by national and local authorities. The line between discretion in individual cases and a too individualistic approach is a thin one. After all, individual decision-making can conflict with principles of equal treatment, the rule of law and legal certainty. For what rights claim do individuals than have, besides being provided with an individual solution that bears no (or little) comparison to what others are provided with.[66] Indeed, in this regard requiring outcomes that take individual human rights circumstances seriously may be less far-reaching than requiring procedures to be tailored to individual needs.

V. CONCLUSION

There are many questions related to indivisible protection of a social minimum by means of procedural review that merit serious attention and require further research. It is clear, however, that the approach that is omnipresent in civil and political human rights adjudication, namely a (very) broad interpretation of rights combined with proportionality review or balancing, does not necessarily lead to the protection a robust social minimum under the European Convention. It is important that we move forward the debate on the justiciability, interpretation and implementation of social rights norms. Yet when carefully fleshed out and taken serious in both theory and practice, the protection of a social minimum under civil rights norms can play an important complementary role.

In this chapter, I showed that there are significant possibilities for protecting especially minimum social rights on the basis of civil rights norms. However, whereas 'rights inflation' appears promising in this regard, it was

[66] Interesting in this regard is the Dutch social domain legislation, that since 2015 has transferred responsibilities from the central state to the municipal level. Rather than specific claims, the idea is that individuals now have a 'right' to 'tailored' services, which are also dependent on whether or not they can rely on family members and networks more broadly speaking. Especially in the light of budgetary cuts, the new *Wet Maatschappelijke Ondersteuning* 2015 (WMO) and the results thereof have led to a lively (legal) debate on administrative, constitutional, and human rights law issues (eg on comparability within and between municipalities, (limited) possibilities for appeal, etc). The link with a procedural, foremost individual needs-oriented approach in the case law of the ECtHR is obvious.

illustrated that insufficient attention to the interpretation stage combined with deferential review, merely underscores a bias against social rights. Procedural review may form an interesting alternative capable of protecting at least minimum social needs. By requiring that minimum social needs of applicants are taking into account at the decision-making stage, the ECtHR requires states to secure minimum social rights, even though these were not originally included in the Convention. Yet relying on such approach for the protection of a social minimum comes with several risks as well. Arguably, in order to be effective, it needs to be combined with reviewing whether provisions were evidently insufficient and also with more attention for minimum social rights content, ie, more explicit recognition of minimum social rights to ensure that procedural review always has the necessary substantive bite.

15

Vulnerability as a Path to a 'Social Minimum'? An Analysis of ECtHR Jurisprudence

DIMITRIOS KAGIAROS

I. INTRODUCTION

THIS CHAPTER EXAMINES the capacity of the European Court of Human Rights (henceforth ECtHR or 'the Court') to establish a social minimum of welfare provisions that states would owe to all individuals within their jurisdiction. The European Convention on Human Rights (ECHR) is a human rights treaty primarily aimed towards the protection of civil and political rights.[1] The jurisprudence of the ECtHR has demonstrated, however, that a strict distinction between first generation (civil and political), and second generation (economic, social and cultural) rights is outdated.[2] The Court seems to embrace the theory of the indivisibility of rights and has argued that the mere fact that an interpretation of the Convention may require the state to provide socio-economic assistance is not in itself a reason against such an interpretation.[3] To that end, the obligations states have to secure the effective enjoyment of ECHR rights,[4] in conjunction with the Court's approach to interpreting the Convention in light of its objective and purpose,[5] have opened up gateways[6] for the civil and political rights protected in the ECHR to generate socio-economic

[1] Some rights that would fall under the umbrella of socio-economic rights are also protected in the ECHR, including the right to education protected under Art 2 Protocol 1 ECHR. See also ch 14 (Leijten) in this volume.

[2] See for instance *Airey v Ireland* (App No 6289/73, 9 October 1979) para 26.

[3] ibid.

[4] C O'Cinneide, 'A Modest Proposal: Destitution, State Responsibility and the European Convention on Human Rights' (30 August 2008), available at ssrn.com/abstract=1370241 or http://dx.doi.org/10.2139/ssrn.1370241.

[5] ibid.

[6] ibid.

obligations on states. Relying on the doctrine of positive obligations in relation to various Convention articles,[7] the Court has succeeded in identifying certain limited Convention-based socio-economic duties to which states must adhere.

Nevertheless, the ECtHR's case law relating to socio-economic rights is to a large extent characterised by timidity and deference to the respondent state.[8] The circumstances in which the Convention will require states to adopt 'socio-economic' measures are exceptional, as the Court does not view itself as a forum for socio-economic litigation nor as a protector against poverty and destitution.[9] Additionally, the few judgments where the Court has found that the state owed socio-economic duties to the applicant are characterised by a lack of uniformity,[10] thus hampering the development of a principled approach to socio-economic jurisprudence at the ECtHR.

This chapter contributes to a specific dimension of the debate on the ECtHR's capacity to protect socio-economic interests and to generate a social minimum of welfare protection. Building on chapter fourteen in this volume, it examines the relationship between the state's positive obligations in the socio-economic sphere and the applicant's 'vulnerability'. Vulnerability, the state of being 'open and exposed to hurts and harms of various kinds'[11] has begun to feature prominently in the ECtHR's case law, including in cases with a socio-economic dimension. This chapter argues that vulnerability can serve as a useful normative justification for the Court to be less deferential to the respondent state and to interpret the Convention in a manner that generates obligations in the direction of a social minimum. Additionally, the chapter discusses the limitations of vulnerability analysis in this context and makes suggestions on how this tool could be developed to further build a path towards a social minimum under the ECHR.

The arguments will be developed as follows. Section II establishes the meaning of a minimum core obligation. This will serve as the basis to determine whether there is any indication that the ECtHR could generate a similar obligation

[7] Primarily Arts 2, 3, 6, 8, 14 and Art 1 Protocol 1 ECHR. See indicatively E Palmer, 'Beyond Arbitrary Interference: The Right to a Home? Developing Socio-economic Duties in the European Court of Human Rights' (2010) 61 *Northern Ireland Legal Quarterly* 225.

[8] It is not uncommon for a case that requires substantial reallocation of resources to be declared inadmissible as manifestly ill-founded. See for instance *Botta v Italy* (Application No 21439/93, dec 24 February 1998); *Zahnalova and Zehnal v Czech Republic* (Application No 38621/97, dec 14 May 2002); *Sentges v Netherlands* (App No 27677/02, dec 8 July 2003). On the approach of the ECtHR to socio-economic rights see indicatively I Leijten, *Core Socio-Economic Rights and the European Court of Human Rights* (Cambridge, Cambridge University Press, 2017) and IE Koch, *Human Rights as Indivisible Rights: The Protection of Socio-Economic Demands under the European Convention on Human Rights* (Leiden; Boston, Martinus Nijhoff Publishers, 2009).

[9] See *Pancenko v Latvia* (Application No 40772/98, dec 28 October 2009) para 2.

[10] On this see J Gerards, 'The ECtHR's Response to Fundamental Rights Issues Related to Financial and Economic Difficulties – the Problem of Compartmentalisation' (2015) 33 *Netherlands Quarterly of Human Rights* 274.

[11] M Neal, 'Not Gods but Animals: Human Dignity and Vulnerable Subjecthood' (2012) 33 *Liverpool Law Review* 186.

under the Convention. Section III examines the nature of positive obligations in human rights law and explains how these have affected the Court's approach in its socio-economic case law. Emphasis will be placed on the fact that positive obligations are obligations of means. They require states to take steps to protect rightsholders from threats to their rights that are attributable to third parties or general situations. The appropriate steps the state must take vary depending on the circumstances of the case and what could reasonably be expected of the state in dealing with the situation before it. Therefore, the chapter concludes that these are obligations that are subjective as they vary among states. In the socio-economic sphere, the Court has granted states a particularly wide margin of appreciation to determine how they will allocate their resources and it has been reluctant to inflate the scope of positive obligations in a manner that would create onerous financial duties for the contracting parties.

Section IV examines instances where the Court, in spite of the subjective nature of positive obligations, has demanded socio-economic provisions from states but in a manner that is *objective*, namely where they are the same for all states and must be immediately complied with, regardless of the specific capabilities of each state. The Court has set such objective socio-economic standards where the applicant is a member of what the Court considers to be a vulnerable group and is wholly reliant on state support for her subsistence. In such cases, the Court will demand that the basic needs of the vulnerable individual are met by the state regardless of the wide margin of appreciation the Court usually grants where the state's capacity to allocate its resources is concerned. The chapter argues that the vulnerability criterion is a tool the Court can rely on to transform what would normally be subjective obligations into objective standards of protection that are meant to apply across all state parties to the ECHR.

This, however, does not generate a social minimum that would protect all from destitution, as the protection is available exclusively to the members of specific groups that the ECtHR has identified as vulnerable. Section V discusses whether expanding the notion of vulnerability to encompass a greater number of individuals in need could become the normative justification the Court relies on to demand social minimum protection from state parties to the ECHR. The chapter concludes that while some expansion of the concept would be useful, the Court is rightfully wary of inflating it. An approach that reconciles the group dimension of vulnerability with the individual needs of the applicant could be the best path the Court could follow towards recognising a social minimum of protection while also protecting its legitimacy.

II. MINIMUM CORE OBLIGATIONS IN INTERNATIONAL HUMAN RIGHTS LAW

The protection states are expected to provide to socio-economic rights in international human rights law is closely linked to the concept of 'progressive realisation'.[12] In the International Covenant on Economic Social and Cultural Rights, this duty to progressively realise socio-economic rights is connected to the 'available resources'[13] the state has at its disposal. Thus, the state is not expected to guarantee that all socio-economic demands will be fulfilled instantaneously. Instead, it must demonstrate that it is working towards the full realisation of the right by taking concrete steps in that direction. Alongside the obligation to progressively realise rights, states have an obligation to immediately fulfil a certain minimum of socio-economic demands regardless of their resources. These represent the minimum core of the right. This core is primarily[14] understood to be inviolable, non-derogable, and must be fulfilled regardless of the subjective capabilities of the state.[15] Thus, even states with limited resources must give priority to the fulfilment of their minimum core socio-economic duties.

In his analysis of such minimum core obligations, Tasioulas argues that they possess three key characteristics. Firstly, minimum core obligations are characterised by their immediacy; 'they demand immediate compliance' rather than progressive realisation from the state.[16] A second characteristic is their completeness, which requires states to ensure that minimum core demands are 'fully complied with at any given time'.[17] Thirdly, minimum core obligations are understood to be universal 'in that they bind all states'.[18] In relation to this final criterion, Tasioulas additionally recognises that these obligations bind all states in the same way, namely their content is understood to be 'invariant across states'.[19] Thus, while progressive realisation creates subjective standards on the states as it is linked to their available resources, minimum core obligations are primarily seen as objective in nature and are the same for all states irrespective of the state's wealth. This understanding of minimum core obligations seems to mirror discussions in political philosophy of a social minimum which Waldron defines as 'a level of material well-being beneath which no-one should be permitted to fall'.[20]

[12] International Covenant on Economic, Social and Cultural Rights, GA Res 2200 (XXI) A (UN Doc A/6316) (16 December 1966) Art 2.

[13] ibid.

[14] Some also argue that it is not an absolute standard based on the wording in UN Committee on Economic, Social and Cultural Rights (CESCR), General Comment No 3: The Nature of States Parties' Obligations (Art 2, para 1, of the Covenant), 14 December 1990, E/1991/23 para 10.

[15] See D Desierto, *Public Policy in International Economic Law: The ICESCR in Trade, Finance, and Investment* (Oxford, Oxford University Press, 2015) 68–179.

[16] J Tasioulas, 'Minimum Core Obligations: Human Rights in the Here and Now' (2017) 20, available at http://documents.worldbank.org/curated/en/908171515588413853/pdf/122563-WP-Tasioulas2-PUBLIC.pdf.

[17] ibid.

[18] ibid.

[19] ibid at 23. Some scholars see it as a variable standard. See for instance C Scott and P Alston, 'Adjudicating Constitutional Priorities in a Transnational Context: A Comment on Soobramoney's Legacy and *Grootboom's* Promise' (2000) 16 *South African Journal of Human Rights* 206.

[20] J Waldron, 'John Rawls and the Social Minimum' (1986) 1 *Journal of Applied Philosophy* 21, 21.

While the ECHR does not include explicit references to progressive realisation and the ECtHR does not employ this terminology, its approach arguably recognises the subjectivity of positive obligations. The following section will illustrate the approach the Court has developed before proceeding in the remainder of this chapter to assess instances where the Court has tentatively departed from such an analysis to identify a minimum core-type duty on the state by relying on the applicant's vulnerability.

III. THE SUBJECTIVE NATURE OF POSITIVE OBLIGATIONS THE CASE LAW OF THE ECTHR

Human rights obligations under international law are not limited to the negative type of protection that traditionally is synonymous with civil and political rights, and call upon the state to refrain from any unwarranted interference with the enjoyment of a right.[21] They also develop a positive dimension which requires the state to act preventatively and protect the individual from wrongful acts that threaten the enjoyment of her rights and are attributable to third persons or general situations.[22] In such cases, even though the prejudice to the right is not directly attributable to the state, the state is still required to take all necessary steps to protect the rights-holder. These steps depending on the circumstances may include an obligation to provide redress to the victim of a violation by a third party, to carry out an effective investigation,[23] to provide material assistance to the rights-holder or to punish the third-party wrongdoer. This positive dimension of rights is where the duty to provide socio-economic assistance would arise, as the state would be required to take action, or at least not to remain passive, in order protect the rights-holder from a situation of destitution that could violate her rights.

However, the duty of the state when its positive obligations are under examination is to *take steps* to protect the rights-holder. All the state must demonstrate is that, given the exigencies of the situation, it was diligent in mobilising its resources to the best of its abilities to fulfil its duty to protect. It does not have an obligation to succeed in protecting the rights-holder.[24] There are further prerequisites for this duty of the state to act to be triggered. For instance,

[21] Civil and political rights, however, also generate positive obligations under the Convention, see A Mowbray, *The Development of Positive Obligations Under the European Convention on Human Rights by the European Court of Human Rights* (Oxford, Hart, 2004).

[22] ibid. See also L Lavrysen, *Human Rights in a Positive State* (Cambridge, Intersentia, 2016).

[23] See for instance *Nachova and others v Bulgaria* (Application Nos 43577/98 43579/98, 6 July 2005).

[24] For a thorough account of positive obligations and the state's duty of due diligence see ILA Study Group on Due Diligence in International Law, First Report Duncan French (Chair) and Tim Stephens (Rapporteur), published 7 March 2014, available at https://olympereseauinternational.files.wordpress.com/2015/07/due_diligence_-_first_report_2014.pdf.

the state must have known (or ought to have known) of the danger to which the rights-holder was exposed.[25]

Once it is established that a duty of the state to protect exists, the Court must then define the scope of this obligation. What must the state have done to protect the rights-holder in the specific circumstances? The tools the Court relies on to respond to this question are helpfully summarised in an oft-cited passage from the Court's Grand Chamber judgment in *Ilaşcu and Others v Moldova and Russia*.[26] In this judgment, the Court asserted that:

> In determining the scope of a State's positive obligations, regard must be had to the fair balance that has to be struck between the general interest and the interests of the individual, the diversity of situations obtaining in Contracting States and the choices which must be made in terms of priorities and resources. Nor must these obligations be interpreted in such a way as to impose an impossible or disproportionate burden.[27]

From this passage, there are three key conclusions we can infer that can inform the discussion on the state's positive obligation to provide a socio-economic protection under the ECHR. Firstly, the scope of the positive obligation is subjective to each state, owing to the diversity of situations to which the contracting parties are exposed. Secondly, in defining the scope of the obligation, due regard must be given to striking a fair balance between the needs of the individual and the general interest. In the socio-economic arena, the state will be afforded a particularly wide margin of appreciation in this regard. Finally, the scope of the positive obligation must be such so as to be within the capabilities of the state. Put more simply, positive obligations cannot require the state to deliver the impossible. Specifically, in the context of socio-economic rights, the Court has made reference to and endorsed the 'proviso of the possible' approach, according to which 'a State cannot be forced to comply with its obligations in the framework of social rights if it does not possess the economic means to do so'.[28]

Thus, when the State's compliance with its positive obligations is examined, the prejudice to the victim is 'a necessary, but still an insufficient condition'[29] to find that the state was in violation of these obligations. The significance of this analysis in relation to the state's socio-economic obligations is that apart from the circumstances of deprivation the individual experiences that may engage her Convention rights, the Court must proceed to establish state fault in order to find a violation, namely that the state failed to take those steps that were necessary to protect the rights-holder. More specifically, the Court must identify

[25] See V Stoyanova, 'Causation between State Omission and Harm within the Framework of Positive Obligations under the European Convention on Human Rights' (2018) 18 *Human Rights Law Review* 309.

[26] Application No 48787/99, 8 July 2004.

[27] ibid at [332].

[28] *Da Silva Carvalho Rico v Portugal* (Application No 13341/14, dec 1 September 2015) at [44].

[29] See in detail O De Schutter, *International Human Rights Law* (Cambridge, Cambridge University Press, 2014) 462–518 at 479.

'a failure of the state that contributed to the prejudice the victim suffered',[30] and/or that there 'were certain supplementary measures which the State could have taken but failed to take, although this would not have imposed a disproportionate burden'.[31]

In relation to this second limb of the required test to find a violation, where the Court must establish that there was state fault that caused harm to the right, the Court in socio-economic cases affords states a very wide margin of appreciation. If the Court were to scrutinise state fault in socio-economic cases intensely, in order to determine the capacity of the state to provide socio-economic assistance, it would inevitably be drawn into sensitive areas of budget (re)allocation. Therefore, it is not surprising that the ECtHR acknowledges that it is out of its remit to place vast financial burdens on contracting parties. In the controversial and much-discussed case of *N v UK*,[32] for instance, the Court held that the United Kingdom was not in violation of Article 3 ECHR when it deported an asylum-seeker that suffered from AIDS-related illnesses, due to the fact that in his state of origin he would be provided with a significantly lower standard of healthcare. The ECtHR stressed on this occasion that, while obligations of a social nature emanate from many of the rights protected under the Convention and require funds from the state, the ECHR is primarily directed towards the protection of civil and political rights.[33] The difference in the level of healthcare provided between the two states was not a sufficient reason to create an obligation for the state to provide 'free and unlimited health care'[34] to all who do not have a legal right to reside in the state. The Court reached its conclusion on the scope of the positive duty in this instance by taking into account the subjective dimension of the positive obligation to provide healthcare under the Convention. As the Court concluded controversially, a different interpretation of the Convention would create a particularly heavy burden on the contracting parties.[35] Similarly, in *Chapman v UK*,[36] the Court stressed that Article 8 ECHR does not guarantee a right to a shelter, due to the fact that such a decision would have obvious financial implications and is therefore a political one. For this reason, it was held that it did not fall under the Courts' jurisdiction to establish a socio-economic duty on states to provide everyone with a home.[37]

The approach to socio-economic rights in these judgments demonstrates that the Court is not identifying the content of a minimum core of socio-economic

[30] See ibid and *Ilaşcu and others v Russia and Moldova* cited ibid at [332].

[31] ibid.

[32] *N v United Kingdom* (App No 26565/05, 27 May 2008).

[33] ibid para 44.

[34] ibid.

[35] In subsequent cases, the Court has been more willing to provide protection to individuals in similar circumstances, by lowering the threshold of exceptional circumstances that would warrant state intervention. See *Paposhvili v Belgium* (Application No 41738/10, 13 December 2016).

[36] App No 27238/95, 19 January 2001 para 98.

[37] ibid.

obligations, nor is it establishing a pan-European social minimum of welfare protection that states are required to deliver. The Court in these instances refuses to extend socio-economic protection under the ECHR on the basis that this may have unintended financial implications that would be too onerous on the contracting parties.

In practice, however, there are instances where the Court has found the state in violation of the Convention for failure to deliver on its socio-economic duties without carrying out an exercise of determining whether these duties were within the state's means. These exceptional cases place duties on member states that seem to be objective in nature. The following section examines such instances in the Court's case law and attempts to assess whether they hold any promise in generating a Convention-based social minimum of welfare protection.

IV. 'VULNERABILITY' AS A MEANS TO GENERATE 'OBJECTIVE' OBLIGATIONS

The approach dictated by the nature of positive obligations discussed in the previous section may seem to paint a particularly disheartening picture for the capacity of the Court to create an absolute baseline of socio-economic provisions from which all contracting parties to the ECHR cannot depart. In practice, however, the Court has demonstrated some attempts to create such objective duties on states. In order to do so, the Court had to identify a normative justification that would allow it to abandon its usual approach to socio-economic obligations and proceed to a finding that an individual's circumstances were so dire so as to create the minimum core-type duty on the state. The key justification the Court has adopted is to focus on the applicant's membership to a vulnerable group. This section argues that while an absolute minimum of social protection is not guaranteed to *all* by the Convention, references to the applicant's vulnerability allow it to guarantee a social minimum to *some*. The justifications the Court relies on to identify these recipients of the social minimum will be discussed in this section.

The concept of 'vulnerable groups' has begun to feature prominently in the ECtHR's case law. The Court's allusion to the applicant's vulnerability is not merely a 'rhetorical flourish'[38] but has legal effects.[39] It is outside of the scope of the chapter to discuss the use of vulnerability in all its forms in the Court's case law. Instead, the focal point will be the use of vulnerability as a means for the Court to justify 'objective' socio-economic duties of the state towards the vulnerable group.

[38] On this see L Peroni and A Timmer, 'Vulnerable Groups: The Promise of an Emerging Concept in European Human Rights Convention Law' (2013) 11 *International Journal Constitutional Law* 1074.

[39] ibid.

The Court in this context has linked vulnerability to applicants who are 'wholly dependent'[40] on state support, and who have found themselves 'faced with official indifference when in a situation of serious deprivation or want incompatible with human dignity'.[41] Under this understanding of vulnerability, the Court has assigned vulnerable status to prisoners,[42] children in a state institution for minors with mental disabilities[43] and to asylum-seekers among others.[44] The key connecting factor seems to be they are all wholly dependent on state support for their subsistence. The state's duties intensify where children asylum-seekers enter a state on their own or in cases where the asylum-seeker is travelling with children.[45] The obligation to protect also increases where the state's passivity to the needs of the asylum-seeker is the cause of, or compounds, their destitution. This would be the case for instance, where the state unduly delays responding to an asylum request, thus prolonging the plight of the applicants.[46]

For these categories of individuals, the state is expected to provide the necessary material assistance to ensure their survival. The Court in these instances does not carry out a thorough assessment of the capabilities of the state to secure these provisions. Especially in the context of persons in detainment, the Court expressly refuses to engage in a discussion on the capacity of the state to offer the rights-holder socio-economic support. Gerards notes the far-reaching socio-economic obligations states owe towards prisoners under the Convention, including the provision of 'glasses, forearm prostheses or dentures, with a special diet or with medication'.[47] In cases relating to such provisions state objections as to their cost do not sway the Court, especially where the Court relies on the vulnerability of prisoners to find Article 3 ECHR violations. In *Poltoratskiy v Ukraine*,[48] for instance, a case where the applicant complained about the very poor prison conditions he was exposed to while on death row, the Court took note of that fact that 'Ukraine encountered serious socio-economic problems'[49] and that authorities were 'struggling under difficult economic conditions'.[50] This did not persuade the Court to alter its approach. The Court held that this 'lack of resources cannot in principle justify prison conditions which are so poor as to reach the threshold of treatment contrary to Article 3

[40] *MSS v Belgium and Greece* (Application No 30696/09, 21 January 2011) para 253.
[41] ibid.
[42] See for instance *G v France* (Application No 27244/09 23 February 2012) paras 72 and 77.
[43] *Nencheva v Bulgaria* (Application No 48609/06, 18 June 2013).
[44] *MSS v Belgium and Greece* (Application No 30696/09, 21 January 2011) and *VM and others v Belgium* (Application No 60125/11, 7 July 2015).
[45] See *VM and others v Belgium* (Application No 60125/11, 7 July 2015).
[46] *MSS v Belgium and Greece* (Application No 30696/09, 21 January 2011) para 263.
[47] Gerards, 'The ECtHR's Response to Fundamental Rights Issues' (2015) 284.
[48] Application No 38812/97, 29 April 2003.
[49] ibid para 148.
[50] ibid.

of the Convention'.[51] This approach leads Gerards to conclude that where the Court is examining the rights of individuals in detainment, the state's positive obligations 'are much stronger and the Court is much less deferential towards the States where budgetary considerations are concerned'.[52] According to Judge Sicilianos in his extrajudicial writings, in these circumstances where the state has sole responsibility for the well-being of the individual, the lines between positive and negative protection become blurred and 'the Court imposes on states a kind of obligation of result'[53] rather than one of means.

This underscores a particularly important function of vulnerability. As Bossuyt explains, vulnerability lowers the threshold for inhuman or degrading treatment, thus creating a link between the deprivation the individual faces and Article 3 ECHR.[54] Due to the absolute nature of the right, any subsequent discussion on the state's capacity to respond to these obligations is rendered nugatory.

A similar approach is followed where asylum seekers are concerned. In the landmark judgment of *MSS v Belgium and Greece*,[55] the ECtHR found Greece in violation of Article 3 ECHR for the living conditions to which the applicant was exposed to while waiting for his asylum request to be processed. The fact that he was left without shelter and material provisions was sufficient for the Court to find that his circumstances had reached the minimum level of severity required for an Article 3 ECHR violation. The Court reached its conclusion by noting the obligations Greece had under EU law[56] to provide a minimum of socio-economic standards to asylum-seekers. This analysis was complemented by reference to the vulnerability of asylum-seekers. In subsequent judgments with similar facts, vulnerability was used as the sole basis to bring the applicant's situation into the realm of Article 3 and to justify the Court's finding of a Convention violation.[57]

The needs of the vulnerable demand an immediate response from the state and thus vulnerable status can serve as a guide to states on how to dispense their positive obligations, namely to which individuals to give priority for socio-economic provisions. By bringing destitution into the scope of Article 3, the state cannot argue that providing socio-economic assistance would be outside its subjective capabilities. Therefore, this approach fulfils the immediacy, completeness

[51] ibid.

[52] Gerards (n 10) 286.

[53] A-L Sicilianos, 'The European Court of Human Rights at a Time of Crisis in Europe' (2016) *European Human Rights Law Review* 124.

[54] M Bossuyt, 'Is the European Court of Human Rights on a Slippery Slope?' in Z Flogaitis, T Zwart and J Fraser (eds), *The European Court of Human Rights and its Discontents* (Cheltenham, Edward Elgar, 2013) 28–29.

[55] Application No 30696/09, 21 January 2011.

[56] Council Directive 2003/9/EC of 27 January 2003 laying down minimum standards for the reception of asylum-seekers in the Member States.

[57] See for instance *VM and others v Belgium* (Application No 60125/11, 7 July 2015).

and universality requirements discussed in section I of this chapter that Tasioulas associates with the social minimum. It does not, however, meet the requirements of Waldron's definition, as it is not a social minimum of provisions that is available to all. It is instead only limited to those groups the Court has deemed to be vulnerable.

This distinction between vulnerable and non-vulnerable individuals in need of social assistance could be faulted for leading to unfair results. In *MSS* for instance, the Court was quick to point out that 'Article 3 cannot be interpreted as obliging the High Contracting Parties to provide everyone within their jurisdiction with a home'.[58] This clarified that the finding of the violation in this case was exceptional and not available to all who were destitute, but instead only to members of a vulnerable group.[59] Thus, the Court's reliance on 'vulnerable groups' has a dual function. On the one hand, it increases the state's obligations to provide material assistance to vulnerable groups by allowing the Court to invoke Article 3 ECHR and consequently to forego a subjective test of the state's resource capabilities. On the other hand, the 'vulnerable groups' construct establishes the limits of this obligation. The duty is only owed to the members of vulnerable groups, thus excluding other individuals that may have equally pressing socio-economic needs but are not able to claim membership to a group the Court has identified as vulnerable.

To illustrate this point by way of an example, if we are to imagine two destitute individuals, one (A) who is a citizen of the state sleeping rough on the streets, and the other (B) an asylum-seeker who is exposed to the same levels of deprivation during the time their request for asylum is being processed, the Court's approach would mean that individuals A and B would have very different prospects of success before the ECtHR. For A to successfully challenge her destitution on Convention grounds, she must demonstrate that, for instance, she was discriminated against and unlawfully excluded from a state-run housing scheme, or that there were procedural flaws in how her case was dealt with, assuming the state in question offers shelters to the homeless in the first place. The ECtHR would most likely afford the state a wide margin of appreciation. The hurdle for B to satisfy her socio-economic demands under the Convention is much lower. The Court's justification for this would be that B has no option but to rely exclusively on the state for her subsistence. Thus, the scope of the positive obligation, the state's duty to protect, is much more pressing in B's case. The state's margin will be narrow, and the ECtHR will most likely find B's treatment to violate the Convention in line with the Court's case law on asylum-seekers. Importantly, this will be an objective duty the state must fulfil, and not one that is based on the subjective capabilities of the state. Consequently, the same degree of deprivation leads to differing human rights obligations under the ECHR as interpreted in the case law of the ECtHR.

[58] *MSS* para 249.

[59] See concurring opinion of Judge Rozakis in *MSS*.

The assumption that A should be more self-reliant and is therefore less deserving of protection may be criticised for failing to identify various layers of vulnerability[60] or the complexities of life that could lead someone to destitution. This aspect of vulnerability as it is understood by the ECtHR also explains why this tool to enhance positive obligations has been criticised. As commentators have pointed out, the term is exclusionary as it suggests that individuals who are not readily identifiable as members of a vulnerable group are viewed as 'self-sufficient, independent and autonomous',[61] and concomitantly less worthy of protection.

One could be tempted to argue that the Court should simply build on its vulnerability analysis to include more classes of individuals in its ambit. If vulnerability unlocks state obligations to provide a social minimum of welfare assistance, expanding the pool of individuals who would qualify as vulnerable would allow the Court to require more from states. With this in mind, the following section will address whether expanding the concept of vulnerability to encompass a broader range of individuals in need of social assistance would in fact be useful.

V. FROM 'VULNERABLE GROUPS' TO INDIVIDUAL VULNERABILITY: AN INFLATION OF VULNERABILITY ANALYSIS?

The previous section has argued that the vulnerable status of an individual can be the means to make subjective obligations objective and to require the state to fulfil a minimum of the individual's socio-economic needs. This raises a related question. If vulnerability serves such a function, and the aforementioned distinctions the Court makes between vulnerable and non-vulnerable individuals can be criticised for leading to unfair results, should the Court broaden the category of those who can lay claim to vulnerability? Prima facie, if the Court were to assign vulnerable status to applicants based on their specific *needs* rather than their membership to a group or the level of responsibility the state purportedly has over them, it could simultaneously adopt a bolder stance in its socio-economic jurisprudence. This could allow the Court to justify narrowing the margin of appreciation or to demand a greater degree of socio-economic provisions from the respondent states.

The Court has clearly not followed an understanding of vulnerability that is linked to the specific needs of the applicant.[62] As Brandl and Czech confirm,

[60] See especially M Fineman, 'The Vulnerable Subject and the Responsive State' (2010) 60 *Emory Law Journal* 251.

[61] Peroni and Timmer, 'Vulnerable Groups' (2013) 1060.

[62] A Timmer, 'A Quiet Revolution: Vulnerability in the European Court of Human Rights' in M Fineman and A Greer (eds), *Vulnerability: Reflections on a New Ethical Foundation for Law and Politics* (Farnham, Ashgate Routledge, 2013) 152.

in the ECtHR's case law 'vulnerability is not derived from an applicant's individual personal circumstances, but from his or her affiliation to a group with special needs'.[63] The Court may identify various degrees of vulnerability within the vulnerable group,[64] or recognise 'double vulnerability'[65] where the applicant possesses characteristics that classify her under more than one group that has been assigned vulnerable status. It does not, however, adopt a vulnerability-based analysis where the applicant is not a member of one of the vulnerable groups recognised as such in the Court's case law. If the Court were to abandon an understanding of vulnerability that is derived from the identity of the applicant, and instead chose to focus on the specific needs of the individual, it could, in theory, more confidently proceed to examine the circumstances of deprivation the individual is facing, and assess whether these would qualify as circumstances 'incompatible with human dignity',[66] thus building on the approach the Court adopted in its asylum-seeker case law.

Such a hypothetical approach would find support in the broader literature on vulnerability. Fineman firmly rejects the notion of 'vulnerable groups', where vulnerability is linked to the identity of the individual. For Fineman, vulnerability is 'universal and constant' due to our embodiment as human beings,[67] a shared characteristic rather than one that relates only to specific marginalised groups.

Fineman cautions against the stigmatising effect[68] that the 'vulnerable groups' construct may have and instead argues in favour of building resilience, which is the 'solution to our vulnerability'.[69] Under Fineman's vulnerability analysis,

> the basis for distinguishing some individuals from better-positioned but equally vulnerable individuals in the first instance would revolve around questions of access to sufficient resources, with a deficit indicating they lacked the resilience that is necessary to address human vulnerability. Significantly, the initial emphasis here is on the distribution or allocation of resources and the structures within which they are produced. This suggests that the first question to be considered is whether institutional, not individual, functioning is inadequate. This inquiry shifts the focus to state

[63] U Brandl and P Czech, 'General and Specific Vulnerability of Protection-Seekers in the EU: Is there an Adequate Response to their Needs?' in F Ippolito and S Iglesias Sánchez (eds), *Protecting Vulnerable Groups: The European Human Rights Framework* (Oxford, Hart, 2015) 249.

[64] Timmer, 'A Quiet Revolution' (2013) 161.

[65] ibid.

[66] The Court employed this terminology in *MSS* at paras 220, 221 and 253.

[67] M Fineman, 'The Vulnerable Subject: Anchoring Equality in the Human Condition' (2008) 20 *Yale Journal of Law and Feminism* 1.

[68] According to Fineman, 'labelling some individuals and herding them into "populations" defined as differently or particularly vulnerable (and therefore somehow inadequate) stigmatises those individuals'; see M Fineman, 'Vulnerability and Inevitable Inequality' (2017) 4 *Oslo Law Review* 133, available at www.idunn.no/oslo_law_review/2017/03/vulnerability_and_inevitable_inequality.

[69] ibid.

> and social responsibility because it recognizes that a deficit in resources often reflects an institutional or societal failing more than an individual one.[70]

Therefore, under Fineman's analysis, the destitute individual A in the example mentioned in the previous section should expect the same level of protection as destitute individual B. Her lack of 'resilience' would not be attributable to her own failings but be viewed as a state failure to protect her interests. Therefore, for Fineman, it would be incorrect to assume that she is more responsible for her plight than B due to the fact that A is not a member of a 'vulnerable group' or is not 'wholly reliant' on state support in the same way as a prisoner or an asylum-seeker. Thus, rather than focusing on the identity of the applicant, the Court could engage in a discussion on whether the applicant's circumstances offend her dignity in a manner that would render her vulnerable and trigger Convention protection.

ECtHR judges have taken some tentative steps in this direction in their extra-judicial writings, but such an approach has yet to enter the Court's analysis. Judge Tulkens, for instance, argues that 'It would be unthinkable not to consider that extreme poverty humiliates the individual in his own eyes and in the eyes of others and is such as to arouse feelings of fear, anguish and inferiority'[71] in a manner that would engage Article 3. Additionally Tulkens questions whether it would really be 'so ridiculous to think that if corporal punishment in schools is considered to be degrading, the same should apply to the situation of someone who "lives" in a slum?'[72] She does however accept that 'almost as a matter of necessity, [there must be] a certain degree of restraint in applying [this] in practice'.[73]

The approach Judge Tulkens recommends has some obvious benefits. It examines the impact of extreme poverty on the individual without reference to her membership to a vulnerable group. It is instead the feelings of 'fear, anguish and inferiority', caused by poverty, that could render the individual vulnerable and trigger obligations on the state to provide a certain baseline of protection.

While this analysis may seem attractive as a means for the Court to broaden the circumstances where an objective state obligation to protect would be triggered, there are important reasons that justify a restrictive understanding of who is vulnerable in the eyes of the ECtHR. A needs-based approach to vulnerability must not be interpreted by the Court as allowing it to generate onerous demands on the member states. As discussed in the previous section, an important function of vulnerability analysis is that it serves as a normative justification to allow the Court to narrow what would normally be a wide margin of appreciation.

[70] ibid.

[71] Judge Tulkens, 'Seminar to Mark the Opening of the Judicial Year of the European Court of Human Rights' (Strasbourg, 25 January 2013) at para 19, available at http://echr.coe.int/Documents/Speech_20130125_Tulkens_ENG.pdf.

[72] ibid at 20.

[73] ibid.

Vulnerability 'operates as a magnifying glass'[74] for the state's duty of protection, allowing the Court to avoid the light touch review usually associated with socio-economic rights. Therefore, the nature of vulnerability is exceptional in that it is a tool that exceptionally allows the Court to use the Convention as a means to satisfy basic socio-economic needs. Thus, while the Court's approach to vulnerability can be criticised, if the proverbial net of vulnerability were cast too wide to include a much broader range of individuals, this tool would be in danger of losing its exceptional character that provides the Court with the justification to make the leap from subjective duties to objective socio-economic demands. Therefore, any development in vulnerability analysis must be cognisant of the limits placed on the Court by its nature as a subsidiary human rights body and the fact that the Convention primarily protects civil and political rights. An inflation of the concept would call into question the Court's legitimacy to interpret the Convention in a manner that creates duties far exceeding those the contracting parties agreed to respect and protect.

A potential solution to this concern could be for the Court to reconcile both approaches to vulnerability in its reasoning. While relying primarily on the concept of vulnerable groups, the Court's analysis could more deftly engage in a discussion on the circumstances of the applicant and how these would trigger the state's duty to provide a minimum of protection. The fact that a person falls within a recognised vulnerable group could be viewed by the Court as a strong indicator of need, thus requiring the state to intervene. It would not, however, be the sole indicator. By further exploring the links between the applicant's situation of poverty and the state's duty to protect, the Court could incrementally[75] develop a more coherent and consistent test to determine the circumstances under which the state would be required to provide a social minimum of welfare. This could open up state responsibilities towards individuals who would not be considered members of a vulnerable group. This approach secures the socio-economic privileges vulnerable groups currently enjoy, but also allows the Court to slowly build its jurisprudence in the direction of specifying a certain minimum of protection that would be available to all who would need it.

The introduction of clearer and more coherent principles that link poverty to the state's duty to protect, would allow the Court to draw on these principles when the applicant's destitution reaches a level of severity that is incompatible with human dignity. This would not constitute a significant departure from the Court's existing legal reasoning. In obiter statements the Court has already identified that 'a complaint about a wholly insufficient amount of pension

[74] See A Beduschi, 'Vulnerability on Trial: Protection of Migrant Children's Rights in the Jurisprudence of International Human Rights Courts' (2018) 36 *Boston University International Law Journal* 56.

[75] On the Court's use of incrementalism see J Gerards, 'Margin of Appreciation and Incrementalism in the Case Law of the European Court of Human Rights' (2018) 18 *Human Rights Law Review* 495.

and the other social benefits may, in principle, raise an issue under Article 3'.[76] A similar approach was adopted in *Budina v Russia*[77] where the Court in obiter statements linked destitution to Article 2 ECHR.[78] Building on this approach would ensure that such statements are not merely 'teasing promises'[79] the Court makes obiter and is unlikely to fulfil, but can instead become the basis for a social minimum of welfare protection under the ECHR.

VI. CONCLUSION

This chapter has attempted to examine the Court's socio-economic case law through the prism of positive and minimum core obligations. It has argued that the nature of positive obligations as obligations that are subjective to each state and are obligations of means, suggesting that the Court may be limited in its capacity to establish a social minimum of welfare protection in absolute terms. The chapter then proceeded to examine an important tool the Court has relied on to require states, regardless of their resources, to intervene to protect individuals from destitution. The Court has established objective duties of protection in circumstances where the applicant is vulnerable and relies exclusively on the state for material support. The Court's case law on socio-economic provisions for asylum-seekers is a particularly useful example of this approach. While the designation of a group as vulnerable and deserving of material assistance with priority against others may raise concerns, the exceptional nature of vulnerability allows the Court to expand the state's duties, thus overcoming the limitations inherent in positive obligations. While it would be useful for the Court to develop its understanding of vulnerability and to focus on the needs of the specific applicant rather than on her identity, the exceptional character of the vulnerability must be safeguarded. Therefore, an approach that reconciles the vulnerable groups approach with the applicant's individual needs would be a promising path for the Court to follow in the direction of establishing a social minimum of welfare provisions.

[76] *Larioshina v Russia* (Application No 56869/00, dec 23 April 2002).

[77] Application No 45603/05, dec 18 June 2009.

[78] On these cases see D Kagiaros, 'In Search of a 'Social Minimum': Austerity and Destitution in the European Court of Human Rights' (2019) 25 *European Public Law* (forthcoming, on file with the author).

[79] C O'Cinneide, A Modest Proposal: Destitution, State Responsibility and the European Convention on Human Rights' (30 August 2008), available at ssrn.com/abstract=1370241 or http://dx.doi.org/10.2139/ssrn.1370241.

16

Constitutionalising a Social Minimum as a Minimum Core

KATIE BOYLE

I. THE MINIMUM CORE AND THE SOCIAL MINIMUM

THE LEGALISATION OF the right to a social minimum is closely connected to the international human rights framework that requires states to take steps to progressively realise economic and social rights (ESR), including the right to an adequate standard of living, to the state's maximum available resources.[1] The right to an adequate standard of living includes the right to food, housing and freedom from poverty. The international framework also provides for the protection of the rights to health,[2] education,[3] employment[4] and social security,[5] among others. As part of this legal framework there is an immediate obligation to ensure a minimum level of protection across the rights. This obligation is referred to as a minimum core obligation. This chapter analyses the concept of the social minimum through the lens of a minimum core obligation.

The chapter is divided into three parts. First the chapter considers what constitutes a social minimum in relation to the legal status of a minimum core obligation. Second, it argues that the right to the social minimum should ideally be protected in the constitution as part of a multi-institutional approach to ESR protection as this enhances democracy. Finally, the chapter analyses what role the court should play in enforcing it under such a framework. This contribution aligns with the emerging 'anti-poverty' stream of liberal constitutionalism.[6]

[1] International Covenant on Economic, Social and Cultural Rights (ICESCR) Art 2(1) and Art 11.

[2] Article 12 ICESCR.

[3] Article 13 ICESCR.

[4] Articles 6–8 ICESCR.

[5] Article 9 ICESCR.

[6] See O'Cinneide on the lack of a social dimension in a liberal constitutional social minimum and the emerging anti-poverty dimension in mainstream liberal political theory in C O'Cinneide, 'The Constitutionalisation of Economic and Social Rights' and FI Michelman on anti-poverty liberal social minimum as an emerging conceptualisation of social democracy in 'Constitutionally

In other words, a social minimum is required for the functioning of a democracy and enhances democratic legitimacy (by enabling participation). And, in turn, this requires a legalisation of rights that compel the state to ensure compliance with both procedural and substantive aspects, drawing from the disciplines of law, philosophy, sociology, economics and politics, to give meaning and substance in determination of what constitutes a social minimum in practice.

The chapter operates on certain assumptions that are important to address as a starting point. Aside from the overarching international legal obligation to ensure a minimum core in the protection of ESR the chapter draws on constitutional theory that suggests providing a social minimum is good for democracy. This is based on a theory of human rights that supports provision of basic necessities in order to be able to participate and function as a human being. The theoretical framework identifies that human beings are entitled to a life of dignity and well-being and each person is entitled to a minimum standard/threshold of human rights protection;[7] that human beings are entitled to autonomy and human rights afford the individual freedom and that the protection of all rights (civil, political, economic, social and cultural) form an important part of self-determination;[8] and that human beings are entitled to social and political participation in society and meaningful participation in democracy is dependent on substantive access to minimum criteria in human rights protection – including a social minimum.[9] Raz theorises that autonomy (or normative agency) is a prerequisite of freedom and that the exercise of autonomy is dependent on the self-fulfilling creation of an autonomous individual, an 'agent', where the agent's activities are not burdened by worries of mere survival.[10] Rawls' theory, based on liberal egalitarianism, supports freedom through meaningful choices about the life one chooses to lead – this requires having the capacity to understand political complexities (supported through education) and having health and income security to plan out a meaningful life. This, he argues, can be supported by constitutionally guaranteeing

Binding Social and Economic Rights as a Compelling Idea: Reciprocating Perturbations in Liberal and Democratic Constitutional Visions' in HA García, K Klare, LA Williams (eds), *Social and Economic Rights in Theory and Practice, Critical Inquiries* (New York, Routledge, 2015) 261–62 and 279–80.

[7] V Gauri and DM Brinks, 'Introduction: the Elements of Legalization and the Triangular Shape of Social and Economic Rights' in V Gauri and DM Brinks (eds), *Courting Social Justice, Judicial Enforcement of Social and Economic Rights in the Developing World* (Cambridge, Cambridge University Press, 2008).

[8] ibid 23–24. See also: C Fabre, *Social Rights Under the Constitution: Government and the Decent Life* (Oxford, Oxford University Press, 2001) ch 1; J Raz, *The Morality of Freedom* (Oxford, Oxford University Press, 1986) chs 14 and 15.

[9] J King, *Judging Social Rights* (Cambridge, Cambridge University Press 2012) 23. See also arguments supported in theories of social citizenship, civic republican social minimum and deliberative democracy – ESR are instrumental in, and support, meaningful participation in political decision-making, FI Michelman, 'Welfare Rights in a Constitutional Democracy' (1979) *Washington University Law Quarterly* 659; Fabre, *Social Rights* (2001) 121–24.

[10] Raz, *Morality of Freedom* (1986) chs 14 and 15.

legally enforceable minimum criteria.[11] This position somewhat differs from the distinction previously asserted by Rawls in relation to 'human rights proper' – Rawls' theory develops towards a more substantive based recognition that minimum criteria are essential to social and political participation – however, he does not expand upon the means through which to achieve this other than to mention that a social minimum is a constitutional essential.[12] Others argue that the social minimum is not enough and that states must take steps to address substantive inequality.[13] The international human rights framework provides a helpful theoretical framework that requires states to move beyond minimum criteria to progressive enforcement of rights. The chapter builds on this theoretical foundation.

The chapter is concerned with enforceable legal obligations through justiciable mechanisms (adjudication in court). It does not explore non-enforceable directive principles as a means of constitutionalisation (such as those operating in Ireland and India). Whilst non-enforceable principles might help mainstream socio-economic objectives they are not legally binding and so are not typically enforceable in court.[14] When they do take on justiciable status, such as in India for example, the reliance on judicial activism to enforce directive principles has caused the principles to be considered nothing more than 'rhetorical language, hopes, ideals and goals rather than the actual reality of government'[15] and enforceability is subject to the whim of whatever judge happens to be sitting on any particular case. The chapter therefore engages with the legalisation of a social minimum in so far as it can be constitutionalised and legally enforced. This relates to the often cited critique of social rights adjudication that questions the feasibility of making ESR justiciable because they are too vague (the indeterminacy critique).[16] It is important to note that all rights are indeterminate to some degree and different institutional actors, including courts, must engage with the meaning of rights, including the social minimum/minimum core obligations in order to give substance to the rights.[17] The chapter therefore

[11] J Rawls, *Political Liberalism* (New York, Colombia University Press, 1996) 227–28.

[12] ibid.

[13] S Moyn, *Not Enough, Human Rights in an Unequal World* (Cambridge, MA, Belknap, 2018). Moyn's account, whilst helpful in elucidating some of the pitfalls of inadequate legal structures largely concerned with civil and political rights, is misplaced in its understanding of the ESR dimension of the international legal framework and its potential if properly implemented. For a critique see G de Búrca, 'Shaming Human Rights' (16 August 2018), forthcoming, *International Journal of Constitutional Law*; NYU School of Law, Public Law Research Paper No 18–47, available https://ssrn.com/abstract=3233063 or http://dx.doi.org/10.2139/ssrn.3233063.

[14] Wiles, in consideration of non-enforceable constitutional provisions, explains as follows: 'explicit legal enforceability is needed in order for social and economic rights to have legitimacy, credibility and consistency as human rights in the long term, as an operative part of the legal system'; E Wiles, 'Aspirational Principles or Enforceable Rights? The Future for Social and Economic Rights in National Law' (2006) 22 *American University International Law Review* 59.

[15] HM Seervai, *Constitutional Law of India*, 1st edn (Delhi, Tripathi, 1984) 759.

[16] See ch 11 (O'Cinneide) in this volume.

[17] K Young, *Constituting Social Rights* (Oxford, Oxford University Press 2012) 8.

operates on the basis that ESR are justiciable if the application of the law renders them so (a positivist and formalistic legal approach).[18] It does not argue for judicial activism but operates on the basis that if the constitution gives the judiciary a set of rules which includes a requirement for the state to comply with ESR, including a social minimum/minimum core component, then courts can legitimately supervise compliance with this obligation.

II. WHAT CONSTITUTES A SOCIAL MINIMUM THROUGH THE LENS OF THE MINIMUM CORE?

The social minimum and minimum core obligation are concepts that can sometimes be referred to interchangeably and they arguably aim to address the same issue (what constitutes a minimum standard for a dignified life). However, the disciplines of sociology, law and philosophy address this question in very different ways. There is more scope to adopt an interdisciplinary approach to holistically address the question of what constitutes a minimum through the disciplines of sociology, law, philosophy and politics among others. The sociological approach to a social minimum tells us that society should set minimum thresholds to ensure people can live a decent life. Sen's capability approach is the long-established framework in which questions about what constitutes a decent life are addressed, including what kind of threshold it entails: minimum, adequate or decent?[19] When examining what is required to facilitate autonomy, participation, and freedom from poverty, questions as to what constitutes a minimum level materialise. Is the minimum a relative threshold (relative to the country's wealth and prevailing circumstances) or absolute (a basic and absolute minimum threshold)?[20] The philosophical approach tells us that normatively a social minimum is absolute[21] – it is a minimum to ensure survival and this aligns with an absolutist approach evident (but contested) in sociology and law. The philosophical literature informs conceptual and legal understandings of what is required to achieve the minimum core of legal rights, in particular economic,

[18] For further discussion of this see K Boyle, 'Justiciability Mechanisms for Economic, Social and Cultural Rights in Northern Ireland, the United Kingdom and Beyond' in A Divers and J Miller (eds), *Justiciability of Human Rights Law in Domestic Jurisdictions* (Cham, Springer International, 2015).

[19] A Sen, *Inequality Reexamined* (Oxford, Clarendon Press, 1992) 39; M Nussbaum, 'Women and Cultural Universals' in M Nussbaum, *Sex and Social Justice* (Oxford, Oxford University Press, 1999) 29–54; M Nussbaum, *Frontiers of Justice, Disability, Nationality and Species Membership* (Cambridge, MA, Belknap, 2006) 70, 75, 76–77; HP Gaisbauer, G Schweiger and C Sedmak, *Ethical Issues in Poverty Alleviation* (Cham, Springer International Publishing Switzerland, 2016).

[20] R Hick and A Lanau, *In-work Poverty in the UK: Problem, Policy Analysis and Platform for Action* (Cardiff, Cardiff University, 2017).

[21] J Tasioulas, *Minimum Core Obligations: Human Rights in the Here and Now*, Research Paper (Nordic Trust Fund, World Bank, 2017).

social and cultural rights.[22] The sociological approach to poverty has developed a relative approach that recognises that different needs and requirements emerge in order to live a life free from poverty and an arbitrary absolute standard is not enough to deal with the complexity of variable and relative human needs.[23] The legal elaboration of the normative content of rights also adopts both an absolute and relative approach to poverty and minimum core obligations (both in international law and in jurisprudence – both discussed below). These oscillating approaches between absolute and relative can cause confusion and exacerbate the indeterminacy of what constitutes a minimum threshold. This chapter proposes that both absolute and relative standards have an important role to play and that the enforcement of a minimum can take on both absolute and relative components with different types of review and remedies available for each.

From a legal perspective, the first conceptualisation of the minimum core principle emerged following the Limburg Principles (1986) that 'each [ESC] right must … give rise to a minimum entitlement, in the absence of which a State party is in violation of its obligations'.[24] This led to the development of minimum core obligations in the progressive realisation of ESC rights. The UN Committee responsible for observing implementation of ICESCR indicated that where a

> state party in which any significant number of individuals is deprived of essential foodstuffs, of essential primary health care, of basic shelter and housing, or of the most basic forms of education [then the State party] is, prima facie, failing to discharge its obligations under the Covenant. If the Covenant were to be read in such a way as not to establish such a minimum core obligation, it would be largely deprived of its raison d'être (CESCR General Comment 3)

As discussed above, the indeterminacy of what constitutes a minimum core obligation has not been resolved in the literature. Young, for example, argues for a relative standard[25] whereas others, more concerned with immediate survival of the most marginalised demand the recognition of an absolute non-negotiable minimum core that enables survival and basic dignity.[26] In practice, the UN legal position has been to place the onus on states themselves to determine what actually constitutes the minimum core in any given context *dependent on a number of variables such as the right in question, the resources available, the measures*

[22] K Shields, *The Minimum Core Obligations of Economic, Social and Cultural Rights: The Rights to Health and Education*, Research Summary (Nordic Trust Fund, World Bank, 2017) 11.

[23] See ch 7 (Eichenhofer) in this volume.

[24] P Alston, 'Out of the Abyss: The Challenges Confronting the New UN Committee on Economic, Social and Cultural Rights' (1987) 9 *Human Rights Quarterly* 352.

[25] K Young, 'The Minimum Core of Economic and Social Rights: A Concept in Search of Content' (2008) 33 *Yale Journal of International Law* 113.

[26] D Bilchitz, 'Towards a Reasonable Approach to the Minimum Core: Laying the Foundations for Future Socio-Economic Rights Jurisprudence' (2003) 19 *South African Journal on Human Rights* 15.

taken and the prevailing social, economic, cultural, climatic, ecological and other (CESCR General Comment 12).

Both the law and literature has developed a 'minimum core' requirement that is legally binding and most likely non-derogable (meaning states cannot justify non-compliance).[27] However, as discussed above, what it actually means in practice is not necessarily always clear. Some of the UN General Comments elaborate on what is required to meet a minimum core threshold in relation to a particular right.[28] One of the most expansive interpretations is contained in CESCR General Comment 14 (right to health) in which the Committee gives an interpretative list with normative thresholds including:

- access to health facilities, goods and services on a non-discriminatory basis, especially for vulnerable or marginalised groups;
- access to the minimum essential food which is nutritionally adequate and safe, to ensure freedom from hunger to everyone;
- access to basic shelter, housing and sanitation, and an adequate supply of safe and potable water;
- access to essential drugs, as from time to time defined under the WHO Action Programme on Essential Drugs;
- the equitable distribution of all health facilities, goods and services;
- implementation of a national public health strategy and plan of action, inter alia.[29]

This approach seeks to identify clear and tangible outcomes in meeting the minimum core obligation in the right to health whilst still allowing significant discretion to the state to substantive interpretation and means of provision. In addition, the Committee stresses that a state party cannot, under any circumstances whatsoever, justify its non-compliance with the minimum core, which is non-derogable.[30] A similar approach is taken in General Comment 15 (right to water) where the minimum core obligation is declared non-derogable.[31]

[27] For a full and comprehensive discussion on the nature of the minimum core obligation in international law see A Müller, 'Limitations to and Derogations from Economic, Social and Cultural Rights' (2009) 9 *Human Rights Law Review* 557, 654.

[28] UN Committee on Economic, Social and Cultural Rights (CESCR), General Comment No 13: The Right to Education (Art 13 of the Covenant), 8 December 1999, E/C 12/1999/10, para 57; General Comment No 14: The Right to the Highest Attainable Standard of Health (Art 12 of the Covenant), 11 August 2000, E/C 12/2000/4; General Comment No 15: The Right to Water (Arts 11 and 12 of the Covenant), 20 January 2003, E/C 12/2002/11 para 37; General Comment No 17: The Right of Everyone to Benefit from the Protection of the Moral and Material Interests Resulting from any Scientific, Literary or Artistic Production of Which He or She is the Author (Art 15, para 1(c) of the Covenant), 12 January 2006, E/C 12/GC/17 para 39; General Comment No 18: The Right to Work (Art 6 of the Covenant), 6 February 2006, E/C 12/GC/18, para 31; General Comment No 19: The Right to Social Security (Art 9 of the Covenant), 4 February 2008, E/C 12/GC/19, para 59.

[29] General Comment 14 para 43.

[30] General Comment 10, para 60.

[31] General Comment 15, para 40.

In General Comments 19 and 17, however, the Committee oscillates to a lesser obligation where the state may justify non-compliance if it can attribute its failure to meet the minimum core threshold to a lack of available resources by demonstrating that every effort has been made to use all the resources at its disposal in an effort to satisfy as a matter of priority its minimum obligations.[32] In General Comment 19, the Committee stipulates that a minimum right to social security should entail essential healthcare, basic shelter and housing, water and sanitation, foodstuffs, and the most basic forms of education.[33] If there is not enough resources to achieve this minimum the Committee suggests consultation on meeting a core group of 'social risks and contingencies' within the state's capacity.[34] Across these different approaches there is an underlying suggestion that there is indeed a minimum core relative to the state's maximum available resources in addition to an absolute non-derogable minimum that applies despite a state's available resources. The former threshold will adjust on a scale depending on the prevailing circumstances and the latter performs a permanent and absolute baseline from which departure can never be justified (a non-derogable obligation).

In terms of how states can demonstrate achieving the minimum core obligation, the means through which to achieve the standards and what they mean in practice in any given context are to a significant degree left to the state's discretion based on an interpretation of the normative elaboration set out in the various General Comments.[35] The nature of the obligation to realise the minimum core can therefore be more easily assessed by reviewing whether the state has taken all necessary measures in order to ensure a basic minimum relative to the country's wealth as well as employing an objective normative threshold as to an immediately enforceable absolute minimum core. In addition, these obligations are not to displace states' obligations to progressively realise the full enjoyment of rights, meaning that at all times there is an obligation on states to progress beyond the minimum to fulfil rights in their fullest sense.

III. WHY THE CONSTITUTION?

Whilst international law requires compliance with minimum core obligations domestic arrangements can differ in terms of how to enforce such rights at the local level. Incorporation of international law can indeed occur through various pathways or 'ports' including the constitution.[36]

[32] General Comment 19 para 60; General Comment 17, para 41.

[33] General Comment 19 para 59(a).

[34] General Comment 19, para 59(b).

[35] General Comment No 3, para 4: 'each State party must decide for itself which means are the most appropriate under the circumstances'.

[36] J Resnik, *Law's Migration: American Exceptionalism, Silent Dialogues, and Federalism's Multiple Ports of Entry* (2006) 115 *Yale Law Journal* 1564.

Many countries embed the right to a social minimum in their constitution reflecting the concept of the minimum core, ie a social floor that ensures no one falls into destitution. According to constitutional theory, a minimum level of subsistence is a constitutional essential for the functioning of a democracy.[37] This is premised on the idea that people need to be able to access basic essentials in order to participate in society and facilitate genuine autonomy.[38] Often the threshold for assessing compliance with a minimum level is based on the concept of human dignity.[39] The approach of an absolute minimum guarantee is evident, for example, in the constitutions of Germany (*Existenzminimum*),[40] Switzerland (*conditions minimales d'existence*),[41] Colombia (*minimo vítal*) and Brazil (*mínimo existencial*).[42]

Constitutionalising social rights is nothing new[43] and different states have taken different approaches to the particular model of constitutionalisation adopted. Some constitutions regard ESR as non-justiciable principles (such as in Ireland, India and Sweden). In some cases the judiciary have developed justiciable rights through a wide interpretative analysis (such as in Canada through equality provisions, or in India through the dynamic interpretation of civil and political rights and with the help of guiding principles on social rights in the constitution). Other constitutions have directly enforceable ESR protection (such as in South Africa, Finland, Argentina and Colombia). More recently some countries are in the process of considering affording ESR justiciable constitutional status including Ireland, Scotland and New Zealand.[44]

[37] J Rawls, *Political Liberalism Expanded Edition* (New York, Columbia University Press, 2005).

[38] R Alexy, *A Theory of Constitutional Rights*, trans J Rivers (Oxford, Oxford University Press, 2002); K Möller, 'Two Conceptions of Positive Liberty: Towards an Autonomy-Based Theory of Constitutional Rights' (2009) 29 *Oxford Journal of Legal Studies* 757.

[39] For a discussion on the role of human dignity underpinning comparative European constitutions, see C Dupré, *The Age of Dignity* (Oxford, Oxford University Press, 2015).

[40] The German Basic Law guarantees an *Existenzminimum*, which means the right to a minimum subsistence level.

[41] Similarly, the Swiss Federal Court has found that an implied constitutional right to a 'minimum level of subsistence (*conditions minimales d'existence*), both for Swiss nationals and foreigners, could be enforced by the Swiss Courts. See Swiss Federal Court, *V v Einwohrnergemeine X und Regierungsrat des Kanton Bern*, BGE/ATF 121I 367, 27 October 1995.

[42] See Brazilian Federal Supreme Court (*Supremo Tribunal Federal*), RE 436996/SP (opinion written by Judge Celso de Mello), 26 October 2005. The Court found that the inefficiency of public managed funds in implementation the constitutional minimum to provide for the needy cannot and should not impede execution of the obligation. This case dealt specifically with the right to education.

[43] See for example the following constitutions each of which provide for 'economic, social and cultural rights' in some regard: Argentina 1853 (reinst 1983, rev 1994), Angola (2010), Macedonia 1991 (rev 2011), Bosnia-Herzegovina 1995 (rev 2009), Cape Verde 1980 (rev 1992), Croatia 1991 (rev 2001), Czech Republic 1993 (rev 2002), Democratic Republic of the Congo 2005 (rev 2011), East Timor 2002, Eritrea 1997, Ethiopia 1994, Iran 1979 (rev 1989), Macedonia 1991 (rev 2011), Montenegro 2007; Mozambique 2004 (rev 2007); Nepal 2006 (rev 2010); Nicaragua 1987 (rev 2005); Portugal 1976 (rev 2005); Rwanda 2003 (rev 2010); Sao Tome and Principe 1975 (rev 1990); Slovakia 1992 (rev 2001); Surinam 1987 (rev 1992).

[44] For a discussion on models of constitutionalisation see K Boyle, 'Economic, Social and Cultural Rights in Ireland: Models of Constitutionalisation' (2014) 3 *Irish Community Development Law*

Of course, some countries do not recognise the social minimum as a constitutional right but provide for a social minimum through the operation of legislation, particularly in the context of welfare legislation.[45]

Some make the case that legislation and administrative measures are the most appropriate means of achieving a social minimum where the allocation of resources ought to be left to the elected branches of government. In other words, it is through politics that the provision of a social minimum should be administered.[46] Waldron, for example, argues that democratic legitimacy is ensured through the operation of political representation[47] and that the substance of rights should be realised through political consensus. This is based on the concept that there is good-faith disagreement between persons about rights and the meaning of rights. This disagreement ought to be resolved by representative legislatures, after reasoned debate, through majority voting. The legislature is therefore best placed to resolve substantive disagreements on the form and substance of rights and how they ought to be protected.[48]

However, there are a number of 'blind spots' in relying on legislative supremacy to ensure adequate rights protection.[49] These blind spots can be categorised under (i) marginalisation (or majoritarian neglect) and (ii) lack of legislative focus. The latter relates to the need to provide the legislature with sufficient focus to ensure that social rights are not inadvertently overlooked or ignored ('the burden of inertia').[50] The former brings more serious concerns around democratic legitimacy. The marginalisation of particularly vulnerable groups essentially means that representative democracy does not represent everyone. The principle of agency is undermined – ie the right to participate in politics to resolve disputes over substance and form of rights cannot be accessed by those who are excluded from the majoritarian system.[51] Waldron and Bellamy – both critics of judicial review – concede that this issue is 'a real limitation to the argument for the legitimacy of legislation'.[52]

Journal 33 and K Boyle, *Models of Incorporation and Justiciability for Economic, Social and Cultural Rights*, Scottish Human Rights Commission (2018), available at www.scottishhumanrights.com/media/1809/models_of_incorporation_escr_vfinal_nov18.pdf.

[45] For a discussion of the different approaches see King, *Judging Social Rights* (2012) 39–40.

[46] See Gearty, 'Against Judicial Enforcement' in C Gearty and V Mantouvalou, *Debating Social Rights* (Oxford, Hart, 2011) 75.

[47] J Waldron, *Law and Disagreement* (Oxford, Clarendon Press, 1999). See also J Waldron, 'The Core Against Judicial Review' (2006) 115 *Yale Law Journal* 1347.

[48] ibid at ch 5.

[49] R Dixon, 'Creating Dialogue About Socioeconomic Rights: Strong-Form versus Weak-Form Judicial Review Revisited' (2007) 5 *International Journal of Constitutional Law* 391.

[50] ibid.

[51] S Benhabib, 'Reason-Giving and Rights-Bearing: Constructing the Subject of Rights' (2013) 20 *Constellations* 38, 46.

[52] King (n 9) 165. R Bellamy, *Political Constitutionalism: A Republican Defence of the Constitutionality of Democracy* (Cambridge, Cambridge University Press, 2007) 26–48 and Waldron, 'The Core' (2006) 1404.

Others argue that the constitution should set a threshold and that the court should have the last say on the determination of ESR, including a social minimum.[53] Mantouvalou argues that:

> Social rights are constitutional essentials at domestic level, as much as civil and political rights are; the two groups of rights are based on common values and have no sharp conceptual differences. Rights to the meeting of basic needs should resist trade-offs and should constitute very weighty considerations for the judiciary when adjudicating, and for the legislature when legislating.[54]

Rather than favour the legislative, executive or judicial branch as final arbiter on rights the constitution can act as an anchor that holds all branches of government to the same standard. King develops a model to constitutionalise a social minimum based on the principles of deliberative democracy that ensures legislative focus on rights and the protection of marginalised groups under an overarching constitutional framework where the court can act as an important accountability mechanism of last resort.[55] This does not necessarily usurp the role of the legislature or executive but requires that the legislative, executive and judicial branches all comply with the same constitutional standard.

This is a multi-institutional approach in a deliberative democracy framework. Rather than leave responsibility for ESR to one arm of the state the responsibility is shared between institutions. Benhabib contributes to this understanding by creating a place for the principles of democratic legitimacy argued by Waldron (through the legislature), King (through the constitution and the court) and argues that each can co-exist (as described by Mantouvalou).

Benhabib argues that representative democracy and the formulation of rights through deliberation in the legislature can indeed complement a substantive rights based constitutional approach to legally enforceable rights – and in the same vein a constitutional arrangement benefits from a legislative system that engages with contextualising rights as justiciable entitlements.[56]

Ultimately, a constitutionalisation of rights under this model must pertain to a form of legalisation, rather than acting as a mere guiding principle. And as such, there is inevitably a role for the court to play in an inter-institutional dialogue on what compliance with a constitutionalised social minimum means in any given context. Hence, returning to the debate on both relative and absolute thresholds and what role the court should play in both determining and enforcing them.

[53] See D Bilchitz, *Poverty and Fundamental Rights, The Justification and Enforcement of Socio-economic Rights* (Oxford, Oxford University Press 2007) 119–34.

[54] ibid, 159.

[55] King (n 9) ch 6.

[56] This formulation is based on Habermas' theory of co-originality of public and private autonomy see J Habermas, *Between Facts and Norms: Contributions to a Discourse Theory of Law and Democracy*, trans W Rehg (Cambridge, MA, MIT Press, 1996) 84–104. See Benhabib, 'Reason-Giving' (2013).

IV. WHAT ROLE SHOULD THE COURT PLAY IN ENFORCING A MINIMUM THRESHOLD?

As above, one difficulty in measuring compliance with the minimum core is the contested nature of what the obligation to a minimum core means. Does it engage with multidisciplinary conceptualisations of a 'social minimum' or is it a standalone normative legal standard? Arguably it could constitute an absolute standard – likewise it could be considered relative to a country's wealth. The UN General Comments suggests there may be both absolute and relative standards at play concurrently. Conceptually this makes it difficult to ascertain whether compliance with international obligations has been met and is one of the main criticisms of the justiciable entitlement to ESR. In other words, a critique of social rights adjudication argues that the obligations are too vague to give any precise legal meaning and are therefore unenforceable (the indeterminacy critique).[57]

A socio-legal approach can help support a court tasked with identifying whether a violation of a minimum entitlement has occurred. For example, should the right to food constitute a right to be free from hunger, should it constitute a nutritious diet which supports a healthy lifestyle, or should it constitute a diet relative to the diets of those around you – and does the threshold change depending on the country? This relates to the sociological question about what constitutes a social minimum, an absolute,[58] adequate[59] or decent[60] threshold. We could contextualise this in the UK, for example, where people rely on foodbanks to feed both themselves and their families, including children. What threshold should the UK be required to meet and is the state meeting its international obligation in law? The UN has raised concerns with the UK on compliance with the right to food but has not explicitly declared a violation of the minimum core.[61] And yet deprivation of essential food is

[57] For a discussion on the indeterminacy critique see ch 11 (O'Cinneide).

[58] As defined in law or elsewhere: compare legal discourse to, for example, S White, 'Social Minimum' in *Stanford Encyclopedia of Philosophy* (2004), available at: http://plato.stanford.edu/entries/social-minimum.

[59] Such as the right to an adequate standard of living (RASL) as provided for in international law: Art 25 UDHR (RASL); Art 22 UDHR (social security); Art 11 ICESCR (RASL); Art 12 ICESCR (health); General Comment 12 (Food); General Comment 4 (housing); General Comment 15 (water).

[60] See for example HP Gaisbauer, G Schweiger, C Sedmak, *Ethical Issues in Poverty Alleviation* (Springer 2016) 54, discussing Raz's approach to a decent standard of living based on the diminishing and satiable principle, J Raz, *The Morality of Freedom* (Oxford University Press, 1986).

[61] In July 2016 the UN Committee on ESC Rights raises concerns with the UK about the reliance on foodbanks and urges the UK to 'develop a comprehensive national strategy for the protection and promotion of the right to adequate food in order to address food insecurity'. The does not state that the UK is in breach of its minimum core obligations nor does it explicitly state a violation of the right to food. CESCR, 'Consideration of Reports Submitted by States Parties under Articles 16 and 17 of the Covenant: [Concluding Observations of the Committee on Economic, Social and Cultural Rights]: United Kingdom of Great Britain and Northern Ireland, the Crown Dependencies and the Overseas Dependent Territories', 14 July 2016, E/C 12/GBR/CO/6, para 54.

a prima facie breach of the minimum core obligation according to CESCR General Comment 3.[62] Arguably the reliance on foodbanks contravenes both an absolute and relative minimum core obligation. If the UK were to incorporate the right to food as provided for in Article 11 ICESCR would this give the court the ability to hold the state to account at the domestic level? What role, if any, should the court play in determination of the right in both absolute and relative terms?

There are three key conceptual approaches to take into consideration in this respect. The first is that the legal framework could require the court to enforce a substantive minimum threshold. If a person cannot access essential food, the court could order the state to provide it meaning there is an immediately realisable right to food (substantive approach). A second approach could require the court could look at the reasonableness and proportionality of the decision-making process around the provision of the right to food – did the decision-maker act fairly and reasonably when engaging with the provision of the right? A third approach could examine the basic requirements of procedural fairness around the decision-making process, ie examine the legality of the decision rather than the fairness of the outcome. The first approach requires a substantive threshold, substantive review and substantive enforcement. The second approach is concerned with both procedural and potentially substantive enforcement through reasonableness and proportionality analysis of the decision-making process. The third approach does not necessarily engage with any substantive standards but is limited to procedural fairness that may, in the end, give rise to some substantive enforcement of a minimum.[63] The first approach is the strongest with regard to ESR enforcement (substantive outcomes) and the last is the weakest (procedural safeguards that may give rise to substantive outcomes, or may not). Examples of these approaches are prevalent in comparative social rights adjudication and courts have at times adopted a hybrid approach using both procedural and substantive enforcement depending on the circumstances.

It is important to break down the duties in relation to the right to social minimum/minimum threshold into their different components as often a right to a process, or a policy, can be confused with a right to an outcome The first approach (the substantive approach) is the duty to fulfil an outcome (x). The second approach is the duty to produce and implement a policy that seeks to achieve an outcome [p(x)]. The second of these approaches falls within a meta-right analogy proposed by Sen that a 'metaright to something (x) can be defined as the right to have policies p(x)'.[64] The third approach concerns fair process in connection with decisions around the right to an outcome [pr(x)]. These different approaches move through procedural through to substantive duties.

[62] According to General Comment 3, para 10.

[63] See ch 14 (Leijten) in this volume.

[64] A Sen, 'The Right not to be Hungry' in P Alston and K Tomasevski, *The Right to Food* (The Hague, Martinus Nijhoff, 1984) 70.

The right to fair process is not the same as a right to an outcome. Neither is the right to a policy the same as a right to an outcome. Nonetheless both of these approaches can lead, in some cases, to substantive outcomes depending on the circumstances. However, ultimately the remedies offered for violations of either p(x) or pr(x) will not be as strong as the remedies available for a violation of (x). The second and third approaches constitute the metaright analogy (not actually a right to something in itself, but a right to particular inputs that may lead to an output).

What law cannot easily determine is the degree to which a right is, or ought to be, realised. One way to work around this is for the court to adopt an absolute standard such as a dignity threshold whilst also assessing the steps taken by the state to reach a relative threshold in line with the continuous improvement of living conditions (Article 11(1) ICESCR). In the latter case the review is of the process and procedures followed to meet a standard rather than establishing whether a standard has indeed been met. Arguably, the more serious the violation, and the more impactful on an absolute minimum core, the more necessary it is for the court to employ strong review and strong outcome-orientated remedies (substantive enforcement). On the other hand, where the state establishes a relative minimum core and broader progressive achievement the more scope there is for justificatory defences and deferential/incremental judgments based on procedural enforcement and reasonableness review.

V. THE SUBSTANTIVE APPROACH

A. The Right to x

In the UK, the Supreme Court recently considered what constitutes the 'minimum necessary to meet the essentials of life'[65] when calculating whether the imposition of tribunal fees in employment law disputes impeded access to justice with reference to minimum income standards developed by the Joseph Rowntree Foundation.[66] The Court held that the imposition of the fees did indeed impact on access to justice and declared the fees unlawful. The judicial review of the Court departed from the traditional approach to review of fair procedures and looked at the substantive aspects of what constitutes a social minimum with reference to independent evidence developed by Joseph Rowntree Foundation. While this type of review is in its infancy,[67] it goes some way to demonstrate the

[65] *R (UNISON) v Lord Chancellor* [2017] UKSC 51, para 90.

[66] ibid.

[67] For a discussion of the development of evidence based judicial review in cases engaging with systemic unfairness see J Tomlinson and K Sheridan, 'Judicial Review, Evidence, and Systemic Unfairness in the UK' IACL-AIDC blog (3 September 2018), available at https://blog-iacl-aidc.org/blog/2018/9/3/judicial-review-evidence-and-systemic-unfairness-in-the-uk.

capacity of the Court to hear evidence on the substantive components of what is needed to 'meet the essentials of life'.

An example of substantive enforcement is evident under the *tutela* system in Columbia. This system enables applicants to appear before the court to declare an 'unconstitutional set of affairs' in violation of the right to a social minimum. The *tutela* device[68] is a fast-track remedial process whereby applicants can seek to enforce constitutional rights, including ESR, if they require immediate protection. In the context of social security the Colombian Constitutional Court developed the concept of *mínimo vital* (based on the German *Existenzminimum*). Although the *mínimo vital* is not explicitly mentioned in the Constitution it has been interpreted (teleologically and dynamically) as implicit to the right to life, the right to health, the right to work and the right to social security.[69] As explained by Sepúlveda,

> in cases of extreme urgency in which the basic subsistence of the individual and her family is in jeopardy, it is possible to file a writ of protection [*acion tutela*] as a fast-track emergency measure for the enforcement of economic, social and cultural rights.[70]

This approach recognises an immediately enforceable right to a social minimum.

Landau argues that the court can become an important institutional voice for the marginalised in such cases.[71] The courts have intervened to ensure that those in desperate need have access to a remedy as quickly as possible. For example, in Colombia, an elderly man living in absolute poverty requested that the state provide him with economic assistance so that he could undergo an eye operation that would allow him to recover his sight. The court found that the legislature had not complied with its duty to adopt a law to address the situation of such persons and ordered the social security system to provide the treatment.[72] This is substantive enforcement of an immediately realisable right.

B. The Right to p(x)

An associated substantive approach can be found under the metaright analogy. The first substantive approach, as set out above, is the right to an outcome linked to the duty to fulfil an outcome (x). The second substantive approach is the right to a policy to achieve an outcome [p(x)].

[68] Article 86 Colombian Constitution.

[69] M Sepúlveda, 'Colombia, The Constitutional Court's Role in Addressing Social Injustice' in M Langford (ed) *Social Rights Jurisprudence, Emerging Trends in International and Comparative Law* (Cambridge, Cambridge University Press, 2009) 150.

[70] ibid.

[71] D Landau, 'The Reality of Social Rights Enforcement' (2012) 53 *Harvard International Law Journal* 189–247. See also Mantouvalou, 'In Support of Legalisation' in Gearty and Mantouvalou, *Debating Social Rights* (Oxford, Hart, 2011).

[72] T-533/92.

In South African jurisprudence the court has adopted a method of review which assesses the reasonableness of ESR implementation by asking whether or not the policy seeking to achieve the outcome was reasonable. For example, the *Grootboom*[73] case concerning access to adequate housing (for those living in slum conditions) demonstrates both the capacity of the court and the limitations of its approach. The court on finding a violation of the right imposed an obligation to devise, fund, implement and supervise measures to provide relief to those in desperate need. This obligation did not create an immediately enforceable right to be rehoused; rather the state was under an obligation to revisit the national housing policy, which the court had declared unreasonable. The court rejected the argument posed by the *amici curiae*[74] that the court ought to follow the recommendations of the Committee on Economic Social and Cultural Rights under paragraph 4 of General Comment No 3 as a guide to interpretation in so far as ESR contain an inherent non-derogable substantive minimum core.[75]

Instead, the court held that the real question before the court was whether the measures taken by the state to realise the right to access adequate housing were reasonable.[76] Despite some positive legislative and administrative measures in place to address the national housing situation the court considered that the state had not sufficiently addressed their obligations in respect of those who were in desperate need.[77] They held that there was nothing in the constitution that conferred an immediate right upon the respondents[78] and the court emphasised that, under the prevailing circumstances in relation to the plight of housing in South Africa, that it would be very difficult for the state to progressively achieve access to housing on a nationwide scale and certainly impossible to achieve this as an immediately enforceable universal right (nor did the constitution confer such a right).[79]

Nonetheless, as highlighted by Pieterse, subsequent case law has developed a 'latent notion of minimum core entitlement' and the Court does not go as far as to say that it would never recognise a constitutional minimum – given that there is a possibility that this could arise as part of a reasonableness review.[80]

[73] *Government of the Republic of South Africa v Grootboom* 2001 (1) SA 46 (CC).

[74] The Human Rights Commission and the Community Law Centre of the University of the Western Cape were admitted as *amici curiae* to the case.

[75] The Court described the minimum core as 'the floor beneath which the conduct of the state must not drop if there is to be compliance with the obligation' at para 31, and rejected this concept as forming part of the obligation under the constitution at *Grootboom* para 32–33.

[76] ibid para 33. The court did not rule out the possibility of litigation based on a minimum core argument but emphasised that establishing a minimum core would be difficult, and even where appropriate, would require sufficient information on the needs and the opportunities for the enjoyment of the right in any given context.

[77] ibid para 66.

[78] ibid para 95.

[79] ibid paras 32–33.

[80] Pieterse argues that there is a latent and flexible notion of minimum entitlement in the court's *TAC* judgment (*Minister of Health v Treatment Action Campaign (no 2) (TAC)* 2002

The reasonableness approach to policy formation can therefore contain both procedural and substantive aspects. Ultimately, a focus on any outcome short of substantive enforcement means that remedies will fall short of immediate transformative change (or adequate remedies) for those in desperate need. Mrs Grootboom was reported to have died 'homeless and penniless' some eight years after the declaratory order was made in the case.[81] Justice Cameron of the South African Constitutional Court accepted that Mrs Grootboom's death was a 'humbling reminder to those in the business of law and of constitutional rhetoric that our craft has limits.'[82]

VI. THE PROCEDURAL APPROACH

A. The Right to pr[x]

Procedural fairness is generally concerned with decision-making processes, and procedural review is when courts ask whether the decision-maker followed due process when coming to his or her decision. Leijten (chapter fourteen) provides a helpful definition: 'rather than looking at the outcome (output) of law and (administrative and judicial) decision-making, [procedural review] is concerned with the way in which decisions were made and motivated' An example of a procedural duty is evident in the UK public sector equality duty (s 149 Equality Act 2010). This duty requires public bodies to have due regard to various protected characteristics when implementing public policy decisions and in the allocation of budgets. Failure to do so can result in a judicial remedy issued by the court which renders the new policy or budget unlawful.

For example, in the case where Birmingham City Council made changes to allocation of their budget in the provision of care for the elderly without considering the adverse impact on those with disabilities, the court intervened and quashed the changes the council were trying to introduce.[83] This is a strong procedural protection to ensure that public bodies have due regard to vulnerable groups in the allocation of resources, however, it does not provide for substantive protection of equality per se. Leijten highlights the wide-reaching potential of a procedural approach to minimum enforcement of ESR as evident in the

(5) SA 721 (CC)) and that this has much potential in guiding a more entitlement based and need-focused jurisprudence, M Pieterse, 'Resuscitating Socio-Economic Rights: Constitutional Entitlements to Health Care Services' (2006) 22 *South African Journal on Human Rights* 473.

[81] See P Joubert, 'Grootboom dies Homeless and Penniless', *Mail and Guardian*, 8 August 2008, available at http://mg.co.za/article/2008-08-08-grootboom-dies-homeless-and-penniless (accessed 23 July 2019).

[82] E Cameron, 'What Can you Do with Rights?', Law Commission of England and Wales, The Fourth Leslie Scarman Lecture, 25 January 2012, available at http://lawcommission.justice.gov.uk/docs/Scarman_2012_Justice_Cameron_What_you_can_do_with_rights.pdf, para 30.

[83] *On the Application of WMG & H v Birmingham City Council* [2011] EWHC 1147 Admin.

ECtHR jurisprudence. Whilst in practical terms procedural review may be the only option available to the practitioner seeking to enforce a right, it is argued here that human rights reform seeking to better protect ESR and the social minimum as a matter of course must try and reach beyond procedural review and thin conceptions of justice. Ideally courts should have both procedural and substantive fairness in mind when addressing violations of rights, including the various components of ESR (the hybrid approach).

VII. THE HYBRID APPROACH

A hybrid approach (encompassing both procedural and substantive review and enforcement) is evident in jurisprudence in Germany. In the *Hartz IV* case the court scrutinised whether the legislature followed the appropriate procedure to set the level of unemployment and welfare assistance and declared the outcome of that process unlawful for failing to meet the social minimum required for a dignified life.[84] It was found that the legislature had erred in the method adopted to calculate the social minimum and so failure to comply with a legitimate process had rendered the outcome unlawful (ie a violation of pr(x)). The law-makers were directed to reassess using correct empirical data.[85] However, the German Constitutional Court went further and declared that the substantive outcome of the flawed process failed to meet a minimum threshold to ensure a right to dignity (ie a violation of x). The court's approach therefore took on both procedural and substantive components arguably engaging with both absolute and relative thresholds. The absolute threshold was measured against the concept of dignity and the relative threshold was measured with reference to the process of calculating a minimum relative to a number of variables, including using correct country specific empirical data.

The hybrid approach is also evident in the work of the Committee of Social Rights in the Council of Europe, which has recommended that states 'recognise, at national level, an individual universal and enforceable right to the satisfaction of basic material needs (as a minimum: food, clothing, shelter and basic medical care) for persons in situations of extreme hardship.'[86] For example, with respect to the adequacy of the level of social assistance the Committee has stipulated that the provisions given must make it 'possible to live a decent life to cover the

[84] *Hartz IV* case – 'existenzminimum' BverfG, 1 BvL 1/09 vom 9.2.2010, Abstaz-Nr. (1–220): www.bverfg.de/entscheidugen/ls20100209_1bv100109.html. For further discussion of the case see A Nolan and M Dutschke, 'Article 2(1) ICESCR and States Parties' Obligations: Whither the Budget?', [2010] 3 *European Human Rights Law Review*, 280–289; 286.

[85] ibid.

[86] Council of Europe: Committee of Ministers, Recommendation R (2000) 3 on the Right to the Satisfaction of Basic Material Needs of Persons in Situations of Extreme Hardship (Adopted on 19 January 2000 at the 694th meeting of the Ministers' Deputies).

individual's basic needs'. In order to assess the level of assistance the Committee considers multiple factors including basic benefits, additional benefits and the poverty threshold in the country, which is set at the median equivalised disposable income and calculated on the basis of the Eurostat at risk-of-poverty threshold.[87] In the absence of the Eurostat indicator the Committee can instead refer to nationally defined thresholds such as the monetary cost of the 'the household basket containing the minimum quantity of food and non-food items which is necessary for the individual to maintain a decent living standard and be in good health.'[88] There are both procedural and substantive components to the assessment of a minimum threshold as well as absolute and relative components to the assessment (covering both basic needs as well as a level of assistance to address poverty relative to a country's wealth).

Here, the question that presents itself therefore is not whether enforcing the social minimum is possible, but whether courts should adopt a procedural, substantive or hybrid approach to assessing if states are meeting a social minimum in terms of both an absolute and relative obligation with both procedural and substantive components. One potential way forward is to use a concept such as dignity to set an absolute minimum that can be substantively enforced whilst imposing a relative duty that can be imposed through both procedural and substantive review including proportionality and reasonableness review (ie that there are fair processes to calculate [pr(x)] and reasonable policies to achieve [p(x)] where (x) is a relative outcome).

Table 16.1 The multiple components of a social minimum/minimum core

Type of right	Type of duty	Type of review	Type of enforcement	Type of defence
The right to x	Substantive – must achieve an outcome	Substantive. Has the applicant's dignity been violated? (assessing the outcome)	Outcome orientated remedy to immediately enforceable minimum	Does not violate dignity/ absolute minimum
The right to p(x)	ensure a policy in place to establish a minimum relative to prevailing conditions	Reasonableness/ proportionality – is the policy reasonable for the purposes of achieving the outcome?	Deferential – revisit a policy to ensure p(x)	Justificatory approach – the policy is reasonable and proportionate

(continued)

[87] *Finnish Society of Social Rights v Finland*, Complaint No 88/2012, decision on the merits of 9 September 2014, §112.

[88] European Social Charter, 'European Committee of Social Rights Conclusions 2015', January 2016, 26, available at https://rm.coe.int/1680593904.

Table 16.1 *(Continued)*

Type of right	Type of duty	Type of review	Type of enforcement	Type of defence
The right to pr(x)	Fairness in the decision-making process	Has the decision-making process been fair? Has the decision-maker considered all relevant factors? Have duties such as due regard been dispensed with fairly?	Revisit the decision-making process	The decision-making process was fair
Hybrid	Take steps to realise a right (through processes or policies) and compliance with a substantive threshold	Substantive and procedural review – does it achieve minimum outcome (measured against dignity) and have steps been taken to ensure relative threshold?	Outcome-orientated and deferential (multiple remedies either procedural or substantive in nature)	The minimum was not violated/ the policy was reasonable/ the process was fair

VIII. CONCLUSION

An interdisciplinary approach is required to further explore the potential of a judicially enforceable constitutional minimum. For example, questions around what humans need to satisfy a minimum must continue to be explored, while also developing methods for calculating a minimum with reference to reliable aggregated empirical evidence, and understanding how states can holistically adopt decision-making early on budgetary processes to ensure that sufficient resources are available to meet both absolute and relative standards. This a multi-layered complex picture and whilst not beyond the bounds of inter-institutional dialogue in a multi-institutional approach it will require all institutional actors (legislature/executive and judicial) to equip themselves with sufficient expertise to ensure an adequate standard of living is enjoyed.

The chapter aims to address some of the outstanding questions around relative and absolute thresholds in the legal enforcement of a social minimum/minimum core, as well as the substantive and procedural components of their enforcement by courts in a multi-institutional constitutional framework. The analysis highlights that a number of antinomies are at play with regard different types of review (procedural v substantive) as well as different types of outcome (relative v absolute). The case made here is that both absolute and relative standards can apply and it is the type of review and enforcement that differs between the thresholds, ideally requiring courts adopt a hybrid approach to procedural and substantive review and remedies.

Both absolute and relative standards can apply simultaneously:

Table 16.2 Absolute and relative antinomies

Absolute minimum	**Relative minimum**
Substantive threshold (dignity/ survival)	Procedural threshold (appropriate steps taken relative to country's wealth)
Right to outcome	Right to policy/fair process
Non-derogable	Derogable if justified
Objective	Subjective
Regardless of state circumstances	Prevailing circumstances
Basic level of living standards	Continuous improvement of living standards
Courts can enforce substantive immediate obligation to fulfil	Courts can review reasonableness of approach to fulfil
Outcome orientated remedies	Deferential remedies (revisit policy or process)

In accordance with international obligations it would perhaps be most appropriate to recognise social minimum/minimum core obligation as a starting point from which the legislature, the executive and the judiciary cannot depart (so recognising that there is a level of destitution below which no person should fall as well as minimum core obligations relative to a country's wealth). Thereafter, the constitutional arrangement could adopt different approaches to the progressive realisation of ESR, not forgetting that the minimum is not sufficient to meet the full international obligations of states to achieve progressively the rights to housing, health, education, employment, social security and an adequate standard of living to the state's maximum available resources. In this sense we must move beyond minimum thresholds that mark only the basic starting point of a much larger ESR picture.

Bibliography

'25 Facts and Stats about NGOs Worldwide', available at techreport.ngo/previous/2017/facts-and-stats-about-ngos-worldwide.html.

Adler, M, *Cruel, Inhuman or Degrading Treatment? Benefit Sanctions in the UK* (London, Palgrave Macmillan, 2018).

—— 'The New Leviathan: Benefit Sanctions in the UK' (2016) 43 *Journal of Law and Society* 195.

Ágh, A, 'The Decline of Democracy in East-Central Europe' (2016) 63 *Problems of Post-Communism* 277.

Alcock, P, *Understanding Poverty* (Basingstoke, Palgrave, 2006).

Alexander, S, 'Humanitarian Bottom League? Sweden and the Right to Health for Undocumented Migrants' (2010) 12 *European Journal of Migration and Law* 215.

Alexy, Robert, *A Theory of Constitutional Rights*, transl J Rivers (Oxford University Press, 2002).

Alkire, S, 'Choosing Dimensions: The Capability Approach and Multidimensional Poverty' in N Kakwani and J Silber (eds) *The Many Dimensions of Poverty* (Basingstoke, Palgrave Macmillan, 2007) 89–119.

—— 'Dimensions of Human Development' (2002) 30 *World Development* 181.

Alkire, S and Jahan, S, 'The New Global MPI 2018: Aligning with the Sustainable Development Goals', HDRO Occasional Paper (New York, UNDP, 2018).

Alston, P, 'Out of the Abyss: The Challenges Confronting the New UN Committee on Economic, Social and Cultural Rights' (1987) 9 *Human Rights Quarterly* 352.

—— 'Ships Passing in the Night: The Current State of the Human Rights and Development Debate Seen through the Lens of the Millennium Development Goals' (2005) 27 *Human Rights Quarterly* 755.

—— 'The Populist Challenge to Human Rights' (2017) 9 *Journal of Human Rights Practice* 1.

Alston, P and Quinn, G (1987), 'The Nature and Scope of States Parties' Obligations under the International Covenant on Economic, Social and Cultural Rights' (1987) 9 *Human Rights Quarterly* 156.

Alston, P and Simma, B, 'First Session of the UN Committee on Economic, Social and Cultural Rights' (1987) 81 *The American Journal of International Law* 747.

Amnesty International, 'Progress, Stagnation, Regression? The State of Human Rights in the Philippines under Aquino', available at www.amnesty.org/download/Documents/28000/asa350022011en.pdf.

—— 'Nigeria: A Criminal Enterprise? Shell's Involvement in Human Rights Violations in Nigeria in the 1990s' (2017), available at www.amnesty.org/en/documents/AFR44/7393/2017/en.

Arneson, RJ (2013) 'Egalitarianism' in EN Zalta (ed), *The Stanford Encyclopedia of Philosophy*, available at plato.stanford.edu/entries/egalitarianism.

Atkinson, AB, *Poverty and Social Security* (Brighton, Harvester Press, 1989).

—— *A National Minimum? A History of Ambiguity in the Determination of Benefit Scales in Britain* (London, London School of Economics, 1990).

—— *Beveridge, the National Minimum, and its Future in the European Context* (London, London School of Economics, 1993).

—— *Poverty in Europe* (Oxford, Blackwell, 1998).

—— 'Income, Health and Multi-dimensionality' in K De Boyser, C Dewilde, D Dierickx and J Friedrichs (eds) *Between the Social and the Spatial: Exploring the Multiple Dimensions of Poverty and Social Exclusion* (Farnham, Ashgate, 2009) 21–34.

—— *Inequality. What can be Done?* (Cambridge, MA, Harvard University Press, 2015).

Atkinson, AB, Cantillon, B, Marlier, E and Nolan, B, *Social Indicators: The EU and Social Inclusion* (Oxford, Oxford University Press, 2002).

Atria, F, 'Social Rights, Social Contract, Socialism' (2015) 24 *Social and Legal Studies* 598.

Babeuf, F-N and S M, 'The Manifesto of Equality' in LP Pojman and R Westmoreland (eds), *Equality* (Oxford, Oxford, Oxford University Press, 1997) 45.

Bäcker, G, Naegele, G, Bispinck, R, Hofmann, K and Neubauer, J, *Sozialpolitik und Soziale Lage in Deutschland* Vol 1 (Wiesbaden, Springer VS, 2008) 365ff.

Barak, A, *Proportionality: Constitutional Rights and Their Limitations* (Cambridge, Cambridge University Press, 2012).

Barak-Erez, D and Gross, AM, 'Introduction: Do We Need Social Rights? Questions in the Era of Globalisation, Privatisation, and the Diminished Welfare State' in D Barak-Erez and AM Gross (eds), *Exploring Social Rights: Between Theory and Practice* (Oxford, Hart, 2011) 1–17.

Barrientos, A, 'Justice-based Social Assistance' (2016) 16 *Global Social Policy* 151.

Becker, B and Mentel, B, 'Aspekte Regionaler Arbeitsmarktmessung in Deutschland' (2010) 4 *Wirtschaft und Statistik* 383.

Beduschi, A, 'Vulnerability on Trial: Protection of Migrant Children's Rights in the Jurisprudence of International Human Rights Courts' (2018) 36 *Boston University International Law Journal* 55.

Bellamy, R, *Political Constitutionalism: A Republican Defence of the Constitutionality of Democracy* (Cambridge, Cambridge University Press 2007) 26–48.

Benhabib, S, 'Reason-Giving and Rights-Bearing: Constructing the Subject of Rights' (2013) 20 *Constellations* 38.

Berggren, H and Trägårdh, L, *Är Svensken Människa* (Stockholm, Norstedts, 2006 [2015]).

—— 'Pippi Longstocking: The Autonomous Child and the Moral Logic of the Swedish Welfare State' in H Mattsson and SO Wallenstein (eds), *Swedish Modernism: Architecture, Consumption and the Welfare State* (London, Black Dog publishing, 2010) 10–23.

Beveridge, W, *Unemployment: a Problem of Industry* (London, Longmans, 1909 and 1930).

Biddle, BJ, 'Recent Developments in Role Theory' (1986) 12 *Annual Review of Sociology* 67.

Bilchitz, D, 'Towards a Reasonable Approach to the Minimum Core: Laying the Foundations for Future Socio-Economic Rights Jurisprudence' (2003) 19 *South African Journal on Human Rights* 15.

—— *Poverty and Fundamental Rights* (Oxford, Oxford University Press, 2007).

—— 'Do Corporations Have Positive Fundamental Rights Obligations?' (2010) 57 *Theoria: A Journal of Social and Political Theory* 1.

—— 'Socio-economic Rights, Economic Crisis, and Legal Doctrine' (2014) 12 *International Journal of Constitutional Law* 710.

—— 'Equality, Liberty and Modern Constitutionalism' in G Hull (ed), *The Equal Society* (Maryland, Lexington Books, 2015) 229–46.

—— 'Fundamental Rights as Bridging Concepts: Straddling the Boundary between Ideal Justice and an Imperfect Reality' (2018) 40 *Human Rights Quarterly* 119.

Bittner, C, 'Human Dignity as a Matter of Legislative Consistency in an Ideal World: The Fundamental Right to Guarantee a Subsistence Minimum in the German Federal Constitutional Court's Judgment of 9 February 2010' (2011) 12 *German Law Journal* 1941.

Bossuyt, M, 'Is the European Court of Human Rights on a Slippery Slope?' in S Flogaitis, T Zwart and J Fraser (eds), *The European Court of Human Rights and its Discontents* (Cheltenham, Edward Elgar, 2013) 27–36.

Boucher, D and Kelly, P (eds) *The Social Contract from Hobbes to Rawls* (London and New York, Routledge, 1994).

Bourguignon, F, *Die Globalisierung der Ungleichheit* (Hamburg, ÖGB Verlag, 2013).

Boyle, K, 'Economic, Social and Cultural Rights in Ireland: Models of Constitutionalisation' (2014) 3 *Irish Community Development Law Journal* 33.

—— 'Justiciability Mechanisms for Economic, Social and Cultural Rights' in A Divers and J Miller (eds), *Justiciability of Human Law in Domestic Jurisdiction* (Cham, Springer International Publishing Switzerland, 2015).

—— 'Models of Incorporation and Justiciability for Economic, Social and Cultural Rights' (Scottish Human Rights Commission, 2018).

Brady, D, Blume, A and Kleider, H, 'How Politics and Institutions Shape Poverty and Inequality' in D Brady and L Burton (eds), *The Oxford Handbook of the Social Science of Poverty* (Oxford, Oxford University Press, 2016) 115ff.

Brems, E, 'Procedural Protection: An Examination of Procedural Safeguards Read Into Substantive Convention Rights' in E Brems and JH Gerards (eds), *Shaping Rights in the ECHR: The Role of the European Court of Human Rights in Determining the Scope of Human Rights* (Cambridge, Cambridge University Press, 2014) 137–61.

Brinks, B, Gauri, V and Shen, K, 'Social Rights Constitutionalism: Negotiating the Tension Between the Universal and the Particular' (2015) 11 *Annual Review of Law and Social Science* 289.

Bruce, M, *The Coming of the Welfare State* (London, Batsford, 1961).

Bundesministerium für Arbeit und Soziales, *Lebenslagen in Deutschland der Fünfte Armuts- und Reichtumsbericht der Bundesregierung* (Berlin, Bundesministerium, 2017).

Cantillon, B, Goedemé, T, and Hills, J (eds), *Decent Incomes for All. Improving Policies in Europe* (New York, Oxford University Press, 2019).

Carr, CL, 'The Concept of Formal Justice' (1981) 39 *Philosophical Studies: an International Journal for Philosophy in the Analytical Tradition* 211.

Carrillo-Álvarez, E, Penne, T, Boeckx, H, Storms, B and Goedemé, T, 'Food Reference Budgets as a Potential Policy Tool to Address Food Insecurity: Lessons Learned from a Pilot Study in 26 European Countries' (2019) 16 *International Journal of Environmental Research and Public Health* 32.

Center for Reproductive Rights and Great Lakes Initiative for Human Rights and Development, 'Supplementary Information for the Adoption of List of Issues on Rwanda Scheduled for Review by the Human Rights Committee During Its 116th Session', Doc No INT/CCPR/ICO/RWA/20243/E (New York, 2015).

Cervero-Liceras, F, McKee, M and Legido-Quigley, H, 'The Effects of the Financial Crisis and Austerity Measures on the Spanish Health Care System: A Qualitative Analysis of Health Professionals' Perceptions in the Region of Valencia' (2015) 119 *Health Policy* 100.

Chambers, R, Longhurst, R, Bradley, D and Feacham, R, *Seasonal Dimensions to Rural Poverty* (Brighton, University of Sussex, 1979).

Checkland, SG and Checkland, EOA (ed), *The Poor Law Report of 1834* (Harmondsworth, Penguin, 1974).

Christensen, A, 'Normativa Grundmönster i Socialrätten' (1997) 78 *Retfaerd* 69.

—— 'Protection of the Established Position. A Basic Normative Pattern' (2000) 40 *Scandinavian Studies in Law* 285.

Christodoulidis, E, 'Social Rights Constitutionalism: An Antagonistic Endorsement' (2017) 44 *Journal of Law & Society* 123.

Churchill, R and Khaliq, U, 'The Collective Complaints System of the European Social Charter: An Effective Mechanism for Ensuring Compliance with Economic and Social Rights?' (2004) 15 *European Journal of International Law* 417.

Clapham, A, *Human Rights Obligations of Non-State Actors* (Oxford, Oxford University Press, 2006).

Cleveland, SH, 'After Kiobel' (2014) 12 *Journal of International Criminal Justice* 551.

Cohen, GA, 'Where the Action is: on the Site of Distributive Justice' (1997) 26 *Philosophy and Public Affairs* 3.

Coleman, D and Isoahola, SE, 'Leisure and Health – the Role of Social Support and Self-Determination' (1993) 25 *Journal of Leisure Research* 111.

Collier, P (2007) *The Bottom Billion: why the Poorest Countries are Failing and What Can be Done about it* (Oxford, Oxford University Press, 2007).

Commission for Historical Clarification, 'Conclusions and Recommendations Guatemala. Memory of Silence' (1999).

Committee on Economic, Social and Cultural Rights (CESCR), 'Report on the First Session', UN Doc E/1987/28 (New York, 1987).

—— 'Report on the Second Session', UN Doc E/1988 (Geneva, 1988).

—— General Comment 3: The Nature of States Parties Obligations (Art 2(1) of the Covenant), UN Doc E/1991/23 (Geneva, 1991).

—— General Comment 4: The Right to Adequate Housing (Art 11(1) of the Covenant), UN Doc E/1992/23 (Geneva, 1991).

—— Report on the Eighteenth and Nineteenth Sessions, UN Doc E/1999/22 (Geneva, 1992).

—— General Comment 12: The Right to Adequate Food (Art 11 of the Covenant), UN Doc E/C12/1999/5 (Geneva, 1999).

—— General Comment 13: The Right to Education (Art 13 of the Covenant), UN Doc E/C12/1999/10 (Geneva, 1999).

—— General Comment 14: The Right to the Highest Attainable Standard of Health (Art 12 of the Covenant), UN Doc E/C12/2000/4 2000 (Geneva, 2001).

—— General Comment 21: Right of Everyone to Take Part in Cultural Life (Art 15(1)(a) of the Covenant) UN Doc E/C12/GC/21 (Geneva, 2001).

—— Statement Adopted By The Committee On Economic, Social And Cultural Rights (Poverty Eradication), UN Doc E/C12/2001/10 (Geneva, 2001).

—— General Comment 15: The Right to Water (Arts 11 and 12 of the Covenant), UN Doc E/C12/2002/11 (Geneva, 2002).

—— General Comment 18: The Right to Work (Art 6 of the Covenant), UN Doc E/C12/GC/18 (Geneva, 2005).

—— General Comment 17: The Right of Everyone to Benefit from the Protection of the Moral and Material Interests Resulting from Any Scientific, Literary or Artistic Production of Which He or She Is the Author (Art 15(1)(c) of the Covenant), UN Doc E/C12/GC/17 (Geneva, 2006).

—— Concluding Observations: Tajikistan, UN Doc E/2007/22 (Geneva, 2006).

—— General Comment 19: The Right to Social Security (Art 9 of the Covenant), UN Doc E/C12/GC/19 (Geneva, 2007).

—— Concluding Observations: Japan, UN Doc E/C12/JPN/CO/3 (Geneva, 2013).

—— Concluding Observations: Sri Lanka, UN Doc E/C12/LKA/5 (Geneva, 2015).

—— Statement on Social Protection Floors: An Essential Element of the Right to Social Security and of the Sustainable Development Goals, UN Doc E/C12/2015/1 (Geneva, 2015).

—— General Comment 22: The Right to Sexual and Reproductive Health (Art 12 of the Covenant), UN Doc E/C12/GC/22 (Geneva, 2016).

—— General Comment 23: The Right to Just and Favourable Conditions of Work (Art 7 of the Covenant), UN Doc E/C12/GC/23 (Geneva, 2016).

—— Statement on Public Debt, Austerity Measures and the ICESCR, UN Doc E/C12/2016/1 (Geneva, 2016).

Committee on the Elimination of Discrimination against Women (CEDAW), Concluding Observations: Guinea, UN Doc CEDAW/C/GIN/CO/7-8 (Geneva, 2014).

Committee on the Rights of the Child, Concluding Observations: Timor-Leste, UN Doc CRC/C/TLS/CO/2-3 (Geneva, 2015).

—— General Comment 19: Public Budgeting for the Realization of Children's Rights (Art 4), UN Doc CRC/C/GC/19 (Geneva, 2016).

—— General Comment 21: Children in Street Situations, UN Doc CRC/C/GC/21 (Geneva, 2017).

Committee on the Rights of Persons with Disabilities, General Comment 4: The Right to Inclusive Education, UN Doc CRPD/C/GC/4 (Geneva, 2016).

—— Guidelines on Periodic Reporting to the Committee on the Rights of Persons with Disabilities, Including under the Simplified Reporting Procedures, UN Doc CRPD/C/3 (Geneva, 2016).

Contiades, X and Fotiadou, A, 'Social Rights in the Age of Proportionality: Global Economic Crisis and Constitutional Litigation' (2012) 10 *International Journal of Constitutional Law* 660.
Coomans, F and Künnemann, R, *Cases and Concepts on Extraterritorial Obligations in the Area of Economic, Social and Cultural Rights* (Cambridge, Intersentia, 2012).
Cranston, M, 'Rights: Real and Supposed' in DD Raphael (ed), *Political Theory and the Rights of Man* (Bloomington, Indiana University Press, 1967) 43–51.
Craven, M, *The International Covenant on Economic, Social and Cultural Rights: A Perspective on Its Development*, doctoral thesis (University of Nottingham, 1992).
Cremer, G, *Armut in Deutschland* (München, CH Beck, 2016).
Dagens Nyheter, 'Begränsa Välfärden för de Med Tillfälliga Uppehållstillstånd', 20 January 2016, available at www.dn.se/debatt/begransa-valfarden-for-de-med-tillfalliga-uppehallstillstand (accessed 11 May 2017).
Dams & the World Bank: www.whirledbank.org/environment/dams.html.
Davis, A, Hill, K, Hirsch, D and Padley, M, 'A Minimum Income Standard for the UK in 2016' (York, Joseph Rowntree Foundation, 2016), available at www.jrf.org.uk/report/minimum-income-standard-uk-2016.
Davis, K, Stremikis, K, Squires, D, and Schoen, C, 'Mirror, Mirror, on the Wall: How the Performance of the US Healthcare System Compares Internationally' (New York, Commonwealth Fund, 2014), available at www.commonwealthfund.org/~/media/files/publications/fund-report/2014/jun/1755_davis_mirror_mirror_2014.pdf.
Dean, H, *Understanding Human Need: Social Issues, Policy and Practice* (Bristol, Policy Press, 2010).
De Boyser, K, Dewilde, C, Dierickx, D and Friedrichs, J (eds) *Between the Social and the Spatial: Exploring the Multiple Dimensions of Poverty and Social Exclusion* (Farnham, Ashgate, 2009).
De Búrca, G, 'Book Review: Samuel Moyn. Not Enough: Human Rights in an Unequal World' (2019) 16 *International Journal of Constitutional Law* 1347.
De Neuberg, C, Roelen, K and Gassmann, F, 'Making Policy Analysis Richer: Multi-dimensional Poverty Research and Social Policy Design' in K De Boyser, C Dewilde and Department of Social Security, *New Ambitions for Our Country: A New Contract for Welfare* (London, HMSO, 1998).
De Rooy, P, *Werklozenzorg en Werkloosheidsbestrijding 1917 – 1940. Landelijk en Amsterdams Beleid* (Amsterdam, Van Gennep, 1979).
De Schutter, O, *International Human Rights Law* (Cambridge, Cambridge University Press, 2014).
De Schutter, O, Eide, A, Khalfan, A, Orellana, M, Salomon M and Seiderman, I, 'Commentary to the Maastricht Principles. Commentary to the Maastricht Principles on Extraterritorial Obligations of States in the Area of Economic, Social and Cultural Rights' (2012) 34 *Human Rights Quarterly* 1101.
Deva, S and Bilchitz, D (eds), *Building a Treaty on Business and Human Rights: Context and Contours* (Cambridge, Cambridge University Press, 2017).
Dicey, AV, *Introduction to the Study of the Law of the Constitution*, 1st edn (London, Macmillan, 1885; 10th edn, 1959) App I.
Dierickx, D and Friedrichs, J (eds) *Between the Social and the Spatial: Exploring the Multiple Dimensions of Poverty and Social Exclusion* (Farnham, Ashgate, 2009).
Dixon, R, 'Creating Dialogue About Socioeconomic Rights: Strong-Form versus Weak-Form Judicial Review Revisited' (2007) 5 *International Journal of Constitutional Law* 391.
Dorling, D, *Inequality and the 1%* (New York and London, Verso, 2014).
Dostoevsky, F, *A Writer's Diary* (Evantston, IL, Northwestern University Press, 2009).
Doyal, L and Gough, I, *A Theory of Human Need* (Houndmills, Macmillan, 1991).
Dupré, C, *The Age of Dignity* (Oxford, Oxford University Press, 2015).
Dworkin, R, *Taking Rights Seriously* (Cambridge, MA, Harvard University Press, 1977).
—— *Sovereign Virtue: The Theory and Practice of Equality* (Cambridge, Mass, Harvard University Press, 2000).
Dwyer, P, *Welfare Rights and Responsibilities* (Bristol, Policy Press, 2000).
—— 'Creeping Conditionality in the UK: From Welfare Rights to Conditional Entitlements?' (2004) 29 *Canadian Journal of Sociology* 265.

Economic and Social Council, 'The Limburg Principles on the Implementation of the International Covenant on Economic, Social and Cultural Rights', UN Doc E/CN.4/1987/17 (New York, 1987).

Egidy, S, 'The Fundamental Right to the Guarantee of a Subsistence Minimum in the Hartz IV Case of the German Federal Constitutional Court' (2011) 12 *German Law Journal* 961.

Eleveld, A, 'Flextensie en de Kwalificatie van de (Meerpartijen) Overeenkomst met de Re-integrerende Bijstandsgerechtigde' (2017) 9 *Tijdschrift voor Recht en Arbeid* 38.

Equality Trust, 'The Scale of Inequality in the UK' (London, 2017), available at www.equalitytrust.org.uk/scale-economic-inequality-uk

Erhag, T, 'Under Pressure? – Swedish Residence-based Social Security and EU Citizenship' (2016) 18 *European Journal of Social Security* 207.

Esping-Andersen, G, *Three Worlds of Welfare Capitalism* (Cambridge, Polity Press, 1989).

European Commission, 'The Measurement of Extreme Poverty in the European Union' (Brussels, Directorate General for Employment, Social Affairs and Inclusion, 2011).

—— 'Taking Stock of the Europe 2020 Strategy for Smart, Sustainable Growth' COM (2014) 130 final (Brussels, 2014).

Fabre, C, *Social Rights Under the Constitution: Government and the Decent Life* (Oxford, Oxford University Press, 2001).

—— *Whose Body is it Anyway?: Justice and the Integrity of the Person* (Oxford, Clarendon Press 2006).

Faust, A, 'Der Staat und die Arbeitslosigkeit in Deutschland 1890–1918. Arbeitsvermittlung, Arbeitsbeschaffung und Arbeitslosenversicherung' in W Mommsen and W Mock, *Die Entstehung des Wohlfahrtsstaates in Großbritannien und Deutschland 1850–1950* (Stuttgart, Klett-Cotta, 1982).

Ferraz, O, 'Poverty and Human Rights' (2008) 28 *Oxford Journal of Legal Studies* 585.

—— 'Brazil: Health Inequalities, Rights and Courts' in AE Yamin and S Gloppen (eds) *Litigating Health Rights: Can Courts Bring More Justice to Health*? (Cambridge, MA, Harvard University Press, 2011) 76–102.

Fessler, P and Schütz, M, 'Private Wealth across European Countries: the Role of Income, Inheritance and the Welfare State', Working Paper Series No 1847 (Frankfurt, European Central Bank 2015).

Fineman, M, 'The Vulnerable Subject: Anchoring Equality in the Human Condition' (2008) 20 *Yale Journal of Law and Feminism* 1.

—— 'The Vulnerable Subject and the Responsive State' (2010) 60 *Emory Law Journal* 251.

—— 'Vulnerability and Inevitable Inequality' (2017) 4 *Oslo Law Review* 133.

Fitzpatrick, S, Bramley, G, Sosenko, F, Blenkinsopp, J, Johnsen, S, Littlewood, M, Netto, G and Watts, B, *Destitution in the UK* (York, Joseph Rowntree Foundation, 2016).

Fotiadou, A, 'A Reply to David Bilchitz' (2014) 12 *Internamtional Journal of Constitutional Law* 740.

Fraser, D, *The Evolution of the British Welfare State* (London: Palgrave 1973).

Gaisbauer, HP, Schweiger, G, Sedmak, C, *Ethical Issues in Poverty Alleviation* (Cham, Springer International Publishing Switzerland, 2016).

Galston, W, 'A Liberal Defense of Equal Opportunity' in L Pojmann and R Westmoreland (eds), *Equality* (Oxford, Oxford University Press, 1997) 170ff.

Gambaro, L, Stewart, K and Waldfogel, J, *An Equal Start?* (Bristol, Policy Press, 2014).

Gammeltoft-Hansen, T, 'Growing Barriers: International Refugee Law' in M Gibney and S Skogly (eds), *Universal Human Rights and Extraterritorial Obligations* (Philadelphia, University of Pennsylvania Press, 2010).

Garland, D, 'On the Concept of "Social Rights"' (2016) 24 *Social and Legal Studies* 622.

Gauri, V and Brinks, DM, 'Introduction: the Elements of Legalization and the Triangular Shape of Social and Economic Rights' in V Gauri and DM Brinks (eds), *Courting Social Justice, Judicial Enforcement of Social and Economic Rights in the Developing World* (Cambridge, Cambridge University Press, 2008).

—— 'Human Rights as Demands for Communicative Action' (2012) 20 *Journal of Political Philosophy* 407.

Gearty, C and Mantouvalou, V, *Debating Social Rights* (Oxford, Hart, 2010).

Gerards, J, 'The ECtHR's Response to Fundamental Rights Issues Related to Financial and Economic Difficulties – the Problem of Compartmentalisation' (2015) 33 *Netherlands Quarterly of Human Rights* 274.

—— 'Procedural Review by the ECtHR: A Typology', in Janneke Gerards and Eva Brems (eds.), *Procedural Review in European Fundamental Rights Cases* (Cambridge University Press, 2017), 127–60.

—— 'Margin of Appreciation and Incrementalism in the Case Law of the European Court of Human Rights' (2018) 18 *Human Rights Law Review* 495.

Gerards, J and Brems, E (eds), *Procedural Review in European Fundamental Rights Cases* (Cambridge, Cambridge University Press, 2017).

Gerstenberg, O, 'The Justiciability of Socioeconomic Rights, European Solidarity, and the Role of the Court of Justice of the EU' (2014) 33 *Yearbook of European Law* 245.

Gilbert, N and Specht, H, *Dimensions of Social Welfare Policy* (Englewood Heights, NJ, Prentice Hall, 1974).

Gilbert, N and Terrell, P, *Dimensions of Social Welfare Policy* (Upper Saddle River, NJ, Pearson Education, 2013).

Glendon, MA, *A World Made New* (New York, Random House, 2001).

The Global Initiative for Economic, Social and Cultural Right, 'The Chixoy Dam Case: Need for Full World Bank and Inter-American Development Bank Accountability', available at www.gi-escr.org/latest-news/chixoy-dam.

Goedemé, T, Storms, B, Penne, T and Van den Bosch, K, 'The Development of a Methodology for Comparable Reference Budgets in Europe – Final Report of the Pilot Project for the Development of a Common Methodology on Reference Budgets in Europe (Contract No Vc/2013/0554)' (Brussels, European Commission, 2015).

Goedemé, T, Storms, B, Stockman, S, Penne, T and Van den Bosch, K, 'Towards Cross-Country Comparable Reference Budgets in Europe: First Results of a Concerted Effort' (2015) 17 *European Journal of Social Security* 3.

Goedemé, T, Penne, T, Hufkens, T, Karakitsios, A, Bernát, A, Franziskus, A, Simonovits, B, Álvarez, EC, Kanavitsa, E, Cussó Parcerisas, I, Romaní, JR, Mäkinen, L, Matsaganis, M, Arlotti, M, Kopasz, M, Szivós, P, Ritakallio, V-M, Kazepov, Y, Van den Bosch, K and Storms B, 'What Does It Mean to Live on the Poverty Threshold? Lessons from Reference Budgets' in B Cantillon, T Goedemé and J Hills (eds), *Decent Incomes for All. Improving Policies in Europe* (New York, Oxford University Press, 2019).

Gómez Isa, F, 'The Reversibility Of Economic Social And Cultural Rights In Crisis Contexts' in E Muniategi Azkona and L Klemkaite (eds), *Local Initiatives to the Global Financial Crisis: Looking for Alternatives to the Current Socio-Economic Scenario* (Deusto, Universidad de Deusto, 2012).

Gough, I, 'Lists and Thresholds: Comparing the Doyal–Gough Theory of Human Need with Nussbaum's Capabilities Approach' in F Comim and MC Nussbaum (eds), *Capabilities, Gender, Equality: Towards Fundamental Entitlements* (Cambridge, Cambridge University Press, 2014).

Habermas, J, *Between Facts and Norms: Contributions to a Discourse Theory of Law and Democracy*, (Cambridge, MA, MIT Press, 1996).

Hänninen, S, 'Pohjoismaisen Hyvinvoinnin Poliittinen Eetos' (2001) 26 *Tiede & Edistys* 19.

Harari, YN, 'The New Opium of the Masses', *The Guardian*, 8 May 2017.

Hauser, R, 'Das Maß der Armut: Armutsgrenzen im Sozialstaatlichen Kontext. Der Sozialstaatliche Diskurs' in E-U Huster, J Boeckh and H Mogge-Gutjahn (eds), *Handbuch Armut und Soziale Ausgrenzung* (Wiesbaden, Springer VS, 2008) 94ff.

Heinig, HM, 'The Political and the Basic Law's *Sozialstaat* Principle – Perspectives from Constitutional Law and Theory' (2011) 12 *German Law Journal* 1879.

Hick, R, 'On "Consistent" Poverty', CASE paper 167 (Centre for the Study of Social Exclusion, London School of Economics, 2012).

—— 'Poverty as Capability Deprivation: Conceptualising and Measuring Poverty in Contemporary Europe' (2014) 55 *European Journal of Sociology* 295.
—— 'Material Poverty and Multiple Deprivation in Britain: the distinctiveness of multidimensional assessment' (2016) 36 *Journal of Public Policy* 277.
—— 'The Coupling of Disadvantages: Measuring Poverty and Multiple Deprivation Before and after the Great Recession' (2016) 18 *European Journal of Social Security* 2–19.
Hick, R and Burchhardt, T, 'Capability Deprivation' in D Brady and L Burton, (eds), *The Oxford Handbook of the Social Science of Poverty* (Oxford, Oxford University Press, 2016) 75ff.
Hick, R and Lanau, A, *In-work Poverty in the UK: Problem, Policy Analysis and Platform for Action* (Cardiff, Cardiff University Press, 2017).
Hirschl, R, 'From Comparative Constitutional Law to Comparative Constitutional Studies' (2013) 11 *International Journal of Constitutional Law* 1, 8–9.
Huijbers, L, 'The European Court of Human Rights' Procedural Approach in the Age of Subsidiarity' (2017) 6 *Cambridge Journal of International Law* 177.
Human Rights Committee and Committee on Economic, Social and Cultural Rights (CESCR), *Summary Record of the Joint Meeting of the Human Rights Committee and the Committee on Economic, Social and Cultural Rights*, UN Doc CCPR/C/SR3273 - E/C12/2016/SR48 (New York, 2016).
Ignatieff, M, 'Human Rights as Ideology' in M Ignatieff and A Gutmann (eds), *Human Rights as Politics and Idolatry* (Princeton, Princeton University Press, 2001).
Indian Law Resource Center, 'Indigenous Survivors of Chixoy Dam Take Case to UN', available at https://indianlaw.org/content/indigenous-survivors-chixoy-dam-take-case-un
International Consortium of Investigative Journalists, '7 Charts that Show how the Rich Hide their Cash' (2017) ICIJ Newsletter, 13 September, available at www.icij.org/blog/2017/09/7-charts-that-show-how-rich-hide-their-cash.
Jheelan, N, 'The Enforceability of Socio-Economic Rights' (2007) 2 *European Human Rights Law Review* 146.
Johansson, H, *I det Sociala Medborgarskapets Skugga: Rätten till Socialbidrag under 1980- och 1990-talen* (Lund, Arkiv förlag, 2001).
Kakwani, N and Son, HH, 'On Assessing Pro-poorness of Government Programmes: International Comparisons' in N Kakwani and J Silber (eds), *The Many Dimensions of Poverty* (Basingstoke, Palgrave Macmillan, 2007) 251–74.
Kampen, K, *Verplicht Vrijwilligerswerk. De Ervaringen van Bijstandscliënten met een Tegenprestatie voor hun Uitkering*, doctoral thesis (University of Amsterdam, 2014).
Kant, I, *The Metaphysics of Morals* (Cambridge, Cambridge University Press, 1996).
Katrougalos, G, 'The Implementation of Social Rights in Europe' (1996) 292 *Columbia Journal of European Law* 277.
Kautto, M, Fritzell, J, Hvinden, B, Kvist, J and Uusitalo H, 'Introduction: How Distinct are the Nordic Welfare States?' in J Fritzell, B Hvinden, M Kautto, J Kvist and H Uusitalo (eds), *Nordic Welfare States in the European Context* (London and New York, Routledge, 2001) 1–13.
Keramidou, I and Triantafyllopoulos, L, 'The Impact of the Financial Crisis and Austerity Policies on the Service Quality of Public Hospitals in Greece' (2018) 122 *Health Policy* 352.
Ketscher, K, *Socialret: Almindelige Principper, Retssikkerhed og Administration, Grundværdier* (København, Forlaget Thomson, 2002).
—— 'Retten til eksistensminimum – og retten til ikke at blive diskrimineret' (2012) *Juristen* 177.
Khalfan, A, 'Division of Responsibility between States' in M Langford, W Scheinin and W van Genugten (eds), *Global Justice, State Duties: The Extraterritorial Scope of Economic, Social, and Cultural Rights in International Law* (Cambridge, Cambridge University Press, 2013).
Khosla, M, 'Making Social Rights Conditional: Lessons from India' (2010) 8 *International Journal of Constitutional Law* 739.
King, J, *Judging Social Rights* (Cambridge, Cambridge University Press, 2012).
—— 'Constitutions as Mission Statements' in DJ Galligan and M Versteeg (eds), *Social and Political Foundations of Constitutions* (Cambridge, Cambridge University Press, 2013) 73–103.

King, M and Thornhill C, *Niklas Luhmann's Theory of Politics and Law* (Hampshire, Palgrave MacMillan, 2003).

Kjellbom, P and Lundberg, A, 'Olika Rättsliga rum för en Skälig Levnadsnivå? En Rättskartografisk Analys av SoL och LMA i Domstolspraktiken (2018) 17–18 *Nordisk Socialrättslig Tidskrift* 39.

Kjønstad, A and Syse, A, 'Grunnlovsreform og Velferdsretten' (2014) 49 *Jussens Venner* 340.

Klees, B, *Arbeitslosigkeit und Ret, ein Handbuch zur Gegenwehr* (Frankfurt/M, Nachrichten-Verlags-Gesellschaft, 1984).

Kleinlein, T, 'The Procedural Approach of the European Court of Human Rights: between Subsidiarity and Dynamic Evolution' (2019) 68 *International and Comparative Law Quarterly* 91.

Koch, IE, *Human Rights as Indivisible Rights: The Protection of Socio-Economic Demands under the European Convention on Human Rights* (Leiden, Martinus Nijhoff Publishers, 2009).

—— 'The Justiciability of Indivisible Rights' (2003) 72 *Nordic Journal of International Law* 3.

Kockheimer, G, *Methoden der Armutsmessung*, (Berlin, Logos, 2012).

Kosonen, P, 'Globalization and the Nordic Welfare States' in R Sykes, B Palier and P M Prior (eds), *Globalization and the European Welfare States: Challenges and Change* (Hampshire, Palgrave, 2001) 153.

Kotkas, T, 'The Short and Insignificant History of Social Rights Discourse in the Nordic Welfare States' in T Kotkas and K Veitch (eds), *Social Rights in the Welfare State: Origins and Transformations* (Abingdon, Routledge, 2017) 15–34.

P Krugman, 'Is Vast Inequality Necessary?' *New York Times*, 15 January 2016, available at www.nytimes.com/2016/01/15/opinion/is-vast-inequality-necessary.html?_r=0.

Kumlin, S, 'Institutions – Experiences – Preferences: How Welfare State Design affects Political Trust and Ideology' in B Rothstein and S Steinmo (eds) *Restructuring the Welfare State: Political Institutions and Policy Change* (New York, Palgrave Macmillan, 2002) 20.

Landau, D, 'The Reality of Social Rights Enforcement' (2012) 53 *Harvard International Law Journal* 189.

Langford, M, 'The Justiciability of Social Rights: From Practice to Theory' in M Langford (ed) *Social Rights Jurisprudence: Emerging Trends in International and Comparative Law* (Cambridge, Cambridge University Press, 2012) 3–45.

Langford, Mm Porter, P, Brown, R and Rossi, J (eds), *The Optional Protocol to the International Covenant on Economic, Social and Cultural Rights: A Commentary* (Pretoria, Pretoria University Press, 2016).

Lansley, S and Mack, J, *Breadline Britain* (London, London Weekend Television, 1983).

—— *Breadline Britain* (London, Oneworld, 2015).

Lavrysen, L, *Human Rights in a Positive State* (Cambridge, Intersentia, 2016).

Le Grand, J, 'Equity versus Efficiency: The Elusive Trade-off' (1990) 100 *Ethics* 554.

Leijten, I, 'From *Stec* to *Valkov.* Possessions and Margins in the Social Security Case Law of the European Court of Human Rights' (2013) 13 *Human Rights Law Review* 309.

—— 'The German Right to an *Existenzminimum*, Human Dignity, and the Possibility of Minimum Core Socioeconomic Rights Protection' (2015) 16 *German Law Journal* 23.

—— *Core Socio-Economic Rights and the European Court of Human Rights* (Cambridge, Cambridge University Press, 2018).

Liebenberg, S 'The Value of Human Dignity in Interpreting Socio-Economic Rights' (2005) 21 *South African Journal of Human Rights* 1.

—— 'Needs, Rights and Transformation: Adjudicating Social Rights in South Africa' (2006) 17 *Stellenbosch Law Review* 5.

—— *Socio-Economic Rights: Adjudication under a Transformative Constitution* (Claremont, Juta, 2010).

Liebenberg, S and Young, K, 'Adjudicating Social and Economic Rights: Can Democratic Experimentalism Help?' in H Alviar García, K Klare and LA Williams (eds), *Social and Economic Rights in Theory and Practice, Critical Inquiries* (London, Routledge 2015) 237–58.

Lind, A-S, *Sociala Rättigheter i Förändring. En Konstitutionellrättslig Studie* (Uppsala, Uppsala Universitet, 2009).

Liu, G, 'Rethinking Constitutional Welfare Rights' (2008) 61 *Stanford Law Review* 203.

Loopstra, R, Reeves, A, McKee, M and Suckler, D, 'Do Punitive Approaches to Unemployment Benefit Recipients Increase Welfare Exit and Unemployment: A Cross-area Analysis of UK Sanctioning Reforms', Sociology Working Paper 2015–01 (2015) Department of Sociology, University of Oxford, available at www.sociology.ox.ac.uk/working-papers/do-punitive-approaches-to-unemployment-benefit-recipients-increase-welfare-exit-and-employment-a-cross-area-analysis-of-uk-sanctioning-reforms.html.

Luhmann, L, *Law as a Social System* (Oxford, Oxford University Press, 2004).

McCrudden, C (2008), 'Human Dignity and Judicial Interpretation of Human Rights' 19 *European Journal of International Law* 655.

Mack, J and Lansley, S, *Poor Britain*, (London, George Allen and Unwin, 1985).

Madsen, MR, 'Between the Law-State and the Welfare State: The Structural Limits of Legal-Political Liberalism in the Danish Welfare State' in M Feeley and M Langford, *The Limits of the Legal Complex: Nordic Lawyers and Political Liberalism* (forthcoming, 2019).

Margalit, A, *The Decent Society* (Cambridge MA, Harvard University Press, 1991).

Marshall, TH, 'Citizenship and Social Class (1950)' in TH Marshall and T Bottomore (eds), *Citizenship and Social Class* (London, Pluto Press, 1992).

Maslow, A, 'A Theory of Human Motivation' (1943) 50 *Psychological Review* 370.

—— *Motivation and Personality*, 2nd edn (New York, Harper and Row, 1954).

Mau, S and Verwiebe, R, *European Societies. Mapping Structure and Change* (Bristol, The Policy Press, 2010).

Meckled-Garcia, S, 'Giving up the Goods: Rethinking the Human Right to Subsistence, Institutional Justice, and Imperfect Duties' (2013) 30 *Journal of Applied Philosophy* 73.

Michelman, F, 'Socioeconomic Rights in Constitutional Law: Explaining America Away' (2008) 6 *International Journal of Comparative Constitutional Law* 663.

—— 'Welfare Rights in a Constitutional Democracy' (1979) *Washington University Law Quarterly* 659.

—— 'Constitutionally Binding Social and Economic Rights as a Compelling Idea: Reciprocating Perturbations in Liberal and Democratic Constitutional Visions' in H Alviar García, K Klare and LA Williams (eds), *Social and Economic Rights in Theory and Practice, Critical Inquiries* (New York, Routledge, 2015) 279–80.

Milanović, B, *Global Inequality: A New Approach for the Age of Globalization* (Cambridge, MA, Belknap, 2016).

Mill, JS, *Utilitarianism* (1863), available at www.utilitarianism.com/mill1.htm.

Miller, D, 'Equality and Justice' (1997) X *Ratio* 222.

—— *National Responsibility and Global Justice* (Oxford, University Press, 2007).

Mjöll Arnardóttir, O, 'The "Procedural Turn" Under the European Convention on Human Rights and Presumptions of Convention Compliance' (2017) 5 *International Journal of Constitutional Law* 9.

Moderaterna, 'Hela Sverige ska Jobba – Moderaternas ekonomiska vårmotion' (2017), available at www.moderat.se/sites/default/files/attachments/hela_sverige_ska_jobba-varmotion_2017_0.pdf (accessed 11 May 2017).

Möller, K, *The Global Model of Constitutional Rights* (Oxford, Oxford University Press, 2012).

—— 'Two Conceptions of Positive Liberty: Towards an Autonomy-Based Theory of Constitutional Rights' (2009) *Oxford Journal of Legal Studies* 29 757.

Morales, L, 'The Discontent of Social and Economic Rights' (2017) *Res Publica* 257.

Mowbray, A, *The Development of Positive Obligations Under the European Convention on Human Rights by the European Court of Human Rights* (Oxford, Hart, 2004).

Moyn, S, *Not Enough: Human Rights in an Unequal World* (Cambridge, MA, Belknap, 2018).

Müller, A, 'Limitations to and Derogations from Economic, Social and Cultural Rights' (2009) 9 *Human Rights Law Review* 557.

Murphy, R and Reed, H, *Financing the Social State: Towards a Full Employment Economy* (London, Centre for Labour and Social Studies, 2013).
Murray, C, *Guaranteed Income as a Replacement for the Welfare State* (Oxford, Foundation for Law, Justice and Society, 2006).
My Right, 'The Alternative Report On Implementation In Bosnia And Herzegovina Of The United Nations Convention On The Rights Of Persons With Disabilities' (Bosnia and Herzegovina, My Right, 2014).
Nagel, T, *Eine Abhandlung über Gleichheit und Parteilichkeit und Andere Schriften zur Politischen Philosophie*, (Paderborn, Schöningh Paderborn, 1994).
Nagel, T, 'Justice and Nature' (1997) 17 *Oxford Journal of Legal Studies*, 303.
Nagata, J, 'Plural Societies' in NJSB Baltes (ed), *International Encyclopedia of the Social & Behavioral Sciences* (Oxford, Pergamon, 2001).
National Audit Office, *Benefit Sanctions*, HC 628, Session 2016–17, 30 November 2016.
National Council of Organization of People with Disabilities, 'Submission for the Consideration of the Republic of Macedonia at the 20th Session of the UN Committee on the Rights of Persons with Disabilities', Doc no INT/CRPD/CSS/MKD/31979/E (New York, 2018).
Neal, M, 'Not Gods but Animals: Human Dignity and Vulnerable Subjecthood' (2012) 33 *Liverpool Law Review* 177.
Netherlands Institute for Human Rights, 'Written Contribution To the Pre-Sessional Working Group of the 59th Session of the Committee on Economic, Social and Cultural Rights' (Utrecht, 2016).
Nickel, J, 'Human Rights' in EN Zalta (ed), *The Stanford Encyclopedia of Philosophy*, available at https://plato.stanford.edu/archives/spr2017/entries/rights-human.
Nobles, R and Schiff, D, *Observing Law Through Systems Theory* (Oxford, Hart, 2013).
Nolan, A (ed), *Economic and Social Rights after the Global Crisis* (Cambridge, Cambridge University Press, 2015).
Nolan, A and Dutschke, M, 'Article 2(1) ICESCR and States Parties' Obligations: Whither the Budget?' (2010) 3 *European Human Rights Law Review* 280.
Nolan, B and Whelan, CT, *Resources, Deprivation and Poverty* (Oxford, Oxford University Press, 1996).
—— *Poverty and Deprivation in Europe* (Oxford, Oxford University Press, 2011).
Nozick, R, *Anarchy, State and Utopia* (Oxford, Blackwell, 1974).
Nussbaum, M, 'Women and Cultural Universals' in M Nussbaum, *Sex and Social Justice* (Oxford, Oxford University Press, 1999).
—— *Women and Human Development: The Capabilities Approach* (Cambridge, Cambridge University Press, 2000).
—— *Frontiers of Justice, Disability, Nationality and Species Membership* (Cambridge, MA, Belknap, 2006).
—— 'Human Dignity and Political Entitlements' in *Human Dignity and Bioethics: Essays Commissioned by the President's Council on Bioethics* (Washington, DC, The President's Council on Bioethics, 2008) https://bioethicsarchive.georgetown.edu/pcbe/reports/human_dignity/chapter14.html.
—— *Creating Capabilities: The Human Development Approach* (Oxford, Oxford University Press, 2011).
Nussberger, A, 'Procedural Review by the ECtHR: View from the Court', in J Gerards and E Brems (eds), *Procedural Review in European Fundamental Rights Cases* (Cambridge, Cambridge University Press, 2017) 161.
OECD, Growing Unequal? Income Distribution and Poverty in OECD Countries' (Paris, OECD, 2008).
—— 'In It Together. Why Less Inequality Benefits all, Overview of Inequality Trends, Key Findings and Policy' (Paris, OECD, 2015).

O'Cinneide, C, 'A Modest Proposal: Destitution, State Responsibility and the European Convention on Human Rights' (30 August 2008), available at ssrn.com/abstract=1370241 or http://dx.doi.org/10.2139/ssrn.1370241.
—— 'Austerity and the Faded Dream of a Social Europe' in A Nolan (ed) *Economic and Social Rights after the Global Financial Crisis* (Cambridge, Cambridge University Press, 2014) 169–201.
—— 'The Problematic of Social Rights – Uniformity and Diversity in the Development of Social Rights Review' in L Lazarus C McCrudden, N Bowles, *Reasoning Rights: Comparative Judicial Engagement* (Oxford, Oxford University Press, 2014) 297–315.
—— 'The European Social Charter and the UK: Why it Matters' (2018) 29 *King's Law Journal* 275.
O'Neill, O, *A Constructive Account of Practical Reasoning. Towards Justice and Virtue* (Cambridge, Cambridge University Press, 1996).
—— 'Agents of Justice' in T Pogge (ed) *Global Justice* (Oxford, Blackwell, 2001).
—— 'The Dark Side of Human Rights' (2005) 81 *International Affairs* 427.
—— 'Cosmopolitan Rights and State Obligations' in O O'Neill, *Justice Across Boundaries: Whose Obligations?* (Cambridge, Cambridge University Press, 2016).
Otto, D and Wiseman, D, 'In Search of "Effective Remedies": Applying the International Covenant on Economic, Social and Cultural Rights in Australia' (2001) 7 *Australian Journal of Human Rights* 5.
Oxfam International, 'Public Good or Private Wealth?' briefing paper (2019) 60–71, available at https://oxfamilibrary.openrepository.com/ bitstream/handle/10546/620599/bp-public-good-or-private-wealth-210119-en.pdf.
Oxford Poverty and Human Development Initiative, *Global Multidimensional Poverty Index 2018: The Most Detailed Picture To Date of the World's Poorest People* (Oxford, University of Oxford, 2018).
Palmer, E, 'Beyond Arbitrary Interference: The Right to a Home? Developing Socio-economic Duties in the European Court of Human Rights' (2010) 61 *Northern Ireland Legal Quarterly* 225.
Panican, A and Johansson, H 'Strategies Against Poverty in a Social Democratic Local Welfare System: Still the Responsibility of Public Actors?' in H Johansson and A Panican (eds), *Combating Poverty in Local Welfare Systems: Active Inclusion Strategies in European Cities*, Work and Welfare in Europe series (London, Palgrave Macmillan, 2016) 155–78.
Paugam, S, 'What Forms does Poverty take in European Societies at the Beginning of the Twenty-first Century?' in K De Boyser, C Dewilde, D Dierickx and J Friedrichs (eds), *Between the Social and the Spatial: Exploring the Multiple Dimensions of Poverty and Social Exclusion* (Farnham, Ashgate, 2009) 3–20.
Pearce, N and Taylor, E, 'Government Spending and Welfare' in A Park, C Bryson, E Clery, J Curtice and M Phillips (eds), *British Social Attitudes 30* (London, NatCen Social Research, 2014) 33–61.
Pennings, F, *Benefits of Doubt. A Comparative Study of the Legal Aspects of Employment and Unemployment Schemes in Great-Britain, Germany, France and the Netherlands* (Deventer, Kluwer Law International, 1990).
Peroni, L and Timmer, A, 'Vulnerable Groups: The Promise of an Emerging Concept in European Human Rights Convention Law' (2013) 11 *International Journal Constitutional Law* 1056.
Piachaud, D, 'Peter Townsend and the Holy Grail' *New Society*, 10 September 1981.
Pieterse, M, 'Resuscitating Socio-Economic Rights: Constitutional Entitlements to Health Care Services' (2006) 22 *South African Journal on Human Rights* 473.
Piketty, T, *Capital in the Twenty-First Century* (Cambridge, MA, Belknap, 2014).
Pillay, A, 'Towards Effective Social and Economic Rights Adjudication: The Role of Meaningful Engagement' (2012) 10 *International Journal of Constitutional Law* 732.
Plant, R, 'So you Want to be a Citizen?', *New Statesman*, 6 February 1998.

Platt, GM, 'Status and Role, Social Psychology Of', in NJSB Baltes (ed), *International Encyclopedia of the Social & Behavioral Sciences* (Oxford, Pergamon, 2001).
Pogge, T (1992), 'Cosmopolitanism and Sovereignty' 103 *Ethics* 48.
—— '"Assisting" the Global Poor' (2007) 13 *The Proceedings of the Twenty-First World Congress of Philosophy* 189.
—— *World Poverty and Human Rights*, 2nd edn (Cambridge, Polity Press, 2008).
—— *Politics as Usual: What Lies Behind the Pro-Poor Rhetoric* (Cambridge, Polity Press, 2010).
—— 'Dignity and Global Justice' in M Düwell, J Braarvig, R Brownsword and D Mieth (eds), *The Cambridge Handbook of Human Dignity* (Cambridge, Cambridge University Press, 2014).
Popelier, P and Van de Heyning, C, 'Subsidiarity Post-Brighton: Procedural Rationality as Answer' (2017) 30 *Leiden Journal of International Law* 5.
Porter, B, 'The Reasonableness of Article 8(4) – Adjudicating Claims from the Margins' (2009) 27 *Nordic Journal of Human Rights* 39.
Pribytkova, E, 'The Human Right to a Dignified Existence: The Ethical Foundations of the Contemporary, Legal Order' in W Brugger and S Kirste (eds), *Human Dignity as a Foundation of Law* (Beiheft, Archiv für Rechts- und Sozialphilosophie, 2013).
—— 'A Decent Social Minimum as a Matter of Justice' in HP Gaisbauer, G Schweiger and C Sedmak (eds), *Ethical Issues in Poverty Alleviation* (Doordrecht, Springer, 2016).
—— 'Protection from Extreme Poverty in the European Court of Human Rights' in HP Gaisbauer, G Schweiger and C Sedmak (eds), *Absolute Poverty in Europe: Interdisciplinary Perspectives on a Hidden Phenomenon* (Bristol, Policy Press, 2019).
—— 'Global Human Rights Obligations Relating to a Decent Standard of Living', JSD dissertation (Columbia Law School, 2019).
Radio Sweden, 'Just what are "Swedish Values"?', available at http://sverigesradio.se/sida/artikel.aspx?programid=2054&artikel=6469485 (accessed 14 May 2017).
Rank, MR, 'Toward a New Paradigm for Understanding Poverty' (2006) 20 *Journal of Law and Policy* 866.
Rawls, J, *Political Liberalism* (New York, Columbia University Press, 1993).
Rawls, J, *Political Liberalism*, expanded edn (New York, Colombia University Press, 1996).
Rawls, J, *A Theory of Justice*, revd edn (Cambridge, MA, Belknap, 1999).
Rawls, J, *Justice as Fairness: A Restatement* (Cambridge, MA, Belknap, 2001).
Raz, J, *The Morality of Freedom* (Oxford, Oxford University Press, 1986).
Reader, S, 'Does a Basic Needs Approach Need Capabilities?' (2006) 14 *The Journal of Political Philosophy* 337.
Resnik, J, 'Law's Migration: American Exceptionalism, Silent Dialogues, and Federalism's Multiple Ports of Entry' (2006) 115 *Yale Law Journal* 1564.
Ringen, S, *The Possibility of Politics: A Study in the Political Economy of the Welfare State* (Oxford, Oxford University Press,1987).
—— 'Direct and Indirect Measures of Poverty' (1988) 17 *Journal of Social Policy* 351.
Roberts, T, 'Poverty' in G River and JM Ryan, *The Concise Encyclopedia of Sociology* (Oxford, Blackwell, 2011) 463.
Rosner, PG, *The Economics of Social Policy* (Cheltenham, Edward Elgar, 2003).
Rothstein, B, *Just Institutions Matter: The Moral and Political Logic of the Universal Welfare State* (Cambridge, Cambridge University Press, 1998).
—— 'The Universal Welfare State as a Social Dilemma', in B Rothstein and S Steinmo (eds), *Restructuring the Welfare State: Political Institutions and Policy Change* (New York, Palgrave Macmillan, 2002) 206–222.
Rothstein, B and Steinmo, S, 'Restructuring Politics: Institutional Analysis and the Challenges of Modern Welfare States' in B Rothstein and S Steinmo (eds), *Restructuring the Welfare State: Political Institutions and Policy Change* (New York, Palgrave Macmillan, 2002) 1–19.
Ryan, A, *On Politics* (London, Allen Lane, 2012).

Ryerson, C (2018), 'Shell in Nigeria: The Case for New Legal Strategies for Corporate Accountability', available at https://legaldesign.org/calblog/2018/7/5/shell-in-nigeria-the-case-for-new-legal-strategies-for-corporate-accountability.

Sachs, JD, *The End of Poverty: Economic Possibilities for Our Time* (New York, Penguin Press, 2005).

Sachs, JD, Fajans-Turner, V, Smith, T, Kennedy-Cuomo, C, Parejo, T, Loni, SS, *Closing the SDG Budget Gap* (New York, Move Humanity, 2018).

Saiz, I, 'Rights in Recession? Challenges for Economic and Social Rights Enforcement in Times of Crisis' (2009) 1 *Journal of Human Rights Practice*, 277.

Salomon, M, *Global Responsibility for Human Rights: World Poverty and the Development of International Law* (Oxford, Oxford University Press, 2007).

Sathanapally, A, 'The Modest Promise of Procedural Review in Fundamental Rights Cases' in J Gerards and E Brems (eds), *Procedural Review in European Fundamental Rights Cases* (Cambridge University Press, 2017) 40–76.

Seervai, HM, *Constitutional Law of India*, 1st edn (Delhi, Tripathi, 1984) 759.

Sen, A (1979), 'Equality of What?' The Tanner Lecture on Human Values Delivered at Stanford University (22 May 1979), available at www.ophi.org.uk/wp-content/uploads/Sen-1979_Equality-of-What.pdf.

—— 'Equality of What?' in S McMurrin, *Tanner Lectures on Human Values*, Vol I (Cambridge, Cambridge University Press, 1980).

—— *Choice, Welfare and Measurement* (Oxford, Blackwell, 1982).

—— 'Poor, Relatively Speaking' (1983) 35 *Oxford Economic Papers* 153.

—— 'The Right not to be Hungry' in P Alston and K Tomasevski (eds), *The Right to Food* (The Hague, Martinus Nijhoff, 1984) 70.

—— 'The Standard of Living: Lives and Capabilities' in G Hawthorn (ed), *The Standard of Living* (Cambridge, Cambridge University Press, 1987).

—— *Inequality Reexamined* (Cambridge MA, Harvard University Press, 1992).

—— 'Capability and Well-Being' in MC Nussbaum and A Sen (eds), *The Quality of Life* (Oxford, Clarendon Press, 1993).

—— *Development as Freedom* (Oxford, Oxford University Press, 1999).

—— 'Elements of a Theory of Human Rights' (2004) 32 *Philosophy and Public Affairs* 315.

—— *The Idea of Justice* (Cambridge, MA, Harvard University Press, 2009).

Sepúlveda Carmona, M, 'The Constitutional Court's Role in Addressing Social Injustice' in M Langford (ed), *Social Rights Jurisprudence, Emerging Trends in International and Comparative Law* (Cambridge, Cambridge University Press, 2009).

Sepúlveda Carmona, M, 'Report of the Special Rapporteur on Extreme Poverty and Human Rights on the Right to Participation of People Living in Poverty' (2013) A/HRC/23/36.

Shields, K, 'The Minimum Core Obligations of Economic, Social and Cultural Rights: The Rights to Health and Education', Research Summary (Nordic Trust Fund, World Bank, 2017).

Shue, H (1996), *Basic Rights: Subsistence, Affluence and U.S. Foreign Policy*, 2nd edn (Princeton, NJ, Princeton University Press).

Sicilianos, A-L, 'The European Court of Human Rights at a Time of Crisis in Europe' (2016) *European Human Rights Law Review* 121.

Simma, B and P Alston, 'The Sources of Human Rights Law: Custom, Jus Cogens, and General Principles' (1988/89) 12 *Australian Year Book of International Law* 82.

Sindzingre, A, 'The Multidimensionality of Poverty: An Institutionalist Perspective' in N Kakwani and J Silber (eds), *The Many Dimensions of Poverty* (Basingstoke, Palgrave Macmillan, 2007) 52–74.

Singer, P, 'Famine, Affluence and Morality' (1972) 1 *Philosophy and Public Affairs* 229.

Skogly, S, *Beyond National Borders: States' Human Rights Obligations in International Cooperation* (Antwerpen-Oxford, Intersentia, 2006).

Smedding, TM, 'Poverty Measurement' in D Brady and L Burton (eds), *The Oxford Handbook of the Social Science of Poverty* (Oxford, Oxford University Press, 2016) 21ff.

Stacey, R, 'Dynamic Regulatory Constitutionalism: Taking Legislation Seriously in the Judicial Enforcement of Economic and Social Rights' (2017) 31 *Notre Dame Journal of Law, Ethics and Public Policy* 85.

Stendahl, S, 'Welfare State Borders: On Local Initiatives to Cater to the Needs of Destitute EU Migrants in Swedish Cities' in W van Oorschot, H Peters and K Boos (eds), *Invisible Social Security Revisited. Essays in Honour of Jos Berghman* (Leuven, Lannoo Campus Publishers, 2014).

—— 'To Reside: To Live, Be Present, Belong' (2016) 18 *European Journal of Social Security* 232.

Stendahl, S and Swedrup, O, 'A Legal Analysis of the Possibilities and Impediments for Citizens Seeking to Enforce their Social Rights' (2016) Deliverable 6.4 of the bEUcitizen project.

—— 'Social Human Rights as a Legal Strategy to Enhance Eu Citizenship' in F Pennings and M Seeleib-Kaiser (eds), *European Citizenship and Social Rights: Entitlements and Impediments to Accessing Welfare* (Cheltenham, Edward Elgar, 2018).

Stichelmans, T (2016), 'How International Financial Institutions and Donors Influence Economic Policies in Developing Countries', A Eurodad discussion paper., available at www.eurodad.org/files/pdf/57f4f4163d760.pdf.

Stiglitz, JE, 'Inequality and Economic Growth' (2016) 86 *Political Quarterly* 134.

Storms, B, '*Referentiebudgetten Voor Maatschappelijke Participatie*' ('Reference Budgets for Social Participation'), PhD thesis (Antwerp, University of Antwerp, 2012).

Storms, B, Goedemé, T, Van den Bosch, K and Devuyst, K, 'Towards a Common Framework for Developing Cross-Nationally Comparable Reference Budgets in Europe, ImPRovE Working Papers' (Antwerp, Herman Deleeck Centre for Social Policy – University of Antwerp, 2013).

Storms, B, Goedemé, T, Van den Bosch, K, Penne, T, Schuerman, N and Stockman, S, 'Review of Current State of Play on Reference Budget Practices at National, Regional, and Local Level' (Brussels, European Commission, 2014).

Stoyanova, V, 'Causation between State Omission and Harm within the Framework of Positive Obligations under the European Convention on Human Rights' (2018) 18 *Human Rights Law Review* 309.

SVT Nyheter, 'Ensamkommande Blir Hemlösa i Väntan på Besked', 19 September 2018, available at www.svt.se/nyheter/lokalt/uppsala/ensamkommande-blir-hemlosa-i-vantan-pa-besked.

Swiatkowski, A and Wujczyk, M, 'The European Social Charter as a Basis for Defining Social Rights for EU Citizens' in F Pennings and M Seeleib-Kaiser (eds), *European Citizenship and Social Rights: Entitlements and Impediments to Accessing Welfare* (Cheltenham, Edward Elgar, 2018).

Tan, K-C (2004), *Justice Without Borders: Cosmopolitanism, Nationalism and Patriotism* (Cambridge, Cambridge University Press).

Tasioulas, J, 'Minimum Core Obligations: Human Rights in the Here and Now' (2017), available at http://documents.worldbank.org/curated/en/908171515588413853/pdf/122563-WP-Tasioulas2-PUBLIC.pdf

—— 'Minimum Core Obligations: Human Rights in the Here and Now', Research Paper (Nordic Trust Fund, World Bank, 2017).

Thorbecke, E, 'Multidimensional Poverty: Conceptual and Measurement Issues' in N Kakwani and J Silber (eds) *The Many Dimensions of Poverty* (Basingstoke, Palgrave Macmillan, 2007) 3–19.

Timmer, A, 'A Quiet Revolution: Vulnerability in the European Court of Human Rights' in M Fineman and A Greer (eds), *Vulnerability: Reflections on a New Ethical Foundation for Law and Politics* (Farnham, Routledge, 2013) 147–70.

Titmuss, R, *Social Policy. An Introduction* (London, Pantheon Press, 1974).

—— 'The Social Division of Welfare' in *Essays on the Welfare State* (London, George Allen and Unwin, 1958).

Tomlinson, J and Sheridan, K, 'Judicial Review, Evidence, and Systemic Unfairness in the UK', IACL-AIDC Blog (3 September 2018).

Torry, M, 'An Evaluation of a Strictly Revenue Neutral Citizen's Income Scheme', Euromod Working Paper EM 5/16 (Colchester, Institute for Social and Economic Research, University of Essex, 2016), available at www.iser.essex.ac.uk/research/publications/working-papers/euromod/em5-16.

—— 'Primary Care, the Basic Necessity: Part I: Explorations in Economics' in A Papanikitas and J Spicer (eds), *Handbook of Primary Care Ethics* (Boca Raton, FL, CRC/Francis and Taylor, 2017) 369–75.

—— 'Primary Care, the Basic Necessity: Part II: Explorations in Ethics' in A Papanikitas and J Spicer (eds), *Handbook of Primary Care Ethics* (Boca Raton, FL, CRC/Francis and Taylor, 2017) 377–84.

—— 'A Variety of Indicators Evaluated for Two Implementation Methods for a Citizen's Basic Income', Institute for Social and Economic Research Working Paper EM12/17 (Colchester, Institute for Social and Economic Research, University of Essex, 2017), available at www.iser.essex.ac.uk/research/publications/working-papers/euromod/em12-17.

—— 'An Update, a Correction, and an Extension of an Evaluation of an Illustrative Citizen's Basic Income Scheme – Addendum to EUROMOD Working Paper EM12/17', Institute for Social and Economic Research Working Paper EM12/17a (Colchester, Institute for Social and Economic Research, University of Essex, 2018), available at www.iser.essex.ac.uk/research/publications/working-papers/euromod/em12-17a.

Townsend, P, *Poverty in the United Kingdom* (London, Allen Lane/Penguin, 1979).

Trägårdh, L (ed), *State and Civil Society in Northern Europe: The Swedish Model Reconsidered* (Oxford, Berghahn Books, 2007).

—— 'Ett val Mellan två Modeller för Sverige' *Göteborgs-Posten*, 2 December 2015, 2.

—— 'Förneka inte Nationen' *Axess*, 1 February 2016, 37–40.

—— 'Between Two Models of Solidarity: Sweden, The Welfare State and Globalization' in D Cagan (ed), *Nordic Ways* (Washington DC, Brookings Institution Press, 2016).

Tuori, K, 'Judicial Constitutional Review as a Last Resort' in T Campbell, K D Ewing and A Tomkins (eds), *The Legal Protection of Human Rights: Sceptical Essays* (Oxford, Oxford University Press, 2011) 365–391.

Tushnet, M, *Weak Courts, Strong Rights: Judicial Review and Social Welfare Rights in Comparative Constitutional Law* (Princeton University Press, 2008).

—— 'A Response to David Landau', *Opinio Juris* Blog, 23 January 2012, available at http://opiniojuris.org/2012/01/23/hilj_tushnet-responds-to-landau.

UNDP, 'Human Development Report 2015: Work for Human Development' (New York, UNDP, 2015) 100.

—— 'Beyond Income: A Broader Picture of Poverty' (New York, UNDP, 2018).

—— 'Human Development Indices and Indicators: 2018 Statistical Update' (New York, UNDP, 2018).

United Nations, 'Sustainable Development Goals Reports' (New York, United Nations, 2016).

—— *Universal Declaration of Human Rights* (New York, United Nations, 1948).

—— *United Nations Convention on the Rights of a Child* (New York, United Nations, 1989).

United Nations Development Programme, 'Guatemala: Laying a Mother to Rest after 31 years', available at www.undp.org/content/undp/en/home/ourwork/ourstories/guatemala-laying-a-mother-to-rest-after-31-years.html.

Vahlne Westerhäll, L, 'Om Sociala Rättigheters Funktion och Konstruktion' in G Regner, M Eliason and H-H Vogel (eds), *Fetskrift till Hans Ragnemalm* (Lund, Juristförlaget i Lund, 2005) 365–386.

Van den Bosch, K, Goedemé, T, Schuerman, N and Storms, B, 'Reference Housing Costs for Adequate Dwellings in Ten European Capitals' (2016) 3 *Critical Housing Analysis* 1.

Van der Walt, J, 'Delegitimation by Constitution? Liberal Democratic Experimentalism and the Question of Socioeconomic Rights' (2015) 3 *Critical Quarterly on Legislation and Law* 303–333.

Van Parijs, P, *Real Freedom for All: What (If Anything) Can Justify Capitalism?* (Oxford, Oxford University Press, 1995).

Van Parijs, P and Y Vanderborght, *Basic Income: A Radical Proposal for a Free Society and a Sane Economy* (Cambridge, MA, Harvard University Press, 2017).

Vandenbogaerde, A, *Towards Shared Accountability in International Human Rights Law. Law, Procedures and Principles* (Cambridge, Intersentia, 2016).

Vandenhole, W (ed) (2015), *Challenging Territoriality in Human Rights Law: Building Blocks for a Plural and Diverse Duty-Bearer Regime* (Oxon–New York, Routledge, 2015).

Villmez, WJ, 'Poverty', in EF Borgattol and RJV Montgomery (eds) *Encyclopedia of Sociology*, 2nd edn, Vol 3 (New York, Macmillan Reference USA, 2000) 2213.

Vizard, P 'The Human Rights and Equalities Agenda' in H Dean Hartley and L Platt (eds), *Social Advantage and Disadvantage* (Oxford, Oxford University Press, 2016).

Vonk, G, 'Repressive Welfare State, the Spiral of Obligations and Sanctions' (2014) 16 *European Journal of Social Security* 188.

Voss, TR, 'Institutions' in NJSB Baltes (ed), *International Encyclopedia of the Social & Behavioral Sciences* (Oxford, Pergamon, 2001).

Vrooman, CJ, *Rules of Relief. Institutions of Social Security, and Their Impact* (The Hague, SCP, 2009).

Waldron, J (1993), 'Rawls and the Social Minimum' in J Waldron, *Liberal Rights. Collected Papers 1981–1991* (Cambridge, Cambridge University Press).

—— (2017), *One Another's Equals: The Basis of Human Equality* (Cambridge, MA, Harvard University Press).

Walzer, M, 'Liberalism and the Art of Separation' (1984) 12 *Political Theory* 315.

White, S 'Should a Minimum Income be Unconditional?' in S Civitarese Matteuci and S Halliday (eds), *Social Rights in an Age of Austerity* (London, Routledge, 2018).

WHO, 'Manuals on Child Mental Health and Psychosocial Development' (Geneva, WHO, 1982).

Widerquist, K, Nogera, J, Vanderborght, Y and De Wispelare, J (eds), *Basic Income. An Anthology of Contemporary Research* (Oxford, Blackwell, 2013).

Waldron, J, 'John Rawls and the Social Minimum' (1986) 3 *Journal of Applied Philosophy* 21.

—— *Law and Disagreement* (Oxford, Clarendon Press, 1999).

—— 'The Core Against Judicial Review' (2006) *Yale Law Journal* 1347.

Warwick, B, 'Debt, Austerity and the Structural Responses of Social Rights' in I Bantekas and C Lumina (eds), *Sovereign Debt and Human Rights* (Oxford, Oxford University Press, 2018) 386ff.

White, S, *The Civic Minimum: On the Rights and Obligations of Economic Citizenship* (Oxford, Oxford University Press, 2003).

—— 'Social Minimum' in EN Zalta, *The Stanford Encyclopedia of Philosophy*, Winter 2015 edn, available at plato.stanford.edu/archives/win2015/entries/social-minimum.

Widerquist, K, 'How the Sufficiency Minimum Becomes a Social Maximum' (2010) 22 *Utilitas* 474.

Wiles, E, 'Aspirational Principles or Enforceable Rights? The Future for Social and Economic Rights in National Law' (2006) 22 *American University International Law Review* 59.

Wilkinson, R and Pickett, K, *The Spirit Level: Why Equality* (London, Penguin Books, 2011).

Wills, JJ and Warwick, BTC, 'Contesting Austerity: The Potential and Pitfalls of Socioeconomic Rights Discourse' (2016) 23 *Indiana Journal of Global Legal Studies* 664.

Young, K, 'The Minimum Core of Economic and Social Rights: A Concept in Search of Content' (2008) 33 *Yale Journal of International Law* 113–75.

—— *Constituting Social Rights* (Oxford, Oxford University Press, 2012).

—— 'Proportionality, Reasonableness, and Socio-Economic Rights' in V Jackson and M Tushnet (eds.) *Proportionality: New Frontiers, New Challenges* (Cambridge, Cambridge University Press, 2017) 227–41.

Index

Note: Alphabetical arrangement is word-by-word, where a group of letters followed by a space is filed before the same group of letters followed by a letter, eg 'legal theory' will appear before 'legally binding minimum'. In determining alphabetical arrangement, initial articles and prepositions are ignored.

Page numbers followed by the letter 'n' refer to footnotes on the quoted pages.

www.ingramcontent.com/pod-product-compliance
Lightning Source LLC
Chambersburg PA
CBHW071303180926
51613CB00001B/118